The Polemics of
Erasmus of Rotterdam
and Ulrich von Hutten

The Polemics of
Erasmus of Rotterdam
and Ulrich von Hutten

Translated from the Latin and Annotated

by

Randolph J. Klawiter

UNIVERSITY OF NOTRE DAME PRESS
NOTRE DAME   LONDON

Published 1977 by
University of Notre Dame Press
Notre Dame, Indiana 46556

Copyright © 1977 by
University of Notre Dame Press

Produced and distributed *on demand* by
University Microfilms International
Ann Arbor, Michigan 48106

Printed in the United States of America

Library of Congress Cataloging in Publication Data

The Polemics of Erasmus of Rotterdam and Ulrich von Hutten.

(Monograph publishing on demand : imprint series)
Translation of Expostulatio cum Erasmo, by U. v.
Hutten, and of Spongia Erasmi adversus aspergines Hutteni,
by Erasmus.
Bibliography: p.
Includes indexes.
CONTENTS: Introduction.—Notes to the Introduction.—Hutten's Expostulation. [etc.]
1. Erasmus, Desiderius, d. 1536. 2. Hutten, Ulrich von,
1488-1523. I. Klawiter, Randolph J. II. Hutten, Ulrich
von, 1488-1523. Expostulation cum Erasmo. English.
1977. III. Erasmus, Desiderius, d. 1536. Spongia Erasmi
adversus aspergines Hutteni. English. 1977.

BR350.E7P64   199'.492   76-30427
ISBN 0-268-01524-4

To my Mother and Father

With filial love and respect

For the countless blessings conferred

Si quid novisti rectius istis,
Candidus imperti;
Si non, his utere mecum.

Horace

Ἱστορία φιλοσοφία ἐστὶν
ἐκ παραδειγμάτων.

Proverb

Contents

Acknowledgements

It is with a profound sense of justice and sincere gratitude that I express my appreciation to the following persons without whose aid and unstinting self-sacrifice the present volume would never have been completed:

To Fathers Germain Marc'hadour and Henri Gibaud of the Université Catholique de l'Ouest, Angers, France, who read the translation and compared it with the Latin original. Their corrections and the fullness of their alternate renderings were of incalculable service to me; if, nonetheless, there are any errors in the English version it is because I chose to follow my own understanding of the text rather than theirs.

To Professor Werner Kaegi of Basle, Switzerland, who so graciously gave me permission to translate his scholarly and beautifully written essay "Hutten und Erasmus. Ihre Freundschaft und ihr Streit" (Historische Viertel-jahrschrift, XXX (1942), 200-278, 461-514) and to use it as an introduction to my translation of the polemics. Because of the length of his study, however, I finally decided against adopting it in its entirety and have instead used it as the basis for the present Introduction, especially with reference to the fundamental differences in character, temperament and aspirations of the two chief protagonists and thus the all but inevitable final rupture between the "revered master" and his over-enthusiastically "devoted disciple."

To Professor Frederick J. Crosson, former Dean of the College of Arts and Letters of the University of Notre Dame, whose encouragement and financial support made it possible for me to acquire all the necessary material employed in this volume; and to the present Dean, Doctor Isabel Charles, through whose good offices funds were made available with which to publish the results of my research.

To Mr. Keith Palka, a doctoral candidate in French literature at the University of Michigan, who read the final version of the typescript and whose unerring sense of English stylistics rendered smooth many a rough and tortured passage whose contents had become so familiar to me that I was wholly oblivious to their verbal shortcomings.

To Mrs. Marcelette Webber, former secretary of the Department of Modern and Classical Languages of the University of Notre Dame, who willingly and, thank God, with an unflagging sense of humor suffered through the un-pleasant task of retyping the countless versions of the manuscript. To her trained eye and sensitivity to the vagaries of English orthography I am like-wise indebted for having been spared several ludicrous and, if read by others, embarrassing errors.

In the final analysis, however, it is to my beloved wife Marilyn to whom I am most indebted for whatever I have made of myself or whatever small accomplishments I might claim. The innate goodness, quiet gentleness and total unselfishness of her life will ever remain my bulwark of strength and source of inspiration.

vii

References

Ad   Erasmus' _Adagia_, LB, II.

Adams   Robert P. Adams, _The Better Part of Valor: More, Erasmus, Colet and Vives on Humanism, War and Peace. 1496-1535_. Seattle: University of Washington Press, 1962.

ADB   _Allgemeine Deutsche Biographie_. Hrsg. durch die Historische Commission bei der Königlichen Akademie der Wissenschaften. Leipzig: Duncker und Humblot, 1875-1912 (56 Vols.).

AK   Alfred Hartmann and Beat R. Jenny, eds., _Die Amerbachkorrespondenz_. 6 Vols. Basel: Verlag der Universitätsbibliothek, 1942-1967.

Aldridge   John W. Aldridge, _The Hermeneutics of Erasmus_. Richmond, Va.: John Knox Press, 1966.

Allen   _Opus Epistolarum Desiderii Erasmi_. Ed. by Percy Stafford and Helen Mary Allen. 12 Vols. London: Oxford University Press, 1906-1958.

Allen (2)   Percy S. Allen, _The Age of Erasmus_. Oxford: The Clarendon Press, 1914 (reprinted New York: Russell and Russell, 1963).

Atkinson   James Atkinson, _Martin Luther and the Birth of Protestantism_. Baltimore, Md.: Penguin Books, 1968.

Auer   Alfons Auer, _Die vollkommene Frömmigkeit des Christen nach dem 'Enchiridion militis christiani' des Erasmus von Rotterdam_. Düsseldorf: Patmos, 1954.

Aus Schr   _Desiderius Erasmus: Ausgewählte Schriften (Studienausgabe)_. Ed. by Werner Welzig. Bi-lingual edition, Latin and German, with Introductions and Notes. 8 Vols. Darmstadt: Wissenschaftliche Buchgesellschaft, 1967 - :

Vol. I - Epistola ad Paulum Volzium; Enchiridion militis christiani (trl. and ed. by Werner Welzig, 1968);

Vol. III - In Novum Testamentum Praefationes; Ratio verae theologiae (trl. and ed. by Gerhard B. Winkler, 1967);

Vol. IV - De libero arbitrio; Hyperaspistes - Liber primus (trl. and ed. by Winifried Lesowsky, 1969);

Vol. V - Julius Exclusus; Institutio principis christiani; Querela pacis (trl. and ed. by Gertraud Christian, 1968);

Vol. VI - Colloquia familiaria (selections trl. and ed. by Werner Welzig, 1967);

Vol. VII - Ciceronianus; Adagiorum chiliades (selections trl. and ed. by Theresia Payr, 1972).

Bainton   Roland H. Bainton, _Erasmus of Christendom_. New York: Charles Scribner's Sons, 1969.

Bataillon   Marcel Bataillon, _Erasme et l'Espagne_. Paris: Droz, 1937.

BdG   Karl Schottenloher, ed., _Bibliographie zur deutschen Geschichte im Zeitalter der Glaubensspaltung. 1517-1585_. Zweite, unveränderte Auflage. 7 vols. to date. Stuttgart: Anton Hierseman, 1956 - .

Béné   Charles Béné, _Erasme et Saint Augustin ou l'influence de Saint Augustin sur l'humanisme d'Erasme_. Genève: Droz, 1969.

Berlichingen   Adolf Freiherr von Berlichingen, _Populär-historische Vorträge über Reformation, Revolution und den 30jährigen Krieg_. Hft. 1-27. Würzburg: Göbel, 1902-1904.

BHN   Nicholas Antonio, _Bibliotheca hispana nova_. 2 Vols. Matriti: J. de Ibarra, 1783-1788.

Bientenholz   Peter G. Bientenholz, _Basle and France in the Sixteenth Century. The Basle Humanists and Printers in their Contacts with Francophone Culture_. Geneva: Droz, 1971.

Bludau   August Bludau, _Die beiden ersten Erasmus-Ausgaben des Neuen Testamentes und ihre Gegner_. Freiburg: Herder, 1902.

BNB   _Biographie Nationale de Belgique_ (publieé par l'Académie royale des Sciences, des Lettres et des Beaux-Arts de Belgique). Bruxelles: H. Thiry-Van Buggenhoudt, 1866-1944 (28 Vols.).

Bö   _Ulrichi Hutteni Equitis Germani Opera quae reperiri potuerunt omnia_. Ed. by Eduard Böcking. 7 Vols. Leipzig: Teubner, 1859-1869.

Bouyer   Louis Bouyer, _Autour d'Erasme_. Paris: Editions du Cerf, 1955 (trl. into English by Francis X. Murphy, _Erasmus and His Times_. Westminster, Md.: The Newman Press, 1959).

Brod   Max Brod, _Johannes Reuchlin und sein Kampf_. Stuttgart-Berlin-Köln-Mainz: Kohlhammer, 1965.

Brunnow   Ernst von Brunnow, _Ulrich von Hutten, der Streiter für deutsche Freiheit. Historisches Gemälde aus den Zeiten der Reformation_. 3 Vols. Leipzig: Teubner, 1842-1843.

BU   _Biographie universelle (Michaud) ancienne et moderne_ ... Nouvelle éd., rev., cor. et considérablement augm. d'articles omis ou nouveaux; ouvrage rédigé par une société de gens de lettres et de savants... Paris: Delagrave, n.d. (45 Vols.).

Büchner   Karl Büchner, _Die Freundschaft zwischen Hutten und Erasmus. Der Brief des Erasmus an Ulrich von Hutten über Thomas More_ (Zweisprachige Ausgabe; Deutsch von Karl Büchner, mit einem biographischen Essay und Anmerkungen des Übersetzers). München: Verlag Alber, 1948.

BWN   Abraham Jacob van der Aa, _Biographisch Woordenboek der Nederlanden_. Haarlem: van Brederode, 1852-1878 (21 Vols. in 17).

Caccia   Natale Caccia, Note su la fortuna di Luciano nel rinascimento. Le versione e i dialoghi satirici di Erasmo da Roterdam e di Ulrico Hutten. Milano: Signorelli, 1914.

Chantraine   Georges Chantraine, 'Mystère' et 'Philosophie du Christ' selon Erasme. Etude de la lettre à P. Volz et de la 'Ratio verae theologiae' (1518). Namur: Secrétariat des Publications, Facultés universitaires, 1971.

Chapiro   José Chapiro, Erasmus and our Struggle for Peace. Boston: Beacon Press, 1950.

Col.   Cf. Thompson (1).

Corp. Ref.   Corpus Reformatorum. Vols. 1-29: Melanthonis opera omnia. Ed. by Carl Bretschneider. Halis Saxonum: Schwetschke, 1834-1860 (reprinted New York-London: Johnson Reprint Corporation, 1963).

DBI   Dizionario Biografico degli Italiani. Ed. by Alberto M. Ghisalberti. Roma: Istituto della Enciclopedia Italiana, 1960 - (to date 12 Vols.: Aaron to Borrello).

DNB   Dictionary of National Biography. Ed. by Sir Leslie Stephen and Sir Sidney Lee. London: Oxford University Press, 1921-1922, corrections and additions, 1923-1963 (21 Vols., 11 Vols. of Supplement).

Dolan   John P. Dolan, The Essential Erasmus. New York: Mentor-Omega Books, 1964.

Drewinc   Harald Drewinc, Vier Gestalten aus dem Zeitalter des Humanismus. St. Gallen: Zollikofer, 1946 (reprinted in Richard Newald, Probleme und Gestalten des deutschen Humanismus. Studien von Richard Newald. Ed. by Hans-Gert Roloff. Berlin: de Gruyter, 1963, pp. 151-325).

DS   Dictionnaire historique et biographique de la Suisse. Ed. by Marcel Godet et al. Neuchâtel: Administration du Dictionnaire historique et biographique de la Suisse, 1921 (i.e. 1920)-1933 (7 Vols., 1 Supplement).

EB   The Encyclopaedia Britannica.... 11th ed. Cambridge, England, New York: University Press, 1910-1922 (32 Vols.).

Eckert   Willehad Paul Eckert, Erasmus von Rotterdam. Werk und Wirkung. 2 Vols. Köln: Wienand Verlag, 1967.

Eckert-Imhoff   Willehad Eckert and Christoph von Imhoff, Willibald Pirckheimer: Dürers Freund im Spiegel seines Lebens, seiner Werke und seiner Umwelt. Köln: Wienand Verlag, 1971.

EI   Enciclopedia Italiana di Scienze, Lettere ed Arti... Roma: Istituto Giovanni Treccani, 1929-1937 (35 Vols., 5 Vols. of Appendices, 1938-1961).

Emden(C)   Alfred B. Emden, A Biographical Register of the University of Cambridge to 1500. Cambridge, Engl.: University Press, 1963.

Emden(0,1)   Alfred B. Emden, _A Biographical Register of the University of Oxford to A.D. 1500_. Oxford: Clarendon Press, 1957-1959 (3 Vols.).

Emden(0,2)   Alfred B. Emden, _A Biographical Register of the University of Oxford, A.D. 1501 to 1540_. Oxford: Clarendon Press, 1974.

EP   _Grande Enciclopédia Portuguesa e Brasileira_... Lisboa-Rio de Janeiro: Editorial Enciclopédia Limitada, 1935- (40 Vols.).

Ergang   Robert Ergang, _The Renaissance_. New York-London-Toronto-Melbourne: Van Nostrand, 1967.

Etienne   Jacques Etienne, _Spiritualisme érasmien et les théologiens louvanistes_. Louvain: Publications universitaires des Louvain, 1956.

EU   _Enciclopedia Universal Ilustrada Europeo-americana_... Barcelona: J. Espasa, 1907-1930 (70 Vols. in 72, 26 Vols. of Supplement).

Exp   _Ulrichi ab Hutten cum Erasmo Roterodamo presbytero theologo Expostulatio_, in Bö, II, pp. 180-248.

Fechter   Heinrich Fechter, _Ulrich von Hutten. Ein Leben für die Freiheit_. Pähl: Verlag Hohe Warte, 1954.

Féret   Pierre Féret, _La Faculté de Théologie de Paris et ses docteurs les plus célèbres. Epoque moderne_. 7 Vols. Paris: A. Picard, 1900-1910.

Ferguson   Wallace K. Ferguson, "The Attitude of Erasmus Toward Toleration" in _Persecution and Liberty. Essays in Honor of George Lincoln Burr_. New York: Century Co., 1931, pp. 171-181.

Förster   Richard Förster, _Lucian in der Renaissance. Rede zur Feier des Geburtstages des deutschen Kaisers Wilhelm_ (gehalten an der Christian Albrecht Universität am 22. März 1886). Kiel: Universitäts-Buchhandlung, 1886.

Friedenthal   Richard Friedenthal, _Luther. Sein Leben und seine Zeit_. München: Piper, 1967 (English translation by John Nowell, _Luther and His Times_. New York: Harcourt, Brace Jovanovich, 1970).

Froude   James A. Froude, _Life and Letters of Erasmus_ (Lectures delivered at Oxford, 1893-1894). New York: Charles Scribner's Sons, 1895 (reprinted New York: AMS Editions, 1971).

Gay   Peter Gay, _The Bridge of Criticism: Dialogues among Lucian, Erasmus and Voltaire_. New York: Harper and Row, 1970.

Gebhardt   Georg Gebhardt, _Die Stellung des Erasmus von Rotterdam zur römischen Kirche_. Marburg an der Lahn: Ökumenischer Verlag Edel, 1966.

Geiger   Ludwig Geiger, _Johann Reuchlin. Sein Leben und seine Werke_. Leipzig: Duncker und Humblot, 1871 (reprinted Nieuwkoop: de Graf, 1964).

Gerrish   Brian Albert Gerrish, _Reformers in Profile_. Philadelphia: Fortress Press, 1967.

Gewerstock   Olga Gewerstock, <u>Lucian und Hutten. Zur Geschichte des Dialogs im
              16. Jahrhundert</u>. Berlin: Ebering, 1924.

Gilmore   Myron P. Gilmore, <u>Humanists and Jurists. Six Studies in the Renaissance</u>.
              Cambridge: Harvard University Press, 1963.

Glöcker   Gottfried Glöcker, <u>Das Ideal der Bildung und Erziehung bei Erasmus von
              Rotterdam</u>. Dresden: Bleyl und Kaemmerer, 1889.

Hagen   Karl Hagen, <u>Zur politischen Geschichte Deutschlands</u>. Stuttgart:
              Franckh'sche Buchhandlung, 1842.

Halkin   Léon E. Halkin, <u>Erasme et l'humanisme</u>. Paris: Editions universitaires,
              1969.

Harbison   E. Harris Harbison, <u>The Christian Scholar in the Age of the Reformation</u>.
              New York: Charles Scribner's Sons, 1956.

Hardison   O.B. Hardison, ed., <u>Medieval and Renaissance Studies. Proceedings of
              the Southeastern Institute of Medieval and Renaissance Studies</u>.
              Chapel Hill: University of North Carolina Press, 1966.

Harper's   <u>Harper's Dictionary of Classical Literature and Antiquities</u>. Ed. by
              Harry Thurston Peck. New York-Cincinnati-Chicago: American Book
              Company, 1896.

Heep   Martha Heep, <u>Die 'Colloquia familiaria' des Erasmus und Lucian</u>.
              Halle: Niemeyer, 1927.

Heer   Friedrich Heer, <u>Die dritte Kraft. Der europäische Humanismus zwischen
              den Fronten des konfessionellen Zeitalters</u>. Frankfurt am Main:
              S. Fischer, 1960.

HHE   Marcelino Menéndez y Pelayo, <u>Historia de los heterodoxes españoles</u>.
              3 Vols. Madrid: Librería católica de San José, 1880-1888.

Hoffmann   Manfred Hoffmann, <u>Erkenntnis und Verwicklung der wahren Theologie
              nach Erasmus von Rotterdam</u>. Tübingen: Mohr, 1972.

Holborn   Hajo Holborn, <u>Ulrich von Hutten and the German Reformation</u>. Trl. by
              Roland H. Bainton from the German. New York: Harper and Row, 1965.

Huizinga   Johan Huizinga, <u>Erasmus of Rotterdam</u>. Trl. by F. Hopman from the
              Dutch. London: Phaidon Press, 1952.

Jacob   E.F. Jacob, "Christian Humanism in the Late Middle Ages" in <u>Europe
              in the Late Middle Ages</u>. Ed. by J.R. Hale, J.R.L. Highfield,
              B. Smalley. Evanston, Ill.: Northwestern University Press, 1963,
              pp. 437-465.

Jensen   De Lamar Jensen, <u>Confrontation at Worms. Martin Luther and the Diet
              of Worms</u> (with a complete English translation of the Edict of Worms).
              Provo, Utah: Brigham Young University Press, 1973.

Jones   Rosemary D. Jones, <u>Erasmus and Luther</u>. London: Oxford University
              Press, 1968.

Kaiser   Walter Kaiser, <u>Praisers of Folly: Erasmus-Rabelais - Shakespeare</u>. Cambridge: Harvard University Press, 1963.

Kalkoff(1)   Paul Kalkoff, <u>Huttens Vagantenzeit und Untergang. Der geschichtliche Ulrich von Hutten und seine Umwelt</u>. Weimar: Böhlaus Nachfolger, 1925.

Kalkoff(2)   Paul Kalkoff, <u>Ulrich von Hutten und die Reformation. Eine kritische Geschichte seiner wichtigsten Lebenszeit und der Entscheidungsjahre der Reformation. 1517-1523</u>. Leipzig: Verein für Reformations-geschichte, 1920.

Kalkoff(3)   Paul Kalkoff, <u>Erasmus, Luther und Friedrich der Weise</u>. Leipzig: Verein für Reformationsgeschichte, 1919.

Kieser   Carl Kieser, <u>Der Streit zwischen Ulrich von Hutten und Erasmus von Rotterdam. Ein Beitrag zur Charakteristik Ulrichs von Hutten und seiner literarischen Zeitgenossen</u>. Mainz: In der Müller'schen Buchhandlung, 1823.

Köhler   Walter Köhler, <u>Desiderius Erasmus. Ein Lebensbild in Auszügen aus seinen Werken</u>. Berlin: Hutten Verlag, 1917.

Könneker   Barbara Könneker, <u>Wesen und Wandlung der Narrenidee im Zeitalter des Humanismus: Brant - Murner - Erasmus</u>. Wiesbaden: Steiner, 1966.

Koerber   Eberhard von Koerber, <u>Die Staatslehre des Erasmus von Rotterdam</u>. Berlin: Duncker und Humblot, 1967.

Kohls(1)   Ernst-Wilhelm Kohls, <u>Die Theologie des Erasmus</u>. 2 Vols. Basel: Reinhardt, 1966.

Kohls(2)   Ernst-Wilhelm Kohls, <u>Die theologische Lebensaufgabe des Erasmus und die oberrheinischen Reformatoren: Zur Durchdringung von Humanismus und Reformation</u>. Stuttgart: Calwer, 1969.

Laible   Wilhelm Laible, ed., <u>Moderne Irrtümer im Spiegel der Geschichte</u>. Leipzig: Dörffling und Franke, 1912.

Lauchert   Friedrich Lauchert, <u>Die italienischen literarischen Gegner Luthers</u>. Freiburg im Breisgau: Herder, 1912.

LB   <u>Desiderii Erasmi Roterodami Opera Omnia</u>. Ed. J. Clericus. 10 Vols. Leiden, 1703-1706 (reprinted London: The Gregg Press, 1962).

Leutsch   Ernst Ludwig von Leutsch and Friedrich Wilhelm Schneidewin, eds., <u>Corpus Paroemiographorum Graecorum</u>. 2 Vols. Hildesheim: Georg Olms Verlagsbuchhandlung, 1958 (reprint of the 1839 edition, Göttingen: Vandenhoeck und Ruprecht).

Lortz   Joseph Lortz, <u>Die Reformation in Deutschland</u>. 2 Vols. 5th edition. Freiburg-Basel-Wien: Herder, 1962 (English translation by Ronald Walls, <u>The Reformation in Germany</u>. New York: Herder and Herder; London: Darton, Longman and Todd, 1968).

Luther   <u>Luther's Works</u>. Vol. 48 (Letters: Vol. I. Ed. and trl. by G. Krodel). Philadelphia: Fortress Press, 1963.

Mann   Margaret Mann, <u>Erasme et les débuts de la réforme française. 1517-1536</u>. Paris: Honoré Champion, 1934.

Marc'hadour   Germain Marc'hadour, <u>Thomas More vu par Erasme. Lettre du 23 juillet 1519 à Ulrich von Hutten</u> (Thèse complémentaire pour le Doctorat ès Lettres présentée à la Faculté des Lettres et Sciences humaines de l'Université de Paris (Sorbonne)). Angers, 1969.

Maurer   Wilhelm Maurer, <u>Der junge Melanchthon zwischen Humanismus und Reformation</u>. Vol. I (der Humanist), Vol. II (der Theologe). Göttingen: Vandenhoeck und Ruprecht, 1967-1969.

Mee   Charles L. Mee, Jr., <u>White Robe, Black Robe</u>. New York: G.P. Putnam's Sons, 1972.

Mesnard   Pierre Mesnard, <u>Humanisme et théologie dans la controverse entre Erasme et Dorpius</u>. Torino: Edizioni di "Filosofia", 1964(?).

Mestwerdt   Paul Mestwerdt, <u>Die Anfänge des Erasmus. Humanismus und 'Devotio moderna'</u>. Leipzig: Heinsius Nachfolger, 1917.

MHL   <u>Monumenta humanistica lovaniensia</u>. Ed. by Henri de Vocht from 1928 until 1968; thereafter by Jos. Ijsewijn. Louvain: Librairie universitaire (after 1968 Vander), 1928- on going (20 Vols. to date).

           Vol. I: Henri de Vocht, <u>Literae virorum eruditorum ad Franciscum Craneveldium, 1522-1528</u> (1928).

           Vol. IV: Henri de Vocht, <u>Monumenta humanistica lovaniensia; Texts and Studies about Louvain Humanists in the First Half of the XVIth Century: Erasmus-Vives-Dorpius-Clenardus-Goes-Moringus</u> (1934).

           Vols. X-XIII: Henry de Vocht, <u>History of the Foundation and the Rise of the Collegium Trilingue Lovaniense, 1517-1550</u> (Vol. X, 1951, Vol. XI, 1953, Vol. XII, 1954, Vol. XIII, 1955).

Murray   Robert H. Murray, <u>Erasmus and Luther: Their Attitude to Toleration</u>. New York: B. Franklin, 1972 (reprint of the 1920 edition).

NDB   <u>Neue Deutsche Biographie</u>. Hrsg. von der Historischen Kommission bei der Bayerischen Akademie der Wissenschaften. Berlin: Duncker und Humblot, 1952- (to date 9 Vols.: Aachen to Hüttig).

NBG   <u>Nouvelle biographie générale</u>. Ed. by Dr. Hoefer. Paris: 1852-1870 (46 Vols., Vol. 1-19 entitled <u>Nouvelle biographie universelle</u>).

Newald   Richard Newald, <u>Erasmus Roterodamus</u>. Freiburg: Verlag Erwin Burda, 1947.

NNBW   <u>Nieuw Nederlandsch Biografisch Woordenboek</u>. Ed. by Philip Christiaan Molhuysen et al. Leiden: A.W. Sijthoff's Uitgevers-Maatschappij, 1911-1937 (10 Vols.).

Olin   John C. Olin et al., eds., <u>Luther, Erasmus and the Reformation: A Catholic-Protestant Reappraisal</u>. New York: Fordham University Press, 1969.

Olin(TB)   John C. Olin, trl. and ed., <u>Desiderius Erasmus: Christian Humanism</u>
              <u>and the Reformation</u>. New York: Harper Torchbooks, 1965.

Ono   Luigi Ferrari, <u>Onomasticon. Repertorio biobibliografico degli scrittori</u>
              <u>italiani dal 1501 al 1850</u>. Milano: U. Hoepli, 1947.

Padberg   Rudolf Padberg, <u>Personaler Humanismus. Das Bildungsverständnis des</u>
              <u>Erasmus von Rotterdam und seine Bedeutung für die Gegenwart</u>. Paderborn:
              Schöningh, 1964.

Pastor   Ludwig Pastor, <u>The History of the Popes from the Close of the Middle</u>
              <u>Ages</u>. Trl. from the German. London: Routledge and K. Paul, St.
              Louis, Mo.: B. Herder, 1938-1961 (40 Vols.).

Payne   John B. Payne, <u>Erasmus: His Theology of the Sacraments</u>. Richmond,
              Va.: John Knox Press, 1970.

Phillips   Margaret Mann Phillips, <u>The 'Adages' of Erasmus: A Study with</u>
              <u>Translations</u>. Cambridge: University Press, 1964.

Phillips(2)   Margaret Mann Phillips, <u>Erasmus and the Northern Renaissance</u>. London:
              English Universities Press, 1949.

Popkin   Richard H. Popkin, <u>The History of Scepticism from Erasmus to Descartes</u>.
              Assen: Van Gorcum, 1960.

Rabil   Albert Rabil, <u>Erasmus and the New Testament. The Mind of a Christian</u>
              <u>Humanist</u>. San Antonio: Trinity University Press, 1972.

Renaudet(1)   Augustin Renaudet, <u>Erasme, sa pensée religieuse et son action d'après</u>
              <u>sa correspondance (1518-1521)</u>. Paris: F. Alcan, 1926.

Renaudet(2)   Augustin Renaudet, <u>Préréforme et humanisme à Paris pendant les premières</u>
              <u>guerres d'Italie (1494-1517)</u>. 2nd ed. Paris: Librairie d'Argences, 1953.

Renaudet(3)   Augustin Renaudet, <u>Etudes érasmiennes</u>. Paris: Droz, 1939.

Renaudet(4)   Augustin Renaudet, <u>Erasme et l'Italie</u>. Genève: Droz, 1954.

Renaudet(5)   Augustin Renaudet, <u>Humanisme et Renaissance</u>. Genève: Droz, 1958.

Reynolds   Ernest E. Reynolds, <u>Thomas More and Erasmus</u>. New York: Fordham
              University Press, 1965.

Ritter   Gerhard Ritter, <u>Erasmus und der deutsche Humanistenkreis am Oberrhein</u>.
              Freiburg: Wagnersche Universitäts-Buhhandlung, 1937.

Rouschausse   Jean Rouschausse, <u>Erasmus and Fisher: Their Correspondence (1511-1524)</u>.
              Paris: Vrin, 1968.

Rüdiger   Horst Rüdiger, <u>Wesen und Wandlung des Humanismus</u>. Hamburg: Hoffmann
              und Campe, 1937.

Rupp   Gordon Rupp, <u>Luther's Progress to the Diet of Worms</u>. New York: Harper
              and Row, 1964 (Harper Torchbooks, TB 120).

Schottenloher   Otto Schottenloher, _Erasmus im Ringen um die humanistische Bildungs-form_. Münster i.W.: Aschendorff, 1933.

Schwiebert   Ernest George Schwiebert, _Luther and His Times. The Reformation from a New Perspective_. Saint Louis, Mo.: Concordia Publishing House, 1950.

Scrinium   _Scrinium Erasmianum_. 2 Vols. Ed. by J. Coppens. Leiden: E.J. Brill, 1969.

Sellmair   Josef Sellmair, _Humanitas christiana: Geschichte des christlichen Humanismus_. München: Ehrenwirth, 1949.

Skalweit   Stephan Skalweit, _Reich und Reformation_. Berlin: Propyläen Verlag, 1967.

Smith   Preserved Smith, _Erasmus: A Study of His Life, Ideals and Place in History_. New York: Harper and Brothers, 1923 (reprinted New York: Dover Publications, 1962).

Sowards   Jesse K. Sowards, _Thomas More and the Friendship of Erasmus (1499-1517). A Study in Northern Humanism_. Ann Arbor: University of Michigan Microfilms, 1952.

Spitz   Lewis W. Spitz, _The Religious Renaissance of the German Humanists_. Cambridge: Harvard University Press, 1963.

Sponge   _Spongia Erasmi adversus aspergines Hutteni_, LB, X, 1631-1672
(or Sp.)   (Bö, II, 265-324).

Stokes   F. Griffin Stokes, _Epistolae obscurorum virorum_. Bi-lingual Latin and English edition. London: Chatto and Windus, 1925.

Stolz   Johann Jacob Stolz, _Ulrich von Hutten gegen Desiderius Erasmus und Desiderius Erasmus gegen Ulrich von Hutten. Zwey Streitschriften aus dem 16. Jahrhundert_. Aarau: Heinrich Reimigius Sauerländer, 1813.

Strauss   David Friedrich Strauss, _Ulrich von Hutten_. 3 Parts in 2 Vols. Leipzig: Brockhaus, 1858-1860 (Parts I and II are a biography of Hutten, Part III is a translation of Hutten's major dialogues).

Surtz(1)   Edward Surtz, _The Praise of Wisdom. A Commentary on the Religious and Moral Problems and Background of St. Thomas More's 'Utopia'_. Chicago: Loyola University Press, 1957.

Surtz(2)   Edward Surtz, _The Praise of Pleasure. Philosophy, Education and Communism in More's 'Utopia'_. Cambridge: Harvard University Press, 1957.

Szamatólski   Siegfried Szamatólski, _Ulrich von Huttens deutsche Schriften_. Strassburg: Trübner, 1891.

Taylor   Henry Osborn Taylor, _Erasmus and Luther_. New York: Macmillan, 1920 (reprinted New York: Collier Books, 1962).

Telle   Emile V. Telle, <u>Erasme de Rotterdam et le septième sacrement</u>.
               <u>Etude d'évangelisme matrimonial au XVIᵉ siècle et contribution</u>
               <u>à la biographie intellectuelle d'Erasme</u>. Genève: Droz, 1954.

Thompson(1)   Craig R. Thompson, <u>The Colloquies of Erasmus</u>. Trl. and ed. by
               Craig R. Thompson. Chicago: University of Chicago Press, 1965.

Thompson(2)   Craig R. Thompson, <u>The Translation of Lucian by Erasmus and St.</u>
               <u>Thomas More</u>. Ithaca: The Vail-Ballou Press, 1940.

Tracy   James D. Tracy, <u>Erasmus: The Growth of a Mind</u>. Genève: Droz, 1972.

UTM   Germain Marc'hadour, <u>L'Univers de Thomas More</u>. <u>Chronologie critique</u>
               <u>de More, Erasme, et leur époque (1477-1536)</u>. Paris: Librairie
               Philosophique J. Vrin, 1963 (Series: De Pétrarque à Descartes,
               Vol. V).

Walser   Fritz Walser, <u>Die politische Entwicklung Ulrichs von Hutten während</u>
               <u>der Entscheidungsjahre der Reformation</u>. München: Oldenbourg, 1928.

Werckshagen   Carl Werckshagen, <u>Luther und Hutten</u>. <u>Eine historische Studie über</u>
               <u>das Verhältnis Luthers zum Humanismus in den Jahren 1518-1520</u>.
               Wittenberg: Herrosé Verlag, 1888.

Winkler   Gerhard B. Winkler, <u>Erasmus von Rotterdam und die Einleitungsschriften</u>
               <u>zum Neuen Testament: formale Strukturen und theologischer Sinn</u>.
               Münster i.W.: Aschendorff, 1974.

Woodward   William H. Woodward, <u>Desiderius Erasmus Concerning the Aim and</u>
               <u>Method of Education</u>. New York: Bureau of Publications, Teachers
               College, Columbia University, 1904 (reprinted 1964).

Introduction

THE POLEMICS OF ERASMUS AND ULRICH VON HUTTEN

"What is a humanist? ... A humanist is one who has a love of things human,
one whose regard is centered on the world about him and the best that man
has done; one who cares more for art and letters, particularly the art
and letters of Greece and Rome, than for the dry light of reason or the
mystic's flight into the unknown; one who distrusts allegory; one who
adores critical editions with variants and variorum notes; one who has a
passion for manuscripts, which he would like to discover, beg, borrow or
steal; one who has an eloquent tongue which he frequently exercises; one
who has a sharp tongue, which on occasion can let free a flood of good
billingsgate or sting an opponent.
... Not all humanists possess all the features of such humanism. ... One
point deserves emphasis above all that I have mentioned. It is this. The
humanist, though his sympathies are deeply rooted in the past, concentrates
his energies on the present. If he wraps himself up in the past and is not
aware what age he is living in, he is a pedant. His works may be useful
reference, but they will convey no message to his generation. All the great
scholars that I have mentioned were true humanists, because they were true
servants of their own times."

Edward Kennard Rand
"St. Jerome the Humanist"
Founders of the Middle Ages

- - - - - - - - -

When we speak or write about a famous man in any field it is
customary to discuss the great deeds he performed, the seminal ideas he
expounded in his works, or the finer human characteristics he embodied in
his daily intercourse with his fellow men - in short, it seems natural to
concentrate upon and admire his successes. In discussing Erasmus' polemics
with Hutten, however, we are forced to dwell for a while upon one of his
decided failures. Such a seemingly negative approach to Erasmus should
not awaken any feeling of animosity toward him as man or scholar, nor
should it lead to any disparagement of his character or his well deserved
fame. On the contrary, Erasmus, like every other human being, deserves to
be understood not only as a human exponent of some universal abstract truth
but also as a unique personality whose greatness flows as much from his
individuality as from his position as representative of some thesis in the
ever developing world of ideas. The quarrel between Erasmus and Ulrich von

Hutten, his erstwhile admirer and devoted disciple, was the tragic culmina-
tion of a friendship of some nine years' duration and resulted primarily -
and one feels compelled to add, inevitably - from the fusion of specific
external events and the temperaments and inner dispositions of the two
individuals involved.

The two first met in Mainz in August 1514[1] where Erasmus read
Reuchlin's Oculare Speculum and was hosted by the active group of local
Humanists,[2] Hutten among them, all of whom undoubtedly sought to enlist
Erasmus' aid in Reuchlin's polemics with the Dominicans at Cologne[3] - a
service Erasmus gladly rendered by writing to Rome in Reuchlin's defense
and again by praising him in the preface to his edition of the writings of
St. Jerome, a work dedicated not by whim to Pope Leo X.[4] At this first
meeting Hutten showed Erasmus a copy of his Triumphus Capnionis, leaving
the ultimate decision concerning its publication to Erasmus' discretion.[5]
In April of the following year, while en route to England, Erasmus again
met with Reuchlin, Hermann Busch and Hutten, this time in Frankfurt am Main,
where the Humanist circle hoped to celebrate one of its favored "Socratic
banquets."[6] Erasmus so captivated the spirit of the young Hutten that in
a letter he wrote to him in Oct. 1515 he intimated that he was preparing a
new edition of his Nemo, in the preface to which Erasmus would be mentioned
with all due honor. For some reason the publication of this second edition
was postponed until 1518, but in the dedicatory preface to Crotus Rubianus
Hutten does praise Erasmus as a truly Christian individual, a thinker basically
opposed to scholastic theology and a restorer of ancient Christian teaching
and scholarship. Judging almost solely from these two personal encounters
(and they only met personally once more, at Louvain in 1520), Hutten saw in
Erasmus not the scholar and the Humanist but rather a polemical spirit and
the opponent of the same hated enemies against whom he himself fought.[7]

In October 1515 Hutten wrote to Erasmus to inform him that,
although he would prefer to remain ever at Erasmus' feet and be closer to
him than Alcibiades was to Socrates, to serve and protect him as was becoming
to a German Knight, he was nonetheless forced by his family to repair to
Italy and study law.[8] While in Italy Hutten travelled extensively, visiting
Erasmus' friends and praising him highly wherever he went as a great Humanist
writer and the educator of the young Prince Charles.[9]

In return for Hutten's flattering comments and undoubtedly captivated by the young man's personality and genius, Erasmus reciprocated with
equally flattering praise of Hutten in the Annotations to his Greek edition
of the New Testament (1516); in a passage on friendship he eulogizes Hutten
as a mind great enough to accomplish for his countrymen what the aristocracy
there could or would not do because of their penchant for war and their
general lack of the refining amenities of true culture.[10]

After wandering throughout Europe for several years Hutten finally
settled down in 1518 at the Court of the young Archbishop Albrecht, a man
reputed for his business acumen, his learning and his admiration for the
newer Humanistic writers, Erasmus above all. Although both Albrecht and
Hutten tried several times to lure Erasmus to Mainz on a permanent basis,
their attempts proved fruitless. With his usual diplomatic aplomb, however,
Erasmus did not wholly alienate himself from the affections of either - he
dedicated a separate reprinting of his famous Ratio verae theologiae to
Albrecht and he proposed that Hutten rewrite the Latin history of the Church,
a task which lay close to Albrecht's heart and one he hoped Erasmus would
undertake. In proposing that Hutten fulfill this task, Erasmus clearly displayed once again his respect for his younger contemporary.[11]

Two letters of the year 1519 between Erasmus and Hutten are important not so much for what they say directly as for what they portend -

at least from the vantage point of hindsight. Hutten's letter of March is
a request that Erasmus intercede with Albrecht on Hutten's behalf to the
effect that Albrecht give him a permanent pension, thereby allowing him to
withdraw from active service at court, a life that had become intolerable
as far as he was concerned. Hutten also mentioned that he was sending
Erasmus his latest works, namely the poems _Febris_ and _Phalarismus_.[12] In
his response to Hutten, Erasmus stated that he had especially enjoyed the
Febris but that since Hutten had attacked Cardinal Cajetan in it by name he
could also understand why it had been forbidden at Louvain. Then in a
jesting but at the same time rather serious vein, Erasmus rebuked Hutten
for even considering joining the proposed armed conflict against the more
reactionary nobles of Germany. Why should he fight with the sword, Erasmus
asks, thereby endangering his great mind and linguistic talents? Fight
rather with the pen, he admonishes, for should Hutten be killed, who could
replace him? To place one's trust in Mars is most ill-advised, for of all
the gods Mars is the most stupid, the most inconstant. It was precisely
this awareness of the more militant aspect of Hutten's character that led
to the final rupture of their friendship. Erasmus might have been hopeful
as far as Hutten personally was concerned, but blind he was not.[13] In a
letter to Cardinal Wolsey of May 1519 Erasmus admitted that the younger
breed of writers in Germany were somewhat too violent and vituperative, but
then after all they were being threatened and goaded unmercifully by their
adversaries. As he stated, however, naming Hutten among others, he could
talk to them and strive to calm them with reasonable argument, but force them
one way or another he could not.[14]

Without a doubt the greatest proof of Erasmus' love and respect
for Hutten is the now famous letter of 1519, in which Erasmus described at

length the personality of his most intimate friend, Thomas More.   At

the end of this letter Erasmus mentioned Hutten's desire to fight for him

and promised him that soon he would have a man to combat who was more

animal than human - an allusion to Edward Lee, who had spearheaded an

abusive attack on Erasmus' New Testament. Erasmus was well aware that

the young German Humanists, especially Hutten, stood at his beck and call;

but that Hutten preferred to declare physical warfare against tyrants and

fight not only with the pen, shows the decided difference in their respective

natures. Erasmus did not approve of the coarseness that exuded from

Hutten's writings, but as long as Hutten was befriended by Archbishop

Albrecht, Erasmus chose to see in him more of the Humanist and less of

the warrior knight.

The first mention of Luther and his reform controversy inter-

jected into the friendship triangle of Erasmus, Hutten and Albrecht, was

made in a letter by Erasmus to Albrecht in October 1519.   At first Erasmus

was rather sympathetic to Luther and his cause, but when a rumor was spread

abroad that he was really the author of Luther's books, Erasmus decided it

was time expressly to deny any connection with the would-be reformer. This

he did in his letter to Albrecht. He also stated, however, that the fault

and the roots of the controversy lay not with Luther but sprang rather from

the aridity of scholastic theology nourished by the excessive trade in

indulgences and the more than pharisaical ceremonies that had encrusted the

spirit of true piety. In a sense Erasmus, while rejecting Luther, did never-

theless defend the spirit which motivated the reformer's actions. The letter

for Albrecht was entrusted to Hutten who, instead of delivering it to the

Archbishop, had it published and distributed.   Erasmus, however, was not

particularly disturbed that the letter had appeared in print, for as yet

Luther had still not openly attacked Rome. After the appearance of Luther's

Babylonian Captivity of the Church, however, Erasmus went out of his way

to disavow any connection with the letter's publication, asseverating to his

many correspondents that obviously his enemies had published the letter as

a means of transforming him into a "Lutheran" and, therefore, openly suspect

and dangerous to the Church. To Albrecht alone did he admit that Hutten

had published the letter and this without his consent.[19]

Matters came to a head in 1520 with the excommunication of Luther

and the proscription of Hutten. On his way to Brussels Hutten visited

Erasmus at Louvain and begged him openly to side with Luther and join in

the full-scale attack on Rome.[20] Not only was the whole idea of open war-

fare repugnant to Erasmus, but it seemed to him a hopelessly lost cause.

Even if Luther's cause were pious and good, Rome and her allies were too

powerful: to undertake open combat against them was decidedly foolish.

Erasmus stated again that he was a warrior of the spirit and not of the flesh

and that although he still loved Hutten it grieved him to see such a gifted

mind swept down into the whirlpool of battlefield slaughter. Hutten, for

his part, still felt that Luther's and Erasmus' goals were the same and

that Erasmus was simply holding himself in abeyance until the propitious

moment to strike openly should arrive. With the conclusion of the Diet of

Worms, however, Humanism as an intellectual movement was polarized into two

contending parties - the one staunchly loyal to Rome, the other staunchly

pro-Luther. Hutten, as is to be expected, contacted Luther and offered his

personal services in the forthcoming struggle; Erasmus, as is also to be

expected, sought as much as possible to remain aloof from either camp.[21]

In August 1520 Hutten wrote a letter to Erasmus which in many

ways can be viewed as the first draft of his later Expostulation. In this

letter he accuses Erasmus of being too weak and non-committal in his defense

8

of Reuchlin; he censures Erasmus for having at first praised the Letters of Obscure Men, a work he now condemns; he reproaches Erasmus for his vacillating attitude toward Luther, reminding him at the same time that regardless of his personal feelings his earlier writings would still stand in defense of Luther's cause; Hutten claims that many were attempting to prove to him that Erasmus was not to be trusted but that he (Hutten) refused to believe this gossip and would continue to do so as long as Erasmus would refrain from fighting against either Reuchlin or Luther; if Erasmus could say noting constructive in the issues at hand, then silence would be the best policy.[22]

Erasmus remained in Louvain until the fall of 1520, but fearing that he would be rather unsafe in this bastion of conservatism unless he were to come out openly against Luther, he moved to Cologne. There he received another letter from Hutten (dated 13 Nov. 1520), in which he badgered Erasmus about remaining in the midst of Luther's enemies. Since it was Erasmus who had reawakened true scholarship and striven to promote evangelical piety, he ought to be aware of how hated he was by the Curialist party, since as far as they were concerned he was the real cause of the reform movement which was sweeping throughout Europe. Would it not be better, Hutten suggested, if Erasmus were to move to Basle where he would be safe and his movements less restricted?[23]

In February 1521 Erasmus did move to Basle, not only to escape his enemies in Louvain and Cologne but also to oversee the printing of his works by Froben. He considered Basle neutral in the Reformation struggle. Eight years later, however, Basle too became one of the strongholds of Protestantism and once again Erasmus was forced to withdraw from the center of the arena. In May 1535, however, on his way to the Netherlands, he returned to Basle to see some more works through Froben's press; while

9

there he was fatally strickened and died in July 1536.

The year 1522 proved to be both the apex and the nadir of Hutten's career. As a comrade-in-arms of Franz von Sickingen, Hutten took an active part in the "Pfaffenkrieg" waged along the Rhein valley by the disgruntled and decaying knightly class. When their campaign ended in complete failure - the armies decimated, Sickingen's strongholds besieged and captured, the insurgents proscribed throughout the Empire - Sickingen withdrew to his castle in Landstuhl (where he was killed in May 1523) and Hutten left Germany for Switzerland. Around the end of July he was in Landstuhl; from there he went to Schletstadt where he met Beatus Rhenanus. It was here that he told Beatus in the company of several others that he would inspire Erasmus with more courage when he saw him again. By the end of November Hutten had arrived in Basle and taken up residence in the inn Zur Blume, where he hoped

25

to spend the rest of the winter.

While in Basle Hutten remained anything but inactive. Among other things he attacked members of Erasmus' circle of friends, especially Basil Amerbach; he wrote an attack on the Electoral Prince of the Palatinate; penned a fierce satire against a doctor in Basle who had undertaken some rather stupid and ineffective cures of Hutten's syphilitic condition; and finally he seems to have agitated too overtly for the expropriation of ecclesiastical possessions. As a result of this flurry of activity, the magistracy of Basle requested him to leave the city, which he did on 19 January 1523. He moved to Mühlhausen, a village not far from Basle, and took up residence in the local Augustinian monastery, whose members were in

26

sympathy with their brethren in Wittemberg.

It was here in March that Hutten received a copy of that fateful letter Erasmus wrote in February 1523 to Marcus Laurinus, Dean of the College of St. Donation in Bruges. In essence the letter is a long defense of him-

self with but one object in mind - to clear his name from any suspicion
of being even remotely a partisan of Luther's. He explained that his move
from Cologne to Basle was necessitated by his desire to oversee the printing
of his works; although some felt his move signified his support of Luther
(whose works had been condemned by Louvain and Cologne as well as the
Sorbonne), this was decidedly not true. Since he was still on excellent
terms with the Emperor and the Pope, there was no truth to the rumor that
Hoogstraten had had his books burned in Cologne - he (Erasmus) might almost
believe that some Lutherans had circulated this story so as to force him
into an open attack on the Curialist party. He wished that both parties
would come to him in Basle and seek his advice, for then he could once again
reiterate what he had always stressed - moderation. Some of his former
friends had recently joined Luther, others were quite hostile to him, but
as long as moderation and sincerity prevailed he could remain friends with
them all. At this point he mentioned that Hutten had been in Basle for a
few days but they had not seen one another; had Hutten come to visit him,
he would have been warmly received, for what Hutten had done in Germany
did not really concern Erasmus. As it was, Hutten could not leave his stove-
heated quarters and, therefore, he did not come to visit him. Since it was
incumbent upon the competent ecclesiastical authorities to pass judgment on
Luther's works and teachings, he (Erasmus) could not and would not do so; in
any event he had not yet even read all Luther's Latin books and could not
read his German writings. In his (Erasmus') correspondence, he had stated,
however, that Luther's works displayed too much bitterness and an obvious
lack of moderation; but it was true that Luther was discussing many points
in the current state of affairs that had to be corrected for the well-being
of Christendom. Since Luther allowed himself the freedom of attacking
everyone - Church Councils and some of the Church Fathers included - everyone

11

was attacking him with equal right; why then should Erasmus not enjoy the
same freedom and perhaps likewise write against Luther, especially since
he was being commanded to do so by those whom it was dangerous to refuse?
To remain above the melee was in a sense prompted by his innate modesty,
for many wise men were already accusing him of having written some of Luther's
works. This is an honor he could not accept and like another John the Baptist
he must exclaim: "I am not he!" Since Luther and his partisans felt that
Erasmus was both a weak Christian and a weak mind, it was far better for him
to cling to the proven Doctors of the Church rather than trust himself to
the new ordinances and dispensations of Martin Luther. The goals for which
he (Erasmus) had always striven were simple and had not altered: evangelical
unity, a peaceful settlement of the evils and abuses besetting the Church,
and a respect for the dignity of the priesthood complemented by the freedom
of the Christian laity. Anyone who pursued these same goals would find a
comrade in Erasmus; those who promoted mere revolution, however, would find
in Erasmus neither a supporter nor a leader. The Lutherans claimed that they
were moved and led by the Holy Spirit; thus far this same Spirit had not
chosen to seize Erasmus, but should He ever do so, perhaps Erasmus might
play the role of a new Saul among the prophets.[27]

The effect of this letter upon Hutten's exhausted and overwrought
mind can be easily surmised. For some time he had felt that Erasmus purposely affected a coldness in matters that demanded passion; although Erasmus
might claim that he was holding himself aloof from the struggle, his correspondence proved that he still supported the tyranny of Rome; his caution
and love of peace were not virtues but only weakness and uncertainty; and
finally, there were definitely untrue statements in the letter - he had been
in Basle for "only a few days"? it was only a "stove" that had kept them
apart? it was he who should necessarily have made the first move? On the

12

third day after receiving a copy of Erasmus' letter he began writing his
Expostulation; it was completed toward the end of April.[28]

Eppendorf advised Hutten to inform Erasmus of his feelings and
so on Eppendorf's second visit from Mühlhausen an exchange of letters between
the two was initiated. In the first letter (from Erasmus to Hutten) Erasmus
attempted to assuage Hutten's anger - he stated that he had just learned of
Hutten's ire from Eppendorf and that although he was still as well disposed
toward Hutten as ever, circumstances had prevented them from seeing one
another in Basle; his request that Hutten not come to see him did not signify
a rejection of Hutten as a friend, but only a desire that Hutten refrain
from burdening him with any odium that could arise from their interview; he
had told Eppendorf that Hutten could come if he really wanted to do so and
if he could bear the chill in Erasmus' house; Erasmus claimed that he still
wished Hutten well and hoped that he had no worse enemy than Erasmus; he
wondered if others were not trying to agitate Hutten into writing against
Erasmus, although he did not deserve such treatment, and did Hutten not
realize that an open break between them would give great pleasure to his own
enemies, especially Hoogstraten; therefore he requested that Hutten expostulate
with him in private via letter; Erasmus also admonished Hutten to consider
his own knightly reputation - should he write against Erasmus, others would
believe he did so only to obtain money since he was in such straitened
circumstances; he said he was warning him of this out of love not fear, but
should Hutten attack him, Hutten's reputation would suffer the more, even
if Erasmus remained silent - which he would not do; therefore, Erasmus says,
consult your reason not your passions; and he closed with the statement "I
await your challenge."[29]

Hutten's response was rather defiant. He promised to send Erasmus
the unprinted Expostulation within three days, although his letter revealed

13

the essence of his pamphlet; he explained that no one was goading him into
writing against Erasmus and he recounted the details surrounding his conversation with Beatus Rhenanus in Schletstadt; he also gave vent to his
indignation about Erasmus' use of a "stove" as the reason that the two had
not met in Basle.[30]

Erasmus then responded, answering Hutten's letter point for point.
Again he warned Hutten against doing anything to damage his reputation
further and closed with the exhortation that if they must disagree, let it
be in private.[31]

By this time the manuscript had been seen by many in Basle and was
forwarded to Zurich, from where Erasmus heard of its contents through correspondence from friends. Hutten answered Erasmus' last letter, more mildly
this time - either because he had had a change of heart or because the news
of Sickingen's death had affected his belligerency for the better. He
promised that their former peace and friendship could be restored if Erasmus
would only remain silent.[32]

When Erasmus finally did receive a copy of the manuscript, Eppendorf
suggested that he might send Hutten some money as an inducement to prevent
him from publishing it. Both Johann Froben and Johann Botzheim offered
Erasmus the funds to be forwarded to Hutten. Erasmus, however, flatly refused to "bribe" Hutten with anything - such an action amounted to surrendering
to attempted blackmail.[33]

In the meantime Hutten had moved from Mühlhausen to Zurich, and
from there he again wrote to Erasmus, suggesting that since what was done
could not be undone, it would be best to attribute the whole misunderstanding
to Ate, the goddess of precipitate and ill-considered evil deeds, and forget
it; in the future he would act more cautiously. In passing he mentioned
that Eppendorf had suggested not publishing the manuscript. It was this same

Eppendorf, however, who rode to Strassburg and contacted Johann Schott,
Hutten's former publisher. The work was in print by the middle of July. 34

Erasmus' initial reaction to the pamphlet was one of indignation
rather than anger, an indignation he expressed succinctly in a letter to
Willibald Pirckheimer - nowhere in Germany had he found such incivility,
shamelessness, vanity and hatefulness as in this one pamphlet of Hutten's,
and how thankless he was for Erasmus' love of him and the many recommendations
written on his behalf to Albrecht of Mainz, princes and cardinals, not to
mention the praise heaped upon him in Erasmus' published books! 35 At first,
Erasmus says, he had thought of not even answering Hutten's vicious allegations,
but upon urging from his friends he dashed off his refutation of the charges
in six days, a refutation that was of laconic brevity (although the Sponge
is almost twice as long as Hutten's Expostulation) and demonstrated Erasmus'
proverbial moderation (although his self-defense often slips into direct ad
hominem attacks on Hutten's character). 36

Both the Expostulation and the Sponge start with a discussion of
Hutten's failure to obtain an interview with Erasmus while he was in Basle.
For Hutten Erasmus' request that he not come was a grave insult; Erasmus'
defense is rather weak if one takes seriously his protestations of love
and affection for Hutten. Although the Sponge was intended to refute the
accusations leveled against him, Erasmus considered it appropriate to revive
the indiscretion on Hutten's part back in 1519, when without knowledge or
permission of the author Hutten published a letter Erasmus had written to
Archbishop Albrecht condemning the violence of the denunciations being
thundered against Luther. 37

Hutten expressed his sense of great repugnance at Erasmus' claim
that the truth doesn't always have to be told. 38 The charge is easily and
credibly refuted not only by Erasmus' explanations but all the more so by

15

an even cursory acquaintance with his personality - something that should
have been evident to Hutten, who so longed to serve as "another Alcibiades
to the new German Socrates." Erasmus' position is simple - the truth qua
truth must always be "told" but it doesn't always have to be "spoken";
where the revelation of truth would effect no positive result and could
possibly cause detrimental reactions, then silence is the best policy.
Hutten should readily have appreciated this position for it was this very
advice he had sent to Erasmus in his letter of August 1520.[39]

Without specific substantiation, Hutten proceeds to vent his anger
about Erasmus' supposed volte-face in the matter of ecclesiastical and social
reformation. Instead of citing documentary evidence Hutten slides into the
slippery by-paths of hypothetical conjecture and slanted rhetorical questions:
has Erasmus changed sides out of fear of the armies the princes are amassing
against Luther? perhaps he is only seeking fresh praise? maybe he is simply
weak and has finally succumbed to some bribery or other? Such innuendoes,
as unbecoming as they are, were easily converted into the two-edged sword
which Erasmus wielded with equal skill and equally unseemly viciousness in
his Sponge.

Two points not as easily parried by Erasmus' dexterous pen were
Hutten's charge that Erasmus used to execrate Hoogstraten[40] but in his letter
to Laurinus he bemoans the fate of the poor man since he had become the butt
of the barbed satires in the Letters of Obscure Men; the second point being
Erasmus' letter to John Fisher describing the fate of Reuchlin after the
recapture of Stuttgart by the Duke of Württemberg.[41] In retrospect it is
easy to see that the first charge is valid only if one is unwilling to take
Erasmus' basic temperament into consideration; he was able to criticize
fiercely but was equally desirous of mending ruptured friendships whenever
possible - peace in all realms of human intercourse was his constant goal.

The second charge is likewise understandable: Erasmus could be rather
gossipy at times, almost frivolously so, but Hutten's passionate nature
would automatically tend to exaggerate any problem affecting him personally.

The heart of both sides of the polemics, however, was Erasmus'
stance <u>vis-à-vis</u> Martin Luther. Hutten's claim that Erasmus at first supported
Luther's endeavor to promote the cause of evangelical truth and piety but
was now striving to combat the cause of Christ, was vehemently denied on
all counts by Erasmus. He had never been Luther's partisan; he found Luther
too belligerent and immoderate; although he fought Roman tyranny and papal
abuses, he had never left the Church; he could not approve of the current
tumults and wars - to reestablish and then preserve peace should be the
common goal of everyone even if this required suppressing some of the truth
until a more wholesome and thorough reform could be effected. Erasmus'
suggestion that all parties submit their views and plans for reform to the
Pope in written form was, however, either facetious or ingenuously simplistic,
given the nature of the Renaissance papacy and the format of the curial
regime.[42]

Since his whole life had been dedicated to furthering knowledge
and promoting a purer form of theology, Erasmus continues, he certainly
was not about to stop now. And furthermore, he was convinced that Luther
would prefer to have him as an enemy than Hutten as a friend, considering
Hutten's violent nature - a not too subtle nor even guardedly oblique
reference to Hutten's participation in the abortive campaigns of Sickingen's
"Pfaffenkrieg." With a semblance of impartial objectivity Erasmus then
proceeds to classify the types of Lutherans one might encounter, rhetorically
asking Hutten which group has claimed him for its own. First there were
the moderate, wise, learned and prudent adherents of Luther who wanted to
change things for the better, reduce the number of ceremonies, insure the

integrity and moral incorruptibility of bishops, abolish the lucrative
trafficking in spiritual matters; but surely none of these would welcome
Hutten in their ranks. Then there were those ignorant and impure followers
of Luther's banners who did not understand what Luther hoped to accomplish
and could not contribute anything to his cause; their wholly negative
attitude and lack of sincerity, however, had caused even Hutten to disclaim
them. Lastly there were some who were out only for what plunder they could
amass - robbers, drunkards, blackmailers, a veritable rabble. Luther himself denounced such individuals and rejected their services; perhaps, however,
this was the group to which Hutten belonged since nothing but Luther's name
alone could offer him, in his destitute circumstances, some slight protection
and nourishment.

Although there were many Lutherans to be seen, Erasmus had yet
found but few who lived according to the dictates and exhortations of the
Gospel. If Hutten should happen to know any, please point them out and
Erasmus would willingly align himself on their side. Moreover, since Erasmus'
character was so weak and unpraiseworthy, let German youth follow the habits
and example of Hutten, an honorable man indeed. Given Hutten's syphilitic
condition and the Emperor's decree of outlawry against him, Erasmus'
sarcasm is apropos if not charitable. Let Hutten wage his wars against
Erasmus; it matters not, since Erasmus' innocence would protect him!

The first dedication of the Sponge was to Zwingli in Zurich and
stated expressly that Erasmus felt it advisable to counteract at its very
source the poison spewed forth by Hutten. In a private letter to Zwingli,
however, Erasmus gave vent to his annoyance that Zwingli would side with
Hutten and offer him not only aid but friendship as well, and Erasmus all
but accused him of being the ultimate cause behind the writing and the one
who had promoted the publishing of Hutten's diatribe.[43]

The initial impression of Hutten's polemical attack on Erasmus was a rather painful one. As is to be expected the Expostulation was criticized rather freely by those in the Humanist camp, and even Hutten's friend Eoban Hesse was angered that Hutten would write such a vicious tract. Although some in Luther's camp rejoiced at seeing Erasmus' hypocrisy unmasked, Melanchthon stated in his correspondence that neither he nor Luther was pleased with Hutten's performance. Even though Erasmus deserved to be censured for his ambivalent attitude toward the reform movement, his age and former merits should have been taken into consideration. As things stood, such a denunciatory pamphlet would only serve to provoke Erasmus and alienate him even further from the evangelical cause, and could ultimately add more fuel to the already active hatred of Luther and his cause.[44]

The publication of Erasmus' rejoinder, however, was criticized even more soundly than Hutten's Expostulation, for it was considered to be basically malicious in intent and only secondarily a matter of self-defense. If nothing else, Erasmus' Sponge polarized the defenders of Hutten's name and reputation, from the gentlemanly rebuke of Hermann Busch to Otto Brunfels' dialogue Responsio ad Spongiam Erasmi, which sought to answer Erasmus point by point. All that his dialogue illustrates, however, is that no matter how puerile and biting Erasmus and Hutten were, they nonetheless were operating within the framework of Humanistic concepts and ideals, whereas Brunfels heralded the onset of a newer and narrower confessional mode of thought.[45]

As we noted above, Sickingen died on 7 May 1523, after the fall of his castle in Landstuhl to the Imperial forces. At the time Hutten was still in Mühlhausen, from where, as we have seen, he wrote Erasmus a somewhat milder letter. This softened tone Erasmus attributed to the shock produced by Sickingen's death. Sometime in late May or early June, however, Hutten left for Zurich as a result of the agitation his presence was causing. It

19

was reported that the inhabitants of the village were even preparing to

46

storm the monastery and capture him.

At this time Zwingli was just initiating his reform activity in
Zurich, reforms that were in closer accord with the spirit of the warrior
knights under Sickingen than with the socio-theologically oriented Luther.
It is not surprising, therefore, that Zwingli offered Hutten aid and comfort,
although the magistracy of Zurich shied away from officially recognizing
his presence in the city. Since Hutten was completely without funds and
was receiving no support from his brothers, he was forced to live off the
charity of his friends or the money he received from blackmailing certain

47

individuals.

His physical condition had also worsened considerably and so
Zwingli sent him to a friend of his in Pfäfers, Johann Jakob Russinger, the
abbot of the local monastery, to partake of the hot water baths in the
neighboring mountains. Due to an unprecedented amount of rainfall, however,
the waters became cold and Hutten was sent back to Zurich, well provisioned

48

with food and horses.

On 21 July Hutten wrote a letter to his friend Eoban Hesse in
Erfurt, begging him to remain true to the cause of the Gospel and requesting
his aid in publishing Hutten's diatribe on the German princes In tyrannos.
But since Hesse was at the time seeking a new position in Marburg, a change
which required the support and favor of the reigning dukes, he could hardly
oppose them or promote such a scathing attack. As a result Hutten's diatribe

49

was lost.

By the end of July Hutten had removed to the island of Ufnau and
was committed to the care of the local pastor Hans Schnegg, although Zwingli
and Oecolampadius were constantly in the vicinity to offer whatever encouragement and succour they could.

Still highly insensed at Hutten's behavior, Erasmus wrote a letter to the Council of Zurich in which he stated that he did not begrudge Hutten his hiding place nor the goodness the Zurich magistrates were showing on Hutten's behalf, but for the sake of good letters as well as the city's reputation it was incumbent on the city fathers to curb Hutten's wild pen.[50] Friends notified Hutten of Erasmus' letter and in turn he wrote the Council praising them for their goodness, their honesty and their love of truth and the Gospel and requesting that they send him a copy of any letters directed to them by enemies trying to poison their minds against him. He had always been a virtuous knight and only wanted the opportunity to defend himself against any who falsely accused him. His love for the Swiss was un-bounded and he would always stand by them.[51] A few days later, however, he became violently ill and died either at the end of August or the beginning of September.[52]

It is hard to say whether or not Hutten ever saw any of the pages of the _Sponge_; the final printed version definitely not. In any event Erasmus himself seemed to feel that he was fighting more with Hutten's ghost than with Hutten his former disciple and friend.[53] Since this is so, one cannot help but wonder why he was not more conciliatory in his second preface, dedicated to the general reader. And, too, one might wish that the magnanimity of his mind had somehow been able to move his heart to expressions of sorrow if not necessarily of forgiveness, for though defending himself he could still have reminded the reader of Hutten's virtues and their years of friendship instead of praising his own modest restraint; and in warning youth to cultivate character as well as culture was he not directly condemning Hutten by implication? As Strauss pointed out in his discussion of the polemics, although Erasmus later claimed in a letter to Luther that he had said nothing derogatory about Hutten's character, was his equivocation not

21

more damning than any outspoken denunciation could ever have been?

Despite breadth of culture and refinement or depth of knowledge and wisdom,

where pique and indignation assume the proportions of a consuming passion,

it would seem we are all capable of falling victim to that aspect of the

human condition so aptly expressed by Nietzsche as "menschlich, allzu

55

menschlich."

The _Expostulation_ and the _Sponge_ speak for themselves in a sense -

the obviously spurious charges, exaggerations and venomous spite of the one

finding their counterpart in the defense of the other - but to comprehend

the bitterness of Hutten's allegations as well as the coldness and at times

spiteful counter-thrusts of Erasmus' reply, one must first endeavor to

56

clarify the total personality of both men.   An understanding of the personal-

ities of Erasmus and Hutten as exemplars of Northern Humanism is essential to

an understanding of their friendship and their final enmity, since their

relationship was wholly Humanistic in origin and development. Thus, any

points of difference between them governed by or oriented toward the Refor-

mation as such, must be reduced to their Humanistic roots. The Luther

question was never specifically central to their mutual interests - at least

initially - since Luther's goals and values were wholly different from theirs.

The position each ultimately assumed toward Luther, however, sprang from

their own divergent characters, and to the degree that their natures differed,

57

so too their response to Luther's challenge to the world order.

A satiric vein is evident in all of the Humanists, but in none

more so than in Erasmus in whom it constituted the very source of his feared

and yet revered power. No realm of personal, social, religious or mental

endeavor was spared the barbs of his pungent wit, to such an extent that one

can justifiably state that a mild scepticism formed the very basis of even

58

his theological investigations.   What _man_, he might ask, ever possessed the <u>fullness</u> of truth? For Erasmus, to be sure, man <u>in abstracto</u> is good; it is only man's ideas and his institutions that are opened to censure - a position fully developed in his <u>Praise of Folly</u>. This attitude was bound to temper Erasmus' view of Luther and the Reformation, and thus it contributed significantly to the break with Hutten, for whom such a commingling of optimism and scepticism was incomprehensible. If any one work encompasses the essential <u>Weltbild</u> of Erasmus, it is his <u>Moria</u>, and for this reason if for no other it deserves our consideration.[59]

Too often the work is listed among the writings of the "fore-runners" of the Reformation, a view that somehow does the work a great injustice, for in no sense does Erasmus seek here strictly to reform anything nor is he being purely polemical. In Folly he seeks rather to represent what he sees. All of man's happiness and goods stem from her; his activities, no matter what form they may assume, are but transformations of her basic nature. Thus even religion falls within her purview, for does it too not stem from love empowered by enthusiasm? The word "folly" encompasses the entire gamut of possible definitions, from mere animal passion and stupidity to the essence of Christian <u>simplicitas</u>, which represents a childlike naturalness and lack of sophisticated reflection. Given this total spectrum of definitions, the disparity between Christian <u>simplicitas</u> and the Greek <u>furor Platonicus</u> is merely a matter of degree and not one of kind or essence, and a fusion of Judaeo-Christian and classical cultures within the totality of God is, therefore, a foregone conclusion.

The world and man's activities therein might indeed be senseless but they are a blessing nonetheless, for man's very happiness depends upon a mixture of passion, self-deception and enthusiasm. Wisdom, then, is not a proper goal of man for it can only rob him of his illusions, and if "to be deceived is indeed a great misery, not to be deceived is the greatest misery of all." If open criticism of anything destroys one's happiness, such criticism ought to be rejected, for is the tranquillitas animi not one with Christian simplicitas? Moria plus simplicitas plus the religious exhortations of the Sermon on the Mount - these constitute Christianity, a religion of naturalness and love, whose external form is the Church. Since only a small group of the elite, in Erasmus' eyes "the Humanists," were able to comprehend this philosophic union of basically eudaemonic elements, the external apparatus of Church was a social necessity and should be accepted as such.[60]

This small circle of elite minds constituted for Erasmus a Respublica Eruditorum bound to no one nation or culture, united alone through their insight into the true condition of man and the friendship of the various members, a group dedicated to the union of the knowledge of the Ancients with the Christian faith.[61] To accomplish this aim one first had to use and then learn to despise the goods and pleasures of this world, all for the sake of philosophy and wisdom; once a humanistic formation has been obtained, it is to be despised in turn for the sake of virtue, which in its turn is despised for the sake of Christian humility or simplicitas, the source of man's happiness. Erasmus' own life well illustrates these ideas as theories rendered into act. His attendance upon many wealthy patrons, his love of elegance and courtly manners, his tastes in food and drink - he indeed first learned to use the "goods and pleasures" of this world; on the other hand the weakness of his bodily constitution forced him to lead the quiet, more regulated life of a scholar. Thus in his very physical nature he embodied a mixture of the love of life and a scorn of the world culminating in a tranquillitas animi as a basic principle of life. Indeed, this principle re-echoed throughout his works (Enchiridion, De pueris instituendis, Institutio principis Christiani) to such a degree that as much

24

as he respected the Ancients he showed no interest in and even warned
against reading about the heroic feats of Grecian and Roman military prowess,
which could only lead man astray through the power of bad example. Thus
long before he ever met Hutten, Erasmus had expressly condemned his younger
contemporary's knightly-warrior ideals.[62]

In Erasmus then we can glimpse at least a twofold world: a
bourgeois world ruled by the Church whose external apparatus might be
senseless but which nonetheless guarantees happiness to the multitude; and
a much smaller world of the erudite who can enjoy and yet see through the
deceptions of life. Both are justified, both should be able to live in peace
without interfering with one another. Of the two principles the rationalistic
one guided Erasmus' thought; the eudaemonic, his life.[63] This alone would
explain his refusal of martyrdom for any truth and his lack of the reformer's
zeal. He himself once said that if driven to it, he would undoubtedly follow
the example of Peter, who through fear and love of life denied his Lord.[64]
And is this love of life not basic to the Encomium Moriae?

This seemingly ambivalent stance of Erasmus was, for him at least,
not at all a matter of conflicting interests, for in his own mind these two
worlds had coalesced into one, reconciled by the double principle of Christian
simplicitas wedded to allegory. In the Praise of Folly the Christian religion
is viewed as one of the fruits of folly, a simple, undogmatic, practical
morality that found its best expression in the early communities of the
Church - a morality, therefore, which as one of the goals of Humanistic
philosophy, could again be revivified by means of the re-edition and study
of the works of the Church Fathers. In his writings allegory assumes a
precedence not to be overlooked, for it serves as the means of reconciliation
between classical and Christian mythology. Socrates, Christ, the apostles -
all are akin to the Silenus of Alcibiades, exhibiting poverty and humility

25

on the exterior but possessing within vast stores of wisdom and experience.
Transferring the Silenus-concept to his contemporary milieu Erasmus could
easily reconcile the use and even in part the abuse of the ecclesiastical
sacramental system and its numerous symbols and ceremonies.[65]

In the _Ratio verae theologiae_ he stated expressly that some truths
are better seen through a prism than viewed directly, and thus the holy is
more majestically effective when perceived in symbols than when apprehended
directly.[66] To protect the weak, ecclesiastical forms are justified - the
strong alone can perceive the spirit immediately.[67] Likewise, within a
Neo-Platonic frame of reference, just as God is reflected in His universe
in a triune progression (the world of angels or ideas, the world of spirits
or concepts, and the world of man or body), so too the community of Christendom has a tripartite structure - clerics, princes and the masses, each one
a recipient of the divine word in proportion to its capacity for receiving
it. Thus, in theory at least, Erasmus had achieved a unity between the
foolishness of this world and the ideal of the scholar, between ancient and
Christian culture, and between pure Christianity and the ecclesiastic dis-
tortions existing in the Church. As a Humanist, therefore, he could work
for a renascence of pristine Christianity while at the same time living at
peace within the existing Church structure. With such an orientation one
could not expect to find in Erasmus the zeal and passionate consequences
of an enflamed reformer. Although to be sure he did attack the worldly
power and pretentions of Rome, he nonetheless defended the Church structure
as a necessity of human nature; and though on the one hand he did advocate
the spread of Scriptural study among the laity, in the next breath he would
emphasize the absolute necessity of a knowledge of Hebrew, Greek and Latin
for those who hoped to interpret Scripture correctly. Without a doubt
Erasmus was sincere and committed to his cause, but his was a sincerity of

26

personal integrity and his cause was human nature itself. That Hutten

finally broke with Erasmus is not at all surprising - one wonders rather

that they remained friends as long as they did.[68]

In Hutten's Nemo, one of his first works, we find a sense of

scepticism somewhat akin to that in the Praise of Folly, but we note as well

something peculiarly different, namely a vitriolic scorn of the limitations

of life expressed with a bitterness completely unchecked by the gentle

laughter of the Erasmian satire. Again in his poem Fortuna his scepticism

is given free rein - nothing but pure luck controls life since fate is blind

and acts without reason, unable ever to answer man's questions concerning

ultimate verities.[69] A sense of irony, though differing in degrees, is

nonetheless present in both Hutten and Erasmus and it was this very mood

that initially fostered their friendship. When Erasmus praised Hutten's

Nemo, the young Humanist was so elated that he hailed him as the Saviour of

the Century. The two men likewise shared a respect for the satirical works

of Lucian, a bond that also forged yet another link between More and Hutten

in Erasmus' circle of personal favorites. Lucian's sceptical views and

excoriating comments on the dissolution of religious solidarity and integrity

in his own day, his biting attacks on the tyrants of the Empire, and his

merciless caricatures of degenerate philosophers found a receptive audience

and a sympathetic echo in the Humanistic outpourings of the Renaissance.[70]

Hutten's scepticism, however, was not wholly devoid of positive

ideals and here too he plucked a responsive chord in Erasmus' breast.

Although Hutten refused to be assimilated by a society he held in contempt,

he did have an ideal toward which to strive, a goal which he expressed

poignantly in his Fortuna as the beata tranquillitas of the scholar's life,

with communion within a closed circle of like-minded friends as the sole

source of traffic with the world, a communion sealed by and embodied in the

printed word.[71]

Given Hutten's native temperament, his early training and his family tradition, it is not surprising to find, from its very inception, a minor fissure in his friendship with Erasmus, a crack that could be ignored for just so long before it split asunder into an irreparable breach. As Erasmus advanced in age he began to see folly as the sole source of the world's happiness, an insight that masked the visage of scepticism with a condescending smile of tolerance if not necessarily of approval. And as long as the coterie of the Humanist elite was restricted to a small circle of individuals who chose to live a semi-retired existence, free from the vexatious demands of political, social or religious absolutes, it was really of little consequence what the unenlightened held to be unalterable truths. Such an attitude, however, was basically at odds with Hutten's own activistic character; as far as he was concerned, truth was truth and under the banner of the generally accepted Humanistic ideals he sought to wage war on the world of falsehood and barbarism. In no sense was the <u>Respublica Eruditorum</u> a cowering band of intellectual anchorites, it was rather a crusading Order which, by infusing the theories of Humanism with the militancy and purposefulness of the knightly warrior class, would revamp the very nature and structure of society. Friendship for such a community as envisaged by Hutten was a bond of all seriousness, which could permit itself the luxury of tolerance only at the expense of its own existence. How much at variance even their views on the nature of friendship happened to be is illustrated all too clearly in the acrid denunciations that Hutten levelled against what he considered to be Erasmus' betrayal of their sacred pledge of brotherhood under the sign of <u>amor Platonicus</u>.[72]

That Hutten seemed unaware of the factors separating him from Erasmus and was therefore more prone to emphasize their apparent unity of outlook, is not to be attributed merely to self-delusion or wishful thinking.

For some time Archbishop Albrecht had played a dominant role in Hutten's life, not because he was solely or even primarily interested in Hutten as an individual but rather because he sought with every means at his command to convert his see into the leading cultural center of the Germanies. Before he was invested with his bishopric, Mainz had defended the cause of Reuchlin; thus Albrecht needed only to advance and expand an already active tradition. Until the Reuchlin affair burst upon the public scene as a polarizing catalyst, the battle against cultural barbarism and religious obscurantism had something vague and unreal about it. That the defense of Reuchlin the man and his intellectual cause would loom so important in Hutten's eyes is therefore not all too surprising. As we mentioned above, in his initial captivation by Erasmus - or perhaps rather by what he thought he saw in Erasmus - Hutten believed this Prince of Humanists would lead their campaign to a glorious conclusion. In his letters defending Reuchlin at Rome as well as in his open praise of Albrecht and Hutten's youthful writings, Erasmus did nothing to discourage Hutten's evaluation of him. In Hutten's eyes, therefore, their goals were identical - the destruction of barbarism wherever encountered and by any means expediency might dictate.

The difference in their respective ages soon began to draw the differences in their characters into sharper focus. A tired as well as sceptical Erasmus saw only too clearly the senselessness of open confrontation and thus he reasonably opted for the peaceful harbor of _simplicitas_ and an Epicurean-Christian ethic; Hutten, on the other hand, still in the prime of life, was all too willing to sacrifice the arbors of _tranquillitas_ and the bowers of scepticism for the open fields of battle. This difference in approach and emphasis was aggravated all the more by an ample dash of vanity and bravado on Hutten's part, for to his chosen intellectual stance he brought alike the dynamism engendered by the urge to accomplish something

great and the burning desire for national freedom. It was only a matter
of time before the conflict churning below the surface would shatter the
crust of even the most fervid Humanist pose.

The first signs of the break occured as early as 1518 in the wake
of the Diet of Augsburg at which Hutten's idea of armed conflict was fostered
by his encounter with like-minded enthusiasts. In the fall of 1518 Hutten
wrote two significant works - the one his dialogue Aula, the other a letter
to his friend Willibald Pirckheimer, the Nürnberg patrician-Humanist. The
speakers in the dialogue definitely represent the various phases of Hutten's
own growth away from the Erasmian-type of scepticism toward his concept of
the warrior-Humanist, from the philosophising scholar to the political
activist.[74] Quite explicit, though perhaps not realizing what he was doing,
he even attacked Erasmus' fundamental ideal when he stated that it is unworthy
of man to limit himself to nothing but studying and writing without ever
undertaking to realize his goals in some concrete social form.[75] The letter
to Pirckheimer expands upon this point when Hutten explains the reasons behind his precipitous flight from the courtly life at Mainz. His nature, he
says, is not such that it could long suffer the inactivity incumbent upon a
devotee of the muses. What man of his day, he asks, would flee from deeds
as the Stoics had done? No, first he must accomplish some great feat - only
then could he retire to the idyllic world of the poet-philosopher. True,
"fortuna" might crush his talents in their infancy but the rewards of success
were worth the risk. Although not stated in so many words, this position
was a forthright renunciation of tranquillitas, the goal of Erasmus' life.[76]

Activism was now the catch-word, but with action qua action in
charge of reconnaissance the sheltered bunker of scepticism had to be
abandoned. At this particular point the two men could still remain friends,
in a somewhat attenuated sense of the word, but once Hutten was launched

into battle beneath the streaming banners of German freedom and national romanticism, all bridges between them were burned. A Humanist he desired to remain, but one cast in the mold of a Cola di Rienzi and not an Erasmus. The upsurge of German nationalism in the 16th century is in essence a reincarnation and adaptation of the Ghibelline principle of medieval politics. Nurtured by a romantic idea of Germany's past, Hutten naively judged his contemporary scene by standards of a by-gone era; he sought to revivify historic glories in his lifetime and to celebrate them in his writings. To a degree these ideas ran parallel to the ideals of Humanism and thus with a little effort and mental juggling the equation of the revival of culture with an active participation in the "Pfaffenkrieg" was an inevitable conclusion, since the only link between the German past and its present was the Knightly Class with the Emperor at its head. This position demanded, however, a total divorce of the Northern Renaissance from its Italian counterpart since each was an endeavor to resurrect a different cultural heritage. In Hutten's mind the German past was superior because it was the agent through which Europe had been rescued from the chaos into which it was plunged at the demise of a degenerate and thus worthless Roman Empire.[77]

The true Germany in Hutten's eyes was the Germany of Tacitus' Germania, rediscovered in manuscript form in 1455 and celebrated at the leading German universities by such renowned scholars as Conrad Celtis and Beatus Rhenanus.[78] In his poem Vadiscus Hutten strove further to regenerate the spirit and the name of Arminius, the warrior savior of the Germanic tribes in their heroic struggle with the tyrants of Rome. In 1515 Hutten had fought at the side of Erasmus against barbarism in general, a lack of education in particular; by 1519 how radical the change! As Arminius had formerly done battle with the Emperors of Rome, so must Hutten now wage relentless war against the Pope of Rome and his clerical legions. The shades of past glory infused with the new blood of activism, clothed in the garb

31

of ideals and crowned with a diadem of truth - what a perfect combination

for revolution or reformation, depending upon one's point of view. Allegory

was no less foreign to Hutten than it was to Erasmus, but for Hutten it had

assumed the potency of an analogical transformation-force.

If for Luther Rome was the religious seat of Antichrist, whose

power was to be overcome by spiritual means, for Hutten it was the seat of

political tyranny to be extirpated with the sword alone. To pay homage to

the foreign Pontiff and reverence his clerical ambassadors was to dishonor

Germany; money sent to Rome was nothing more than degrading tribute. As

the Saxons under Arminius had once saved Germany from enslavement under the

Roman yoke, so again under Frederick the Wise could they repeat their deeds

of valor and rush to the aid of the Emperor Charles V who was as truly

engaged in the Investiture Struggle as was Henry IV before him.[80]

Hutten - Humanistic idealism - political freedom / Luther -

religious idealism - freedom of conscience: the unity of the ultimate

purpose of these two forces is obvious, at least in theory. If in the eyes

of Erasmus the contours were far less distinct, the dichotomy hardly so

clear - so much the worse for him! Truth is truth and will admit of no

compromise! He who attempts to do so, cloaking his pusillanimity in the

shabby rags of doubt and its derivative tolerance, is not only a coward but

a traitor to the cause of God who is truth itself.[81]

In _Nemo_ Hutten had fought the world, in _Vadiscus_ his enmity is

directed solely against Rome. By background and temperament Hutten felt

himself to be a military leader - be it as guardian of the _Respublica_

Eruditorum, a defender of Reuchlin, a protector of Erasmus, or a deliverer

of the besieged Luther. If divine truth were threatened, one had no choice

but to act. When Hutten met Erasmus for the third and last time in 1520,

he tried to explain to him his ideas and his plans of action. Erasmus could

only smile at such foolhardiness. When, however, the plans were executed
and then consigned to the flames of failure, Erasmus' smile of scepticism
turned to a frown of concern and he asked Hutten not to visit him lest the
guilt of Hutten's actions be transferred by association to Erasmus' own
ideas. The stage was thus prepared for the final act: enter Hutten,
physically sick unto death, politically a banned and hunted man, mentally
distraught because of the failure of his every plan, religiously convinced
of the truth of Luther's cause and yet personally somewhat suspect by the
reformer himself. [82]   In need of encouragement and hope he appears before
his former mentor and friend, only to find himself in this last refuge
persona non grata. Urged on by Erasmus' enemies, supplied with half-truths
and bold-faced lies, hurt in his sense of pride and stung in his sense of
integrity by the apparent lack of same in the man who was once almost a
deity in his eyes, Hutten reacted in the only way he knew how - in truly
Humanistic fashion he penned an attack against Erasmus as the living symbol
of perversity and inconstancy, seeking to destroy him in the eyes of posterity.
In all else he might have failed, in this he would succeed; his form of
Humanistic truth would prevail in the act of the written word. Erasmus'
response is basically a self-defense, although at times he sadly digresses
into the slippery alleys of personal abuse and unnecessary recrimination.
The truth undoubtedly does lie more heavily on his scales than on Hutten's,
but in the final analysis it really does not matter, for the causes of the
polemics are of far greater importance and more compelling interest than
their ultimate effects.

Although both Erasmus and Hutten could at first ridicule the world
in which they lived, their courses of development diverged too sharply to
permit any enduring cooperation. Erasmus learned to ridicule and doubt even
the means and terms by which he scorned the world and, recognizing this

position, he could not in conscience judge any single man or group. Hutten's growth, however, led more unswervingly along the path of strong conviction and dogmatic ridicule and thus step by step he was led to condemnation and confrontation. Their final meeting in Basle, which was actually no meeting at all, could never have resulted in such bitter enmity if the basis of such hatred were not already at hand. The misunderstandings and mishaps involved and even the Luther issue were in no sense the cause - this lay rather in the irreconcilable differences of their natures, which completely[83] destroyed whatever points of contact and interest they once had shared.

Notes: Introduction

1. Allen, II, Eps. 300 (cf. n. 12, p. 4), 332 (cf. Introduction); Allen, III, Ep. 967 (cf. n. 72, p. 589); Holborn, Ch. 4, "Polemic against Scholasticism. Acquaintance with Erasmus", pp. 49-72; Werner Kaegi, "Hutten und Erasmus. Ihre Freundschaft und ihr Streit", _Historische Vierteljahrschrift_ (Leipzig), XXX (1924), 200-278, 461-514; hereafter referred to as "Kaegi"; Strauss, I, 110, 216; Sponge, pars. 376-377.

2. Allen, II, Ep. 305; Spitz, "Wimpfeling - Sacerdotal Humanist", pp. 41-60, "Celtis - the Arch-Humanist", pp. 81-109; Cornelis Augustijn, "Die religiöse Gedankenwelt des Erasmus und sein Einfluss in den nördlichen Niederlanden", _Rheinische Vierteljahrsblätter_ (Bonn), XXVIII (1963), 218-230; Ritter.

3. Cf. n. 1 above, Holborn; Spitz, "Reuchlin - Pythagoras Reborn", pp. 61-80; Strauss, I, Ch. 7, "Reuchlins Kampf mit den Cölnern und Hutten's Theilnahme an demselben. 1511-1517", pp. 188-230; Brod; Geiger.

4. Allen, II, Eps. 333, 334, 335 (cf. esp. p. 88); Geiger, pp. 339-343; "The Apotheosis of that Incomparable Worthy, John Reuchlin" (Col., pp. 79-85).

5. Cf. Sponge, pars. 376-378; Strauss, I, 216-217. For a discussion of the Hutten's activities in Reuchlin's defense and his participation in the writing of the _Epistolae obscurorum virorum_ (hereafter referred to as EOV) cf. Strauss, I, 231-275; Hutten's poem _Triumphus Doctoris Reuchlini sive Ioannis Reuchlini viri clarissimi encomium_ (Bö, III, 413-448); Francis Griffin Stokes, _Epistolae Obscurorum Virorum_ (The Latin Text with an English Rendering, Notes and an Historical Introduction). London: Chatto and Windus, 1925; the three volumes of the EOV appear in Bö, VI, 1-80 (Volumen primum), 181-300 (Volumen alterum), 515-534 (Volumen tertium). For other writings in connection with the Reuchlin affair cf. _Defensio Ioannis Pepericorni contra famosas et criminales Obscurorum Virorum Epistolas_ (Bö, VI, 81-176); _Ex obscurorum virorum salibus cribratus dialogus_ (Bö, VI, 301-322); _Lamentationes obscurorum virorum_ (Bö, VI, 323-395); _Ortvini Gratii epistola apologetica,_

(Bö, VI, 396-416); <u>Hochstratus ovans dialogus festivissimus</u>(Bö, VI, 461-488);

Hutten's letter to Rich. Crocus (22 Aug. 1516) in which he says that Erasmus

had approved of the EOV(Bö, I, 123-124). Concerning Erasmus' attitude to-

ward Reuchlin and the EOV cf. Allen, II, Ep. 300, 11. 1-30: (the learned

world supports Reuchlin against Pfefferkorn; the 1513 condemnation by

Hoogstraten is really a defense of Reuchlin's case; in any event Reuchlin

should avoid abusive language in the future); Allen, II, Ep. 324 (again

praise of Reuchlin and his scholarship); Allen, II, Ep. 335, 11. 303-307

(in the dedication of his edition of Jerome's works to the Pope, Erasmus

praises Reuchlin's erudition and calls him the ornament of Germany); Allen,

II, Ep. 413, 11. 13-17 (Erasmus states that the Basle preacher Capito was

more learned in Hebrew than Reuchlin; concerning Hutten's fury at this remark

and Erasmus' justification of the statement cf. Expostulation, pars. 85-87

(hereafter referred to as "Exp") and Sponge, pars. 97-99); Allen, III, Ep.

622 (Erasmus is displeased with the EOV; some are indeed witty but they are

basically offensive because they mention individuals by name; people are

accusing Erasmus of writing some of the letters just as they had accused him

of composing the satire <u>Julius Exclusus</u>; for the sake of good letters the

EOV ought to be suppressed); Allen, III, Ep. 636, 11. 26-34 (although Erasmus

favors Reuchlin and he himself is at war with Hoogstraten, he must condemn

the virulence of the <u>Triumphus Capnionis</u>); Allen, III, Ep. 694, 11. 21-33,

108-114 (Erasmus praises Pirckheimer's defense of Reuchlin (cf. Eckert/Imhoff,

pp. 239-268) because he writes in a learned yet friendly manner; he warns

Pirckheimer, however, against befouling himself by fighting with dirty men -

which Reuchlin's enemies are); Allen, III, Ep. 808, 11. 13-24 (condemnation

of the EOV; again he states that he had nothing to do with them and that he

does not know who the author is); Allen, III, Ep. 961, 11. 23-48 (he had

nothing to do with the <u>Julius Exclusus</u>, Hutten's <u>Nemo</u>, the EOV or Luther's

works; he neither could nor would write such things); Allen, III, Ep. 967,

11. 67-88 (Erasmus had only a passing acquaintance with Reuchlin, but he
had warned him to write with less asperity; it is wrong to confuse the cause
of good letters with the Reuchlin or the Luther affairs); Allen, IV, Ep.
1006, 11. 1-48 (Erasmus was grieved at Reuchlin's _Defensio_ ... _contra_
calumniatores suos Colonienses because it was so abusive, although Reuchlin
himself was a very mild man; many have accused Hoogstraten of being greedy
and tyrannical, but Erasmus has tried to soften such views; Hoogstraten's
own _Apologia_ (Feb. 1518), however, also lacked the mildness and moderation
one would expect from a Christian theologian); Allen, IV, Ep. 1033, 11. 19-
45, 192-211 (Erasmus again disclaims any participation in the Reuchlin or
the Luther affairs; he always condemned the poisonous battles between the
partisans of Reuchlin and Hoogstraten; the ignorant members of the Dominican
Order attack Reuchlin because, though a layman, he is so learned in the
biblical languages); Allen, IV, Ep. 1141, 11. 14-30 (Reuchlin's enemies are
again attacking him because Luther used his name to bolster his own cause;
Luther did this against Erasmus' advice); Allen, IV, Ep. 1217, 11. 93-94
(he was never involved in the Reuchlin affair); Allen, VII, Ep. 2045, 11.
164-177 (again a denial that he was ever involved in the EOV; the Dominicans,
however, were so stupid that they thought the Letters were really a defense
of their Order). An interesting footnote to history is the fact that in a
letter to Reuchlin (22 Feb. 1521) Hutten reproached this man he so venerated
because Reuchlin had broken with his nephew Melanchthon because the latter
refused to come to Ingolstadt to live and because he had advocated Luther's
position at the Leipzig Disputation. Hutten accused Reuchlin of not supporting
Luther and wishing his cause suppressed; cf. Ludwig Geiger, _Johann Reuchlins_
Briefwechsel. Tübingen: Litterarischer Verein in Stuttgart, 1875, p. 328
(Bö, VII, 803-804); C. Th. Keim, "Ein Wort über Reuchlin's Bruch mit Luther
und Melanchthon" _Theologische Jahrbücher_ (Tübingen), XIII (1854), 288-294;

37

Eckert/Imhoff, "Die Apologie für Johannes Reuchlin...", pp. 239-268.

6. Allen, II, Eps. 325, 327 (Bö, I, 43-44); Manfred Krebs, "Reuchlins Beziehungen zu Erasmus von Rotterdam", in <u>Johannes Reuchlin 1455-1522</u>. <u>Festgabe seiner</u> <u>Vaterstadt Pforzheim zur 500. Wiederkehr seines Geburtstages</u>. Ed. Manfred Krebs. Im Selbstverlag der Stadt Pforzheim, 1955, pp. 139-155 (cf. esp. pp. 144-145).

7. The dialogue <u>Nemo</u> is a play on the word nobody: nobody is real, can know everything, is free from error, can serve two masters, etc. The expanded version (published 1518) is far more biting: nobody can succeed in life by means of virtue, prefers others to self, can be pious and a courtier at the same time, can unite all Germans under one head, can free Germany from the Italian yoke, dares to censure the Pope, rewards good studies, etc. The dedication to Crotus Rubianus is a further attack on the society of the day: Humanistic learning is scorned by the knights, theologians and lawyers. The knights want nothing but brigandage, the theologians prefer hair-splitting scholasticism to true piety and virtue, and the lawyers are more interested in their glosses of Roman law than in the older German customs. The theologians also reject the works of Erasmus and Reuchlin. Such men attack only the defenseless and, for that reason, refuse to wage war against the Turks. Hutten definitely prefers to remain a "nobody" than to join their ranks (cf. <u>Nemo</u> (Bö, III, 107-118); "Hutten ad Crotum Rubianum in Neminem Praefatio" (Bö, III, 175-184, cf. p. 183, par. 40); Allen, II, Ep. 365 (Bö, I, 102-103)). For a discussion of the first edition (1512?) cf. Strauss, I, 103-104; the second edition, Strauss, I, 148-150; the dedicatory letter to Rubianus, Strauss, I, 150-154.

8. Holborn, Ch. 5, "The Termination of Studies in Italy, 1515-1517", pp. 73-86; Strauss, Ch. 6, "Hutten's zweite Reise nach Italien. 1515-1517", pp. 147-187.

9. Allen, II, Ep. 588 (Bö, I, 135-136); Allen, III, Ep. 611 (Bö, I, 146-148);

Holborn, Ch. 7, "Politics and Pamphleteering, 1518-1519", pp. 101-116; Strauss, I, 147-187.

10. Bö, I, 163-164 (Erasmus Roterodamus in Annotationibus in primam ad Thessalonicenses: "... At in aliis quidem saepenumero videmus magna vitia vel aetati condonari vel eruditioni. In his omnibus quos recensui, vitae morumque probitas cum eruditione ex aequo certat. Sed pene exciderat unicum illud Musarum delitium Udalricus Huttenus adolescens et imaginibus clarus, etc.). This eulogy of Hutten was also printed in the 1519 and 1522 editions but was thereafter removed. Cf. Eckert, "Novum Instrumentum", I, 213-258; Tracy, pp. 167-178.

11. Allen, III, Eps. 614, 631, 661 (Bö, I, 188); Allen, III, 745 (Erasmus' response to Ep. 661 above (Bö, I, 231-232)); Hutten's letter to Albert, Mar. 1519, as Preface to his work on Livy (Bö, I, 249-251); Hutten to Francis I, 28 Feb. 1519 (Bö, I, 242-246); Kaegi, pp. 214-215; Kalkoff (1), Ch. 4, "Huttens Verhältnis zur kurmainzischen Regierung", pp. 119-140, Ch. 6, "Die Universität Mainz und der Humanismus zur Zeit Huttens", pp. 168-220, Ch. 7, "Die Mainzer Geistlichkeit und Huttens Satire", pp. 221-267; Kalkoff (2), Ch. 2, "Richtlinien zur Beurteilung Huttens im Rahmen bisher unbekannter Tatsachen: 1. Huttens Stellung und Tätigkeit im Dienste des Erzbischofs von Mainz", pp. 42-72.

12. Allen, III, Ep. 923 (Bö, I, 248).

13. Allen, III, Ep. 951 (Bö, I, 260-262).

14. Allen, II, Ep. 967, 11. 68-122 (Erasmus states that although he had only a passing acquaintance with Reuchlin, he had warned him against too much asperity in his Apologia; he had read only a few pages of Luther's works since he had no time for such things; although he was no partisan of Luther, he had heard many reports about his excellent moral life - even Luther's enemies could not attack him on that account; to touch the money bags of the clery, however, was bound to stir up much trouble which in the end would

only harm good letters; Hutten will some day be a great name in Germany; Hutten, Eoban Hesse and Beatus Rhenanus were fighting for the advancement of good studies in Germany - this type of man Erasmus would support; Bö, I, 269-271).

15. Allen, IV, Ep. 999 (Bö, I, 278-286); Büchner; Marc'hadour; Reynolds; for another sketch of More and his family cf. Allen, IV, Ep. 1233.

16. Gustav Bauch, "Aus der Geschichte des Mainzer Humanismus", <u>Archiv für hessische Geschichte und Altertumskunde</u> (Darmstadt), N.F. V (1907), 3-86, cf. esp. 76-80; Bö, I, 195-217 (Hutten to Pirckheimer, 25 Oct. 1518: "Hutteni ad Pirckheimer epistola vitae suae rationem exponens"); Bö, I, 346-348 (Hutten to Lee defending Erasmus' New Testament); Allen, IV, Eps. 1037 (cf. esp. the Introduction, pp. 108-111), 1061, 1087; Bludau.

17. Allen, IV, Ep. 1033 (Bö, I, 315); cf. n. 37 below.

18. Sponge, pars. 325-328; Bö, II, 311.

19. Allen, IV, Eps. 1152 (Bö, I, 421), 1153, 1167, 1217; Allen, III, Ep. 933 (From Luther, 28 Mar. 1519: Luther was seeking Erasmus' support; Erasmus responded (Allen, III, Ep. 980, ll. 17-21) that he had not read all of Luther's books but he did agree with the spirit of those he had read, although his (Luther's) language was too violent).

20. Hoborn, Ch. 8, "Expectation and Preparation for the Reform in 1520", pp. 117-134; Kalkoff (2), pp. 185-187; Strauss, II, Ch. 2, "Entschiedenes Auftreten gegen Rom; Verhältnis zu Luther. 1519-1520", pp. 18-60, Ch. 3, "Huttens Reise an den Hof des Erzherzogs Ferdinand. Enttäuschung. Päpstliche Verfolgung. 1520", pp. 61-72. Hutten's activity during 1520 is reflected clearly in his correspondence, cf. esp. Bö, I, 320-321 (to Melanchthon, 20 Jan. 1520: extends his greetings to Luther and states that Sickingen will protect him with troops if necessary); Bö, I, 324-325 (to Melanchthon, 28 Feb. 1520: Hutten would like to meet Luther; could he possibly come to

Steckelberg?); Bö, I, 355-356 (to Luther, 4 June 1520: since they both were fighting for the cause of Christ, He would surely bless their efforts; what a glory Luther's excommunication really is - though evil men exult, God will bless Luther; Hutten always agreed with Luther's ideas and wishes to fight with him; Sickingen again asks Luther to come to the safety of the Ebernburg; cf. Strauss, II, 62-64); Bö, I, 400-403 (to Albert of Brandenburg, 13 Sept. 1520: begs the Archbishop not to allow the Pope to trample the rights of Germany under foot; he still loves Albert though others are trying to keep them apart and condemn him without a trial; Hutten will trust in God even though the Pope should use the arm of the state against him. This letter was prompted by Pope Leo X's demand that Albert arrest Hutten; cf. Bö, I, 362-363 and Albert's response, Bö, I, 363-365); Allen, IV, Ep. 1161, 11. 10-39 Hutten begs Erasmus to flee to Germany and expresses the hope that Emperor Charles V will aid in the reform of the Church, or at least not hinder it; since this is unlikely, a great war is unavoidable); Bö, I, 435-437 (to Luther, 5 Dec. 1520: Hutten again begs Luther to come to Sickingen's fortified castle; since some of their former allies still believe that it is unholy to oppose the Pope, they are being deserted - protection for Luther is thus necessary).

21. Sponge, pars. 84-85, 128, 173-374; Heer, "Erasmus, Luther und die lutherischen Erasmianer", pp. 213-241; Holborn, Ch. 11, "Hutten's War on the Romanists", pp. 174-187; Kalkoff (2), Ch. 5, "Huttens Verhältnis zu Luther bis zu ihrer gleichzeitigen Verurteilung durch den Papst", pp. 157-209, Ch. 6, "Hutten als ungebetener Mitstreiter Luthers im Vergleiche mit Erasmus und Friedrich dem Weisen", pp. 210-233; Lortz, pp. 67-68 (Hutten), 127-135 (Erasmus); Strauss, II, Ch. 2; Jones; Heinrich Bornkamm, "Erasmus und Luther," Luther-jahrbuch (Munich), XXV (1958), 3-22; Paul Kalkoff, "Erasmus und Hutten in ihrem Verhältnis zu Luther", Historische Zeitschrift (Munich), CXXII (1920), 260-267. Concerning the progress of the estrangement between Erasmus and

Hutten cf. Allen, IV, Ep. 1113, ll. 36-38 (Hutten hopes to see the unification of Germany under Charles V; with letters of recommendation from Erasmus he has left to see Ferdinand (Charles' brother); cf. esp. n. 36); Allen, IV, Ep. 1119, ll. 33-34 (Hutten no longer moderates his style as he once did); Allen, IV, Ep. 1135, ll. 1-15 (the Pope wants Hutten arrested; an open war is unavoidable; cf. n. 2); Allen, IV, Ep. 1152, ll. 1-11 (Erasmus did not give Hutten permission to publish his former letter to Albert; this was either an accident or perfidious treachery); Allen, IV, Ep. 1161, ll. 5-25 (Luther is the liberator of Christendom and will free Germany from Roman tyranny); Allen, IV, Ep. 1167, esp. ll. 92-101, 268-283, 390-404 (Erasmus wishes to be neutral in the Luther affair; he has warned Luther to be less violent; because he had opposed the printing of Luther's books in Basle he had alienated Luther's partisans in Germany); Allen, IV, Ep. 1184, l. 25(Erasmus used to love Hutten's genius); Allen, IV, Ep. 1217, ll. 12-34 (Hutten had no permission to publish Erasmus' conciliatory views on Luther); Allen, V, Ep. 1313, ll. 1-27 (although there are evils to be corrected, unrestrained fury cannot do it; open warfare will crush Luther and the cause of reform); Allen, V, Ep. 1352 (Erasmus always wanted the abuses in the Church to be corrected, but because he will not take a partisan stance he is attacked by both sides; he pleads with the Pope to defend his (Erasmus') reputation and lead the way to reform for the glory of Christ); Allen, V, Ep. 1526, ll. 12-30, 47-73 (Erasmus still chooses to remain aloof from the battle but requests the Duke to control Luther's wild excesses; he states that he has begged both sides to meet and discuss their differences, but neither will agree to do so); cf. n. 54 below.

22. Allen, IV, Ep. 1135 (Bö, I, 367-369); Strauss, II, 259-260.

23. Allen, IV, Ep. 1161 (Bö, I, 423-426); Strauss, II, 260-261.

24. M.A. Nauwelaerts, "Érasme à Louvain. Ephémérides d'un séjour de 1517 à 1521", Scrinium, I, 3-24; R. Crahay, "Les censeurs louvanistes d'Érasme",

Scrinium, I, 221-249; M.-M. de la Garanderie, "Les relations d'Érasme avec Paris au temps de son séjour aux Pays-Bas méridionaux (1516-1521)", _Scrinium_, I, 29-53; P.G. Bietenholz, "Erasmus und der Basler Buchhandel in Frankreich", _Scrinium_, I, 293-323. Concerning Erasmus' removal to Freiburg cf. Allen, VIII, Eps. 2158, 2196; Allen, IX, Ep. 2470.

25. For Hutten's movements from July to November 1522 cf. Strauss, II, 241-243. That Hutten arrived in Basle by 28 Nov. 1522 is proven by a letter of that date, cf. Bö, II, 153 (Glareanus to Zwingli); concerning his residence in the inn Zur Blume cf. Theophil Burckhardt-Biedermann, _Bonifacius Amerbach und die Reformation_. Basle: R. Reich, 1894, p. 15.

26. Strauss, II, 266 (ns. 2 and 3); Bö, II, 157 (from Oecolampadius to Hedio, 21 Jan. 1523: as a result of the machinations of the local clergy Hutten was forced to leave the city; the writer does not know where he went); Allen, V, Ep. 1437, 11. 24-39; Allen, VII, Ep. 1934; Johann Jacob Hottinger, _Historia der Reform in der Eidgenossenschaft_. Zurich: Bodmer, 1708, p. 118.

27. Allen, V, Ep. 1342 (Bö II, 158-177); a German translation with explanatory notes can be found in Kieser, pp. 1-64. Concerning some of the points in this letter to Laurinus cf. J. Beumer, "Erasmus von Rotterdam und sein Verhältnis zu dem deutschen Humanismus mit besonderer Rücksicht auf die konfessionellen Gegensätze", _Scrinium_, I, 165-201; Ernst Wilhelm Kohls, "Erasmus und die werdende evangelische Bewegung des 16. Jahrhunderts", _Scrinium_, I, 203-219; B. Hall, "Erasmus: Biblical Scholar and Reformer", in _Erasmus_. Ed. T.A. Tracy. Albuquerque: University of New Mexico Press, 1970, pp. 81-113. Erasmus explains in various ways to different people his reasons for not seeing Hutten while he was in Basle: Allen, V, Ep. 1331, 11. 57-59 (he did not want to see Hutten although he still loved him; he had other things to do); Allen, V, Ep. 1342, 11. 689-696 (Hutten could not leave his stove-heated rooms and, therefore, could not come to visit him); Allen, V, Ep. 1356, 11. 5-15 (Erasmus did not forbid Hutten to come, he

only requested him not to do so lest his presence burden Erasmus with more hatred from his enemies; this is the version he expands in the Sponge); Erasmus' letter to Melanchthon, however, is most revealing, cf. Allen, V, Ep. 1496, 11. 1-16 (through involvement with Hutten he could easily insult his own patrons who already hated Hutten - news of their meeting would fly to Rome, Brabant, England and to the Emperor's court; Erasmus also feared that he would be forced to invite Hutten to live with him and then support him because his financial situation was so helplessly straitened; he also feared contagion from Hutten's syphilis which might infect even the air in Erasmus' house; Erasmus feared Hutten might beg him for financial assistance which he was in no position to give him; he feared also that Hutten's strong evangelical spirit would disrupt his household and prove detrimental to Erasmus' own labors; and finally, Hutten's bitterness and innate tendency toward boasting must surely have increased as a result of his troubles - this is something Erasmus could not live with).

28. Strauss, II, 271-272; Otto Brunfels, Responsio ad Spongiam Erasmi (Bö, II, 341, response to par. 389).

29. Allen, V, Ep. 1356 (Bö, II, 178-179); Strauss, II, 272-276 (cf. Gottlieb J. Planck, Geschichte ... unsers protestantischen Lehrbegriffs ... 6 vols. Leipzig: Crusius (Vogel), 1791-1800, Vol. II, p. 107, n. 143). Concerning Erasmus' attitude toward Eppendorf in this whole affair cf. Allen, V, Eps. 1376, 1383, 1437 and Allen, VII, Ep. 1934.

30. Although the correspondence between Erasmus and Hutten (which followed Erasmus' letter of 25 March 1523) is not available, there are references to it, cf. Sponge, pars. 18-21, 42-49 and 383-386; cf. also Erasmus' letter to John Botzheim, Allen, VII, Ep. 1934, 11. 200-320.

31. Sponge, pars. 42-49, 383-386.

32. Sponge, pars. 18-21.

33. Allen, VII, Ep. 1934 (Bö, II, 429-434); Bö, II, 382-383 (from Zwingli to Bonifatius Wolfhart, 11 Oct. 1523: money from various people given to Eppendorf for Hutten); Allen, V , Ep. 1383, 11. 1-15 (Hutten blackmailed his friends).

34. Strauss, II, 277; Sponge, pars. 22-23. On the title page of the Schott edition of the Exp. there appeared two portraits, one of Erasmus and the other of Hutten; there was also a medallion with two heads designated as Melanchthon and Luther. These are all reproduced in Julius von Pflugk-Harttung, ed., Im Morgenrot der Reformation. Hersfeld: Vertriebsanstalt christlicher Kunstwerke, 1912, p. 584; cf. also Josef Benzing, Ulrich von Hutten und seine Drucker. Wiesbaden: Harrassowitz, 1956. Concerning Erasmus' negative reaction to the portraits cf. Allen, V, Eps. 1376, 1459, 1477.

35. Allen, V, Ep. 1376. Concerning some of Erasmus' recommendations on Hutten's behalf cf. Allen, III, Ep. 745 11. 15-18, 67, Ep. 967 11. 105-111, Ep. 968 11. 20-22, Allen, IV, Ep. 1009, 11. 67-71.

36. Allen, V, 1437; Sponge, par. 424; Exp. (Bö, II, 180-248); Spongia (LB, X, 1631-1672 and Bö, II, 265-324): the polemics were translated into German twice, cf. Stolz (1813) and Kieser (1823).

37. The letter in question is Allen, IV, Ep. 1033 (Erasmus states that he had warned Luther to write with more gentleness and less arrogance; even Luther's enemies admit that he is a good man; what reproach would be warranted even if Erasmus did support Luther?; if Luther is innocent he should not be crushed by rogues, if he is guilty he should be corrected; he is condemned by theologians who do not understand him - they only thirst for his blood because he attacks abuses upon which they feed; Luther only offered propositions for debate - for this he should not be punished; he wrote against the burden of human ordinances which do need correcting; Luther has written

with more imprudence than impiety and has shown greater deference to the Bible than to scholastic principles; to support the worldly power of the Pope is to serve him ill - those who do this have incited the Pope against Luther; heresy once meant dissenting from the Gospel - now it is equated with knowledge and eloquence; to preserve one's peace of mind and soul it is best not to become involved in these troubles). Two years later there was a decided change in Erasmus' attitude toward Luther, cf. Allen, IV, Ep. 1202, 11. 1-19 (Erasmus castigates Luther's immoderation; he warns against the danger Luther's attacks pose to the peace of the Church and the future progress of true reform); cf. n. 17 above.

38. Allen, IV, Ep. 1167 (basically an expression of Erasmus' desire to be neutral in the Luther affair; Erasmus had warned Luther to be less violent, and by opposing the printing of Luther's books in Basle he had alienated many friends in Germany; although much of what Luther says is true, printing his books would only lead to more tumults and hatred); cf. Exp., par. 73 and Sponge, pars. 242-243.

39. Cf. Note 22 above.

40. Exp., pars. 58-59, 67-70; Sponge, pars. 67-71, 76-88. Concerning Erasmus' relationship to and feelings about Hoogstraten cf. Allen, II, Ep. 300, 11. 4-6 (Hoogstraten's condemnation of Reuchlin's works is his (Reuchlin's) best defense); Allen, III, Ep. 636, 11. 22-33 (the best men favor Reuchlin in his quarrel; Erasmus, however, cannot approve of such violent invectives from either side); Allen, III, Ep. 856, 11. 24-36 (Erasmus often wanted to warn Hoogstraten not to risk his reputation by writing such pamphlets; from reading Hoogstraten's invectives one gains a poor impression of his character); Allen, III, Ep. 878, 11. 12-14 (Hoogstraten and Egmondanus (Nicholas Baechem) are much together in Louvain - "birds of a feather" reference); Allen, III, Ep. 889, 11. 40-41 (Hoogstraten was expelled from Cologne); Allen, IV,

Ep. 1006, 11. 27-37 (Erasmus is grieved at the violence of Reuchlin's
attack on Hoogstraten, but Hoogstraten is equally open to this criticism);
Allen, IV, Ep. 1033, 11. 31-45 (Erasmus is displeased with the poisonous
battles between the partisans of Reuchlin and Hoogstraten); Allen, IV,
Ep. 1040, 11. 1-5 (Hoogstraten has a copy of the letter Erasmus wrote to
Luther (30 May 1519) and accuses Erasmus of supporting Luther); Allen, IV,
Ep. 1085, 11. 4-10 (both Hoogstraten and Lee are attacking Erasmus again);
Allen, IV, Ep. 1141, 11. 18-19 (Hoogstraten has some theses in mind that
will force everyone to submit to the Inquisition); Allen, IV, Ep. 1166,
11. 53-56 (Hoogstraten is responsible for the burning of Luther's books
in Cologne); Allen, V, Ep. 1299, 11. 96-101 (Hoogstraten is out to destroy
good letters); Allen, VII, Ep. 1821, 11. 23-24 (a few of Erasmus' enemies
have died, Hoogstraten among them). Concerning Hoogstraten cf. Ludwig
Geiger, "Jakob Hochstraten", ADB, XII, 527-529; Karl Goedeke, Grundriss
zur Geschichte der deutschen Dichtung aus den Quellen. 2nd ed. Dresden:
Ehlermann, 1884, Vol. I, pp. 449-451; N. Paulus, "Zur Biographie Hochstratens",
Der Katholik (Mainz), LXXXII (1902), I, 22-40.

41. Cf. Exp., par. 97; Sponge, par. 102. Concerning Erasmus' relationship to
Reuchlin and his opinions of the Letters of Obscure Men cf. n. 5 above;
Allen, IV, Ep. 1129; Rouschausse.

42. Sponge, par. 409; Olin; Mee (an interesting study about the differences in
temperament, training and attitudes of Luther as reformer and Leo X as the
embodiment of the Renaissance papacy).

43. Allen, V, Ep. 1378 (Erasmus' letter to Ulrich Zwingli, Aug. 1523 - used as
the first Preface to the Sponge); Allen, V, 1384. Cf. also Gottfried W.
Locher, "Zwingli und Erasmus", Scrinium, II, 325-350.

44. Strauss, II, 297 (ns. 1 and 2). Concerning Melanchthon's reaction cf.
Corp. Ref. I, 626 (Melanchthon to Spalatin, 1523), 626-627 (Melanchthon to

Joachim Camerario, 23 Aug. 1523), 627 (Melanchthon to Oswald Ulianus, 24 Aug. 1523), 677-678 (Melanchthon to Baumgartner, 15 Oct. 1524; cf. Bö, II, 416-417). Cf. further Bö, II, 378-379 (From Nicolaus Gerbelinus to Johannes Schwebelius, 30 Sept. 1523: both Luther and Melanchthon disapprove of the open quarrel); Bö, II, 379-380 (From Luther to friend "N", 1 Oct. 1523: Luther is displeased with both Erasmus and Hutten; Erasmus was far from possessing true Christian piety and Luther certainly does not need Hutten as a defender; also found as letter No. 661 (to Konrad Pellican) in D. Martin Luthers Werke. Kristische Gesamtausgabe. Weimar: Böhlaus Nachfolger, 1933, Briefwechsel, II (cf. Introduction, pp. 158-160)); letter of Luther to Erasmus, ca. 18 Apr. 1524 in Luthers Works. Vol. 49 (Letters, II, No. 144; trl. and ed. by Gottfried G. Krodel). American Edition. Ed. Helmut T. Lehmann. Philadelphia: Fortress Press, 1972: both Erasmus and Hutten were in the wrong since their quarrel was injurious to the cause of truth and piety; cf. Allen, IV, Ep. 1443. Concerning Hutten's relationship to Melanchthon cf. Maurer, II, 83-85.

45. In defense and praise of Hutten cf. Brunnfelsii pro Hutteno ad Erasmi Spongiam Responsio (Bö, II, 325-351); Iudicium Erasmi Alberi de Spongia Erasmi Roterodami... (Bö, II, 373-378); for poems, letters, epigrams, etc., in praise of Hutten and expressing grief at his death cf. Bö, II, 354-372; Triumphus Veritatis by Hanss H. Freyermut (Bö, II, 419-424); Allen, V, Eps. 1405, 1406 (from Brunfels, Dec. 1523: letters defending his Responsio); Allen, VI, Ep. 1614 (the friendship between Erasmus and Brunfels can be restored if Brunfels so desires).

46. Strauss, II, 307 (ns. 1 and 2, cf. Johann Jacob Hottinger, Helvetische Kirchen-Geschichten. Re-edited by Ludwig Wirz. 5 vols. in 6. Zurich: Orell, Füssli, 1808-1819, Vol. II, p. 118); Allen, V, Ep. 1437.

47. Allen, V, Eps. 1376, 1383; Strauss, II, 307-309.

48. Strauss, II, 309 (ns. 3 and 4), 310 (n. 1); Bö, II, 255.

49. Strauss, II, 310-315.

50. Allen, V, Ep. 1379.

51. Bö, II, 257-258.

52. On the uncertainty as to the exact date of Hutten's death cf. Strauss, II, 317-320; Allen, V, Ep. 1388; an excerpt from the *Chiliani leibii annales A.D. MD XIII* (Bö, II, 359-360); excerpt from *De Philippi Melanchthonis ortu ... naratio* of Ioachimus Camerarius (1566; Bö, II, 361-362); Johann Jacob Hottinger, *Helvetische Kirchen-Geschichten*. Pt. 3. Zurich, 1708, pp. 98-99, 118-119 (Bö, II, 372-373).

53. Allen, V, Ep. 1389 (Second Preface to the Sponge, ca. Oct. 1523).

54. In many of his letters Erasmus tried to justify his writing of the Sponge; among others cf. Allen, V, Ep. 1376, 11. 17-24 (Erasmus never suspected such a vicious attack from Hutten; how ungrateful Hutten was for all of Erasmus' many recommendations on his behalf (cf. Allen, III, Eps. 745, 968, Allen, IV, Ep. 1009)); Allen, V, Ep. 1383, 11. 1-15 (Hutten blackmailed his friends); Allen, V, Eps. 1378, 1384 (To Ulrich Zwingli, Aug. 1523 and 31 Aug. 1523; cf. Sponge, pars. 17-19 and Brunfels' *Responsio* (Bö, II, 327-328)); Allen, V, Ep. 1411, 11. 16-18 (Erasmus is being attacked by both parties and then by his friend Hutten); Allen, V, Ep. 1429 (a rebuke to the city of Strasburg for allowing the Exp. to be printed there; it displeased Luther and Melanchthon as well (cf. Bö, II, 402); cf. also Allen, V, Ep. 1477 (Erasmus denounces the publication of Brunfels' *Responsio* in Strasburg; cf. Bö, II, 412-413)); Allen, V, Ep. 1437, 11. 8-106 (Erasmus discusses in detail his relations with Hutten and Eppendorf; for another lengthy version of these relations cf. Allen, VII, Ep. 1934); Allen, V, Ep. 1445, 11. 36-59 (an answer to Luther's letter to Erasmus (Allen, V, Ep. 1443) in which Luther expressed disapproval of both the Exp. and the Sponge; Erasmus defends himself by saying that he was moderate in his reply to Hutten since he did

not mention Hutten's dissolute life, his disease, his corruption, his foolish military ventures, his extortion or cutting ears off monks, his highway robberies; Erasmus even kept Hutten's name out of the narration of the printing of his letter to Albert of Brandenburg; Erasmus also states that thus far he had not written against Luther although powerful individuals had requested him to do so and that in the end he might be of more value to Luther than certain individuals who were writing in his defense); Allen, V, Ep. 1496, 11. 5-16 (Erasmus condemns Hutten's friends who fanned the flames of hatred; cf. n. 27 above, Allen, V, Ep. 1500, 11. 10-15 (from Melanchthon: he is displeased with the polemics for they can only injure the cause of truth, piety and good letters); Allen, V, Ep. 1523, 11. 1-17 (in answer to the above, Erasmus states that he is not worried about his own reputation, but fears the consequences of continued tumults which would indeed harm the cause of the Gospel and good letters). For a discussion of the relationship between Erasmus and Melanchthon cf. Maurer, II, 85-90); Allen, VI, Ep. 1645; Allen, VI, Ep. 1700; Allen, VII, Ep. 1804, 11. 165-168 (Eppendorf goaded Hutten into writing against Erasmus); Allen, VII, Ep. 1893, 11. 39-42 (Eppendorf was the cause of the whole tragedy); Allen, VII, Eps. 1991, 1992; Allen, IX, Ep. 2441, 11. 30-37 (Hutten's attack on the papal bull against Luther fanned the flames of war).

55. For some interpretations of the relationship between Erasmus and Hutten cf. Bainton, Ch. 8, "The Worse Century", pp. 172-200; Froude, Lecture XVI, pp. 319-337; Holborn, Ch. 12, "Hutten's Controversy with Erasmus", pp. 188-202; Huizinga, Ch. 17, "Erasmus at Basle, 1521-1529", pp. 151-160; Newald, Ch. 16, "Verdächtigungen", pp. 222-235.

56. Holborn, Ch. 10, "Worms 1521", pp. 162-173, Ch. 11, "Hutten's War on the Romanists", pp. 174-187; Kalkoff (1), "Einleitung: Ulrich von Hutten und die Reformation", pp. 1-30 (cf. n. pp. 11-14: Hutten in den "Colloquia

familiaria" des Erasmus); Kalkoff (2), pp. 239-240; Rüdiger, "Ulrich von Hutten und der deutsche Humanismus", pp. 86-102, "Desiderius Erasmus und der europäische Humanismus", pp. 103-136; Juga Russell, "Erasmus und Hutten. Ein Kapitel deutscher Tragik", <u>Deutschlands Erneuerung</u> (Munich), XV (1931), 433-438; Strauss, II, Chs. 3-7.

57. Berlichingen, "Erasmus von Rotterdam, der Vorläufer Luthers", pp. 69-88: T.B. Birch, "Informing versus Reforming. Erasmus versus Luther", <u>Review and Expositor</u> (Louisville, Ky.), XXXIV (1937), 156-174; Heinrich Bornkamm, "Erasmus und Luther", <u>Luther-Jahrbuch</u> (Munich), XXV (1958), 3-23; Franz Fritsche, "Hutten, Sickingen und Luther", <u>Evangelische Kirchenzeitung für Österreich</u> (Bielitz-Berlin), V (1888), 113-116; A. Galley, "Erasmus und Luther", <u>Der alte Glaube</u> (Leipzig), III (1902), 105-108, 123-128, 147-153; Gerrish, "Erasmus", pp. 60-85; Huizinga, "Erasmus as Humanist", pp. 39-46, "Erasmus' Mind", pp. 100-116, "Erasmus' Character", pp. 117-129; W.H. Hutton, "Erasmus and the Reformation", <u>The Quarterly Review</u> (London), CCIII (1905), 411-440; Paul Kalkoff, "Erasmus und Hutten in ihrem Verhältnis zu Luther", <u>Historische Zeitschrift</u> (Munich), CXXII (1920), 260-267; Paul Kalkoff, "Der geschichtliche Ulrich von Hutten in seinem Verhältnis zu Luther", <u>Luther-Jahrbuch</u> (Munich), V (1923), 22-55; Gerhard Ritter, "Die geschichtliche Bedeutung des deutschen Humanismus", <u>Historische Zeitschrift</u> (Munich), CXXVII (1922-1923), 393-453; Werckshagen; Holborn, Ch. 9, "Hutten and Luther", pp. 135-161; Strauss, II, 95-101, 134-137, 145-155, 182-189, 251-257; Eckert, "Erasmus und die Reformatoren", II, 327-412; Sellmair.

58. Bouyer, "La théologie d'Erasme", pp. 141-177; Heer, "Erasmus und Italien", pp. 62-82; Kohls (1); "Die Antibarbari", I, 35-68; Mestwerdt, pp. 260-262; Popkin; Johannes von Walter, "Die Ja -und Neintheologie des Erasmus", Laible, pp. 165-180; LB, X, 1696 A-C.

59. Bainton, "Italy: The Praise of Folly", pp. 78-100; Ivo Bruns, "Erasmus als

Satiriker", <u>Deutsche Rundschau</u> (Berlin), CIII (1900), 192-205; Arthur E.
Du Bois, "Humanism and Folly", <u>The Sewanee Review</u> (Sewanee, Tenn.), XL (1932),
446-459; Eckert, "Der christliche Narr", I, 130-159; Huizinga, "The Praise
of Folly", pp. 69-78; Kaiser, "Erasmus' <u>Stultitia</u>", pp. 15-100; Könneker,
"Erasmus' <u>Moria</u>", 248-329; Newald, "Das Lob der Narrheit", pp. 93-104;
Smith, "The Praise of Folly", pp. 117-128; Tracy, pp. 111-125.

60. LB, IV, 450 C ("Sed falli, inquiunt, miserum est; imo non falli, miserrium");
Halkin; for a lengthy defense by Erasmus of his <u>Praise of Folly</u> and his
edition of the New Testament cf. Allen, II, Ep. 337; Bö, II, 400-401 (from
Conradus Mutianus to Erasmus, 1 Mar. 1524: praise of Erasmus as a source
of knowledge and tranquillity).

61. Fritz Caspari, "Erasmus on the Social Function of Christian Humanism",
<u>Journal of the History of Ideas</u> (New York), VIII (1947), 78-106; Gilmore,
"Fides et Eruditio", pp. 87-114; Glöckner; Harbison, "Erasmus", pp. 69-102;
Jacob, "Christian Humanism", pp. 437-465; Mestwerdt, pp. 245-70; Ray C.
Petry, "Christian Humanism and Reform in the Erasmian Critique of Tradition",
Hardison, pp. 138-170; Rudolf Pfeiffer, "Erasmus und die Einheit der klassischen
und der christlichen Renaissance", <u>Historisches Jahrbuch</u> (Leipzig), LXXIV (1955),
175-188; Spitz, "Erasmus", pp. 197-236; S. Dresden, "Érasme et la notion de
'humanitas'", <u>Scrinium</u>, II, 527-545; Kohls (2); Padberg; Tracy, pp. 68-77
(<u>De formando studio</u>), pp. 77-82 (<u>Adagiorum</u>); Eckert, "Adagiorum chiliadestres",
I, 82-96.

62. Adams, Ch. 6, "The Genius of the Island: Designs for a New Social Order -
Erasmus' <u>Against War</u> (1515)", pp. 88-111, Ch. 7. "The Genius of the Island:
Erasmus' <u>Christian Prince</u> (1516)", pp. 112-120; P.S. Allen, "Erasmus on Peace",
<u>Bijdrajen voor Vaderlandsche Geschiedenis en Oudheidkunde</u> (The Hague), VII
(1936), 235-246; Roland H. Bainton, "The <u>Querela Pacis</u> of Erasmus: Classical
and Christian Sources", <u>Archiv für Reformationsgeschichte</u> (Leipzig-Berlin),

XLII (1951), 32-48; Chapiro; Köhler, p. 133; "Military Affairs" (Col.,
pp. 11-15), "Hunting" (Col., pp. 42-43), "The Soldier and the Carthusian"
(Col., pp. 127-233); Eckert, "Die Antibarbari", I, 82-96, "Enchiridion",
I, 97-122; Kohls (1), "Die Epistola de contemtu mundi", I, 19-34, "Die
Antibarbari", I, 35-68, "Enchiridion", I, 69-176; Tracy, pp. 31-37 (De
contemptu mundi), pp. 37-44, 61-68 (Antibarbari), pp. 83-110 (Enchiridion);
LB, IV, 588 A-B.

63. Allen, III, Ep. 858, cf. esp. p. 362, 11. 8-12 (Olin (TB), pp. 107-133).

64. Allen, IV, Ep. 1218, 11. 31-34.

65. Erich Benz, "Christus und die Silene des Alcibiades. Wandlungen eines
platonischen Bildes im Zeitalter der Reformation bei Erasmus und Sebastian
Franck", Aus der Welt der Religion (Berlin), N.F. III (1940), 1-31; Woodward,
p. 49; "Sileni Alcibiadis" (Ad, 770C-782C; Phillips, pp. 269-296); LB, V,
29 A-B; Schottenloher.

66. LB, V, 118 B-C; J.P. Payne, "The Hermeneutics of Erasmus", Scrinium, II,
13-49.

67. LB, V, 37 B-C; C.J. de Vogel, "Erasmus and His Attitude towards Church
Dogma", Scrinium, II, 101-132; Gebhardt; for what has been termed "a veritable
manifesto of the religion of pure spirit" cf. Allen, III, Ep. 858.

68. LB, V, 88C-89D; Kohls (1), I, 69-176; Eckert, "Gebet und Meditation", II,
463-498.

69. Ulrichi Hutteni Nemo (Bö, III, 107-118; Strauss, I, 103-104, 148-150);
Hulderichi Hutteni Eq. Germ. Fortuna Dialogus (Bö, IV, 75-100 Strauss,
III, 9-49: "Fortuna").

70. Albert Bauer, "Der Einfluss Lukians von Samosata auf Ulrich von Hutten",
Philologus (Leipzig), LXXV (1918), 437-462, LXXVI (1920), 192-207; Ergang,
"The Renaissance in Germany", pp. 286-310; Strauss, I, 177-179.

71. Bö, I, 3-4, 8-9, 17; Bö, IV, 75-100, cf. pars. 2-3, 17-18, 50, 83, 107;
Strauss, II, 1-17.

72. Ferguson, "The Attitude of Erasmus toward Toleration", pp. 171-181; Murray, pp. 179-212; Albert Hyma, "The Contributions by Erasmus to Dynamic Christianity", Scrinium, II, 157-182.

73. Allen, IV, Ep. 1161 (Bö, I, 423); Eckert, pp. 436-439.

74. Drewinc, "Hutten", pp. 215-284; Spitz, "Hutten - Militant Critic", pp. 110-129; Spitz, "Pirckheimer - Speculative Patrician", pp. 155-196; Strauss, II, 18-60; J. Thikötter, "Ulrich von Hutten und Franz von Sickingen. Zum 400jährigen Gedächtnis", Deutsch-evangelische Blätter (Halle), XIII (1888), 77-103.

75. Bö, IV, 49, par. 15; Newald, pp. 222-234; Smith, pp. 129-158.

76. Ulrichi Hutten Equitis ad Bilibaldum Pirckheymer, Patricium Norimbergensem, Epistola vitae suae rationem expones (25 Oct. (11 Nov.) 1518; Bö, I, 195-217: the goal of his life is the union of good letters and practical affairs; although he does not like court life (cf. Aula), he is too young for the sedentary life of a scholar - he must accomplish something in life first; his nature demands contact with all kinds of men; his defense of Reuchlin proved his love of studies; barbarism will someday be driven out of Germany - Hutten will clear the field of enemies and then Pirckheimer can peacefully sow the seeds of knowledge; Erasmus, Reuchlin and Pirckheimer - each has contributed to the awakening of good letters in Germany; a eulogy of Nürnberg as the crown of German cities; good letters need patrons - Hutten hopes the Emperor will encourage them; Pirckheimer himself combines active and scholarly pursuits - Hutten will also do so; his activity in Mainz encourages both loves of his life; praise of Erasmus edition of the New Testament, Budé's commentaries on the Pandects, etc.; closes with the triumphant shout "Oh, century! Oh, scholarship! It is a joy to be alive...!"; cf. Strauss, I, 319-330); Eckert-Imhoff, "Die Deutung der Reformation als christlichen Humanismus", pp. 277-285; Hutten's letter to Pirckheimer, pp. 334-349.

77. Bö, IV, 58-59; Hagen, "Ulrich von Hutten und Deutschlands politische Verhältnisse im Reformationszeitalter", pp. 165-268; Paul Joachimsen, "Vom Mittelalter zur Reformation", <u>Historische Vierteljahrschrift</u> (Leipzig), XX (1920-1921), 426-470; Kalkoff (2), pp. 234-494; Skalweit, pp. 58-72; Strauss, II, pp. 73-243.

78. Paul Joachimsen, "Tacitus im deutschen Humanismus", <u>Neues Jahrbuch für das klassische Altertum</u> (Leipzig-Berlin), 14. Jahrgang, XXVII (1911), 697-717, cf. esp. pp. 706-709.

79. Hutten's active role in the "Pfaffenkrieg" was but an attempt to put into deed what he had been advocating for years in his writings. A short list of his major letters and works will clarify this point. His nationalistic yearnings are evident in his letters and exhortations to the Emperor and the princes of Germany as well as in his major dialogues: <u>Epistola ad Maximilianum Caesarem</u> (1516; Bö, I, 106-113), Hutten to Sickingen (1 Mar. 1519; Bö, I, 247); <u>Huldericus de Hutten liberis in Germania omnibus</u> (27 Mar. 1520; Bö, I, 349-352); <u>Exhortatio ad Germanos ut resipiscant</u> (29 Sept. 1520?; Bö, I, 352-353); "In sequentem librum de unitate ecclesiae conservanda praefatio" (1520; Bö, I, 325-334); Hutten to Emperor Charles V (Klageschrift, Sept. 1520; Bö, I, 371-383); Hutten to Duke Frederick of Saxony (11 Sept. 1520; Bö, I, 383-399); <u>Omnibus omnis ordinis ac status in Germania principibus nobilitati et plebeis</u> (28 Sept. 1520; Bö, I, 405-419); <u>Bulla decimi Leonis contra errores Martini Lutheri</u> (Bö, V, 301-334; cf. Strauss, II, 96-99); <u>Herr Ulrichs von Hutten anzöig wie allwegen sich die Römischen Bischöff oder Bäpst gegen den teütschen Kaysseren gehalten haben</u> (Bö, V, 363-395; cf. Strauss, II, 112-115). Hutten's major dialogues: 1) <u>Febris prima</u> (Bö, IV, 27-42 - Latin original and Hutten's translation; Strauss' translation "Das Fieber. Erstes Gespräch", Strauss, III, 50-60; discussion of same, Strauss, I, 314-315: an attack on the luxurious life

of the rich, especially the clergy, with a particular thrust at Cardinal

Cajetan); 2) <u>Febris secunda</u> (Bö, IV, 101-144 - Latin and German; Strauss'

translation "Das Fieber. Zweites Gespräch", Strauss, III, 61-93; discussion

Strauss, II, 12-17: concerning the misery and evils of concubinage which

affects Rome and the whole Church; Germany must reduce the number of clerics);

3) <u>Fortuna</u> (Bö, IV, 75-100; Strauss' translation "Fortuna", Strauss, III,

12-49; discussion Strauss, II, 5-11: Hutten's desire to make his fortune

so as to be able to live in leisure and dedicate his mind to philosophic

speculation, with a wife at his side to beautify his life); 4) <u>Vadiscus</u>

<u>sive Trias Romana</u> (Bö, IV, 145-268 - Latin and German; Strauss' translation

"Vadiscus oder die römische Dreifaltigkeit", Strauss, III, 94-185; dis-

cussion Strauss, II, 27-38: a manifesto against Rome accusing the papal

court of having killed truth, piety, freedom and the Christian religion);

5) <u>Inspicientes</u> (Bö, IV, 269-308 - Latin and German; Strauss' translation

"Die Anschauenden", Strauss, III, 185-219: discussion Strauss, II, 38-46:

the strengths and weaknesses of Germany were paraded at the Diet of Augsburg;

attack on the clerical estate and the oppressive tyranny of Rome whose

tool was Cajetan); 6) <u>Monitor primus</u> (Bö, IV, 337-349; Strauss' translation

"Der Warner. Erstes Gespräch", Strauss, III, 265-288; discussion Strauss,

II, 148-151: a former friend of Luther's tells him why he has changed

sides - he is going to Rome to become a cardinal because the situation has

become too dangerous - obvious reference to Erasmus); 7) <u>Monitor secundus</u>

(Bö, IV, 350-362; Strauss' translation "Der Warner. Zweites Gespräch",

Strauss, III, 289-312; discussion Strauss, II, 138-139, 147-148, 151-156,

202-203: Sickingen's arguments win over the weakening "warner" to the war

for reform of the Empire and the Church); 8) <u>Bulla vel Bullicida</u> (Bö,

IV, 310-336; Strauss' translation "Die Bulle oder der Bullentödter",

Strauss, III, 227-264; discussion Strauss, II, 145-147: papal bulls, the

symbol of the evil of Rome, mistreat Germany; Sickingen will lead the

Germans in their struggle against this Roman tyranny) 9) <u>Praedones</u>
(Bö, IV, 363-406; Strauss' translation "Die Räuber", Strauss, III, 313-389;
discussion Strauss, II, 156-166: the greatest robbers in the Empire are not
the knights or the robber barons but the monks, priests and courtiers;
Sickingen will lead the war that must be waged against them); 10) <u>Arminius</u>
(Bö, IV, 407-418; Strauss' translation "Arminius", Strauss, III, 390-412;
discussion Strauss, II, 325-329: a new Arminius must arise to drive out
the Romans invaders once again). Concerning Erasmus' political writings cf.
Eckert, "Schriften zur Staatslehre und Politik", I, 160-212; Tracy, pp.
127-166.

80. <u>Clag an Friedrich von Sachsen</u>; (Bö, I, 383-399) <u>Invective an Aleander</u>
(Bö, II, 12-16); Brunnow; Kurt Eggers, "Die Freiheitsidee des Ulrich von
Hutten", <u>Nationalsozialistische Monatshefte</u> (Munich), VII (1937), 681-687;
Friedenthal, cf. esp. pp. 278-391.

81. Bainton, "Under Fire", pp. 151-171; Kuno Francke, "Ulrich von Huttens
Lebensideale", <u>Internationale Monatsschrift</u> (Berlin), VII (1913), 151-170;
Smith, "The Quarrel with Luther", pp. 320-371; Spitz, "Luther - The Reformer",
pp. 237-266.

82. Luther, passim; cf. n. 57 above; Kalkoff (1), pp. 268-407.

83. Holborn, pp. 188-202; Kaegi, Pt. III, pp. 461-514; Kalkoff (2), pp. 495-536;
Strauss, II, pp. 244-329; Gustav Schnürer, "Warum wurde Erasmus nicht ein
Führer der kirchlichen Erneuerung", <u>Historisches Jahrbuch</u> (Munich), LV.
(1935), 332-349.

Expostulation
of Ulrich von Hutten
with
Erasmus of Rotterdam
Priest and Theologian

ULRICH VON HUTTEN, KNIGHT

TO ERASMUS OF ROTTERDAM, THEOLOGIAN

GREETINGS

1. At long last, my dear Erasmus, it seems to have dawned on you just how painfully you hurt my feelings - and those of our mutual friends as well - by so unjustly refusing to speak to me or even see me when I was in Basle a short time ago.[1] Desiring above all to justify your conduct toward me, you have explained your actions, as far as I can judge, in different ways to various individuals, as for example in your letter to a certain Laurinus.[2] This letter was sent to me from Basle by some intimate friends of mine as soon as it appeared in print, and I must say that I am indeed astounded by what might be called this figment of your imagination. Allow me to quote you: "Hutten was here as a guest for a few days, but neither he nor I visited each other. However, had he come to see me, I certainly would not have refused to talk to him, since he is an old friend of mine..."; and then a little further on: "But since he was not able to leave his overheated room, because of poor health, and I am not able to bear such heat, it happened that we were unable to see each other."[3]

2. Now I ask you, my dear Erasmus, what sort of fabrication, no, what sort of lie, is this? Was that the reason we failed to see each other? As

59

soon as I had arrived in the city, was it not you who requested that I refrain from visiting you because of the odium my presence would cause you, a burden it would certainly be improper of me to impose on a friend? [4]

3. Again, my dear Erasmus, if the whole affair is such a trifling matter, as indeed everyone can see it is, why seek to justify your conduct in writing? If, on the other hand, you realize that you are guilty of a certain misconduct toward me, then how do you have the audacity to lie about something so well known to everyone, attempting to defend yourself by such ambiguous subterfuge?

4. Would you have us believe that, after frequently standing in the Main Square for three hours at a time conversing with friends, I was really unable to leave my heated quarters during the more than 50 days I spent in Basle - whether for reasons of health or whatever other trifling matter - and thus could not have come to pay you a visit or two? [5]

5. Is it indeed worthy of your character to depict in false colors something so well known and thus clothe the truth in the shabby garb of lies? And furthermore, I am not at all certain which angers me more, your craftiness or the fact that you have dealt with me so discourteously.

6. As a lover of sincerity I detest with my whole being all forms of deceit, and nothing offends me more than to realize that I am being treated neither with honor nor affection. You probably thought, however, that I would not start any sort of trouble about something so insignificant. Thinking, too, that I would not even bother to censure this insult, you considered yourself safe as far as I was concerned. Thus you sought only to remove from the minds of others any suspicion of overt incivility on your part.

7. Indeed, if this is what you think, you do not really know me at all! How could I possibly not consider it a grave insult to be so mistreated by you, my friend, to whom my fidelity has always been known, my good will always obvious and from whom I have never been alienated by any offense of

which you can accuse me or I myself am aware?

8. Do you really have the audacity to deny that you refused even to see me, knowing full well the number of witnesses I can call upon to testify that you did so? Or is it perhaps that you did not quite believe that I would ever take cognizance of the whole affair and thus you did not fear to concoct any old story that just happened to strike your fancy?

9. I assure you, however, that my primary concern has always been the scrupulous observance of the many obligations imposed by the very nature of friendship. And since there is no sin from which I have more consistently fled than from the accusation by a friend that I have mistreated him, so there is nothing that fills me with greater indignation than to realize that someone offends me in this same regard.

10. You might, therefore, now begin to realize just how bitterly painful it was for me to have you insult me in such a manner. How could it have been otherwise? As you yourself have publicly stated - a statement to which in conscience I acquiesce - I have always treated you with the greatest deference, almost as if prompted by a sense of awe. And now you do not consider it worth your while even to converse with me!

11. During our entire friendship, a friendship which I so passionately honored, no one ever treated you inimically who, for that very reason, was not also an enemy of mine; and now you hold this friend in such low regard that upon the most trivial suspicion of evil-minded individuals you refuse to associate with him.

12. What could possibly be more boorish? what more unworthy of my zeal for you? Undoubtedly you had to think of your own safety - that by welcoming me you could endanger yourself. Indeed, I believe the members of the Roman Curia [6] must be lying in wait for you alone, attentively observing your movements to ascertain whether or not you have anything to do with me.

13. Although countless cities throughout Germany as well as innumerable

private citizens of good repute have most sincerely extended their hospitality to Hutten,[7] fearing neither danger nor odium to themselves, Erasmus alone would seem subject to some imagined danger and unable to sustain the ill-will engendered by my presence. I truly cannot see how the former alternative might even be possible nor how the latter can be worthy of you.

14. Of my many friends not one has thus far alienated himself from me because of the connivings of the Roman Curia nor even thought it necessary to avoid my company. Now certainly the fear of any odium that might arise because of a mutual relationship is hardly sufficient reason for you to refuse to speak with a friend. If a short time ago you had joined forces with me in armed conflict,[8] then indeed you might run the risk of some danger; but that anyone should hate you just because you conversed with me, that I cannot understand at all.

15. Furthermore, when have I ever expected a friend to share any sort of danger with me, even when I ventured upon far less perilous undertakings? Is it not true that I was so wholly committed to Reuchlin's defense to the very last day of his life that I even asked him to avoid me, so that whenever his enemies, who always had far more to fear and to suffer from me than from him, complained to him about those things which I had done, he could solemnly swear that anything that had happened had been done without his knowledge?[9]

16. And to make them believe that I had not communicated or deliberated with Reuchlin, I consented to being warned against attempting anything on his behalf; to which I responded that everything I was doing concerned me alone and in no sense pertained to him - indeed, it was at my own risk and for my own cause that I was fighting.

17. Thus it was that the wretches had no peace from me even though they might from him and, while he remained silent or did something else, I pursued them hatefully enough. But why should I tell you these things as though I

62

wished to boast of my own merits? Did you yourself not commend me in your
earlier writings for the fact that I am not in the habit of compromising
anyone but myself?
        10

18. Desiring thus to harm no one, all of a sudden I should now seek to
harm you, no doubt the dearest friend I have ever had? Do you really
believe that I would have asked or even agreed to talk to you if I had
thought that my presence would have endangered you in any way? No, indeed,
this I would never have done. Quite the contrary, I would gladly have
foregone that pleasure since I have never sought to force myself upon you.
                                                                    11

19. But who could really believe that my enemies have suddenly become so
rabid that they would now consider pursuing such trifling matters, having
thus far disdained to take note of far graver provocations?

20. In honesty I must say that it is not at all likely that anyone would
have bothered molesting you on my account, since they have ignored me
personally with the greatest contempt. Granted there were grounds for
your misgivings, just what would you then dare to do for a friend since
you refuse to suffer even the slightest inconvenience?

21. Or what support might I expect from you should fate ever decree that
the power of my enemies wax so strong that I am forced to beg for aid and
assistance, seeing you refuse even to speak to me while I still enjoy favorable circumstances?   Is it perhaps credible that you would aid me in any
        12
manner whatsoever were I suddenly to be pursued by my enemies, although you
would not allow me even to visit you while these very same enemies were
attempting absolutely nothing?

22. In the meantime the municipality of Basle has joyfully offered me its
official protection and hospitality and has also most graciously offered me
financial subsistance. One public official after another has come to pay me
his respects and many individuals from every social class have eagerly sought

63

to visit me, one might even say they rushed to see me.   Even some of my

enemies have already become reconciled with me. Erasmus alone holds him-

self aloof, shut up in his room, fearing that the allegiance which he swore

to the Roman Pontiff might be suspect were the Pope to discover that he

had conversed with Hutten.

23. What other reason could you have had, if not this? Or might it

possibly be you seriously feared that an insufficient insult to me would

betray your troubled conscience? Would your duplicity not have become

only too obvious were I to reproach you concerning certain matters, which

14

I indeed seriously intended to do!

24. Nor are you unaware of why I am so annoyed with you - first because of

myself, whom you have criticized quite odiously in your writings, and then

15

because of the recently deceased Reuchlin,   whose name you have most

wretchedly besmirched, exposing him as much as you can to dishonor and

disgrace.

25. Furthermore, I wanted to admonish you concerning the Gospel and the

16

matter of freedom,   since it has come to my attention from various sources

that you no longer hold the same views on these subjects as you did formerly;

either you have changed your mind about them or what you say does not

correspond to what you believe.

26. I might also have brought forward several other matters of interest to

us both. However, on the very day I arrived in Basle I was immediately

accosted by our mutual friend, the Knight Heinrich von Eppendorf, who first

conveyed your greetings to me and afterwards requested that I not expose

17

you to any sort of odium while I was in the city.

27. I did not understand at all what he meant by this and then he finally

came right out and stated that you begged me not to visit you because you

feared that it could prove harmful to you were my enemies to discover that we had seen one another.

28. Even though this request sorely grieved and embittered me, I was nevertheless willing to forgive almost anything for the sake of your virtues, our friendship and public opinion in general. You see, at that time I still had not become aware of how your hostility toward me had corrupted you or that even then you held in readiness that dart you would hurl against the guardians of truth and the defenders of liberty.

29. Therefore I refrained from communicating with you by letter, hoping that somehow you would change your mind and, having summoned me, you would be willing to listen to me. In order to appeal to you I repeatedly walked back and forth in front of your house [18] with some of my friends, even though I had no pressing business in the neighborhood, and I am very certain that you must have seen me there more than once.

30. Later I happened to leave Basle somewhat sooner than I had anticipated, but when my friends found out that I had decided to spend the rest of the winter not far from the city, [19] some of them began to communicate with me by letter, others came out in person to visit me.

31. When by chance our conversations happened to involve you, I discovered from their reports just what sort of things you were daily saying about Luther and his supporters and that you were openly threatening us - indeed with weighty tomes - hoping in this way to destroy our movement.

32. This immediately aroused in me the suspicion that there was some truth in what others had told me about you. But even then I held myself in check, until that letter you wrote to Laurinus, the one I mentioned earlier, was brought to me - the day before yesterday, I believe. Your letter is absolutely frought with hateful abuse, [20] providing indisputable evidence of the complete reversal of your previous opinions, or, if you have not changed your mind, it gives eloquent testimony to an assumed dissimulation by which you hope to

65

ingratiate yourself with those individuals who would find it impossible to consider you their friend unless you proved yourself our enemy.

33. I was surprised by this, one might say I was completely stunned. Suffering all manner of consternation and mental torment, I kept asking myself what, in the final analysis, could have caused you to renounce your former opinions and now uphold the exact opposite position? Was it not only a short time ago you aided us in putting the Roman Pontiff in his place, with a vengeful pen castigating Rome itself as a cesspool of depravity and crime? Did you not curse papal bulls and indulgences and damn ecclesiastical ceremonies? Was it not you who scourged the curial system and execrated canon law and pontifical pronouncements? In short, did you not mercilessly flay the entire hypocritical structure of that estate? And now this same
21
Erasmus has entered into alliance with the enemy?

34. While pondering this matter rather anxiously, various ideas occurred to me which allowed me to surmise just why you had deviated so from your-self: first of all your insatiable thirst for recognition and your lust for fame which they say make you unable to bear any excellence that threatens to rival yours; and then there is a certain weakness in your character which has always displeased me as something unworthy of your greatness, but which
22
leads me to believe that sheer dread made you yield to their threats.

35. However, while pondering the matter even more intently, it seemed to me that neither of these two reasons was sufficient enough to have effected such a change in you: granted you might envy Luther because everyone is now talking about him or because far and wide his writings are being read almost more extensively than your own, and granted, too, you were convinced that by overthrowing him you could expect praise and honor for yourself, I still could not believe that because of envy or ambition you would be driven to an indiscriminate attack on an entire movement which is neither his alone nor
23
initiated by him. I was sure your first consideration would be for yourself

66

and should prompt you to keep your feet firmly where you had planted them as well as pay heed to so many estimable men who, as you know full well, are deeply involved in this matter.

36. But even if by chance you did yield to a fear of our enemies, I still could not imagine that you would have such audacity as suddenly to rise up so fiercely against those who but a short time before had been your friends. It seemed unlikely to me that anyone could suddenly become so bitterly opposed to his friends merely because he feared a common foe; and in this instance [24] I do find you bitter and pitiless.

37. Furthermore, I could not convince myself that you would so fiercely condemn your former opinions because you had found something better or that the sudden recognition of having been in error would impose upon your conscience the obligation not only to reverse your previous position but even to retract and wholly reject it with all your strength and power.

38. For if this were so, you would not have reviled authors with whom you share so many of those very faults with which you charge them and you would have advanced reasons for your actions. Such reasons, however, you fail entirely to offer. Nor would you have made such a concerted effort - which indeed seems to be the main object of your letter - to have our adversaries believe that you had never done or said anything against them, and this by toning down the most obvious as well as the most biting passages in your writings, either through a decidedly strained interpretation [25] or at times by glossing them over through deceitful pretense. It certainly would have been quite sufficient on your part merely to confess your error and beg forgiveness for your sin.

39. It therefore occurred to me that you had perhaps been bribed or that you might be anticipating some sort of preferment. These thoughts were prompted by what you yourself say about the magnificent brief you received

from Pope Adrian surpassing, in its terms of endearment, respect and out-
right praise, anything you had received before. [26]

[27]

40. You also mention that Cardinal Schiner, the Bishop of Sitten, had

promised to give you out of his own pocket a yearly pension of 500 ducats

as well as a generous travel allowance if you should decide to move to Rome.

41. There is also the Reverend Father Silvester Mazolini, as well as a

few others, who likewise summon you to Rome, promising you great recompense;

and there is even one who has offered you a certain benefice, hardly to be

despised, which will be surrendered to you whenever you desire it.

42. And yet you say there are those who unjustly claim that you have

deserted the defense of truth because you have been corrupted by greed,

and by way of self-defense you insist that had you been able to be dragged

into the present war merely by the promise of reward, you would have been

[28]

dragged into it long before now.

43. These considerations can only arouse everybody's suspicion that one

to whom inducements have so frequently been offered must in the final

analysis have accepted something. And, too, it is easy to believe this

since the more often a man is tempted, the easier it is for him to succumb

[29]

in the long run; and besides, the more one attempts to defend himself

against some accusation, the more others will assume there is justification

for suspecting him.

44. Even though these suspicions were bound to be of momentous weight, my

mind still refused to accept this conclusion because I just could not under-

stand how you could allow yourself to be corrupted by such shameful bribery,

since you already have enough wealth and, moreover, you are now of an age

when you will need very little for the future.

45. From these multifarious ideas I at length arrived at one definite

conclusion by means of which I resolutely feel that your behavior can fully

be explained. The explanation lies above all in that certain cowardice

inherent in your character, a timidity which causes you at the slightest provocation to fear the worst and thus to despair, reducing to naught your confidence in the progress of our common cause. Your fears have increased now all the more since you see a great many of the foremost princes of Germany banding together against us, and thus you have been led to believe that you must not only abandon us but also resort to any and every means at
your disposal to curry their favor. ³⁰

46. Afterwards, when they had most gratefully accepted you as one of their own and had even lavishly praised your sense of duty, acclaiming you a man of unreserved loyalty, the arrangement rather began to please you. Still, you did not dare wholly to confide yourself to them until you had first commended yourself by some service or other.

47. Therefore, after considering the matter somewhat, you decided the wisest course of action would be to write openly against the Lutherans, since Luther's enemies were greatly desirous of finding someone suitable to oppose him and had already been urging you for quite some time to assume
this task. ³¹ Thus you were swayed in part by the fear of punishment, in the event that Luther's foes should ultimately be victorious and in part by the hope of their favor, if you were to surrender unconditionally to their demands before the tragic conclusion of the whole undertaking.

48. Since there was such gusto in your first onslaught against us, I conjecture that you probably were hoping to crush our spirits and force us into some sort of unconditional surrender, for if you were to succeed in accomplishing this, not only would your future be secure but you would also be considered a truly great man and accorded an extraordinary amount of honor.

49. If your reasoning were guided by any consideration at all, it was undoubtedly this; but if it were, I strongly urge you not to be too easily

deceived. There is yet sufficient cause to remain anxious, for if the whole affair should run a course different from what you expect, I predict nothing but pitiable misfortune for you. Think it over well, my friend!

50. You have now reached an age when it is not necessary for you to have worries, nor should you fear death nor strive after glory. On the contrary, it is fitting that you should enter into this stage of your life like a pilgrim who, joyfully nearing the end of his journey and freed from the woes of material care, spurns all public approbation and scorns all worldly triumphs.

51. Nevertheless, you still seem desirous of attaining new glory, so much so that you do not even deem it unworthy of you to try to ingratiate yourself with the lords of this world at the expense of your former convictions. Nor do you seem to realize how unbecoming it is for you to gain their attention by such advances.

52. You really should not allow yourself to be so influenced by the present state of affairs, since those who are seducing you to their cause by all manner of entreaties and bribes, would indeed not do so - being as mighty as they are - nor would they so anxiously engage in consultation concerning us, if they did not foresee some immense danger to themselves.

53. But now that you recognize this fact, what conclusion must you draw since your hopes depend wholly upon them? Those whose resolutions are based upon mere fate or the favorable results of chance have always harbored a fragile hope. I would have you be aware that my admonitions refer more specifically to the reputation of your name than to any danger to your person, although even in this regard a sense of fear is not entirely lacking.

54. Although your life may be safe, your reputation is nevertheless at stake and it would behoove you to be far more concerned about this fact. You should consider that there are a great many people who for years now have been quite aware of your chameleon-like character and are repelled by

it; since until now, however, you have vacillated only in matters of no real significance, and considering, too, your other eminent accomplishments, they have chosen to tolerate your minor inconsistencies. But when they see you now yield to your emotions in a matter of such great importance, to what extent must they not in turn yield to indignation!

55. And how will those others, who have always held you in the highest esteem and have never conceived the slightest suspicion of guile or frivolity or dissimulation on your part, how will they react when they see you now succumb to such a cowardly weakness? Will not they who formerly spoke of you with such glowing praise, now spit all the more contemptuously at the very mention of your name?

56. Oh, had I only been able to prevent such a misfortune! Never would I have done anything more willingly than to save you from such an imminent danger; but now I fear it is too late, you have gone too far. Assuredly I still desire to help you even though I am not certain whether my feelings on this point are still agreeable to you, especially since you not only attack our cause in general but expressly scourge me in particular and treat those whom I hold dear in a manner more odious than a friend can tolerate, while, at the same time, you praise to the skies those who are our mortal enemies.

57. But I have already delayed now far too long my discussion of that matter which was the primary concern of this expostulation. Before discussing your calumny of Luther, however, I should like to address a few words to you concerning the manner in which you seem to treat both your friends and your enemies, depicting as it were before your eyes and impressing on your mind your ambivalent position, since it would appear that you yourself do not see this clearly nor take it sufficiently into account.

58. Trivialities I shall overlook. In a certain letter to Hoogstraten you

71

state the following: "By chance I happened upon a certain little book,
lying neglected in some library or other, containing several letters ful-
minating against you, Venerable Father. Unless I am mistaken, the first
one was by Reuchlin, the second by the illustrious Hermann Count of Neuenahr,
the third by Hermann Busch and the fourth by Hutten. In no way would I
have been able to endure the bitterness of all these letters, had I not read
beforehand the works by which, it would seem, they had been provoked into
their outrageous lack of restraint. It was, therefore, with a not unmixed
sorrow that I read these letters, sighing both for the fate of the authors
themselves as well as for your own, for I could not help fearing repeatedly
that even good and fair-minded men might judge such bitter revilings as
accusations hurled against an individual who was not altogether innocent."

59. So, my indignation with Hoogstraten has all of a sudden become a savage
lack of restraint, whereas you always used to refer to it as fair and just,
indeed an act of piety? And you even fear now that the things I wrote
against Hoogstraten might somehow be judged as merited by him to some degree?
As though he had not merited any such treatment or that I had merely invented
fictitious, groundless and false grievances!

60. If this is so, then I shall condemn myself and say that no one ever
more deserved to be banished from Germany than Hutten, a man who viciously
slanders good men and reviles the innocent with words of savage virulence.
If this is not the case, however, then I can state without hesitation that
I would desire against no one a vengeance more severe than against him who
would lay to my charge, although innocent, a crime so hideous and so hateful.

61. I have always abhorred lying as a great disgrace and I can think of
nothing more detestable than not to speak and do all things honestly and
with the greatest frankness; from my childhood onward I have constantly
endeavored to act sincerely and candidly toward everyone.

62. More than anything else this effort on my part has commended me far and wide - of this I have had more than abundant evidence - and it is against my will that your grievous insult forces me to boast of myself. Thus when I have written even against powerful men, nothing has protected me more than the fact that what I wrote appeared to be true, and this by the soundness of the cause for which I fought.

34

63. My writings, the indices of my mind, are in the hands of the public; from its judgment I do not flee - let it decide if anywhere a lie can be discovered about anyone, inserted there by my own deceit. Indeed, let even the princes of Germany not spare me nor refrain from the cruelest form of punishment if I should ever be convicted of such a crime.

64. In that case, however, I would pass judgment against myself and to this declaration I here bear public witness. There are those who studiously search my writings to see whether or not something cannot be uncovered by means of which to drag me into a law suit. Were they able to find anything, how easily they would crush me since they already bear me such ill-will.

65. If in this I deceive my fellow men, then may our Heavenly Father, who sees and knows all things, destroy me and scatter my remains to the corners of the earth; and if under the pressure of circumstances I have ever lied about anyone, may He never be merciful to me.

66. Even you were formerly ready to attribute integrity and sincerity to me, and were it not that you have now decided most indecently to flatter Hoogstraten, given the opportunity, I know for certain that you would most vigorously defend my reputation since you would not want anyone to believe

35

that such a shameful disgrace could befall me.

67. And as far as that goes, who would find it necessary to lie about Hoogstraten? Why would anyone have to resort to fabrications and lies if he wanted to write against a man who is not only wholly inundated by the

73

mass of his shameful deeds and encompassed and polluted by the greatest crimes, but one whose very conscience is degraded and who is always ready to do anything underhanded and to rush headlong into it?

68. Everyone knows this only too well; what defense, therefore, do you have to make for that beast? I am not asking now what you said in those flattering letters of yours; rather, I would ask what it is you often said about him in the past in the presence of the most honorable men. Away with your dissembling and blush if you are still capable of shame! This scoundrel, whom you now praise, you used to decry as a plague sent to earth by the wrath of God to destroy scholarship and men of genius, a worker of havoc and a calamitous devastator of the noblest pursuits of man. You further castigated him as a pitiless cause of destruction of all culture and refinement and as an incendiary who in our times has set ablaze such a conflagration that it is to be feared lest all those truly devoted to learning be consumed in its flames. And for this very reason, to whom did you not turn asking all to attack him most bitterly?

69. Whom have you not exhorted to sharpen their pens against him? Out of a sense of discretion, however, I shall refrain from quoting here those things you wrote to me about him, although I cannot say whether others will follow my example. Nor is it necessary, for have we not heard you yourself say that this source of all evils must be destroyed, since from it flow the hatred and jealousies, the discords and conflicts which threaten to inundate all of Germany and which before long will ravage the land with slaughter and murderous treacheries? [36] For such a task some Hercules [37] is needed who will slay this Hydra [38] and drag this Cacus [39] from his lair to the punishment he so justly deserves.

70. That at least is what you thought then; now you seem to have changed your mind and have decided to flatter Hoogstraten so that he might be

74

favorably inclined toward you. But what does that have to do with me?

Just because you wish to enjoy the favor of one particular individual,

is it fitting to call down on my head the wrath of everyone else? Or am

I the one who should ignore the hostility of righteous men so that you

might ingratiate yourself with those who are evil?

71. You would do well, Erasmus, to moderate your fickleness and weigh

carefully what you write about whom. It would also behoove you to remember

that you have been forewarned no longer to contrive your fawning on others

at the expense of my reputation. I would indeed have discovered means by

which to wreak vengeance upon you for the vicissitudes of my fate, were you

not the very man - and for me this fact is of great importance - through

whose powerful support learning was encouraged and the humanities furthered

and because of whom many in Germany make daily progress in their knowledge

of the Ancients; and I also willingly confess that I, too, owe my growth
      40
to you.

72. Given these circumstances, your talents and merits are of greater

importance as far as I am concerned than the wrongs I have suffered at

your hands or the sorrow you have caused me. You, however, should also

practice moderation and show some concern about your own honor. What, I

might ask, is more disgraceful, more unworthy of you than publicly to praise

Hoogstraten as an honest man when you know that he is anything but that and

to commend that monster of depravity at the price of heaping odium upon

your friends?
                                                                        41
73. You will probably protest that on occasion it is necessary to dissemble;

but I for one cannot at all esteem such simulation in any Christian, least

of all in a learned man and a theologian. Why, even a pagan writer condemns
                              42
duplicity in friendship.   For, as he says, it falsifies, nay utterly

destroys one's sense of truth; and thus to base a relationship with other men upon hypocrisy and dissimulation is all the worse for a person of your profession.

74. That liberty might remain unimpaired, it is all right for us to assume the most difficult tasks and to suffer the most adverse circumstances, just as long as we see to it that you personally give offense to no one in any quarter and that no suspicion whatsoever be laid to your charge! Were victory to crown our endeavors, no one would be more willing than you to take advantage of the situation; and yet, if any danger at all seems imminent, you do not hesitate to attack even your best friends with railing abuse. And so, in order to recommend yourself to that Reverend Father as one eagerly supporting his cause, you clench an angry fist at the Lutherans.

75. "I immediately realized," you say, "the cunning deceit of those men whom I really do not know by what name to call, although some call them Lutherans. It is evident that by this manner of agitation they sought to incite me, a guileless and credulous man, against Jacob Hoogstraten"; and then you exclaim, "Oh, cunning plan."
43

76. On the contrary, my dear Erasmus, in these matters it is your own nature that is cunning and false, of too little honesty and lacking in gentlemanlike qualities, assuming of course that the Hollanders even have a word for such shameful deeds - or do your fellow countrymen designate fraud
44
by the epithet "guileless"? Was it we who spread the rumor that Hoogstraten had your books burned? Come now, most learned of theologians, what is your sense of shame that it would allow you intentionally to accuse honest men so falsely?

77. I appeal to your conscience - tell us what you know about these matters, what you have ascertained. Was it not common knowledge and dare we not openly admit now that, during the sessions of the Diet of Augsburg, Hoogstraten did not bother to conceal the fact that he felt he ought to have you arrested

as a heretic and publicly have your books burned as heretical doctrine and that it was only our zeal in protecting Reuchlin that hindered him in this undertaking?

78. As soon as he had settled the Reuchlin affair, he was prepared to attack you. Since this was common knowledge at the time, could the rumor not easily have started that he had already done what he had determined to do anyway? And, after all, of what use would it really have been for us to fabricate such a story? "Just to incite me against Hoogstraten," you will say. But at the time we were convinced that there was no one more incensed or more hostile toward him than you.

79. Granted, however, it just might have been our intention to win your support and enlist you on our side; how could we possibly have done it so easily in this manner, since you certainly would not have dared to do any-thing against him or against anyone else before knowing exactly what was at stake? Or is Switzerland so far from Brabant that we might have hoped you would receive no news from there for a whole year?

80. Take yourself and that simplicity of yours somewhere else, Erasmus; our Germany produces far different qualities in a man. For quite a while we have been aware of similar deceptive traits in your character, but out of respect for you and because we hoped for better things from you in the future, we let them pass unnoticed and did not throw them up to you.

81. By way of clarification allow me to recapitulate the situation: When the Letters of Obscure Men first appeared, you praised and applauded them more than anyone else, attributing to the authors something akin to a triumph. You stated in so many words that no more direct way had ever been devised for attacking ecclesiastical obscurantists, admitting in short that such barbarous Latin was indeed the best method of ridiculing such barbarians. Thus it was that you congratulated us on this felicitous undertaking, and

45

since these nonsensical spoofs were not printed as yet, you even copied
several of them out by hand, saying "I just have to send these to my friends
in England and France."

82. Not long afterwards, however, when you saw that the whole rabble of
third-rate theologians had become violently angered and that these agitated
hornets were raving mad from one end of Europe to the other, threatening
death and destruction to the authors of the letters, you immediately began
to grow fearful and so, to make certain that absolutely no suspicion would
be cast in your direction that you yourself were the author or approved and
applauded the lampoons, you wrote that letter to Cologne 46 just dripping
with your brand of sincerity, hoping to forestall any derogatory rumor by
blatantly depicting yourself as one grieving at the sad fate of those poor
gentlemen. Taking the stance that the whole affair greatly displeased you,
you angrily struck out against the book and its authors.

83. By doing so you furnished our enemies with the sharpest of arrows, an
action that stemmed from the weakness of your character which did not allow
you to remain firm in your convictions. However the public in general
might interpret your motives, you attempted in an underhanded manner to
besmirch the good name of others. In one particular instance I simply cannot
refrain from defending the name of a recently deceased friend of ours, an
innocent man upon whom you strive to heap all manner of shame and disgrace.

84. I am speaking of course about Reuchlin, a man who in his lifetime was
illustrious because of his erudition and whose whole life was graced by an
admirable innocence, a man nonetheless of such modesty that his noble qualities
were praised by others far more than they were recognized by himself. I do
not know whether or not you felt that he was honored to excess by his friends;
I do know for certain, however, that you harshly abused a man who himself
loved you beyond measure.

85. At first, to be sure, you did this with a very light touch, but you did it nonetheless, in a manner neither becoming to you nor appropriate to the matter at hand. For who among all our contemporaries knowing Hebrew would agree that it was right of you in a certain letter [47] to give preference to Capito over Reuchlin concerning their respective knowledge of Hebrew letters, and this solely because you desired to minimize another man's greatness which made you chafe; a preference accorded a man who, as everyone knows, has barely progressed beyond the rudiments of the language?

86. Of course, among those just studying the language, the opinion of an Erasmus might be able to supercede the judgment of everyone else, were it not for the fact that only a short time ago you yourself admitted that you were just beginning to learn Hebrew. I do not in any sense wish my statements to be interpreted as though I were seeking to belittle Capito, for he has never given me cause to do so, nor does there seem to be very much about the man for anyone to envy. I wonder, however, what could have moved you so invidiously to compare with one another two men who in the unanimous consensus of the world are altogether unequal.

87. If Capito is the man he ought to be, your false praise should annoy him far more than any abuse he might receive at the hands of someone else. I do not believe that he is really so ignorant of his own qualities that he does not recognize how great the distance is between the honor due him and that accorded Reuchlin, especially in that branch of knowledge in which Reuchlin is considered to have surpassed everyone else. And, too, Capito surely cannot be pleased by a eulogy from you which is as far from the truth as possible and thus does not only not honor him but actually calls down upon him the odium of others.

88. True, he praised your translation of the New Testament to the skies - but is this sufficient reason or a worthy motive for you to favor him so

immoderately! Reuchlin, too, had done this, but his good-will was not very pleasing to you, for others had already begun to place him on a par with you and, as one who was doing as much as you to promote the classical languages, some even referred to him as the "other eye of Germany."

89. This did not seem at all bearable to you - indeed, in order that you alone should be mighty, you felt it only fair that everyone else's reputation should be brought low. I recall, too, that while in France I heard various scholars, who were furious with you at the time for writing what you had against Lefèvre,[48] say that it was quite like you not to be able to enjoy your own fame without disparaging that of others.

90. I did not believe this, however, until you yourself convinced me of the truth of the accusation. For, considering all the evidence at hand, what other reason could there be for your disparaging remarks about the merit of a man who was so kindly disposed toward you, except that you were wholly unable to accept him graciously as an equal? And yet of his own accord he himself was accustomed to yield all preference to you, since he always judged himself to be too far your inferior ever to merit being compared with you.

91. Nor did we go so far as to compare the two of you - we admired you too much; we did feel, nevertheless, that he should not be cheated out of his justly deserved recognition. While honoring you most highly indeed, we still could not condemn the endeavors of others who, to the best of their ability, were striving to promote the cause of greater learning.

92. Oh, if only you could erase that letter from everyone's memory! For what clearer testimony to your unfairness will ever exist than this perverse judgment of yours? Just because certain insignificant individuals have commended your work, you praise them; on the other hand, you strive to detract from the reputation of a man who in the consensus of all is a consummate

80

scholar and who never sought to compete with you for public acclaim. You alone seek to belittle his accomplishments which the long-standing opinion of those in this field, the most learned among them as well as everyone else, has always conceded to him. And even the Jews, who alone are able to pass competent judgment in this area, have lauded his Hebrew scholarship, although envious of the fact that his achievements were accomplished by one who was not a Jew.

49

93. Again I quote your own words: "Ludwig Baer, a Sorbonne theologian and, as they say, the foremost authority in his profession, literally kisses and worships my work, etc." (You are speaking here about your translation of the New Testament). "Wolfgang Capito, a clergyman in Basle, a man far more learned in Hebrew than Reuchlin, feels the same way." If you were at all concerned about the truth, how eagerly you would retract this statement!

94. Or is it possible that you cannot tolerate to have contemporaries who also bear the mark of excellence? Although the achievements of those who lived and worked before your time did not (as far as I can see) prevent your own fame from equaling theirs, why should you cast a jaundiced glance at those who are satisfied to be of some repute, albeit at some distance

50

behind your own?

95. Let others also have some measure of fame and, although you strive so diligently to acquire glory for yourself, do not envy theirs! With respect to literary talent there is no one in this day and age who would compare himself to you; why, therefore, begrudge Reuchlin, a person of such great modesty, the praise given him by all for his unique knowledge of the Hebrew language and for his insight, granted to but few, into certain cryptic, esoteric lore, especially since you yourself have never coveted this knowledge and are ready to admit that you had formerly learned something from his writings?

96. Nonetheless, I never would have reproached you concerning this matter, had your groundless envy spent itself merely in spiteful remarks. In your envy, however, you have also accused Reuchlin of something which could hardly be conceived of as more hateful; just to speak of it causes me to shudder, and yet speak of it I must.

51

97. Although everyone was thoroughly convinced of Reuchlin's fidelity and integrity - so much so that not even his enemies could reproach him on this account - you heaped upon him the charge of perfidy and betrayal when, in a letter to John Fisher, Bishop of Rochester, you wrote: "The matter is as follows, if one can credit rumor with some truth: When there was danger that the Duke of Württemberg would recapture Stuttgart, Reuchlin advised some of the citizens to flee elsewhere, promising to accompany them. They fled but he, fearing for the safety of his household goods, changed his mind and stayed at home. Later, when the Duke had been defeated once again, certain friends of Reuchlin's obtained assurances from the victorious army that they would not plunder his house. Those citizens, however, whom he had so deceived, caused the old man a great deal of trouble upon their return. So he moved all of his belongings to a place of safety and is now leading a tranquil life in Ingolstadt."

52

98. Who is it that concocted this lie, Erasmus, if you are not the author of this "scoop"? Who was the seer of that dream? I ask you in the name of the immortal Christ, did you not consider it necessary to find some credible witnesses to verify your story before spreading such shameful rumors about a fellow Christian? Or did you perhaps believe that Reuchlin, already a dying man, had so few friends you did not have to fear that, at some time or other, someone in his name would call you to account for this calumny?

53

99. Anyhow, that is what you thought, I imagine. I, however, consider myself bound by loyalty not to desert the cause of a friend you so falsely

accused, and no matter how offended you might be, I for one believe that this stain must definitely be removed from his reputation. And even though this most worthy man should die within the minds and hearts of everyone else, you will never get me at least to pass over this iniquity in silence.

100. To be sure, I shall never demand of you something that the rest of us believe friends mutually owe one another, silence namely - even if this rumor about Reuchlin had been confirmed in your eyes by serious-minded authorities, would your devoted love for him not move you to conceal the matter as much as possible instead of prompting you immediately to spread the story further by repeating it even in your correspondence? As I said, I shall not demand this of you since it is evident you are lacking in human consideration to such a degree that no one before this would have believed it possible.

101. But tell me, if it is required of everyone else who accuses others of something to substantiate the accusation with the testimony of witnesses, why do you feel yourself spared this obligation, especially since you desire to heap such dishonor on Reuchlin, not only by word of mouth but by passing on to posterity written documents to that effect? Do you fail to realize that no one would allow another person to be so traduced by you without proof of his guilt, were he a stranger or even an enemy? And now, since the whole affair concerns a friend, how much more did it not behoove you to have a just and sufficient reason before saying anything!

102. "Some say so," you write, and you attach such weight to what they say that you add: "if their story is true"! If you have doubts about the truth of their report, then why do you divulge it with such confidence, when a man's reputation and indeed the whole meaning of his life are involved? Indeed, if the whole matter is derived from nothing more than a false source of information and based on an uncertain rumor, you should have set no store

54

by it, but should rather have firmly maintained a suspicion as to the honesty of the informants.

103. Nonetheless, I choose not to believe what certain others resolutely assert, namely that the whole story was neither reported, written nor conceived by anyone else nor heard by you from another source, but on the contrary was fabricated by you alone, desiring to spread odium around
55
Reuchlin's good name.

104. Granted the rumor did come to you from someone else, I still cannot understand why you had to publicize it immediately, especially since you had no witnesses to verify its truth. Would it not have been far more proper for you to be among the very last to believe such a story, even if everyone
56
else were repeating it in conversation or in print!

105. The rumor conveyed to you by those scandalmongering acquaintances of yours was so dim that it never reached me, although I was always thoroughly acquainted with all of Reuchlin's affairs. It was to me that he willingly confided everything favorable as well as unfavorable to him; often he revealed to me the entire condition of his life and he even poured out into my bosom as it were all of his cares and anxieties. He was especially accustomed to inform me if anything new were being leveled against him or if his enemies were out to stir up trouble for him.

106. At that time he had completely withdrawn from public affairs, some
57
years previously in fact, and he never meddled in anything; even the tyrant in whose lands he was living had granted him this immunity.

107. Those things, therefore, which succeeded in escaping my knowledge, though I was his most intimate friend, were nonetheless told to you by people whose reliability is doubtful; and still, what you have drawn from such sources, you would offer abroad as public fare? Oh, Erasmus, where is your loyalty! This, then, is to be the reward our beloved Reuchlin receives

84

at your hand as payment for his steadfast love of you, this his compensation?

108. What Hoogstraten, that inveterate perjuror, never accused him of, nor any of his enemies ever imputed to him, you invent as a reproach to his name! That disgrace which the frenzy of none of the Dominicans ever contrived or the bitterness of none of our third-rate theologians ever hurled against him, you, his friend (such as you are), inflict upon him, producing it from some secret archives in order to defame and vilify an innocent man.

109. Although you might have blundered into this affair with your characteristic levity, believing yourself secure from any future censure concerning the matter, serious though it is, we shall not be unmindful of our duty nor desert the memory of our friend. If his integrity deserved to be defended by everyone while he was alive, we shall see to it that his reputation and good name are also protected against your calumny now that he is dead.

110. You should be aware, therefore, that it is incumbent upon you to convict Reuchlin of the crime imputed to him, for if you do not, we shall convict you - this fact is already fixed and settled in my own mind. If you have anything to use in your own defense, hold it in readiness and do not remain idle, for I will not abandon this undertaking, and the easier it becomes for me to forgive you what you have done to me, the more steadfastly will I persevere in my endeavors, primarily because death has already robbed Reuchlin of any chance to speak in his own behalf; indeed, we dare not hope that he will appear among us again from beyond the grave to defend his cause against you.

111. It is not at all necessary for me to assume the defense of those yet alive - and there are several whom I might mention - who have also been

treated in an equally dishonest fashion by you, since each himself is free

to take you to task for the wrong done to him, and I am sure that none of

them will be found wanting in this matter. 58

112. I will, therefore, insert here only a few observations about the

enemies whom you and all of us have in common, to show you by way of a few

examples that you are able to bear enemies in a manner no more dignified

than the way in which you treat your friends. You might thereby see that

we know and are aware of how you have lowered yourself by perversely doing

all these things, both abusing in such a hateful manner those who merited

better treatment at your hands and then wherever possible flattering with 59

vile adulation those most hostile to you. Enough has already been said

above about Hoogstraten.

113. In how many bitter letters have you not complained to your friends

about the theologians at Louvain and Cologne, to the effect that they are

not only perniciously opposed to classical studies but are as well the 60

foremost seedbeds of all barbarism in Germany! And in a similar fashion

you used to liken them to a kind of Lernean Hydra exhaling their deadly

poison far and wide, thereby destroying in so wretched a manner the minds

of many devoted to learning; and their schools you used to compare to the

fatal nests of the most evil of birds, from which poured forth in every

direction those Harpies of the mind befouling all the pleasure and joy of 61

everyone engaged in the pursuit of classical learning.

114. That indeed is the way you used to speak to us. But now that you

see we are sufficiently inflamed and passionately incited against the enemy,

you reverse your stand and in a most flattering manner you commend yourself

to these very people. In your praise of their schools you now almost prefer

them to the academies of Athens and you reproach us for having the audacity 62

to attack these modern day Platos and Theophrastuses.

115. This is the way you always operate: first you incite us against those who are our most bitter enemies, seeking everywhere to cause people to oppose them; but then, as soon as you see that the heat of passion has been enkindled through your efforts, you begin to praise those same men publicly and to trumpet their merits far and wide. To some of them you even write in terms of fraternal affection, addressing them in your letters in a most loving fashion, all the while pretending that the aversion on both sides does not exist. And if there are some who are really furious with you, you soothe their wrath with caressing words; and sometimes, in order to please them or in your eagerness to placate them, you even savagely maul one or the other of us.

116. Who does not know how much you were opposed to these very schools when they condemned Luther's articles? Now you tell them how excellently they have comported themselves, and in writing to the theologians at Louvain you boast that you were always most resolutely on their side in their dis-
63
putations against Luther.

117. In like manner you also now treat the Dominicans, of whom you were always rather wary and against whom you were often known to be more than hostile; now, however, by various manners of persuasion you attempt to
64
make them believe you were never ill-disposed toward their Order.

118. You used to curse the Roman Curia as something most inimical to good morals and highly dangerous for Christian teachings and faith, but now it has become for you the holy universal Church itself, in which men surpass
their
even the lilies in the brilliance of/purity and where anything said by any
65
member of the Curia, no matter how knavish, is likened to a rose.   But more about this a little later.

119. You used to describe Jerome Aleander to us as the most abominable of men, born only for plotting deceptions and executing dirty tricks, a man

87

always faithless and treacherous, always malicious and evil-doing who had

66

cultivated scholarship only to injure it.

120. It seems to me that you were also the first one who secretly spread

the rumor that he was a Jew by birth. There are also people not unworthy

67

of belief who assert   that when Aleander served as the papal legate at the

Diet of Worms, it was you who said that you did not believe it possible for

68

free men to exist in Germany if he, a traitor like Sinon,   were permitted

to leave Germany alive, since he had been sent here solely to devise all

manner of deceits and plots in order to unleash the hatred of passion and

promote physical devastation; and as soon as he had vanquished Luther, whom

he was to attack first of all, he would then proceed to attack all the most

learned and intelligent men among us.

121. And, indeed, we do not doubt that what you said was true; we are

astonished, however, that here and there bookdealers are at present selling

eulogies about the man with you as the supposed author, despite the fact

that you have leveled such adverse criticism against him; and yet, in more

69

than one place, you write   about him as if none of the things I have

mentioned were true: he loves you in an unparalleled manner and you hold

him dear; you live with him on most agreeable terms and at times you prolong

your conversations until late into the night; and you have even mutually

agreed to travel to Rome together.

122. Oh, what sweet intimacy to have so suddenly sprung from bitter hatred

and enmity! Do not think, however, that these things disturb me, as though

I envied you the friendship of such a man - nothing is further from my mind.

Go ahead and keep him for yourself and all those like him; love them and in

turn let them love you! As for me, I will easily refrain from being a rival

for their affection.

123. I am recounting all this at such length only to show you how beautifully

you keep changing your mind all the time and to illustrate the fact that
at present there is almost no single mortal enemy of higher learning with
whom you have not had some corrupt double dealing.

124. Everyone knows for certain that Aleander had come fully instructed to
&tack you so that afterwards he might more easily crush the rest of us,
since, as he himself said, you were the foremost instigator of all the
rebellions in Germany and the innovations everywhere else; and it is equally
well known that nothing would have prevented him from handling you in his
own way except that after a full deliberation of the matter it was decided
that it would be more advisable to proceed with greater tact and seduce you
from your cause so that the Roman Curia might keep you in reserve for its
own purposes. It would, however, have been more useful for us, as well as
for you yourself, had he done otherwise, for then no matter how the affair
had turned out, your reputation would have suffered less.

125. Moreover, it was not a story fabricated by the Lutherans that Pope
Adrian was contriving hostilities against you; and yet once again, shamelessly

and contrary to your conscience, you laid the blame on us.   There was
rather a constant, widespread rumor afoot - a rumor originating in some
letters sent at that time from Spain to you and a few others - to the effect
that even when he was a Cardinal and Bishop of Tortosa he let it be known
he was taking steps against you and that once he had written a letter to
Rome in which he greatly censured the leaders of the Curia for spending so
much time disputing with Luther. It was you rather who should be seized,
the source of all harm and the tinder of all rebellions; it was you who
instructed Germany how to oppose the Roman Pontiff, you who were almost the
sole instigator of all the innovations. Once you were suppressed, it would
be all over with Luther and his sympathizers, since it was from your books
and your spirit that all of us derived what we said and wrote.

126. For this reason I quite readily believe that the book he was said

to have written against you is by no means wholly a spurious invention,

although, as far as I can remember, I had never heard about it previously.

Although you learned of this matter before any of the Lutheran party had

done so - and this I dare affirm by oath - you nonetheless have the temerity

to impute to us the disgrace of having fabricated this rumor, knowingly and

willingly launching this most deceitful calumny against us, thereby hoping

to preclude any danger threatening you through him and, at the same time, by

viciously attacking us, hoping to show how favorably inclined you are toward

Rome.

127. In some of your other writings you are unable to moderate the praise

you lavish upon such a Pope (although he has not been Pope long enough for

you possibly to conjecture whether good things or bad can be expected of

him); and yet before he was elected Pope, you openly declared that he was

not a particularly good man. Prompted, however, by your never failing

caution, you erect to his name a golden statue, even before he has brought

any project to a successful conclusion; and although he might wholly believe

everything you say about him, were he endowed with any modesty whatever, he

would cry out against your excessive praises: "Oh, Erasmus, I am indeed

not as remarkable as you say I am"; but you, like the friends of Timon,

would reply with proper guile, "But, Adrian, you will be so in time."[72]

128. But then perhaps one cannot praise a Pope too highly! How does it

happen though that you are also now trumpeting far and wide eulogies about

Glapion?[73] Formerly you used to curse the man's wickedness and bemoan the

fact that he was a wily fox who would use every dirty trick just to have the

chance to crush you; he was the worst possible teacher, the most evil

counselor, who turned the Emperor's ears away from every wholesome admonition,

instructing him instead in every form of perversity; through his influence

90

the noble character of the young Emperor was being corrupted and led astray along evil pathways.

129. Oh, had you only warned people about these deceitful things instead of openly proclaiming such untruthful praises, then many things would be better in Germany and we would have a more impartial Emperor. And should you ask me what I think of Glapion, I would respond - having once decided to confess the truth without restraint - that I have never met a more worthless man nor one who is more abundantly equipped to pursue every manner of deception.

130. Without a doubt, as an egregious hypocrite he surpasses everyone in simulating and dissimulating, and there is nothing about him that is not appropriate, suitable and adapted to deceiving - his mouth, eyes, brow, head, hands, speech, gait, in short everything; he knows how to accommodate himself to everyone and to assume any necessary pose or what has to be said or done at any given time or place - only nothing true, everything treacherous and with studied pretense.

74

131. When the Emperor sent him to us at Ebernburg, Franz von Sickingen and I and several others who were also present heard him admit (and from this one deception of his anyone can infer the rest of them) that neither he nor even those most hostile to Luther would deny that Luther was the first to open to all Christians the door through which one might enter into the true knowledge of the most hidden meanings of Holy Scripture.

132. But when I then inquired wherein so great a sin on his part might therefore lie, a crime which could outweigh such great merit, he answered: "I haven't the slightest idea." Nonetheless, no one hated Luther more bitterly than he, and if anything cruel and harsh to be used against Luther was being considered at the time, it was devised first in his workshop. Nor did anyone else fight more obstinately to have Luther condemned - unheard, undefended

and without a formal charge - a fight he managed to win.

133. He was thus able to keep himself concealed for a time, showing his

colors only when it seemed opportune for him to do so. How fitting that

he should be now reviled, now praised by none other than you, for in many

ways you are very similar to this Vertumnus!

134. Among friends you never approved of Silvester Mazolini, nor do you

have any reasons for approving of him now, although you wish to do so.

Nonetheless, you praise him and publicly proclaim him a good man who is

kindly disposed toward you. It is evident that you do this only because

of your ill-will toward Luther and, in order to appear as opposing him all

the more, you flatter his enemies.

135. And for no other reason was Caracciolo, in most respects an evil man,

restored to the benefit of your favor, than because together with Aleander

he carried out some anti-Luther business for the Pope. In this alone

consists all his virtues which you seek to extol.

136. Your honor roll also includes Eck who, according to your own statement,

is the most vain and arrogant man alive. You even used to say that he

deserved to be exposed to the contempt and open derision of everyone as

well as to be hissed off the stage. But now it seems that you have changed

your mind to such an extent that you are furious with certain individuals

who merely satirized him on some posters they put up.

137. Even the Dominican Jean Lefèvre finds favor in your eyes,   a man by

nature cruel and unfeeling, who has never been found acceptable by any good

person and one who advised that the most merciless measures be taken first

against Reuchlin and now against Luther. If that is not a crime, worthy of

your disapproval, then what do you say about the fact, known to everyone,

that no one more than he has always desired the destruction of classical

studies? I should think this would anger you exceedingly, and yet in a letter to the Bishop of Mainz   you state that it grieves you because your

powers are too weak to commend so great a man in proportion to his merit.

138. In your writings, a similar good fortune is shared by Johann Heigerlin,

a Canon and the Vicar-General of the Bishop of Constance and, of all the

flatterers of Rome, the most haughty.   He wrote a lengthy volume against

Luther which, you once said, deserved to be thoroughly smeared by everyone

with excrement; a fair judgment, since the ass brayed such nonsense in his

book.   But now you have reasons to compare him with truly great men, for

he stands in favor at Rome and not long ago he delivered to you that famous

brief from Pope Adrian   and, what is probably the most compelling reason

of all, he is hostile to Luther.

139. Who would have believed that Ludwig Baer and Johann Gebwiler would

have found a champion in our ranks - those two deadly plagues of Basle who

are sunk in avarice, blinded by ambition and of all the flatterers of Rome

the most abominable and who alone in that city have for a long time now

most obstinately opposed the renascent sciences and the emerging studies of

the fine arts?! They obtained you, however, whom anyone can purchase for

himself if he wishes. These two do not acknowledge their virtues to be

adorned by your praise, but they do rejoice that their vices are confirmed.

140. Such men you welcome into your home, but me you exclude;   you deem

them worthy of daily conversations, while you refuse to grant me - whom you

have not seen in three whole years - even a friendly interview.

141. No one in Germany, I believe, would ever have heard of Jacobus Latomus,

Nicolaus Baechem or John Briard, if you had not exposed them to ridicule in

exceedingly numerous and very hostile letters, endeavoring loud and long to

convince us that nothing bad enough could be written against these men who

had conspired so wickedly and so obstinately against classical studies and

who at the same time most viciously disparaged the virtues of others.

142. Afterwards we found this to be true and thus both under your influence and from having satisfied ourselves about their guilt, we shall
not cease to judge them as their conduct deserves. But now I read quite
different sentiments in your letters, where at times you treat them rather
ambiguously, though at other times in a friendly vein. To Briard you even
concede a tribute which, as far as I know, has been awarded to but few
since the creation of the world, namely that although he is highly praised
by everyone, he is still not praised sufficiently.   Oh, what equality of
judgment! Is it proper for a Christian theologian to speak in this way
about such a good-for-nothing, such a venomous beast?

143. But why should I mention several more, since other matters have to be
settled? There remains, however, Edward Lee who, if I remember rightly,
was the last one you threw to the mercy of our pens.   In a recently
written recantation, or rather a condemnation of us by means of a defense
of him, you have again changed your mind and removed him from the "list of
the proscribed."   To you alone, it seems, is granted the right, whenever
and as often as you desire, to cast your vote for or against a person, to
breathe on others icy blasts or mild breezes, to flatter with praise or
defame with violent reproach.

144. If indeed you had wanted to avail yourself of such a privilege in all
matters and to allow yourself a prerogative that no one should claim and
that no good man would want, still in the case of Luther you should have
taken into consideration so many friends who for the most part have deserved
better treatment at your hands, friends who nonetheless are hardly less
willing to be separated from him than they are to be torn from the truth
itself or led into ways contrary to the Gospel. These friends grieve that
you should wound them so sorely, not merely forsaking them but even making
common cause against them with their enemies.

145. The gifts of your new allies beguile you to such a degree that ours easily lose their luster for you. Thus the morsel placed in your mouth (from Rome, I believe) enticed you so, that what we have to offer only sickens you. For this reason you clasp these new men to your bosom, while us you cast out of your heart. If I should ask "What is your motive?" you would not want to answer. One can, therefore, but conjecture here, one cannot tell with certainty.

146. This shift in purpose is such, however, that it could not have taken place had you not considered the matter carefully. Everyone is certainly surprised and would like to know your reasons, for what is more novel than to hear about you: "Erasmus has surrendered himself to the Pope and has received orders from him not to fail the authority of the Apostolic See"? What is this? Has Hercules submitted to the authority of Omphale and, with distaff in hand, does he complete the day's task allotted by her?[91]

147. Oh, Erasmus, how greatly you act against your own honor! Everywhere you let yourself be used as a tool by men who are wholly unworthy of you, and by serving their perverse ambitions and unspeakable lusts you endanger your reputation and your eternal salvation. I beseech you, therefore, to consider well what sort of men it is to whom you subject yourself and render such service.

148. They are in truth those who despise all honesty, transgress both laws and piety, corrupt good morals, hinder faith, violate innocence, ridicule religion, wage war against truth and are enemies of the Gospel.[92] To such as these you desert and are prepared to carry out their commands!

149. Already you have begun eagerly to do their work; straightaway you have given them a proof of your zeal. The colors have been raised, the trumpet summoned to battle, the spear cast. It is you who have broken the peace, you who inflicted the first wound. So short a time ago you were the unassuming

Erasmus; now suddenly you are a rabid flatterer of Rome.

150. Can there be a greater, a more sudden alienation? Who in the future will recognize you, who will believe that such things could have happened? But yesterday you exhumed piety, you brought the Gospels back from their dungeons into the light of day and restored faith and religion; now all of a sudden you openly avow the desire to trample this selfsame work underfoot, to expel, overthrow and utterly annihilate it!
93

151. Is it that you are no longer in possession of your faculties? "I am," you say. Then what reason can you give us for having changed your position so radically? Is it perhaps that the cause began to displease you so much that you had to abandon it out of necessity?

152. This indeed you do not say; but rather: "Many people have encouraged me to do this - first, only to mention a few, the Reverend Father Marinus Caracciolo, Apostolic Nuncio to the Emperor; further his Excellency Jerome Aleander, unquestionably the foremost scholar of our age in Hebrew, Greek and Latin; and then the Reverend Father Joannes Glapion, the erstwhile preacher at the Emperor's court, who, at the request of the Emperor, often wrote to me concerning this matter no less diligently than lovingly. Long ago William Blount, Lord Mountjoy, urged me to the same end and recently the illustrious Duke George, Prince of Meissen, did likewise. In addition, men of great importance have already persuaded the Emperor that I am suitably equipped to carry out this charge. What more do we really need then? Since the whole world is sharpening its pen against Luther, why should you be indignant with me alone if I should also react, being commanded to do so by persons whom it would hardly be safe not to obey?"
94

153. These are fine reasons and most effective for motivating someone stupid, but certainly not an Erasmus! From the reasons you have just alleged it is very clear how agreeable all this is to you and to what an extent you

are titillated by the greetings of important people, their familiar forms

of address and the magnificent clouds of incense they burn in your honor,

as well as by their princely trumpery, courtly pomp and the gratuitous

favors they shower upon you. And you make it quite clear that you consider

these things to be a source of glory for you, even though you call upon

Laurinus to witness that you are not at all desirous of this type of insignificant renown. [95]

154. Nevertheless, if you had not been so eager for this honor, those

people would have enticed you in vain; and furthermore, you could not have

been alienated from us, had you not considered it a mighty honor that the

whole Roman Curia - which, though packed with men of every race and from

every nation, had gradually been forsaken and driven by us into the narrowest

straits - was able to breathe freely again upon hearing the report of your

changing sides, whereas prior to this it had had no sure hope of enlisting

any aid against us.

155. And why should this not be to your advantage? Indeed, for this very

reason Erasmus is already considered great in Rome. If he should go there,

a great many of these worthy dignitaries would without a doubt go forth to

receive him, accompanied by the jubilant pageant of an immense multitude.

And then, how great would be the joyous reception within the city itself,

with magnificent triumphal processions and wondrous acclamations in honor

of the mightiest defender of the Catholic Church, the invincible conqueror

of heretics who, like another Camillus, [96] restored anew through his valor

the commonwealth of Rome that had fallen into ruin!

156. I can well imagine that you entertain these and similar thoughts both

night and day, and since you so often boast of the letters you receive from

the most prominent people, the praises accorded your works by these individuals

or that prince, the honor paid you by this or that city, the money sent you or the promises made to you, you give us a good idea of your extraordinary vanity.

157. Beware, however, that this success does not deceive you and push you into unbearable adversity; be sure that all who now charm you with excessive flattery, do so for your own sake! Indeed, from some of them I greatly fear for you. But even granted that all of them keep their word and you deserve those panegyrics from Rome and those triumphal processions I was talking about, are you willing to risk your reputation merely to recover it in the end from the hands of such reprobates?[97]

158. "You will not desert the dignity of the Apostolic See." So be it. We on the other hand will oppose it! But show us where that See is which alone should be called apostolic, so that we might come and likewise adore it. You say: "I believe it is the Roman Church, which is not to be differentiated from the Catholic Church."[98] May I perish on the spot in both soul and body if you do not know to what extent this Roman Church deviates from the Catholic-Apostolic Church!

159. Produce the Scriptural text that teaches that the Church of Rome is this Church and thus the head of all the others, or that the Bishop of Rome possesses by right absolute lordship over the other bishops, that it is the Divine Will to call him His Holiness, and that at will he can revoke the Gospel and the laws received from Christ and prescribe new norms of living or decree other laws in their place. What text states that it is impious to dissent from his opinions or that we must obey him no matter how bad he might be? By what right does he extend his feet to have them kissed by the princes of this world, by what authority does he dispense the kingdoms of this world according to his own will or sell heaven or have men buy from him the salvation of their souls or the souls of others?

160. Just show me the text, I say, one issuing from Christ or at least an

apostle, and you will convert me too from my opinion and compel me to stand by you in defense of the dignity of this See. But if the Roman See is in such a plight - as it is - that all who truly are Christians are bound to wish it overthrown and abolished (and should this happen, everyone would consider it beneficial for the Christian commonwealth), what then could be more sacrilegious than to say, as you did in the sentence I quoted above, that no pious individual was unfavorable toward the Roman Pontiff? [99] On the contrary, what pious person could be favorable toward him, whose whole position is based upon sheer hypocrisy which, as long as it prevails, forces true piety to languish?

161. "But the Christian world has followed the authority of that See for so many centuries," you say. [100] What if everyone has erred for so many centuries? Would you forbid us to return to the right path once our error has been recognized or to flee from danger into safety? And most obviously we have erred. You were among the first to recognize this and, as far as you were able, you led men back again into the true path. Many followed you and are grateful. But now, since you see that it is to your advantage, you call us back once more into error. Everyone is astounded! The reason you give is that "this authority has been confirmed by the consensus of the world over so many centuries."

162. All of Greece and Asia, however, and in addition the greater part of the Christian world, have not followed this authority. Where moreover is that "whole world" which of its own accord is sharpening its pen against Luther? I presume it must be some other world that is doing this, perhaps one of Democritus'! [101] For in our world there are many who are not bent on writing against Luther and there are others, you will soon find, who in a very short time will be sharpening their pens against you on Luther's behalf.

163. You experience no qualms in using big words to describe insignificant

things; but this does not impress us in the least, for neither your vain boasting nor your deceitful railing against Luther will cause any change in our purpose. But let me return again to your great lords!

164. In your opinion do these men, whom you say one ought to obey, command us to do what is right? "Because they command it, I consider it right," you say. Can you find no counsel within yourself? Do you not have an intellect to direct you or a desire to be guided in life less from without, to be less dependent upon others?

165. To quote you again: "The Lutherans must at least concede that the man who, as they wisely say, is fearful, scarcely learned and of no competent judgment in matters of this nature, should now and again endorse the judgments of so many approved men." Whence all of a sudden this ignorance, this stupidity in you - you who but a short time ago possessed such an abundance of knowledge? Where has all of this substance so quickly disappeared, on which so many claim to have thrived? Has your knowledge been so far reduced that you who used to teach everyone else, and with such great success, must now yourself be taught by just any master?

166. How shameful this pretense, how unsuitable a trick for you to use so as to deceive! Only one of two choices was proper - either to stand firm on our side or, if you did wish to change sides, to state your reasons for rejecting us and desiring to join our enemies.

167. You assert that it is Luther's arrogance and excessive vulgarity which displease you. Granted he might have these failings, what does that have to do with his cause, which is the cause of truth and the Gospel? It is not against the truth and the Gospel, however, that you contend, but rather against the Lutherans; and you might perhaps like to know why I, whom you never considered to be a Lutheran, should become involved in this affair? I neither call myself a Lutheran nor do I like to hear myself labeled as one.

168. But I will tell why I am moved by this affair, if you will first answer me this: what is it in Luther that the Roman Pontiff disapproves of most of all, and why does he so greatly desire him to be utterly destroyed? You might advance some specious answers here by way of meaningless pretext, but if you are willing to reply in good conscience, you must concede that it is because he opposed the tyranny of the Roman Pope, not indeed as the first one to do so, but as the one who did it with the greatest vigor; it was he who restored the Gospel to its rightful place as no one before him had done; it was he who discredited human sanctions and tore the mask of dissimulation off the face of pseudo-bishops; it was he who laid bare before the world papist frauds, reduced papal bulls to naught, overthrew papal favors and barred from Germany indulgences and other similar chicaneries.

169. You will admit those are the real reasons. But having decided to attack Luther, you emphatically proclaim that "you acknowledge the Roman Church to be the true Church, from which not even death can separate you,"[104] whereas in fact you have often deviated from it. And further, you assert that anyone who opposes the Roman Pontiff is thus your enemy as well, since "you have always been and always will be subservient to the Roman See, to which you consider yourself deeply bound in many ways."[105]

170. You would not brag so much, I dare say, or use such parasitic,[106] high-sounding compliments, unless you knew the real reason for the hostility against Luther was just as I said: the irate Romanists could easily have forgiven him what, in their opinion, he had falsely stated concerning free will, the sacraments and certain other matters of this nature; they attack him, however, because he stood in the way of their profit making and barred the road to their gain; because of him their deceits fall flat and their tricks are revealed.

171. And this is the reason why in Rome so many creatures of Pope Leo are

101

now destitute, so many bishops and protonotaries forced to reduce their expenditures, why the very court of that most High Lord is being emptied, his consistories deserted, ambitions frustrated and his copyists and so many notaries in the city driven to famine.

172. All these things I attacked even before Luther did so and I have firmly continued to do this with all my strength to this very day because I consider it a mark of a good man to confess the truth, to avenge justice wherever possible and always to be of service to one's native land. I also feel that as a Christian I should give up my life for the truth if necessary. Therefore, I would rather be called a Lutheran - since those who do these things are now so named - than desert my duty.

173. Therefore, although I consider Luther neither my teacher nor my associate in this affair, and thus undertake what I am doing independently because I hate to seem to belong to any faction whatsoever, nonetheless I desire always to be numbered in the foreranks of those who oppose the tyranny of the Roman Pontiff and dare to protect the truth and turn themselves from the decrees of men to the doctrine of the Gospel. Since such have now come to be commonly referred to as Lutherans, I will gladly bear the disgrace of also being called a Lutheran, lest I seem to deny my support of this cause.

174. Nor will any designation ever so displease me that, to be rid of it, I will allow even the suspicion of having abandoned a praiseworthy undertaking. Here you have my reason for acknowledging the designation "Lutheran"; it would also be easy to make everyone else believe that for these very same reasons you too are a Lutheran, in fact an even greater one than I or anyone else, because you are a better writer and a more eloquent orator.

175. For as I have shown above, you have done the same things and, what is more, you did them before the world ever knew that Luther and I were born, although now you would purge yourself of them and desire to appear

102

as never having committed anything of this sort. You must, however, either destroy the greatest part of your writings or be considered a member of this party (since it is now called a party) by all who judge more the matter itself than the outward form it assumes.

176. If, however, they either accept your justification or expect from you some future advantages, which will largely compensate the damages they have suffered, and if in your writings you are to attack the Lutherans, i.e. the champions of truth and the defenders of Christian liberty, of your own accord, you will invite us to be your adversaries. I for one, without taking note of the name of any party, considering only the cause which you persecute, will defend that cause against you to the limits of my ability.

177. I would not want you to force this necessity on me, but since you have preferred to play the parasite to those people rather than stay on good terms with me, I will suffer us to be separated; while you then go over there, where it is considered advantageous to esteem as sacrosanct 107 the authority of the Roman Pontiff, I will remain here, where in the interest of Christianity it is considered just to remove from office anyone who seizes tyrannical authority in the Church.

178. Being secure, you may carry on your business there among influential men who offer you gifts and are ready to give you financial enticements, bishoprics and benefices not to be despised - all this if you are willing 108 to write against Luther. As for me, I will take my chances here among men who are incorrupt, serious, truthful, sincere, honorable, resolute and free, whom neither gifts sway nor honors alter nor dangers deter, men who worship justice, keep their faith, care for religion and do not desert truth.

179. And what concern is it of mine if you are obligated to the Roman Curia for so many reasons? For the sake of the common good I will combat that tyranny as resolutely as you persistently defend it for your own private

good. In doing so my task will be easier, my conscience freer since everything I have to say is true and clear and straightforward; your situation
will be worse, for you will be forced to feign and invent, to concoct,
counterfeit and deceive.

180. But then you also assert that one does not always have to tell the
truth and that the way one speaks matters more 109 - this sacrilegious
utterance of yours ought to be shoved down your throat again (indeed, the
matter at hand compels me to express this with some animus) if those who
now force heretics to recant or send them to the stake, properly did their
job.

181. For what can be more godless and contrary to the teaching of Christ
than to assert that the truth does not always have to be told, for the sake
of which He wanted us to die? Then, in order to expose us to even greater
hatred, you accuse us of inciting tumults and dissensions, imputing to us
as a crime those things which are proper to the matter itself.

182. Did Christ not predict that because of Him and His word there would
be hatreds and dissensions, wars and slaughters? 110 Therefore, were the
papists able to bear the Gospel, they would not become so angry at Luther,
nor would he offend others if a Christian way of life could prevail without
inconveniencing them.

183. Why do you not show us the way in which both the truth may obtain
its due and those most gently be stopped who now excite to wars? To be sure,
it is fitting for you to counteract these developments with such advice,
since you boasted that you would never fail Christendom and that you alone
were able to heal these discords. 111 Your statement, that it is not up to
you to hurl those people from their throne, is, therefore, entirely irrelevant.

184. We do not demand this of you anyhow; we desire only that you work hard
at spreading the teaching of Christ as widely as possible. "Christ lives,"

you say, "and holds in His hand a whip with which He will drive such people
out of the temple."[112]   We know this; but in the meantime raise your voice

as well, call out and do not desist, proclaim to the people of God their
evil deeds![113]   This is what, as a theologian, you should be doing.

185. Indeed, it is a compelling duty from above that a man, to whom the

keys of the knowledge of God have been given, must always strictly and

immutably reveal and proclaim the truth, however great the danger. "But

this cannot be done without tumult," you say.[114]   Perhaps it cannot; but

tell me, which is better, that these tumults be avoided or that the word

of God be spread? Just because certain people are in an uproar does not

seem to us sufficient reason for deserting the work already begun; and if the

party which opposes the truth of the Gospel cannot be suppressed without

causing the worst of tumults in the whole world, we shall nonetheless strive

to suppress it.

186. Christ desires to be preached both in season and out of season, as
Paul teaches,[115]   and thus one should not cease in one's efforts on His

behalf, no matter what stands in the way. "But such discord will involve

innocent people." You do point this out and we abhor it; but even if it is

true, it is in no way of such importance that the cause of Christ should be

considered of lesser account.

187. The real objection made against you by those rabid Lutherans is not

the one you mention, namely that you are too mild and too flattering to

princes and that you are too much of a pacifist.[116]   You indeed have not

listened attentively to the people - their complaint is that you never speak

or act with consistency and that for the slightest reason you flatter and

agree not only with princes but even with the meanest person whom your

weakness views as someone to be feared.

188. And then, what utter nonsense you babble in your flattering! "Who

would not honor the dignity of the man who, through his evangelical virtues,
117
reproduces Christ before our eyes?"   Everyone would, if such a person
could be found! But tell me then in good conscience, has there been a Roman
Pontiff in the last 800 years who conducted himself according to the Gospel?
Or, in our own time, has there been one who had even the slightest honesty
in him, although some people have been prompted to bestow unmerited praise
on them?

189. Therefore, since no seriousness appears in you any longer, nor any
consistency whatever; and since you previously used to join forces with us,
while now you waver and even desert to the enemy; and since you most falsely
declare, against all reason and common sense, that no pious person fails
118
to honor the Roman Pontiff,   who, as everyone sees and knows, has the
worst of men for his partisans; for these reasons, I repeat, you have become
a total stranger to us. That you have come to such a state of insanity that,
against your conscience, you approve of things so manifestly absurd, can
only be deplored.

190. And if indeed you do not wish to be cured, we willingly allow you to
perish with them rather than live as one of us, for we have no need of your
kind of men - fickle and of unstable faith; our work is to be accomplished
by the strong and the steadfast.

191. I cannot sufficiently marvel at the boast you make, namely that
certain Lutherans sought to entice you to their side by cunning tricks,
119
while others even wanted to seize you by force.   And thus you logically
demonstrate that the Lutherans are not evangelical, since it is not in
keeping with the Gospel to compel anyone into one's own party by trickery
and force; especially since it is well known that bearing this name is not
any less dangerous than bearing the name of Christian used to be.

192. We admit that this is not in keeping with the Gospel, and for that

very reason we approve no less of your lord in Rome who tries to compel

us by force and violence to submit to his authority; and when we resist,

he threatens us with thunderbolts from heaven, as if these were within his

power.

193. As for the men who sought to ensnare you by such cunning tricks and

threatened you with force, I would like to know who did such violence to

you and where. Tell me, I beg you, are you serious about this or do you

jest? But you cannot be jesting since you have asserted two or three times

that they were Lutherans who tried to drag you into their camp, first by
                                        120
guile and then by force.   Whoever they are who used such machinations

(if indeed they exist), they are men of little faith and no self-confidence,

nor is there a spark of Luther's spirit in them.

194. Perhaps here, in your desire to condemn us, you reckon among our

followers certain village clowns and good-for-nothings who haunt the market

place and who, in their desire to be noticed, say and do things which depart
                                                                        121
from normal behavior and then shield their vanity behind the name of Luther.

You know full well these fellows draw nothing from Luther and you dare not

assert that they are worthy to be put on a par with the most respectable

men. Nor can I easily believe that your hatred is so great that you would

want us burdened with this insult.

195. What force, moreover, can the Lutherans use, I ask you, considering

the great conspiracy of the German princes against us from every side?

While in Basle I did not hear that anyone was trying to turn you or anyone
                                        122
else into a follower of Luther.   And I am sure that in Wittenberg nobody

is thinking along these lines since, on the one hand, they have always

believed you were one of them and, on the other hand, the closer men live

to Luther, the more they share his spirit.

196. Luther's attitude, however, is such that he would not give a farthing

to be rid of the fear of that defection from him which you are trying to incite. By preaching the Gospel he has attracted to himself, or rather to Christ, the masses as well as a good part of the nobility. He hopes to continue to do so and he does not fear in the least that either you or anyone else will accomplish anything against the Gospel. He also knows with certainty that there will be no lack of people to welcome the word of God into their hearts. Thus he is not at all concerned about winning men for Christ by guile or compelling them by force; his confidence lies in the power of the word.

197. Where then, I ask again, are these forsaken Lutherans, who, in their loneliness, I suppose, have need of like-minded associates? Whether I turn to the east, or gaze toward the west, or direct my eyes to the south or scan the north - I myself see none.

198. I wonder, then, where they may be hiding; why do they escape my notice? If they are near at hand, how did it happen that when I was in Basle, the veritable army of Lutherans who surrounded me never sensed the presence of these obscure figures? And, moreover, why did they themselves not communicate their plan to me so that, in common with them, I could endeavor to make a new proselyte of you? If, however, they are at some distance, what force can they exert against you in such a city as this, among such people?

199. I find rather distasteful a tale so lacking in verisimilitude; it seems sheer fiction. I know for certain, however, that you are most hostile toward Luther himself. For what reason I cannot say for sure, unless, as I said earlier, the rumor is true that you cannot bear to have other heroes flourish beside you and you envy everyone who shares in your celebrity.

200. If this report is not incorrect, Luther provides you plenty of ground for envy; his name is already so famous throughout the world that even

123

children, from the cradle on, are taught to invoke it, and his reputation has reached even those who are not of our faith.

201. It is high time you learn to be satisfied with your own glory without detracting from that of others. We measure your greatness by a strength peculiar to it, and as yet nothing has been taken from it because of Luther, in whom we admire a spiritual quality and that barely incomparable penetration of mind when it comes to understanding the mysteries of Holy Scripture.

202. His love for you is undoubtedly true and sincere; and you yourself used to honor his virtue and approve of his life. "But he had not yet flung
124
the apple of discord into the world," you may reply.   My dear Erasmus, anyone who proclaims the Gospel does so. You meant to say, I presume, that "envy had not yet begun to dominate me, nor had the allurements from Rome yet begun to tempt me."

203. Therefore, stop falsely accusing this good man, lest He at least (if no one else), who judges all things with impartial eyes, hold you accountable for it. If there are no longer any reasons for you to love him (I would also like to touch upon this), I cannot see why you should hate him. And even if there are some, you would do better to remain aloof from the conflict and, as you have been accustomed to do, apply yourself in the meantime to other, far more useful labors.

204. At your age their tempo should be eased, not increased. What, moreover, will you gain by these dialogues which you spread abroad and which are
125
supposed to strike terror into us?   You will merely turn into enemies those friends whom you court with such danger to yourself and who prevailed on you to make an about-face which, in my opinion, is most ill-advised.

205. How does it happen that all those who pressured you into writing against Luther are either very evil or very powerful or both? Further, whether the quarrel is just or unjust, can be gathered from the fact that those who condemn this man do so by force and injustice, they condemn him unheard,
126
without defense and without granting him a proper trial.   No one attacks

109

him with reasons so that he can refute them; instead, they harass and censure him with abusive language. Your writings indicate what you formerly used to think about this sort of treatment.

206. Another thing: if there were reasonable grounds for discrediting Luther's cause, there would be no opposing the princes of Germany, who to a man have conspired to destroy us utterly and (it is claimed) to tear us out by the roots. I know them to be so disposed that they would do nothing more readily and eagerly than get drunk on our blood (and they do not lack the power to do it), if only they could give some semblance of honesty to the 127 action they have been considering for a long time already.

207. Now, however, the awareness that this would be a great injustice and the fear of arousing the intervention of the people by such an outrageous assault, keep them from daring to try. Thus, being restrained in this respect, they see that their purpose can be realized in another way, namely through the pen, and so they woo you by entreaties to write and fight on their behalf, although there is no one they would rather see destroyed.

208. And you will fight, as you have already begun to do. One reason for deciding to do so is that everything among our adversaries appears beautiful, while with us everything seems frightful, something you have to shun; another is that their recent successes have made you despair of our good fortune. It is, however, chiefly from fear of the hardships which you would suffer, should we be overcome, that you have allowed yourself to be won over.

209. To these reasons were added those well-known invitations from men of high rank - the rewards and promises, the glory and the expectation of triumphs. Thus you have been bought away from us and have sold yourself to them. May Christ turn it all for the best! All of this happened contrary to our expectation, but since it did happen, we shall accept it with the greatest equanimity.

210. Until now you have not declared yourself one way or the other; like
another Metius you are awaiting your chance with extreme caution.   But
seeing the strength of our adversaries increase to such a great degree that
you almost despair of our victory, you join the side which you consider to be
the victor, doing so not in good conscience, but either impressed by the
fate of each camp or won over by bribes or the fear, which I mentioned above,
that should we be vanquished, our adversaries would treat you no less
leniently than any one of us - and I for one have never doubted this.

211. And so, cognizant of where your interests lie in this affair, you
decided to exert yourself in every way possible, including the most shameful
flattery, to assure beforehand the good will of the future victor. How
like your hopeless frailty! You imagine you have already achieved this, nor
do you doubt in the least that you have our enemies steadfastly on your side.

212. But ponder what certainty there is in such a course, consider well
whether it will eventually be in your power to redeem this one perfidy by
means of another. For my part, I am certain that (whatever you may hope or
trust) the papists will treat you as one who has surrendered and been caught
by them rather than as a friend or one reconciled to their cause.

213. From bitter experience they at first feared your pen, and not without
cause; and then they believed we would be able to do nothing once you were
taken from us. This was a false persuasion, at which we have good cause to
rejoice; for if this assumption made them so eager to draw you to their side
(as I for one imagine), their hope will be disappointed, and shortly they
will see how wrong their opinion was and that it was in no way because of
you that, contrary to their boast, we have not been destroyed and annihilated
before this.

214. For the time being let them congratulate themselves on having secured
and stolen you from us; we shall not promote our cause with any less care -

in fact, it is not faring badly at all! They have cut down the prop upon which they believed we leaned for support, but soon they will see what it is that actually upholds our cause. They considered you the one who alone could do what many of us vainly claimed credit for; now that you are drawn away and turned against us, they will find out whether or not the truth remains defenseless.

215. In their opinion you were our protection, our fortress; now they have taken possession of you, they hold you. It is time for the world to realize how easily right is defended. Therefore, it does not disturb us at all that they have obtained what they desired and that you have reached the haven for which you longed.

216. They alone are tranquil of spirit who have some definite goal. Adaptable as you are to sudden changes in affairs, you are never certain where you can step or stand firm or settle, since you hasten toward that to which not honesty leads but ambition lures, to which not duty calls but the pleasure in promised favors drives you along. You are doomed to be fearful that in a short time you will be faced with the necessity of yet another change - one, moreover, which you cannot make, no matter how much you would like to. Your situation may reach such a pass that you - you who sought an opportunity to reap from these tumults first security and then some great return of immense personal glory - will receive from right and left a reward worthy of your faithlessness; with no hope of favor from either party, you will be stranded in a no man's land, having been forsaken by both sides.

217. Even though I shall not have wholly ceased to love you, I will still praise our enemies, and rightly so, if, whatever the outcome of this affair may be, they treat you - and it is my guess that they will do this in any event - in a manner worthy of one who is a traitor to both parties, one whom they dare not expect to find any more faithful to them than he was to us.

218. I know what a master you are at manipulating the minds of men by saying what they want to hear. However, the more often such flattery has profited you in the past, the more carefully you ought now to consider what you are doing, lest you eventually reap misfortune from it. For do you really believe that those individuals will come to love you, or rather will ever cease to hate you, from whom they received the first blow of their downfall? No, by Christ, it will never happen. And all the less, the more vigorously we proceed with the task we have begun.

219. For - and this will be their worst annoyance - as long as we keep up the fight, your writings will continue to wage war on our side. Nor are you any less with us now that you have defected to them, than when you were active in our cause with such diligence and fidelity.

220. Actually against your will we have reinforcements of your providing - your books namely, which are better than those you will write in the future, if
130
indeed you write any more, and if disgust with your basely changed life does not drive you to death first. Therefore, whatever you might do over there will be highly and disquietingly dubious; what you have done for us here is admirable.

221. And what can you achieve elsewhere of great importance? what feats perform? what illustrious monument erect to your memory? what fame, what distinction acquire? Here you championed the truth, there you will support deceit; here you fought in defense of liberty, there you must indulge in cringing flattery and in the end all you will purchase is servitude. Here your companions were the best of men, those most worthy of approbation be-cause of their lives and their erudition; there, your associates are the very ones you so often attacked as barbarians and, surrounded by a horde of men who shrink from no baseness or dishonor, no crime or felony (men, besides, who have no true love for you - of this I am certain), you will assault all that is sacred before God and man.

113

222. Even supposing that you behave heroically among them and fulfil their heart's desire by conquering us to adorn their triumph, what, may I ask, will be the glory from your victory which will drag in its wake great destruction of evangelical truth and freedom, as you yourself can foresee must happen or rather as you have, like Caiaphas of old, prophesied against you will.[131]

223. You yourself admit that the Gospel will suffer force, once we have been suppressed; and yet you dare to favor our suppression? What could you do that would be more pernicious, more impious? Here at last you reveal yourself, your sense of justice comes to light and your innermost feelings are made public. What need is there then for you to multiply your face-saving declarations? Through this one admission you have completely unmasked yourself, so that everyone can easily recognize both what you have deserted and on whose side you now stand.

224. And yet, although you deserve to be severely punished by everyone, indeed the interest of our cause demands this, the memory of your merits often returns to me, even when I am most angered at you, so that I am not fully at one with myself, whether your present activities deserve greater hatred or whether your great and immortal achievements of former days ought to be cherished with more lasting gratitude. If only you yourself did not retract those former works and reject your highest and most splendid merit on behalf of Christendom by wishing to make it seem as though you had never resented the tyranny of the Bishop of Rome and his infamous Curia!

225. That is what robs you of the esteem of many; that is why such bitter enmities arise against you. If only I had been able to admonish you in time, I would have urged you with great concern and the utmost zeal not to dishonor and defile, for any reason, so many excellent qualities and, further, I would have urged you to see things as they are and not to destroy here a

greater love and respect than you can possibly hope to acquire over there.

226. But already all admonition comes too late, my compassion is superfluous. You have been snatched away from us, you have yourself deserted our ranks, to my great and sincere sorrow and to the boasting and applause of our enemies. How I deplore this change of yours from the bottom of my heart! I see misfortune lying in store for you because of this desertion, and I see you betrayed by yourself and all but lost; for should you ever desire to come to your senses again, you are sure to be welcomed back among us, but it will not be simple to justify your desertion of them. They will watch you everywhere and at all times, and with great care they will keep you in their
132
service, whether you are willing or not.

227. Should you still desire to regain your senses, there might perhaps yet be a way for you to return to us. But you neither desire to return, nor, were you to desire it, could you do so for shame; so irretrievably have you fallen under their control, so securely have you allowed them to bind you. You have even given them a pledge of your loyalty by that thrice
133
cursed letter   in which, as it were, you sounded the call to arms and incited the minds of both camps to battle.

228. Nevertheless, having gained their trust in this manner (at least you believe you have their trust), you still wish to seem to stand by us. Taking up that expiatory basin and washing your hands with ritual water
134
like the iniquitous judge,   you cry out: "I am indeed innocent of oppressing the Lutherans." And then you bid us to flock to you and receive the counsel which you alone know how to give for the great advantage of human affairs. You also entreat the leading princes - although you consider it a sin to
                                    to
refuse them anything - not to delegate/ you the task of contending with the
      135
Lutherans.

229. You want your impartiality to be recommended by everyone, for through-

115

out your life you have endeavored with all your might not to cause your friends any trouble - a claim wholly at odds with your character! Was any man ever found who said and did everything more variously, inconsistently and deceitfully? Are you not ashamed at your age to promise one thing in words and perform something else in deeds? Say rather with the comic figure Gnatho: "I have at last made it a law for me to agree with everything."[136]

230. Who indeed is so versed in eloquence that he could properly initiate and maintain the right course in responding to your various statements, since you are so changeable and many-sided? To me at least you appear so, and thus I really do not know "by what joint I can lay hold of this ever shifting Proteus."[137] But your future shifts will be wasted on us; never again will you deceive us.[138]

231. Who among us is so stupid as not to understand on what trumpery you base this appearance of honesty? You do not desire our downfall? But you have already begun to devise it; you yourself have cast the die with the loud threats thundered against us and the great terror you would breathe among us.

232. You offer us advice; but who indeed would accept it from one who is already pledged to the adversary, one who is a declared foe? Are we to consult you concerning something for our benefit, while at the very moment you promise us counsel you proclaim that you will never desert the Apostolic See - as if everyone were in breathless expectation on your account? If you do desire to mediate peace between the two sides, why then do you wage war on one of them like an enemy, and so tumultuously at that?[139]

233. How easily you could have kept out of the whole affair and remained without anxiety by offering as a pretext your age or your well-known occupation with matters highly beneficial to the whole community.[140] And further, your claim to be impartial cannot be sincere, for the charges you

116

level against us belie it, since some of them are most unfair.

234. And if you have always been devoted to peace and never wished to harm anyone, how does it happen that we above all are the main target for the wrong you are doing? In the first place, who among us forced you to alter your habits and your way of life? Why do you attack us so unmercifully, you who in other respects are ready to show moderation? Are we the first and only ones to denounce in Erasmus a congenital faint heartedness? By no means!

235. I have heard from some of your friends, whom you had badly treated in the past and who called upon God and man to witness their complaint, that you were not only fickle but deceitful and treacherous as well. At that time no one would listen to them, for you had won the ears and hearts of everyone; and so you considered it sufficient to impute to fate those things they were accusing you of, or to attribute them to the Homeric goddess Ate,[141] which you did beautifully but, as we see now, quite erasmically.

236. And yet, with such a nature, you say you accord perfectly with the Germans as far as character is concerned. In no way, however, are the Germans like that; such frivolity and inconsistency are most foreign to their nature, for those qualities belong to men who at any moment can be turned now one way, now another, with nothing firm about them, but everything subject to the unpredictable turns of a fickle fortune. Go, therefore, to Italy, to those Roman cardinals with whom you have struck an alliance, behave in this way where everyone is at leisure to live according to his own character and temperament. Or return to your French-German compatriots, if by chance this vice is a national trait they share with you.[142]

237. Unless you curb certain instincts which are intolerable to us, I think that by a general resolution of all Germans you will be begged, indeed requested, to emigrate elsewhere, so that by your example you can no longer

taint our youth with frivolity and inconsistency, to which vices the nation is unaccustomed. This is especially so since the authority of your name is able to promote such a falsehood and people consider you worthy to imitate; and among the youth almost everyone believes that, having profited from you in his studies, he should also form himself according to your character, since your books must reflect your true likeness.

238. As much as I have always urged everyone to emulate your scholarship, no less will I now urge them to flee your character. I will not let pass any opportunity to reveal your pretense, and everywhere I will see to it that your reputation for sincerity, which thus far you have so cunningly managed to establish, will no longer be of any avail to you in cloaking your indecencies.

239. If people listen to me, you will henceforth rely in vain on those tricks which you practice as occasion demands, nor will you be able to charm anyone with your fabricated ambiguities. You have compelled me to undertake this action against you, although I would prefer to act in your favor, if only you would choose to be other than you are. But since you have decided, contrary to virtue and piety, to support evil-doers, I shall banish from memory, although reluctantly, those many things which used to constitute for me the main bonds of my friendship with you. For why should I remember your good deeds which you yourself desire to see obliterated and removed from the minds of men and consigned to eternal oblivion? Not only do you reject and retract the most noble and beneficial things you have done, you even promote the contrary. Again I say, I pity you.

240. But you do not wish to seem worthy of pity, so blind have you become at the hands of your perverters. How easily you could have resisted them, if only you had wanted to play the man! Assuredly, at the very least you should have remembered that you would be a perpetual object of shame to us,

for the more often one of us was prompted and inspired by you to engage in our present struggle, the more you will have to blush whenever one of us might happen to meet you face to face.

241. How are you going to bear this shame or how will you be able to face me if I should ever meet you? But maybe this is not the first time you have done such a thing? Perhaps in the past you have been caught at it and the habit has now thickened your skin? For my part, I would consider it a difficult task and I wonder if there is anyone who can do such things without blushing. For this very reason I have never feared that such an accusation would ever be leveled against you.

242. Against those very things which you yourself used to sow and plant, inspire and foster, you now speak out in anger with that violent eloquence of yours, as though you had to atone for them by some sort of bloody expiatory offering. Could there be a greater transformation into the contrary of one's actions? What you are now doing is prompted neither by a passion of the mind nor an upsurge of the spirit, neither at the prompting of your conscience nor because you now distrust the cause of which you so often approved. It is rather (at least as I judge it) because you are led by ambition and because you see too many, especially all the most powerful, now opposed to us, so that you do not believe we will be able to carry through what we have begun.

243. Perhaps, too, you have received some bribes; your own letter gives rise to this suspicion, since you boastfully refer to the fat offers made to you. Assuredly something great and compelling has happened, for certainly no honest reason has alienated you from us.

244. But supposing this suspicion were groundless and you have been seduced away from us by no such motive, then answer me this, I pray: under what honorable pretext do you hope to attack that party whose suppression, if it

119

should ever happen - and you yourself realize this - would bring with it great destruction of evangelical truth and freedom?

245. Is your faith in Christ of so little importance to you? or perhaps your resolve to speak and write only favorably about those people so firm, that you do not wish to act in any other way, even if one should have to give up something of the Gospel? Have you failed to consider what a great loss your honor and reputation will suffer because you seek to insinuate yourself into their esteem and, at your age, endeavor to obtain, by fair means or foul, the favor of the most powerful men?

246. I would not even have dared to suppose that you could do such a thing. On the contrary, I would not have hesitated to swear on your behalf that you would remain true to your duty and that those, who for five years have sought to ensnare people's minds would never succeed in enticing you with any form of allurement. To such a degree did I believe you were committed to the truth.

247. And yet, I was not unaware that those people were contriving among themselves some means to win for their side someone from our ranks, one who thinks as we do, in order to use him as the standard bearer in their attack against us. But who would have believed that you of all men would forsake your allegiance in this matter? Still, my opinion of you was wrong, as was that of all honorable men; whereas the hope of our adversaries was not disappointed in the least. Why then should I not exclaim: "Nowhere is
144
faith secure!"?

248. You who were the first and almost sole nursery of sound doctrine, profitable and wholesome for many, are you now to be set against us as one who retards the spreading of truth? You whom men delighted in as their head and standard bearer in combating the enemies of Christ, are you now to be wholly their man? Who would have suspected such a monstrosity? In truth I

120

have seldom experienced anything so contrary to expectation.

249. As a result, however, you will be the only one to whom they look for help, from whom they will derive their hope and in whom they can confide. When they were all exhausted and weary, here you come to rescue them, to bolster their courage and rouse their energy. Not so very long ago their cause had collapsed, but here you come in time to encourage them with needed assistance; when their cause was hopeless, they found you, the man who could restore the balance.

250. My most sincere love for you, my good-will which is fully known to you and which you often experienced, my devotion, my eagerness, the anxiety aroused in me each time you uttered those complaints about your enemies - none of these exerted any influence toward keeping you faithful to your duty. But then, why do I speak of myself?

251. Were you not at all concerned about deserting that side on which right and equity, divine law and piety stand? fleeing instead to that party which is upheld solely by human resources and wanton tyranny? Why then not take the next step and declare war on the Gospel as well? You have allied yourself so readily with its enemies!

252. Yet there was a time when people used to speak of you with unrestrained joy and were ready to congratulate one another, saying: "At long last we have found a diligent and industrious laborer in the exegesis of the Sacred Scriptures. A restorer of true piety has been given to us, one who, having overthrown superstition, will renew the Christian religion now so degenerate; dispelling the mists which envelop the truth, he will make it clear and recognizable. He will unmask the deceits of the Roman Pontiffs; the innovations brought about by them without cause or at the prompting of ambition and avarice, he will reduce to their ancient basis and natural state. He dares to cry out against the tyrants and, breaking the chains with which they

have bound Christian liberty, he will set it free."

253. This was your title to greatness, your true glory, your fame shining brilliantly among all nations. Now you have suddenly assumed a new character, and as if you were retreating from error, you flee to the enemy's camp, having deserted our standards, abandoned your post and betrayed the defending garrison. Since their concern is to foster deception and to fortify crime, tell me, what other choice do you have but to impugn the truth?

254. I pity you, Erasmus, and from the bottom of my heart I deplore your fate which is indeed pitiful. [145] Nevertheless, if you listen to me, you will turn back and, no matter how far you have progressed, you will retrace your steps, mindful of the ancient proverb: "It is better to run back than to run in the wrong direction." [146] For you are leading your reputation and honor into the greatest danger, something which cannot be impressed upon you often enough.

255. Those who have seduced you away from us are indeed not ignorant of this. But it was the plan of these perverse individuals to obtain someone from beyond their immediate circle whom they could easily jettison without the least danger to any of them. When they had considered the matter thoroughly, you seemed the only one suited for this purpose and they immediately persuaded themselves that you alone were able to instill trepidation in us.

256. Granted you are able to accomplish this, what sort of prudence is it, I ask you, to consider what you can do and not what you should do? Will you be the sure hope of the most evil of men? You the defense which they had already despaired of? the fortress sustaining them and protecting them against us? And, if it please Christ, you will be the support in which they confide all their hope with great confidence?

257. How gladly I would remove this way of thinking from your mind! But

you will not listen to me, you consider it unseemly to accept advice from a young man. I wish, therefore, that I could force you to come to your senses again and thus rescue you, even though against your will, from the evils surrounding you - not in the way those Lutherans do, who, you say, try to drag you into their sect by force, but only through the zeal of friendship. I would willingly cause you this annoyance for a short time, since afterwards it would become a source of great consolation.

258. The latter, however, I dare not do, the former you will not permit. In any case, you have already resolved not to desist from what you have begun; and too, you will neither admit that in attacking the truth a feeling of shame ought to overwhelm you, nor even grant that this course of action is a matter of conscience. You will remain under the authority of the Supreme Pontiff, defend the Roman Church and attempt to replenish the Curia which we have now nearly decimated; you will protect papal law from annihilation and restore those notorious canons we have almost destroyed.

259. Oh, what a change for the worse you have undergone, what a perversity you have committed! Writings of this type will indeed be a great prop to them, books of this spirit will suit their humor perfectly! And what then are we to do? Make solemn public vows perhaps, visit churches, make the full round of their altars near and far and beseech Christ to defend us from one such as you? No, quite the contrary; since we ourselves are secure, we will pray for you as for a friend, that you may recover your senses and return to sanity, lest through this ungracious and unexpected deed you, who up to this very day have merited the highest public praise, should in the end destroy the efficacy of your former glorious services and obliterate the memory of everything you have done well up to now.

260. But the things they promise you are better than what you might lose here with us. I only wish this were true! While wishing that it were so,

I cannot see at all what new fruits you might harvest among them that will be any more abundant than those you have been gathering all these years, nor what new glory you might add to the solidity of your former glory. Instead, I can see and I know for sure that through your present undertaking you will lose all the fruits of your past life, and will precipitate into miserable ruin that true and incomparable glory you have achieved by means of virtue and toil.

261. How easy, is it not, for seekers of false praise to find disgrace? Therefore, I repeat again and again: What do you think will be rumored about you among the people? What will they say, what will they think? Will there be one out of a thousand who will not believe you are only looking for some magnificent gift, some exalted honor? I only wish this universal opinion were wrong!

262. But I doubt very much that you will justify yourself sufficiently to anyone in this matter; even I stand with the rest of them in feeling that you did not withdraw from your former position without having received some recompense.

263. Whatever the source of your new confidence is, I know full well you are not one to derive such courage from sheer uncertainty - there must be a definite cause that first aroused you to action and now even makes you petulant. How otherwise does it happen then that those who wield power over you - since you recognize those men in Rome to be heads of the Church - approach you with entreaties and the most flattering briefs to move you to perform this service on their behalf?

264. Must this not give rise in everyone's mind to not only the mere suspicion but even the strongest conviction that, in a disgraceful bargain of this nature, you can reject authority and that if someone allures you with the hope of some lucrative income and the offer of by no means negligible

fees for your efforts, you can easily change camps?

265. Join their ranks then, continue the task you have begun and apply yourself strenuously to the Pope's interests! I will not hinder you in any way from completing your undertaking, but for your own good I wish you would refrain from it and out of love for you I would dissuade you from it. You, however, remain staunch, plunge ahead and behave as our enemy through and through. And by way of indicating your intent more clearly, such is the character you suddenly assume that your very first onrush against us is so violent that we are robbed of all hope of ever bringing you back to us again.

266. Go ahead, fulfil the expectation of those who for so long have sought someone to lead the forces which assail the truth! Get ready! The matter at hand is now ripe and a worthy occupation for your old age. Exert your powers and remain steadfast in your attempt, so that you might climb those slippery heights from which many before you have plunged!

267. Your adversaries are not unprepared; indeed, that Lutheran party, which you hope to annihilate, awaits the challenge it will not refuse. Their spirits are high and, since they are honest men, supported by sure hope and relying on a clear conscience, they will shy from none of the fronts on which you may choose to encounter them. On the contrary, that you might see how confident we are, you will discover that the keener your fight against us, the greater our ardor will be in defending the cause of truth.

268. You, admittedly, are good at writing both plentifully and eloquently but we, rather than spending any care on literary elegance, will recommend ourselves by our lives and our deeds; we will gain men's confidence through the steadfastness of our hearts in the pursuit of truth. Nor do we doubt that we will accomplish as much through a plain presentation of truth as

125

you are able to do by means of the vain ostentation of words. Where the
conscience is untroubled, there the powers of expression are not lacking.

269. And yet, as I have already said, a part of you will remain in our
camp and out of reach of your new allies. Your struggle will be not so
much with us as with your own character and your writings. You will speak
elegantly against yourself and against your own eloquence. A battle will
147
rage within your writings and one will be a rejoinder to the other.

270. Since you would have it no other way, there is nothing we will do
to prevent you from continuing as you are. We do not tremble, we have no
fear, we do not waver. We have already progressed so far in stirring the
hearts of many in favor of true religion that there is no danger of our
being brought low by you.

271. How indeed should we treat your zealously hostile spirit in this
affair since you are not only threatening us with war but clearly waging
it already? Should we entreat you in the name of faith and friendship not
to desert our side? No, our cause is too honorable; it does not need to
beg protection from anyone, much less from one who esteems faith and friendship so lightly and holds at a distance those who would admonish him. Or
ought we perhaps to invoke the powers of heaven that they divert your assault
away from us? But again, we, as the champions of truth, know neither fear
nor doubts nor, relying upon that holy confidence of ours, do we dread your
extraordinary gifts of nature, the might of your genius or the strength of
your eloquence. We too have our own resources.

272. What then is to be done? We must fight this out to the very end and
engage in hand-to-hand combat so all can see what a perverse thing you have
done and with what a violated, nay utterly prostituted conscience you have
undertaken it. This is truly the only way, this the best decision, since
neither regard for religion nor our warning, tendered in love, has any effect
whatsoever upon you. Farewell!

Notes: *Expostulation*

1. Cf. Introduction, n. 25.

2. Allen, Ep. 1342 (to Marcus Laurinus, 1 Feb. 1523; hereafter referred to as "Laurinus"); cf. Introduction, n. 27.

3. Laurinus, 11. 689-696; Sponge, par. 51.

4. Sponge, par. 53.

5. Sponge, par. 52.

6. Hutten uses the term "curtisanos" (acc. pl. of "curtisanus"). The word "curtisanus" is a 15th century spelling of the 14th century word "curtesanus" meaning a courtier; the 15th century word "curtezanus" meant a papal official or adherent. It is my opinion, however, that Hutten had the papal officials, especially the Curia, in mind when he used the form "curtisanos."

7. Sponge, pars. 22, 37, 45.

8. Hutten is referring to his participation in the "Pfaffenkrieg" waged by Franz von Sickingen against the Electoral Princes of the Palatinate and Trier and the Landgrave Philip of Hesse. Caspar Sturm, the imperial herald, later wrote an eye-witness account of the war and Sickingen's death. The dates of Sturm's life seem to be unknown although he served under Emperor Maximilian, Emperor Charles V and Ferdinand of Austria. It was he who conducted Martin Luther to the Diet of Worms under the Emperor's safe-conduct. Besides his account of the "Pfaffenkrieg" (1523), he also wrote a medieval-type chronology of Europe for King Ferdinand, Die vier namhafftesten Königreich (Frankfurt, 1538). His eye-witness account of the "Pfaffenkrieg" is called Warlicher bericht wie vo(n) den dreyen Churfürsten und Fürsten, nämlich Tryer, Pfaltz und Hessen weylandt Franz von Sickingen überzoge(n). Auch was sich im selbige(n) mit eröberung seiner und anderer Schlösser ...begeben, etc. Mainz: Joh. Schöffer, 1523. Concerning Sturm cf. Otto Clemen, "Eine

unbekannte Schrift des Herolds Kaspar Sturm," in <u>Beiträge zur Reformations-</u>
<u>geschichte aus Büchern und Handschriften der Zwickauer Ratsschulbibliothek.</u>
3 Hefte. Berlin: C.A. Schwetschke und Sohn, 1903, Heft 3, pp. 1-4; Th.
Kolde, "Der Reichsherold Caspar Sturm und seine literarische Tätigkeit,"
<u>Archiv für Reformationsgeschichte</u> (Leipzig-Berlin), IV (1906/1907), 117-161;
Roethe, "Kaspar Sturm", ADB, XXXVII (1894), 41-42.

9. Cf. Introduction, n. 5.

10. Sponge, par. 28; cf. also par. 66 below; Allen, Ep. 1195, 11. 137-143 (to
Aloysius Marlianus, 25 March 1520/21; hereafter referred to as "Marlianus");
cf. also Eps. 1114 and 1119, n. 33.

11. Sponge, par. 30.

12. Sponge, par. 32.

13. Sponge, par. 33.

14. Sponge, pars. 40-41.

15. Died 30 June 1522.

16. Possible reference to Luther's <u>Freedom of a Christian Man</u> (1520), cf. Martin
Luther, <u>Three Treatises</u>. Philadelphia: Fortress Press, 1960, pp. 265-316.

17. Sponge, pars. 5-6.

18. Sponge, par. 52.

19. In Mühlhausen; cf. Introduction, n. 26.

20. Sponge, par. 210.

21. Sponge, pars. 173, 213-214.

22. Sponge, par. 334.

23. Sponge, par. 211; cf. Introduction, ns. 20-21.

24. The letter to Laurinus.

25. Sponge, par. 353.

26. The papal brief is dated 23 Jan. 1523 (Allen, Ep. 1338); cf. Laurinus, 11.
631-643 and Sponge, par. 235.

27. Sponge, par. 238.

28. Laurinus, ll. 651-652.

29. In a footnote to this passage Böcking cites the proverb: "Quod quisque sperat, facile credit" and refers to Vergil's Eclogues, VIII, 108: "Credimus? an, qui amant, ipsi sibi somnia fingunt?" To this Erasmus might readily have answered in the words of Julius Caesar: "Quae volumus et credimus libenter ..." (Commentarii de bello civili, II, 27).

30. Sponge, pars. 37, 242.

31. The issue on which Erasmus did finally write against Luther was the question of free will, cf. his De libero arbitrio (1524; LB, IX, 1215A-1248D); Luther responded with his De servo arbitrio (1525; D. Martin Luthers Werke. Kritische Gesamtausgabe (Weimarer Ausbabe). Weimar: Hermann Böhlaus Nachfolger, 1908, Vol. XVIII, pp. 600-787; the work is edited by A. Freitag who also wrote an excellent Introduction, pp. 551-599). Erasmus responded with a much longer and more organized treatise, the Hyperaspistes diatribae adversus servum arbitrium Martini Lutheri (1526/1527; LB, X, 1337A-1536F). The first two works are available in an excellent translation in the series "The Library of Christian Classics", Vol. XVII: Luther and Erasmus - Free Will and Salvation. Philadelphia: Westminster Press, and London: SCM Press, 1969 (De libero arbitrio, trl. and ed. by E. Gordon Rupp in collaboration with A.N. Marlow, pp. 33-97; De servo arbitrio, trl. and ed. by Philip S. Watson in collaboration with B. Drewery, pp. 99-334). Cf. also Ernst F. Winter, trl. and ed., Erasmus - Luther: Discourse on Free Will. 2nd Printing. New York: Frederick Ungar Pub. Co., 1961; Pierre Mesnard, Erasme de Rotterdam, essai sur le libre arbitre. Algiers: R. Chaix, 1945; J. I. Packer and O. R. Johnston, Martin Luther on the Bondage of the Will. Westwood, N.J.: F.H. Revell, 1958; Winfried Lesowsky, trl. and ed., Erasmus von Rotterdam: De libero arbitrio/ Hyperaspistes. Aus. Schr., Vol. IV, 1969.

32. Allen, Ep. 1006, 11. 63-72; Sponge, pars. 61-70.

33. The EOV, cf. Introduction, n. 5.

34. For a partial listing of Hutten's works cf. Introduction, ns. 5, 7, 76, 79.

35. Introduction, ns. 10, 14, 35; Sponge, par. 28; cf. par. 17 above.

36. Among others cf. Allen, Ep. 808, Ep. 1299, 11. 91-101, Ep. 1330, 11. 49-56.

37. In Greek and Roman legend Heracles or Hercules was a mighty hero, deified and worshiped as the god of extraordinary physical strength and courage. He was the son of Zeus and Alcmene (the wife of Amphitryon). In a fit of madness - caused by Hera, the jealous wife of Zeus - he killed his own wife and sons; to purify himself and expiate his crime he performed twelve perilous labors, the completion of which then brought him immortality (cf. Harper's, pp. 789-794).

38. In Greek mythology the Hydra was a monstrous dragon dwelling in Lake Lerna in Argolis; it was represented as having nine heads, each of which, if it were cut off, would immediately be replaced by two new ones unless the wound were cauterized. The destruction of this monster was one of the twelve labors of Hercules (cf. Harper's, p. 790).

39. In Roman mythology Cacus was a giant, the son of Vulcan; he lived near the spot on which Rome was founded. After he stole some of Geryon's cattle, which were in Hercules' keeping, Hercules dragged him from his lair and slew him (cf. Harper's, p. 239; Ovid, Fasti, I, 543-586; Livy, I, 7; Vergil, Aeneid, VIII, 190-273).

40. Sponge, par. 237.

41. Allen, Ep. 1167, 11. 164-173.

42. Cicero, De amicitia, XXV, 92.

43. Laurinus, 11. 616-621.

44. In his adage "Auris Batavia" (Ad, 1083F-1084F) Erasmus praises the Hollanders for their complete lack of guile: "Ingenium simplex, et ab insidiis, omnique

fuco alienum, nullis gravibus obnoxium vitiis, tantum ad voluptatem, praecipue conviviorum aliquanto deditius" (1084C-D); cf. Phillips, p. 210: "It is a straightforward nature, without treachery or deceit, and not prone to any serious vices, except that it is a little given to pleasure, especially to feasting."

45. Hutten made the exact statement concerning Erasmus' approval of the EOV in a letter to Rich. Croke dated 9 Aug. 1516 (Bö, I, 124, ll. 6-15).

46. Allen, Ep. 622; cf. also Allen, Ep. 636, ll. 1-11 and Ep. 808, ll. 13-25.

47. Allen, Ep. 413; cf. par. 93 below.

48. Apologia ad Fabrum Stapulensem (Louvain, 5 Aug. 1517; LB, IX, 17A-50E); concerning Erasmus' attitude toward Lefèvre d'Etaples (Faber Stapulensis) cf. Allen, III, passim, esp. Ep. 778, pp. 223-230; Sponge, pars. 333-334.

49. Allen, Ep. 413, ll. 10-15; cf. Sponge, par. 97 where Erasmus uses the words "doctior Reuchlino" (comparative degree) instead of the "Hebraice longe doctissimus" (intensified superlative) which is found in his letter to Fisher.

50. Sponge, par. 97.

51. Sponge, par. 102.

52. Allen, Ep. 1129, ll. 6-14; Sponge, pars. 102-113.

53. Sponge, par. 109.

54. Allen, Ep. 1129, ll. 1 and 6; cf. n. to l.1.

55. Sponge, par. 111.

56. Sponge, par. 112.

57. Ulrich I von Württemberg

58. Sponge, par. 333.

59. Sponge, par. 114.

60. Sponge, pars. 115-120.

61. In Greek mythology the Harpies were ravenous and filthy winged monsters with the faces and bodies of women and the wings of a bird; their feet and fingers

were like sharp claws. They served as ministers of divine vengeance by carrying off the souls of the dead and defiling the food of living victims. They were either two or three in number, although Homer mentions only one, Podarge. Originally they were the personification of stormwinds sent by the gods to carry off offenders against them (cf. Harper's, pp. 771-772; Homer, Iliad, XVI, 150; Vergil, Aeneid, III, 211-244).

62. Plato, perhaps the most famous philosopher of Greece, 429/428BC-347BC (cf. Harper's, pp. 1271-1274); Theophrastus, c.372-287BC, was a disciple of Aristotle whom he succeeded as head of the Peripatetic School. Although he wrote many scientific works he is best remembered for his 30 short prose sketches, the "Characters" - vivid vignettes portraying various personality types: the flatterer, the grumbler, the boastful man, etc. (cf. Harper's, p. 1567); Sponge, par. 117.

63. The letter to which Hutten refers is probably Allen, Ep. 1164, in which Erasmus states: "Disputationibus vestris adversus Lutherum semper constantissime favi..." (11. 64-65). Erasmus' response to this charge (Sponge, pars. 121-123), however, refers to an earlier letter, Allen, Ep. 1153; cf. also his two letters to the theologians of Louvain defending himself against the charges of being pro-Luther (Allen, Eps. 1217 and 1301).

64. Sponge, pars. 125-126.

65. For similar analogies cf. Persius, Satirae, II, 38 and Claudianus, Laus Serenae, 1, 89; Sponge, pars. 127, 213, 249.

66. Sponge, pars. 128-144.

67. Sponge, par. 333.

68. Sinon was a Greek soldier during the Trojan War who pretended to desert the Greeks and sought refuge among the Trojans. He persuaded King Priam to drag the wooden horse built by the Greeks into Troy and then proceeded to release the soldiers hidden inside and joined in the general sack of the city, thus

betraying the confidence the Trojans had placed in him (cf. Vergil, Aeneid, II, 57-194).

69. Laurinus, 11. 105-110; Sponge, par. 140.

70. Sponge, par. 200.

71. Sponge, par. 145; Laurinus, 11. 623-643.

72. Timon (the Misanthrope) was an Athenian who lived during the Peloponnesian Wars (second half of the 5th cent. BC). As a result of disappointments and the ingratitude of his fellow citizens, he withdrew completely from the world except for his friendship with Alcibiades, whom he is said to have favored because he (Timon) believed that someday Alcibiades would destroy Athens (cf. Harper's, p. 1585; Lucian's Timon and Shakespeare's drama Timon of Athens).

73. Sponge, par. 152; both Hutten and Erasmus seem a little confused on the matter of Glapion. Erasmus does mention him in the letter to Laurinus (11. 245-256) but he certainly does not praise him there; on the other hand neither does he refer to him simply as the Emperor's confessor as stated in the Sponge, par. 152; he does so, however, in Allen, I, I, p. 35, 1. 15.

74. Glapion was sent to negotiate with Sickingen while Luther was on his way to the Diet of Worms (1521).

75. This is a decidedly groundless charge; from the plethora of material available concerning this question cf. Atkinson, Martin Luther and the Birth of Protestantism, pp. 141-207; Friedenthal, Luther, His Life and His Times, pp. 212-294; Jensen, Confrontation at Worms; Rupp, Luther's Progress to the Diet of Worms; Schwiebert, Luther and His Times, pp. 275-531.

76. Vertumnus was an ancient Etruscan deity, adopted later by the Romans; he came to be regarded as presiding over gardens and orchards, and was worshiped as the god of the changing seasons (cf. Harper's, p. 1650); Sponge, pars. 155, 194.

77. Sponge, par. 156.

78. Sponge, par. 157.

79. Allen, Eps. 1150, 1151, 1152, 1156.

80. Allen, Ep. 1152, ll. 12-15; Sponge, pars. 158-159.

81. Laurinus, ll. 320-326; Sponge, pars. 160-161; cf. also Allen, Ep. 1335, ll. 36-62, Ep. 1357, ll. 5-10, Ep. 1382, ll. 67-73.

82. The work referred to is probably his Opus adversus nova dogmata Lutheri. Rome: M. Silber, 1522. Erasmus might also have seen the manuscript of the work Malleus ... in haeresim Lutheranam, jam denuo ... recognitus, etc. Ed. J. Romberch. Apud Ioannem Soterem: Coloniae, 1524 (re-edited by Anton Naegele in 2 pts. Münster: Aschendorff, 1941, 1952 in the series: Corpus catholicorum, Nos. 23/24, 25/26).

83. The brief is dated 1 Dec. 1522, cf. Allen, Ep. 1324.

84. Sponge, pars. 162-165.

85. Sponge, par. 164.

86. Sponge, pars. 166-168.

87. Allen, Ep. 563, ll. 23-24.

88. For Hutten's defense of Erasmus against Lee's attacks cf. Bö, I, 346-348; cf. also Allen, IV, Eps. 1037 and 1061 (esp. the Introduction, pp. 108-110 - a survey of the quarrel between Erasmus and Lee) to which Hutten is responding; Sponge, pars. 169-171.

89. The work referred to is the expurgated reprint by Froben (at Erasmus' instigation) of Lee's Annotations, Basle, May 1520, with a Preface by Erasmus; cf. Allen, Eps. 1100, 1037 (Introduction, p. 110).

90. Sponge, pars. 172, 179.

91. In Greek legend Omphale was a Lydian queen in whose service Hercules wore women's clothes and did women's work for three years to expiate a murder. Later she became his mistress and bore him several children (cf. Harper's, pp. 1134-1135); Sponge, par. 239.

92. Sponge, par. 241.

93. Sponge, par. 174.

94. This paragraph is a composite of statements from several letters, the major letter to Laurinus already cited; an earlier one to him (Allen, Ep. 809, ll. 289-291, 816-824); a letter to Campegio (Allen, Ep. 1167, ll. 221-224, 421-426); to John Botzheim (Allen, I, I, ll. 11-20).

95. Laurinus, ll. 266-267; Sponge, par. 265.

96. Marcus Furius Camillus (d. c. 365BC) was a Roman general and several times dictator of Rome. In c. 396 he took Veii and in c. 390, after the sack of Rome by Brennus, he defeated the Gauls. The Romans acclaimed him the second founder of their city (cf. Harper's, p. 263; Plutarch, Camillus; Livy, V, 46-55).

97. Sponge, par. 288.

98. Allen, Ep. 1167, ll. 415-426, Ep. 1195, ll. 27-28, 122-124; Sponge, par. 249.

99. Marlianus, ll. 39-41; Laurinus, ll. 885-896; Sponge, pars. 245-246.

100. Laurinus, ll. 993-994; Sponge, par. 246.

101. Democritus, called the Abderite and the Laughing Philosopher, c. 460BC-c.357BC, adopted and further developed the atomistic theory of being. He had a very cheerful disposition and was wont to laugh at the follies of man rather than censure them. According to him, the soul was the manifestation of the real existence of the body, but even it died with the body. Since the gods were also mortal, his ethical system was based on pleasure as the end of life, a pleasure tempered, however, by the avoidance of excess in any form (cf. Harper's, pp. 488-489); Sponge, pars. 196, 248.

102. Laurinus, ll. 989-992.

103. Laurinus, ll. 765-767, 783-784.

104. Marlianus, ll. 28-30.

105. Allen, Ep. 1167, ll. 444-447; Sponge, pars. 250-251.

106. Hutten uses the term "Gnatonicis", an adjective derived from the name Gnatho, a character in Terence's drama The Eunuch who is a consummate, dedicated parasite. The term has thus come to mean a parasitic flatterer; Sponge, par. 355.

107. Cf. par. 169 above; Laurinus, ll. 885-896; Sponge, par. 249.

108. Laurinus, ll. 248-332, 644-659; Allen, Ep. 1217.

109. Marlianus, ll. 105-120; cf. par. 73 above; Sponge, par. 274.

110. Matthew, X, 34-36, Luke, XII, 51-53.

111. Laurinus, ll. 816-824; Allen, Ep. 1217, ll. 35-56; Sponge, par. 253.

112. Laurinus, ll. 896-906; Sponge, par. 253.

113. Isaiah, LVIII, 1; Sponge, pars. 253-254.

114. Allen, Ep. 1167, ll. 365-367.

115. II Timothy, IV, 2.

116. Laurinus, ll. 603-604.

117. Laurinus, ll. 892-893; Allen, Ep. 1195, ll. 39-42; Sponge, pars. 234, 252.

118. Marlianus, l. 40.

119. Marlianus, ll. 23-26.

120. Marlianus, ll. 23-26; Allen, Ep. 1167, ll. 109-116, 235-241; Laurinus, ll. 603-612, 684-689, 725-732, 740-743; Sponge, par. 267.

121. Sponge, par. 224.

122. Sponge, par. 401.

123. Sponge, par. 212.

124. Allen, Ep. 1228, l. 25. Hutten speaks of the "Apple of Eris" which has become the symbol of discord. In Greek mythology Eris, the goddess of discord, was the sister of Ares (Mars) and the daughter of Nyx (night). In revenge for not having been invited to the wedding feast of Peleus and Thetis, she threw among the guests a golden apple bearing the inscription "To the Fairest". A dispute arose among Aphrodite, Hera and Athena concerning who should receive

the apple. Paris was asked to decide the question. He in turn voted in favor of Aphrodite who rewarded him by assisting in the abduction of Helen of Sparta, thus giving rise to the Trojan War (cf. Harper's, pp. 1175-1176); Sponge, par. 203.

125. Allen, I, I (Catalogus omnium Erasmi Lucubrationes), pp. 34-36; Sponge, pars. 186-187.

126. Cf. par. 132 above and n. 75; Sponge, par. 195.

127. Sponge, pars. 242, 265.

128. Metius Fuffetius, the dictator of Alba, was torn assunder by chariots driven in opposite directions on the order of Tullius Hostilius, the third King of Rome, because of his treachery toward the Romans (cf. Harper's, p. 1041; Livy, I, 23-28); Sponge, pars. 198, 257.

129. Sponge, par. 271.

130. Sponge, par. 269.

131. John, XI, 49-52; Caiaphas, the son-in-law of Annas, was the Jewish High Priest from 27 to 36 AD; he presided at the council which condemned Jesus to death and took part in the trial of Peter and John (cf. Matthew, XXVI, 57-68, Acts, IV, 6); Sponge, par. 190.

132. Sponge, par. 289.

133. To Laurinus.

134. The reference is to Pontius Pilate, Roman Procurator of Judea, 23-36 AD, cf. Matthew, XXVII, 24-25.

135. Sponge, pars. 310-312.

136. Terence, The Eunuch, II, ii, 21-22; Cicero, De amicitia, XXV, 93; Sponge, par. 355.

137. Horace, Epistolae, I, 1, 90; Sponge, par. 352.

138. Sponge, par. 353.

139. Sponge, par. 257.

140. Apostolius et Arsenius, VII, 72a (Leutsch, Vol. II, p. 415); Sponge, pars. 313, 424.

141. In Greek mythology Ate was the personification of infatuation or moral blindness in which right and wrong, advantageous and ruinous conduct cannot be distinguished. She is the subject of an extensive allegory in Homer's Iliad (XIX, 90-133; cf. also IX, 502-512) in which she appears as the daughter of Zeus. She is also called the daughter of Strife and the sister of Lawlessness (cf. Harper's, p. 147); Sponge, pars. 22-23.

142. The inhabitants of the Lowlands, esp. the Belgians (cf. n. 44 above and Sponge, par. 296).

143. Sponge, par. 292.

144. Vergil, Aeneid, IV, 373.

145. Sponge, par. 403.

146. Lucian, Lucius, The Ass, 18; this same quote appears in Hutten's Invectiva in Lutheromastigas sacerdotes (Mar. 1521; Bö, II, p. 34, 11. 18-19).

147. Cf. par. 219 above and Sponge, pars. 269-270.

First Preface to the *Sponge*[1]

(Basle, August 1523)

Erasmus of Rotterdam to the most learned Ulrich Zwingli, Preacher in the renowned Swiss City of Zurich. Greetings.

Since your city of Zurich was the first to receive the poison dispatched from here, most learned Zwingli, it seemed fitting that Zurich should be the first place to receive the antidote, not because I fear Hutten's accusations might harm my good name with you or any other sensible man, but because I feel I should aid those also who are not too well-disposed toward me or else, through a defect in their nature, are more ready to believe whatever harms a person's good name rather than what commends it.[2] For what good and prudent man would not execrate the example set by Hutten, whom I have never harmed, neither by word nor deed?[3] On the contrary, I have often praised him even in published works, and no one was ever more generously, sincerely or repeatedly extoled in my letters of recommendation to men in high positions. Suddenly, however, as though he had been lying in wait, he has launched such a pamphlet against a friend who at that very moment was praising him most candidly and lovingly, while he was engaged in penning that work of his.[4] The last thing I expected was that such a melo-drama was taking shape in Hutten's heart. What more foreign to German honesty and all feelings of humanity could have been contrived? What more welcome and pleasing to the enemies of sound learning? What worse blow to these studies themselves? What more ruinous to the cause of the Gospel or, if you will, even to that of Luther, which he boastfully claims to support.

The war he had declared was against the Roman clique, but then, without

any previous protest, he attacks his dearest friend with a pamphlet so

bitter that he has not yet written anything more poisonous even against an

enemy.[5]   And, as I hear, he has meanwhile augmented his little book, as if

it did not contain enough poison; nor is there any likelihood that he will

ever stop, now that he has declared war on both the Muses and the Graces.

I for one do not begrudge him the kindness of the Swiss in pro-

viding him with a hiding-place in which to remain safe from those who are

hunting him down to execute him.[6]   Steps should be taken, however, to assure

that while hiding in safety among them, he does not so abuse their hospitality

by hurling such books at the heads of any or all the universally acknowledged

cultural leaders.[7]   He spares neither the Pope, the Emperor, the German

princes, nor even the most honorable men of the Swiss nation, Ludwig Baer

among them. Since he is writing these things while hiding among the Swiss,

it is to be feared that, because of this, something hateful or misfortunate

might eventually happen to that nation, a nation we so desire to see flourish

in public peace and general prosperity.[8]   Now, there is nothing easier than

to incite discord, no evil once aroused more difficult to quell.[9]   Farewell.

Preface to the Second Edition of the Sponge[10]

Erasmus of Rotterdam to the Unprejudiced Reader. Greetings

Hutten's death has robbed my _Sponge_ of some of its charm, if indeed

there is any charm in books of this nature. Had I foreseen it, I would

either not have answered him at all or would have answered differently.[11]   As

it is now, there are certain things in my response which Hutten alone would

have understood. In my opinion, he had not yet read the whole of it before

his death (although certain people affirm that he did), since he died on the

29th of August, at which time Froben had barely finished printing the work.

Death came as a real blessing to Hutten, for it undoubtedly spared the
poor wretch many pressing and threatening cares. [12]   What a pity it did not
overtake him sooner, that is before he fell into such extreme folly that,
thanks to this treacherous book, he brought loathing and discredit on himself first of all, as well as on classical studies, on the cause of the
Gospel and on the good name of Germany; for in this attack only the least
part of the evils affects me! [13]   And yet, if men were led by right reason,
it would be unjust for anyone to feel enmity toward classical studies just
because one individual happens to use them perversely, or to become hostile
to the spreading of the Gospel solely because Hutten impudently forced
himself upon it - since even Luther repudiated him as an enemy to his cause.
It would be even more unfair to judge the character of a whole nation from
the flaws of one man. Did not Scythia have its Anacharsis and Athens give
birth to many fools? [14]   I would indeed have shielded my friend against the
disgrace of violating our friendship without cause, if certain individuals
had not so purposely seen to it that we should not speak to each other. [15]
Now at least I congratulate myself that I have been able thus far to
preserve the well-known moderation I always keep in any rejoinder. And if
Hutten had attacked me again - which, in my opinion, he would have done,
had he lived, either because he had already forfeited all sense of shame in
himself, or because there would have been no lack of persons ready, as the
saying goes, to upset the apple cart [16] - he would have come to realize that
my response is indeed no harsher than a sponge. [17]

I am not going to disturb the repose of Hutten's spirit provided
that, though dead, he does not come forward to begin the quarrel all over
again. It seems to me that by now we have had far more than enough insanity.
Since what has already been done, cannot be undone, should we not lay the
evil to rest? [18]   Men are right in advising us to extract whatever good we

can from misfortunes and I personally will profit from the harm done;

hereafter I will be more wary in making friends, more cautious in cultivating
them, more sparing in my praise, more circumspect in commending others.

In the spirit of Solon's celebrated saying, I shall grow older learning
something new every day.   And, too, from this affair our youth may learn

to strive no less after a sound character than after a sound culture, so

that the wanton passions of the spirit may be controlled by the bridle of
reason.   There are many who at first indulge their vices and excuse the

whoring and riotous behavior of their youth, feeling that gambling and

extravagance are marks of the gentleman. In time, however, their resources
decrease, their debts increase,   their good name is imperilled and the

favor of princes, whose liberality supports them, dies. Soon poverty in-

duces them to robbery; at first they cloak their brigandage with the

honorable title of "warfare"; but later, when nothing satisfies their

extravagance (which can be likened to the sieve of the Danaides), they

devise desperate plans in which no distinction is made any more between
friend or foe, wherever plunder is involved.   Then finally, like a horse

who has thrown its rider, their arrogance rushes headlong to its own
destruction.

I am really not all that astonished about Hutten, for I know better
than I could wish how ill-advised nearly all his plans were.   I am forced

to deplore a total lack of judgment in those who pushed him onto the stage

to act out such a senseless play, and who continue to applaud such a stupid
performance.   They want to be considered favorable to classical studies

and yet no one has done them greater harm; they are eager to support Luther

and yet they could not have harmed his cause more; they loved Hutten, but no

enemy ever inflicted greater evil on him. They hate the enemies of Luther,

but no one has yet treated them to a more enjoyable spectacle; they are

Germans to the core, but in 300 years no one has more dishonored the good name of Germany!

I am not deceived as to whose advice prodded him on or by whom this play was directed. I am admittedly endowed with a simple mind and by no means suspicious, but I am not so wholly imperceptive nor am I such a blockhead or so stupid that I should be the only one not to realize what everyone else realizes. But still I would wish not to know what I know and to forget what I remember, if in doing so it could put an end to this gladiatorial contest. I fear, however, that some addicts of such quarrels will thwart this wish. Although they know how courteously I treat Hutten in my Sponge, such people are nonetheless not at all ashamed to spread the rumor that I published my book after Hutten's death, and they picture me as fighting only with his ghost.[28] I immediately responded to Hutten's Expostulation in July - Johannes Froben and several others saw my manuscript. He was ready to print it then, but at the time no press was available, and, too, I thought it more advisable to delay publication lest another attack should appear just before the Book Fair, to which I would have no time to respond. Now, since it appears that Hutten died on the 29th of August, on a tiny island quite a distance beyond Zurich, and since it is also well known that Froben began printing the Sponge on the 13th of August and finished it on the 3rd of September, how is it possible that I should have published this work only after Hutten's death, especially since Hutten (according to their letters) died suddenly? Reckon the time it would have taken to bring the news of his death here, even posthaste, and then examine the date by which the printed bundles of the Sponge were already on their way - you will discover that not four hours would have remained for publishing it. From this, then, judge how shameless they are who broadcast such lies! However, if the one whom I suspect should betray himself, he will realize how truly[29] little I hated Hutten.

Farewell, dear Reader, and learn from my misfortune.

Erasmus' *Sponge*

THE SPONGE OF ERASMUS AGAINST THE ASPERSIONS OF HUTTEN

1. Now, if you have the time, listen in turn to the Laconian orator respond
to the Asian, not only briefly ^{30} but politely as well, for it is only with
a sponge that I will wipe off the muck with which he has splattered me,
and in return I will heap on my antagonist no reproach or abuse. Such is
my behavior because of our former friendship, and also because it has always
been my constant habit.

2. I know that Hutten's noble spirit cannot bear contempt. Therefore,
since in the past he has provoked many with his caustic writings and thus
far not one has considered him worthy of a reply, this honor he will receive
from an old friend. I pray you, however, most distinguished reader, to be
attentive to me in this matter, for I want you to be not merely a witness
to this conflict, but an advocate and judge as well.

3. This tragedy had its prologue when Hutten arrived in Basle and I would
not grant him an interview. You cannot imagine the trouble he is trying to
stir up because of this. A straightforward, clear relating of the truth,
however, will disperse all the smoke. ^{31} Not a word will be fabricated. The
matter then stands as follows:

4. Heinrich Eppendorf - who, as often as I shall mention his name in this
narrative, will be mentioned with all due respect ^{32} - was the first one to
inform me that Hutten was in Basle. Immediately delighted at this news, I
began to inquire about his health, whether he was safe, whether the magistrates
were inclined to help him and other such things we normally ask about those
whom in all sincerity we wish well. Without a doubt I was at that time as
sincerely well disposed toward Hutten as was anyone else.

5. Everything was all right, thank God, apart from his health which, I was
sad to hear from Eppendorf, was in a very poor condition. Finally I asked

Eppendorf gently to persuade Hutten to refrain from visiting me, if he just wanted to greet me, since such a visit would be of no advantage whatever to him but would increase ill-will toward me, from which I had already suffered more than enough.[33] For the rest, however, nothing had changed in my former affection for him and, moreover, should he ever need my assistance in any matter at all, I would be entirely at his disposal.

6. Eppendorf agreed to deliver the message to Hutten and I do not doubt that he delivered it even more appropriately than I had recommended him to do, endowed as he is with such politeness.[34] Anyway, he affirms that he conveyed my message in the politest terms possible.[35]

7. When he came to see me again after a day or so, I asked him whether Hutten had well received my request. "To be sure," he said, "Hutten smiled pleasantly and interpreted it in good part." Once again I averred my affection for him and offered my services should Hutten ever want them.

8. Quite a few days later I more confidentially asked Eppendorf to tell me frankly whether Hutten seemed to accept my entreaty in the same spirit in which I had meant it and whether he gave any indication of being offended. He said he had observed no such reaction in Hutten but, as he was about to leave, he added that Hutten was eager to speak with me. When I asked him whether Hutten himself had said this, he said no, but that perhaps there was something he was eager to say to me.

9. I replied then that, although I did desire to avoid any ill-will, this was nevertheless not of such great importance to me that I could not easily disregard it if Hutten had something serious to discuss with me. If speaking with me really meant so much to him, I would go to him myself were I only able to bear stoves, whereas he, being in such poor condition, perhaps could not do without one. However, if he could endure the coldness in my room, I would willingly converse with him as long as he liked and I would see to it

that the fireplace was burning brightly. To this Eppendorf responded that, because of his weakened physical condition, Hutten always had to stay in stove-heated rooms.[36]

10. In the meantime Hutten left for Mühlhausen. Eppendorf told me of the dangers Hutten had very successfully eluded, which made me very happy. Eppendorf can also testify how fearful I was at the time that some misfortune might befall Hutten.

11. And so, when Eppendorf was preparing to return to Mühlhausen, I commissioned him to warn Hutten not to rush from his safe place into any danger, since not a few people were hunting him down; he should beware of everybody.

12. He had published a really absurd pamphlet against a doctor in Basle,[37] and I expressed my amazement to Eppendorf that Hutten had so much leisure time in which to amuse himself with such writings, given his illness and the number of difficulties confronting him. Eppendorf replied that Hutten was relaxing his mind with such jests. In response I said that I would prefer it if, at his age, he would choose some theme in which all the energy of his genius might be released and through which he could transmit to posterity the memory of a great name. Eppendorf replied that Hutten was solely concerned with perfecting his style.[38]

13. While I, like an upright and honest friend, was anxiously pondering these things about my Hutten, Eppendorf returned from him and announced that Hutten was terribly angry with me and that he was preparing some sort of violent book against me. Since this happened so unexpectedly and contrary to what I deserved from him, I was simply overwhelmed by surprise.

14. I asked what all this was about and Eppendorf answered that Hutten was furious because he had not been allowed to speak with me. "But," I asked, "did you not say that he accepted my request in good part?" "This is true," Eppendorf replied, "but after leaving Basle, he began to be very offended and

it seems that he cannot be appeased."

15. Now the rumor about this was already spreading even farther, so much so that Beatus Rhenanus, also worried about it, came to see me. With my permission he summoned Eppendorf too and we consulted together. I stated that I could not be responsible for what this person or that one suddenly began to think; it was sufficient for me if I displayed a disposition at which no one could be justifiably angered.[39] "For, my dear Eppendorf," I said, "as far as the interview is concerned, you know that he has no cause to be angry with me."

16. They both thought Hutten could be appeased by a letter before he published his book. I replied that it seemed best to me to ignore the situation since dispositions of his type rage all the more violently if someone attempts to appease them.[40]

17. Since both of them continued to disagree with me, I wrote to Hutten, stating that my conscience was not aware of having committed any evil against him and that if anything had been falsely reported to him or if he were suspicious in any respect, he should privately expostulate with me in a letter; I had no doubt that I could satisfy him on every point. In the meantime, he ought to consider whether what he was stirring up would profit good letters, the cause of the Gospel and the present state of his own affairs.[41]

18. My supposition did not deceive me. Eppendorf brought back a most stinging letter from Hutten, for he already considered me a timid man, trembling with dread. He accused me on several points: I had given preference to Capito over Reuchlin in Hebraic studies; in a letter to Hoogstraten I had censured Hutten himself; I had besmirched Reuchlin with the stain of perfidy; I had flattered the theologians of Louvain and several others; finally, I had suddenly deserted the cause of the Gospel and directed all my energy toward overthrowing it.[42]

19. He promised, however, that he would send me the book by a servant within three days. In point of fact, however, the copy, which had already passed through many hands here, had been sent to Zurich and others were to tell me what Hutten had written against me.

20. I replied in writing to each of the charges contained in his first letter, reminding him of many points which were no less in his interest than in mine. He answered a little more mildly - Franz von Sickingen had been killed by this time - and suggested that, since the pamphlet had already been sent to the printer, I might as well remain silent about it and, if I so desired, peace and even friendship would then be restored [43] between us as it was before.

21. At last the pamphlet was delivered, neither sealed nor bound. Although Hutten was already no longer able to suppress it, there were nevertheless some who earnestly urged me to send Hutten some money, so that (would you [44] believe it!) I could persuade him not to have it published. I answered firmly that it would have been best had a book of this type never been written, but since it was already scattered about, having left the author's hands, there was nothing better to do than to have it published, the sooner [45] the better. Moreover, I offered to provide the funds if Hutten agreed.

22. In the meantime Hutten had moved on to Zurich. From there he wrote that Homer's Ate was to blame for his behavior and that henceforth he would [46] act more prudently. After this, nothing transpired between us.

23. That all of this was so, no one can testify more fittingly than Eppendorf, since he is well aware from my many writings and from numerous intimate conversations that I still maintained a pure and friendly affection for Hutten and [47] that from no one less than from him did I expect such hostilities.

24. Where, then, is this discourtesy which Hutten magnifies in his speech? Where the contempt for such a great man? Where the fear of his furious [48] expostulation which I would be unable to sustain? I gently asked that he

not without cause burden with odium a friend already burdened more than enough. I did not refuse to speak with him, if it were about something serious, and I offered him the services of a friend, even to the point of giving him as much money as my straitened circumstances would allow. In the end I agreed to an interview, if it meant so much to him, even if he had nothing serious to discuss.

25. For this task an obliging and graciously eloquent mediator was chosen - one who, being noble-minded, sympathetic and gracious, would be able to mitigate the situation should there be anything unpleasant about it. It is evident, therefore, how out of place is Hutten's so often repeated complaint that I refused to grant him an interview. At the time I was so disposed toward him that I would not have considered it too burdensome even to ride as far as Constance, if I had felt that it really mattered so much to Hutten. Thus all the less is it true that I wanted to avoid conversing with him.

26. To such an extent did I value the friendship between us, which the Muses had brought into being several years before and which from the very beginning certain mutual services helped to foster. My writings testify to the fact that it was in no ordinary manner that I loved Hutten's disposition and talent. His libertinism I attributed to his youth, and I hoped this would be corrected in the course of time. In his writings I saw a rich, brilliant and ready store of words, and sufficient character, and I hoped that reason, judgment and prudence would be added with age, experience and study. [49]

27. Now, if one compares the state my affairs were in at the time (and still are) with the condition of Hutten's affairs, he will certainly judge it a matter or prudence that I shunned an interview with him, a meeting which would have meant little to him but a lot of trouble for me; and the one who will be judged discourteous is not he who tried to avoid this visit, but the one who took offense.

28. But yet he bitterly attacks me on my own testimony: have I not commended his uprightness by saying he was not wont to bring down ill-will on anyone? I admit that I did commend Hutten's noble-mindedness since he, unlike others who were publishing books anonymously or under fictitious names, did sign his works so as to burden no one but himself with suspicion. **51** But what does this have to do with the matter?

29. If I did praise Hutten's rectitude, this fact alone should have reminded him not to be other than true to himself. If one extols a wine as excellent, should he afterwards be accused of untruth if the wine happens to turn sour? Would to God Hutten had proved me wrong only in this!

30. "Of my own free will," Hutten says, "I would have abstained from that pleasure which I always derive from your company, had I seen that it would **52** have burdened you with odium." If, then, he was prepared to do this of his own accord, and since it was certain that our meeting could only cause trouble for me, why should he be indignant with me for having so courteously requested him to do what he fully intended to do without even being asked?

31. I am not curious to know what enemies Hutten might have; so I do not fear any ill-will toward me on their part. A report of this meeting, however, would have reached the Pope in Rome, the Emperor in Spain, Brabant, where I have very active informers, and England, where there is no lack of those who would make of me a Lutheran even against my will. If there is even a **53** grain of truth in a report, these people gladly invent much more. It was the odium of such rumors that I feared. Hutten could easily have ascertained this from my letter to Laurinus.

32. "But," Hutten will ask, "what aid in times of distress may one expect from a friend who shuns the odium of a meeting while one's affairs are still **54** untroubled?" To this I respond: those are one's truest friends who know how to keep themselves untroubled for the time when their friends need them

and, therefore, fear any danger from which their friends might derive
        55
absolutely no advantage.

33. But I indeed do not wish now to examine how untroubled his affairs are;
I would certainly wish they were more favorable for him, so that he himself
                    56   57
might choose to be worthy of a better fate.   Everyone, he says,   wishes
Hutten well, one magistrate after another comes to pay his respects, many
from every social level eagerly rush to visit him, Erasmus alone stays
cloistered at home.

34. Who ever saw Erasmus leave his house in the wintertime just to visit
someone? Besides, I do not need to extol the kindness of this city's
magistrates, which I too have experienced more than once. It was a great
kindness, indeed, that they let Hutten in, but an even greater one that they
let him out again. And I would add this to their praise, that they prefer
their services to be kept secret rather than boasted of - in this their
        58
modesty consists.

35. Would to God Hutten would only conduct himself in such a way as con-
tinually to enjoy the kindness of good men! But the very ones who received
him so hospitably, warned him to refrain from any sort of speech that could
incite tumults; how much less would they approve of such pamphlets! There
are some who are not troubled by ill-will: many obscure individuals, for
example, or those who are powerful enough to disdain it. But what does that
have to do with me? As it is, I can scarcely withstand ill-will and I have
                                                    59
nothing with which to protect myself except my innocence.

36. He, however, will cease to wonder that I rather fear ill-will, compared
to which no plague is more noxious, who considers that some time ago the
Cardinal of Mainz dismissed Hutten from his household for no other reason
than that he did not wish to be burdened with odium on account of him. And
Franz von Sickingen, why did he send Hutten away, except to avoid odium?

And why do those most closely related to Hutten prefer that he not live on the family estate, unless they fear odium? All this is common knowledge. Is it only Erasmus, then, who fears odium?[60]

37. "One ought not to be despised, whom kings and princes have considered worthy of their encouragement."[61] Hutten's fame is certainly not threatened by me. One does not despise, who seeks to avoid ill-will; or is it perhaps that I despise the King of France, who awaits me as eagerly in France as I would wish to be there for the sake of my health? Nevertheless, fearing ill-will, I have stayed away, since the relationship between him and the Emperor is still too unsettled.[62]

38. When I was in Bruges a short time ago, I avoided conversing with a king who loves me,[63] not because I held him in contempt but rather because I feared the ill-will of the papists this would entail, an ill-will which I could not wholly escape.

39. If only Hutten had moderated his ambitions in like manner![64] Just as he was once welcomed among the French with honor because of the respect accorded the prince whom he represented, he would even now enjoy the favor of the powerful and would be loved and respected by all without any ill-will.[65]

40. Now just look at what a hateful reason he invents for my refusal to grant him an interview! One might say our knight was born not for riding but for slandering. He asserts that I knew he wished to remonstrate with me and, since I had a guilty conscience, I avoided speaking with him.[66] But from where did Hutten derive such new authority, that I, an old man, would be unable to bear the reproaches of this young man?[67]

41. How does it happen that Hutten has suddenly been transformed into a censorious Cato?[68] When addressing me formerly, he used to exhibit a certain respectful propriety which was certainly more befitting his age than his present impudence of tongue and pen.[69] And how was I to guess that he wanted

153

to remonstrate with me?

42. While in Schletstadt, as he writes in his letter to me, he had charged Beatus Rhenanus to tell me that he found something lacking in me. But in fact, Beatus Rhenanus neither wrote me a single word from Schletstadt, nor, having returned from there after Hutten had already departed, did he ever mention that he had spoken with Hutten. This I found out for the first time in the letter which Hutten wrote me from Mülhausen.

43. It happened by chance that Eppendorf and Beatus were present while I was reading the letter. When I arrived at the passage under discussion, I said, "Beatus, you are being summoned into court; you have need of a lawyer." Then Beatus frankly admitted what the whole thing was about and he gave his reasons for never having mentioned it.

44. Pondering the matter for a while, he then explained it all to us in such a way that I was forced to admit the lack of any German honesty in Hutten, who had manipulated this affair with a certain cunning so as to have something with which to defile my conscience. He had not actually charged Beatus with anything in secret or in a serious tone or of a nature that it would have been worth the trouble for me to know it. He had merely declared to all present that I was not very favorably disposed toward Luther; he interpreted this as fear and said he would inspire me with courage.

45. He added similar insinuations and a few other messages, thinking Beatus was about to return to Basle; but there was no threat in his words nor any indication that he was sharpening his pen against me. And, furthermore, he did not speak in secret, but in the uproarious midst of a laughing and joking
70
company.

46. In the meantime, moreover, he spoke so respectfully about me that Beatus could not have suspected the approaching tragedy. Then, since some business detained Beatus in his home town, Hutten released him as it were from his

154

charge, indicating that he himself would soon be going to Basle and would inspire me, a far too fearful man, with courage. Thus Beatus kept silent, in no way suspecting the evils about to arise.

47. Nor would they have arisen, if an interview with Hutten had been possible; with ten words I could have assuaged his anger. As it happened, Beatus returned to Basle some time after Hutten had left the city. When he greeted me in the presence of several friends, among them Ludwig Baer, he asked me how I was getting along with Hutten and I answered, "Very well." At the time I was wholly convinced of this.

48. While Beatus was visiting me once again, Eppendorf showed us a letter Hutten had written to him, in which Hutten asked him to warn me not to abuse Luther: he was very well disposed toward me, but he could not consider me a friend unless I refrained from attacking Luther. Since at that time nothing was further from my mind, our peaceful relationship was sure to last.[71]

49. Although in the meantime nothing new had occurred between us, the astonishing news soon arrived that Hutten was violently incensed and was writing something against Erasmus. I thought it fit to recount these things in such detail so as to make it clear that I neither had heard anything from Beatus nor could have suspected anything about Hutten's animosity.

50. Therefore, once this foundation is removed, the whole structure of lies Hutten built on it comes crashing to the ground. Why did he not charge his loyal friend Eppendorf here with the same things with which he had charged Beatus there? Beatus, however, reported that Hutten's disposition toward me was calm and dispassionate. Now, if I had been aware of Hutten's frame of mind, embittered somehow by suspicion, it would not have been necessary for him to beg to visit me; on the contrary, I myself would have healed the nascent evil, either by a personal visit or in writing. I will shortly reveal how trifling those things were about which he wanted to remonstrate with me.

51. But, he contends, I betrayed my guilty conscience in my letter to Laurinus by using a stove as a pretext for not meeting with him, thereby trying to escape the accusation of being inhospitable.[72] To this I would answer that, given the opportunity, I am accustomed to mention my friends with pleasure in my writings and, since there were many reasons for my refusing to see Hutten, in wording my letter I referred only to the one which[73] had nothing odious about it, even though Hutten himself calls it hateful[74] in a certain letter of his.

52. It is indeed ridiculous when he says that he frequently walked past my house in order to induce me to come out and converse with him; and, furthermore, that I was well aware of this, since, as everyone knows, I am accustomed to sit at my window in the wintertime to watch the passers-by. But why was it necessary to lure me out in such a manner? The door of my house was almost always wide open, contrary to the general custome of this city, and he could have come in and asked to speak with me; and even if the door were closed, he could have knocked.

53. But you begged me not to come visit you, he says. Oh, what sudden bashfulness![75] What, however, would have been more modest, to go visit some- one, even though he had begged you not to come, or to write such a book against an unsuspecting friend? He should have expostulated with me at least by letter before beginning this tragedy, writing as many letters as he does. Is it a habit of his to declare war on his enemies only after notifying them in advance, but when it comes to a friend, to attack him[76] without warning?

54. But he will say perhaps that he had given Eppendorf an inkling of his animus toward me. How as I to guess this, since Eppendorf firmly stated that he had detected no sign of estrangement in Hutten? That this is true, Eppendorf himself does not deny and he has frequently acknowledged it, not

only to me but also before a number of others, among them Beatus, Glareanus
76a
and Botzheim.

55. You can see, therefore, dear reader, that in this matter I did nothing
that was impolite, haughty, unfriendly or prompted by pride or a guilty
conscience. Let us assume, however, that I did commit some act against the
laws of propriety; now, since Hutten admits that I was such a great friend -
indeed he scarcely had another as good - and since he also admits that all
of Germany is greatly indebted to my labors, should he not first have re-
monstrated with me in private before publishing such a book, the most virulent
he has ever written against anyone? And yet he calls it a mere "remonstrance";
in a certain letter he even refers to it as a "very gentle remonstrance,"
77
considering the atrocity of my behavior.

56. Where then are these mutual friends who are so grieved because I refused to see Hutten? Eppendorf knows I did not refuse to do so, and even
he disapproves of Hutten's behavior, stating as much in a letter to me; this
78
Hutten cannot deny. But enough about this "refusal" of an interview with
Hutten!

57. Now let us proceed to those faults of mine that so greatly enraged
Hutten's spirit, gentle as it is by nature. Obviously they must be ex-
cessively vile! Our friendship, he admits, was no ordinary one and he also
admits that I have rightly merited - and still do merit - glorious praise for
what I have done to benefit scholarship. In this respect he attributes more
79
to me than I acknowledge.

58. To himself he attributes above all a love of truth, which is something
proper for a German. He likewise attributes to himself a love of literary
culture, a characteristic befitting a scholar. He denies that he ever
allowed anyone to incite him against a friend, as befits a wise and gallant
knight. I am sure he also knows that nothing should be accepted as true

which comes from the lips of scandalmongers, through whom whole kingdoms

have been destroyed again and again; nor is he unaware with what reluctance

a friendship should be broken, especially one that was in no sense a common

type, and that no suspicion ought to be harbored lightly against a proven

friend.[80]

59. Finally, since he also claims for himself moral probity, it cannot have

escaped his attention how much respect a young man owes a grey-haired old

man,[81] one who is his friend and who has well deserved praise in the past,

and is still well-deserving; for what else do I do now with my incessant

labors but promote the cause of the Gospel? I must, therefore, have committed

a horrible crime to compel Hutten, a champion of humanity, to publish against

Erasmus a book fraught with so many lies, so many insults, so many acrimonious

reproaches and, furthermore, to do this by violating all the codes of gracious

conduct, oblivious of my former kindnesses, spurning the respect he owed my

grey hairs - and they have greyed largely through my labors in the service

of the community - and then attacking me without expostulating with me

beforehand, something even enemies usually do before engaging in open combat!

60. I do not gainsay his love of truth, but the matter itself indicates

that his course of action against me was prompted by the most unreliable of

persons.[82] In any event, let us now hear my terrible crimes, after disposing

of which I shall discuss the most horrible of all, namely whether it is true

that at one time I used to stand on the side of the Gospel but now, having

suddenly shifted my stance to the complete opposite, I am striving to subvert

the whole Gospel together with Christ.[83] This very book of Hutten's found

me here toiling with all my heart to advance the cause of the Gospel, and

since I never rested at any time from my efforts, despite such great turmoil

and danger, I repeat, can his allegation be true?

61. This is the first charge: among my letters there is one to Jacob

Hoogstraten which begins, "Formerly, when I was lecturing..."; whoever

takes the time to read it through, will immediately see how shameless the

accusation is which Hutten alleges. In that letter I remonstrate with

Hoogstraten for attacking Reuchlin more acrimoniously than becomes a

theologian, for reproaching the incomparable Count of Neuenahr in his

writings in a hateful manner and for attacking me, without cause and un-

deservedly, in the book he wrote about the Cabala and directed against

Reuchlin.[85] In all of this, I believe I omitted no arguments to justify

my position.

62. But Hutten was offended because I addressed him as "Reverend Father,"

as if indeed kings do not honor one another with their customary titles

even in the midst of war.[86] Certainly no one except Hutten was so suspicious

about this point that he would accuse me of flattering Hoogstraten by such

titles. There were even some who suspected I used them in derision.

63. Hutten was seriously offended, however, because in the same letter I

am supposed to have censured him personally and, concerning the letters

which Reuchlin, Hermann Busch, the Count of Neuenahr and Hutten had most

crudely written against Hoogstraten, he claimed I stated the following: "In

no way would I have been able to endure the bitterness of all these letters,

had I not read beforehand the works by which, it would seem, they had been

provoked into their outrageous lack of restraint."[87]

64. Thus far I have been quoting verbatim from my letter. Who, however,

is so lacking in judgment or of such perverse discernment that he cannot see

I was only stating these things from Hoogstraten's point of view, who without

any doubt whatsoever did find those letters exceedingly caustic? And what

Hoogstraten had in fact written to me, I was but quoting back to him, who

in his own writings had given cause for such an acrimonious rejoinder.

65. The same deliberate tactics have made me state that I was not skilled

in theology nor capable of making a judgment in that field. Hutten then
asks with the same lack of discernment whence this sudden ignorance? not
recognizing, or at least pretending not to know, that here again I was
merely repeating the words of others, not my own, and that I was only ex-
tracting from these statements what I could use against the same individuals.
That is indeed the most efficacious manner of argumentation which can turn
against the enemy the very weapons he uses against you.

66. Here, I know, he will call me a crafty sophist. Nonetheless, in the
art of rhetoric this is referred to as versatility, and if one has not
mastered it, he can never hope to be eloquent. And, too, if neither Christ
nor the apostles refrained from this manner of argumentation, certainly it
is but fair to condone my use of it.

67. Hutten was angered even more by what followed in my letter: "It was,
therefore, with a not unmixed sorrow that I read these letters, sighing for
the fate of the authors themselves as well as for your own, since I could
not help fearing repeatedly that even good and fair-minded men might judge
such bitter revilings as accusations hurled against an individual who was
not altogether innocent." Why should this so anger Hutten? I clearly
stated that to good and fair-minded men these letters would not seem to have
been written against a wholly innocent man. "But," Hutten says, "you speak
indirectly and figuratively." To be sure, doing so was advantageous for the
cause I was supporting. In this, Hutten has no cause for complaint, for I
did not blame him for lack of restraint or for lack of substance; on the
contrary, it was Hoogstraten I was accusing.

68. Perhaps Hutten would have wanted me to write something like this: "You
filthy cesspool, how dare you defile men of heroic stature with your muck-
filled books?" Such a style might become Hutten, but not Erasmus. If
Hoogstraten could be corrected, then civility was called for; if, however,

he were incorrigible, then my moderation would be more injurious to him among men of upstanding character than would be any foul-mouthed reviling on my part.[92]

69. Furthermore, since this passage pertains equally to four men, why was Reuchlin never offended, whose letter displeased me indeed, not because I was overly disturbed at what was being written against Hoogstraten, but rather because I was sincerely saddened that such a fine old gentleman would be aroused to such a distemper as that letter displays? And why was Hermann Busch also not offended? As for the Count of Neuenahr, a man of most discerning judgment,[93] he was delighted with my letter and thanked me for it, something Hoogstraten never did.

70. Finally, why did Hutten not expostulate with me concerning this matter while he was still in Brabant, since the book had already been published by that time? All of this, therefore, is really so clear that, as they say, even a blind man could see it.[94] Why then that torrent of words which Hutten pours forth about his calm and moderate publication, about his own wonderful loyalty and love of truth and about my frivolity and dissembling?[95]

71. Hutten did not begin to be an enemy of Hoogstraten at my request, for he had already written his Reuchlin's Triumph[96] against Hoogstraten before he had ever seen or known me personally. On my advice he suppressed this work for two years; and yet he asserts that in the meantime I spoke about Hoogstraten with the utmost bitterness. Just another sample of my craftiness, as he sees it.

72. Before proceeding to the rest of his accusations, it might be wise to call the reader's attention - in a few short words - to what constitutes the over all rhetoric of the pamphlet under examination. It is based on mere assumptions, fiction, sheer verbiage and exaggeration; the sprinkling of abuse serves only as seasoning.

73. By assumption I mean this statement, for example: "Erasmus imputes to Reuchlin the charge of perfidy." How exceedingly shameless of him to say such a thing! Equally shameless are the other charges he invents.[97] One might ask, "What could have moved Erasmus - who in the past praised Reuchlin so highly - suddenly to reverse his position so that he now zealously attempts to brand Reuchlin's name with such an abominable mark of disgrace?"[98]

74. The reason Hutten invents here is my lack of human decency and an envy which could not bear to have some people call Reuchlin "the other eye of Germany."[99] But, my dear Hutten, if you assume something to be true, it must either be established as true in itself or, if you wish to excel as an orator, you must prove it with suitable arguments. Then, too, the reasons stated ought to be such that they credibly accord with the temperament and character of the man accused. Hutten, however, often has me say not the sort of things I actually said, but what could have been said in such a situation. He does this not for the sake of truth but for his own advantage.

75. This might perhaps be allowed to authors who depict the ancient past, a biographer of Alexander the Great for example; but the same liberty does not apply to a recent event to which so many witnesses are still available. Furthermore, he fails to consider stylistic propriety by attributing to me speeches far more splendid and magnificent than my accustomed speech. But then, for him nothing is too trifling to be magnified with words of tragic proportion, although speech ought to conform to the subject as a garment does to the body.

76. This admonition will shed some light on the whole text for the reader. Consider now what sort of lies he invents at the very beginning of his account. First of all, I am supposed to have praised Hoogstraten. Let him then, I pray, point out the passage where I praised Hoogstraten! That particular letter which he finds so fawning is at once replete with candor and not lacking in barbs. Who cannot detect the irony in the place where I

call him an "old" friend, not an "intimate" one?

77. Let us now hear Hutten's fatuous verbiage: "This scoundrel, whom you now praise, you used to decry as a plague sent to earth by the wrath of God in order to destroy scholarship and men of genius, a worker of havoc and a calamitous devastator of the noblest pursuits of man. You further castigated him as a pitiless cause of destruction of all culture and refinement and as an incendiary who in our times has set ablaze such a conflagration that it is to be feared lest all those truly devoted to learning be consumed in its flames."[100]

78. Who will not immediately recognize Hutten's style here, not Erasmus'? He says that I used to encourage everyone to sharpen his pen against Hoogstraten; let him name just one such person and he wins! Surely he considers it a rhetorical device when he states that for the sake of courtesy he will not produce these murderous letters; his aim is rather to allow greater scope for suspicion. I am not adverse to having these letters produced, as long as all of them are, for they will prove conclusively that I was never allied with the Lutherans.

79. For a long time now Hoogstraten's arrogant disposition has displeased me, for it is hostile to good letters, born to incite tumults and thirsty for fame acquired through the misfortunes of others.[101] I have never coveted the man's friendship, nor have I desired to engage in a feud with him, the repose necessary for my studies being my primary concern.

80. What, however, is more boorish than to relate what was said at informal drinking parties or in conversations between friends, something which neither the speaker nor the listeners can remember?[101a] If, on the other hand, a matter is discussed earnestly, then one's true opinion is made apparent.

81. Even before I met Reuchlin, I wrote him that he ought to inveigh against Hoogstraten and his associates with greater moderation. I was prompted here

163

by my good-will toward Reuchlin, not toward Hoogstraten. Now if Reuchlin

was used to pouring all his secrets into Hutten's bosom, I do not doubt

in the least that he also showed him these letters. [102]

82. When the Count of Neuenahr wrote to me, asking for my advice as to

whether he ought to make his peace with Hoogstraten, who then desired a

reconciliation and had promised a retraction of the things he had said, I

advised him to forgive the injury in a true Christian spirit. [103]   Later,

when Edward Lee had most bitterly attacked me, the Count urged upon me my

own advice, exhorting me to do for Lee what he had done for Hoogstraten at

my persuasion. [104]   All of this can be substantiated in our correspondence.

83. When Hermann Busch was about to publish a work, to which he gave the

title A Bulwark for True Culture, [105]   I admonished him to temper the harshness

of his style. It was moderated and the book is now read by scholars without

offense. Such is my advice whenever a matter is treated with seriousness.

I have always exhorted to moderation. At meals or in conversations with

friends I do jest, uttering whatever comes into my head, often more freely

than is advantageous; "And this is my greatest fault," to quote Parmeno in

a play by Terence. [106]

84. Who, however, would not judge that I should be banished from the society

of all men, if I now - with conditions as aggravated as they are - wished to

produce what friends wrote to me at length in confidential letters or,

relying on my discretion, discussed in my presence, even if these friends

have now become enemies? [107]   When Hutten told us that he had declared war

on the Romanists, I asked him in jest what he was going to do to the Dominicans.

He replied with a smile that they too were Romanists.

85. Then, too, while dining together I used to ask him when Hoogstraten

would hang from the gallows. He replied that he would attend to that shortly.

This was said, however, in such a way that no one would have failed to recognize from our facial expressions that both of us were joking.

86. Now really, how can Hutten deduce from all this that, while attempting to gain the favor of a certain person, I seek to make him appear hateful in the eyes of everyone else?[108] As I see it, my writings added something to Hutten's reputation and popularity, and did not draw down upon him one grain of ill-will. Did he come into everyone's disfavor because I mentioned those four letters? Why, the authors themselves had already published them!

87. Let him imagine I used to be more than hostile toward Hoogstraten and that later I was reconciled with him - what business is that of Hutten's? Did I ever enter into such an agreement with Hutten - the type kings are accustomed to make - that I could not befriend anyone with whom he happened to be at war? Hutten is free to love those I do not love and hate those I cherish; the same right, however, should be granted to me as well.

88. It is Christian to bear enmity toward no man; should enmity arise, however, it is human to comport oneself with civility and to have done with it at the first opportunity.[109] There is, however, not one passage in my works where I flatter Hoogstraten, nor have I sought to mend my friendship with him, nor in any way troubled or injured Hutten. Nevertheless - and may the Muses forgive him - this man has thought it timely to utter commonplaces against dissimulation in friendship, as though our friendship were at stake if I treated Hoogstraten in an elusive manner. Why then does he not also censure Zopyrus for not having dealt frankly with the Babylonians?[110]

89. Hutten now strings together accusation upon accusation, just as one ties one thread to another. In the recently published letter to Laurinus I related the rumor spread by certain individuals that Hoogstraten had had my books burned in Brabant.[111] This, I suppose, was done by those who hoped to provoke me by such a trick into publicly attacking Hoogstraten; and further, so as not to offend all those who support Luther, I added that I did not know by

165

what name I ought to call them, although some called them Lutherans. Now

there are some who are recommended by this name, although they are anything

but Lutherans - factious, unlearned, stupid, dissolute, slanderous individuals,

who have nothing in common with Luther except that they curse the Roman

Pontiff.

90. Hutten claims I fabricated all this in order to shake an angry fist at

the Lutherans. What will Hutten say if I now produce a hundred witnesses

who will testify that this very rumor had been brought here more than once?

And what if I produce detailed letters to this effect written by friends

to me as well as to others? He will wholly rid himself of all sense of

shame, if in fact he still has any; indeed, what else can he do? As it is,

I was the only one never to believe the rumor about Hoogstraten's auto-da-fé,

since nothing of the kind had been written to me from Brabant, even though

I knew well what he would like to do, if it were in his power to do every-

thing he liked.

91. At this point Hutten throws in the old tale that seven years ago

Hoogstraten threatened to attack me as soon as he had destroyed Reuchlin

and that the only thing that delayed his doing so was the diligence of
                                    112
Reuchlin's friends in protecting him.   Even if this were true, what does
                                             113
it have to do with the matter at hand?   Could it be Hutten wishes to

persuade me that Hoogstraten was and still is ill-disposed toward me? To

accomplish this would necessitate a long and thoroughly prepared document.

Or perhaps he means to suggest that the rumor recently spread abroad is

really true? The facts, however, prove it is completely groundless. Nonetheless,

the waves of his accusation swell into a tide.

92. "I at first applauded the Letters of Obscure Men, but soon overcome by

fear, I sent a letter to Cologne in which I let it be known that such books
             114
displeased me."   Now, dear reader, hear what really happened and recognize

Hutten's cunning for what it is! I had obtained a manuscript copy of one

letter describing "the Teachers' Banquet" - nothing more than a harmless
115
joke ascribed to Hutten.   It afforded me the greatest pleasure and was

read so often among us friends, that I nearly knew it by heart. After my

return to Basle I lost my copy and so I dictated it from memory to Beatus

Rhenanus; at the same time I wrote to some of Hutten's friends, requesting

that they send me the text just as it had been written. I frankly admit

that this is exactly what happened. Now, what is so sinful about my taking

pleasure in a letter which was humorous and yet injured no one's good name?

93. Somewhat later the book appeared in print, containing several libellous,

obscene and venomous letters. When it was read to us, we laughed again, but

still the numerous company of scholars who at the time were staying at

Froben's house will testify that, although I approved the humor in many of
116
the letters, I nonetheless condemned the precedent it was setting.   Nor

did I ever approve of the work in any other way.

94. Reuchlin was indicted in the book as a heretic; this was in jest, to

be sure, but the fact remains he was so labelled and I do not believe even

he was pleased with the work. Upon my return to Brabant, I discovered that

many thought I had composed it. Although I was not unaware of who the authors

were - the three, that is, to whom rumor attributed it - I directed no

suspicion against anyone, but merely sent a letter to Caesarius removing the
117
false suspicion from me.   This letter was then secretly transcribed in

Cologne and soon appeared in print. What is the shameful crime in this?

The matter really displeased me, so I removed the false suspicion from myself

without blaming anyone else.
118
95. A second and similar book soon followed.   When it was offered to me

as a gift in Louvain, I refused to accept it. I likewise refused similar

dialogues written almost immediately thereafter in Cologne, nor have I ever deigned to read them.   I condemned such things because I could see that

they would effect nothing other than dragging good letters and Reuchlin's

cause into disrepute and that our enemies would be further provoked rather

than silenced.   How is this a proof of my being feeble or fickle?

96. Two years ago a dialogue appeared which, unless I am mistaken, was

entitled Hoogstraten Exulting and which seemed to have been written as a

favor to me.   But is it not true that I constantly and publicly condemned

it and tried in all ways to have it kept from the press?   That I am not

inventing this is known by both the one who wrote the dialogue and the one

who counseled him to do so.

97. Behold, however, another and more horrible charge: in a certain letter

I stated that Capito was more learned than Reuchlin in Hebrew letters.

Good God, what a furor Hutten raises because of this, just as if I had

poisoned the man! It is well known that Reuchlin was the pioneer Hebrew

scholar among the Germans; but would it be to his discredit were another

more learned than he to follow him? I personally consider this something

glorious. I wish six thousand would follow me and surpass me in every field,

and this even during my lifetime. Would Reuchlin be wronged if, after

placing him at the summit of fame, I were to prefer Capito to him in the

sole area of Hebrew scholarship?

98. "But," Hutten will object, "you compare a most obscure man with a most

famous one." But even then Capito was not unknown; his essays had already

won him recognition among scholars. And even if he had been relatively

obscure, all the more reason for drawing him out into the light by our

honest praise. Thus I felt about Capito at that time, and I did so not

without reason. Do not his fellow Hebraists nowadays endorse my judgment?

99. Here, dear reader, you have Hutten's shameless assumption; now see

what reasons he invents to support his charge. "I was galled by Reuchlin's

fame because many put him on a par with me as a promoter of languages
and used to acclaim him as the other eye of Germany." I, who have always
favored the study of languages and good letters with so much zeal, was I
not able to suffer a man who was sharing these pursuits, especially one who
                    124
was my friend?

100. I confess I was not able to read without laughing what he wrote about
"the other eye of Germany." So then I was trying to oust Reuchlin in order
to make Germany one-eyed? Who does not know how sincerely and constantly
                    125
I supported Reuchlin?   I do not hesitate to call upon the testimony of
all those with whom I have lived on intimate terms to prove that my character
is free from the disease of envy and that there is no vice from which I am
further removed.

101. Hear now another charge equally as shameless: "I attribute so much
to Capito only because he had praised my edition of the New Testament, just
                                                        126
as Ludwig Baer had also done." What diverse matters he unites here!
Indeed, I appealed to the verdict of the theologians Baer and Capito concerning my New Testament in order to counteract the shouts of theologians
who wanted nothing to be read unless first approved by themselves! If only
what has met the approval of theologians ought to be read, then that work
of mine should be read, for although it was condemned by the theologians at
                                                                        127
Louvain, it did gain the approval of some other very distinguished theologians.
Consequently, nothing was more shameless or ill-timed than Hutten's tirade
about my disparagement of the merits of others.

102. Now, however, I come to that dreadful and horrible crime which Hutten,
that gentlest of men, asserts he will never forgive - he even shudders to
speak of it: in a certain letter to the Bishop of Rochester I accuse Reuchlin
of perfidy! In the case of such horrible villainy it is worth the effort
to quote the very words of my letter: "The matter is as follows, if one can

credit rumor with some truth: When there was danger that the Duke of Württemberg would recapture Stuttgart, Reuchlin advised some of the citizens to flee elsewhere, promising to accompany them. They fled but he, fearing for the safety of his household goods, changed his mind and stayed at home. Later, when the Duke had been defeated once again, certain friends of Reuchlin's obtained assurances from the victorious army that they would not plunder his house. These citizens, however, whom he had so deceived, caused the old man a great deal of trouble upon their return. So he removed all of his belongings to a place of safety and is now leading a tranquil life in Ingolstadt."[128]

103. Thus far I have cited the words of my own letter. Now, dear reader, here is the gist of the situation. First, my friendly feelings toward Reuchlin are attested not only by my writings but also by the close companions of my life. Years ago - I was in England at the time - Reuchlin, harassed by his detractors, wrote to me, requesting that I arrange with like-minded friends to assume the defense of his innocence.

104. I accomplished more in this matter than he had requested; not only did I obtain for him the love of many, but I also recommended his cause to a few cardinals in Rome. Among the Englishmen I won over to him, Reverend Father John, Bishop of Rochester, was the most eminent. He was in fact almost infatuated with Reuchlin and thought so highly of him that, in comparison with him, he felt I knew nothing. He also sought an opportunity to leave England in order to confer with Reuchlin in person, as though with an oracle of all mysteries.

105. Having once inspired this affection in the bishop, I continued to nourish it, in no way offended because Reuchlin was obscuring the bishop's good impression of me; on the contrary, I rejoiced that he had a man of such excellence on his side. Rochester even consulted me about some gift he

had wanted to send to Reuchlin to honor him! How unenvious of Reuchlin I was on this occasion he himself can best testify.

106. Afterwards I often wrote to Reuchlin about the bishop's good-will toward him, hoping thereby to comfort him with some consolation. Conversely, if there was any news about Reuchlin's affairs, I took care to let the bishop hear of it, for I knew that such news pleased him very much. Thus, in that letter which offended Hutten, I was only informing the bishop both about the danger in which Reuchlin had been and about the tranquil state in which he was now living. Moreover, I wanted him to know where he should send anything he might want to give him.

107. Furthermore, I never even dreamed of charging him with perfidy. To deceive is not always treachery, since he also deceives who secretly lays gold under the pillow of a sick friend; and a friend also deceives, who arrives unexpectedly for a visit. Now if I had wanted to accuse him of perfidy, I would not have added the words "having changed his mind"; for merely to change one's mind is no perfidy, since necessity often compels one to do so, and often there are reasons of such a nature that it would be foolish not to change it.

129

108. It is in vain, therefore, that Hutten thunders against me with such tragic words, since what he charges is completely false, even if I did not refute it. Who moreover, except Hutten alone, ever interpreted that passage in such a manner? Even supposing I had harbored such a plan, would I have written it to that man who loved Reuchlin more than anyone else?

109. The letter was also published while Reuchlin was still living. "But he was on the verge of death," Hutten will claim. Who could predict how long Reuchlin was going to live? Since he enjoyed such a vigorous and robust old age,

130

I certainly hoped he would continue to stay with us for a long time, and would to God he had! I who, after his death, wrote an _Apotheosis_ commending him to the loving affection of the young, would I have wanted

to brand his name with the mark of perfidy while he was a dying man and I
need not fear his reproaches?

110. But now Hutten demands witnesses, solicitors, evidence, in short all

the trappings of a court trial. He might lawfully demand these things, if

I were suing our friend; but nothing is further from the truth. My relation

of what happened is simple and friendly, and thus it does not entail much

effort on my part; indeed the matter speaks for itself.

111. But Hutten is here attempting to cast on me the suspicion that I in-

vented my informants, as though I had not learned these details from others

but had fabricated them myself so as to besmirch Reuchlin with the stain of

infamy. I beg you, dear reader, is there anything more malicious or perverse

than what Hutten would like to impute to me, his friend, for some reason or

other? Now, what I wrote to the Bishop of Rochester was reported to me at

Louvain by Dr. John Salius while the Emperor Charles was staying there. I

thought the more highly of this man because he displayed an extraordinary

love for Reuchlin and recounted certain services he had rendered Reuchlin in

the past.

112. When this letter, along with many others, was finally published in

Basle (I was in Brabant at the time), why was it not altered if it were in-

sulting to Reuchlin? For my part, I had given certain learned friends the
authority to make whatever alterations they desired.   "Why did you not

make the changes yourself?" Hutten might ask; my reply - because I did not

suspect anything wrong. "Why then did you give such a commission to others?";

because, being better informed about conditions in Germany, they were in a

better position than I to decide what should be done. "Why did your friends

not make these changes then?"; because they did not have the eyes of a Hutten

who had resolved to leave nothing untried in maligning Erasmus, hoping that

by doing so he would merit the highest praise.   "But why are you so
uncertain about what you write?"; because even Salius himself could possibly
have been deceived.

113. But how could Reuchlin's reputation be affected by what I wrote,
whether it was true or not? Just because Hutten was certain that everybody
would wonder why I had wished ill to one as beloved and praised as Reuchlin,
he invented the reasons: discourteousness and envy. But then why had I not
envied him when he was a civic magistrate and an imperial councillor and
when his fortune and reputation were flourishing, rather than at the time
when the fallen magistrate had become a professor? How crudely, how clumsily
these lies are concocted!

114. At this point, honest reader, I would have you consider well how un-
abashedly shameless Hutten must be; for he, who sounds so outraged because
one of his friends has been smeared with the stain of infamy, proceeds
without cause to invent on his own all manner of charges against another
friend. After he had raved against me, then, in this most groundless of
quarrels - with charges, suitable or not - he proceeds to my other crimes in
the following words: "We want you to realize that we know and are aware of
how you have decided to do everything perversely, and somehow to abuse hatefully the well-deserving, while, at every opportunity, you cringe before
those whom you consider to be most dangerous to you."

115. And here once again he has me speak at his discretion about the two
universities of Louvain and Cologne; but he has me do so in a style any
reader would recognize as Hutten's own, his style of tragedy. Here is the
gist of the charge: while in conversations with friends I severely condemned
these two universities, but in my letters I now speak of them very respectfully.

116. What nonsense I have to listen to! Have I ever been at war with any
university? And just because a few stupid individuals there fight against

good letters, is Louvain not still a most flourishing university? And do
I not also have many friends at Cologne who wish me well and support better
studies? When have I ever approved of those who are evil? Or why should I
attack those who are good?

117. Behold the verbiage he uses to dress up this nonsense: ".... you
reverse your stand," he says, "and in a most flattering manner you commend
yourself to these very people. In your praise of their schools you almost
prefer them to the academies of Athens and you reproach us for having the
audacity to attack these modern day Platos and Theophrastuses."[136] Who
cannot see that this grandiloquence in no way corresponds to the situation?

118. I suspect that Hutten was offended by a letter I wrote to the Louvain
theologians, responding to certain points which Nicolaus Baechem had most
odiously and without cause attacked as heretical.[137] In the heading to the
letter I address them as "Honorable Brothers" and in a certain other letter
I refer to them as "Venerable Fathers" and "most respected Masters." Among
them too there are some who wish Erasmus well and who are displeased with
Baechem's and Vincentius' conduct; and there are some others not past all
cure.[138]

119. First of all, it is ridiculous to incriminate my use of customary
titles of address which, as we have already noted, one enemy concedes to
another even in the midst of war.[139] Furthermore, what concern is it of
Hutten's if I do defend my cause before them? What would be more stupid
than to hurl abusive epithets at those whose approbation of our cause we
zealously strive to obtain?[140] Moreover, what is more unfair than to lash
out at an entire class when it does not deserve it?[141]

120. For the sake of argument let us assume all of them are our enemies;
it is certainly a matter of civility and prudence to hurt as few as possible,
for then it can happen that the others might become our friends or, although

enemies, grow milder.   For my part, I will not deny that I wish to live

in peace, if possible, not only with the Louvain theologians but also with

the whole Order of Preachers. As for his ravings that I flattered our

enemies after having aroused a conflagration against them and that to humor

them I frantically strike out now at this friend, now at that one, I will

presently reveal how false they are.   For the moment though, I will

continue with the present indictment.

121. Hear now another proof of my inconsistency, as Hutten sees it, although

it is actually a proof of his own impudence. He asserts that I violently

opposed the faculties of Cologne and Louvain when, in their official

Opinion, they condemned several of Luther's articles;   now, he says, I

approve what I formerly condemned, as is evident in a certain letter to the

theologians at Louvain where I boast of my constant support of their dis-

putations against Luther.

122. Here, dear reader, I beg you to take note of Hutten's malicious

endeavor to find fault with everything. I never approved nor disapproved

of those articles, for I did not want to oblige certain people by providing

them with the handle they were grasping for.   At my instigation Baechem

was summoned before the Rector to cite at least one article in Luther's

writings that I had ever defended, even while drinking with friends; as he

had nothing to say, he produced a passage about confession in a letter I had

written to the Cardinal of Mainz.

123. In this passage I say that Baechem had publicly condemned something

he had not understood. This does not mean defending what Luther had written,

but only exposing the shamelessness of a man who, without understanding the

matter under discussion, had raised an outcry before the laity.   "After

that," he says, "you support their disputations." What does this have to

do with the Opinion? In that document they do not dispute, they give an official pronouncement, nor were they teaching, they were condemning. I have always disapproved of turbulent ranting before the laity, in which many lies are broadcast, and I exhorted those theologians to give up shouting and to refute Luther with arguments and, if he had erred, to set him straight.

124. Afterwards they began to do so with sufficient moderation and I approved of this. The theses of their disputations were neither approved nor disapproved of by me - I approved only this, that they gave up their mad ravings in order to dispute and to teach. Hutten interpreted this stance as if it meant that I endorsed whatever they had defined against Luther in the course of their debating. Prior to this he had also falsely assumed that I had wholeheartedly endorsed whatever they had condemned in their censures. Let anyone who can now deny Hutten's genius for maliciously distorting even those things said with the best of intentions.

125. He adduces something similar about the Order of Preachers, toward which I was supposed formerly to have been hostile, but now I am endeavoring to persuade everyone I had never wished that religious body any ill. 149 I have never been so mad as to wish any Order ill, as my words and deeds everywhere amply testify. If it were right to hate the whole Order of Preachers just because it has many members who are bad, then one should hate all Orders since there is not one which does not have a great number of bad members; indeed, one would then have to hate all Christians, since the bad among them outnumber the good.

126. So there is nothing inconsistent in this; my writings and my actions 150 proclaim rather what I have always firmly believed. What, however, shows greater good-will, to hate an entire Order because of the bad members it contains or to favor an Order because of its good members? The Dominicans have several men who not only wish Erasmus well, but support good letters as well as the cause of the Gospel. If I have not always advised all my

friends not to impugn any Order or any nation, then Hutten will have proven

that I was hostile to the Dominican Order.

127. He reproaches me with a similar inconsistency with respect to the

Roman Curia, about which I am supposed to have spoken at one time as harshly
151
as Hutten could make me speak, but now I extol it with wondrous praises.

"Now" - he has me say - "it (the Church) has become for you the holy universal

Church itself ... where anything said by any member of the Curia, no matter
152
how knavish, is likened to a rose."   What do such statements proclaim

other than Hutten's incredible impudence? Who ever approved of the morals

of the Roman Curia? But yet, who condemns the whole Church because of them?

I believe that some of its members are men devoted to Christ. And who on

earth would contend that whatever one of the Curia says, wicked as he might

be, is as fragrant as a rose? Are such assertions not those of a man

intemperately abusing others with his pen and making light of his written

attacks? But since Hutten prefers to postpone this charge to its proper

place, we too shall respond to it in its proper place.

128. In the meantime let us speak of Aleander, concerning whom Hutten

censures my inconsistency, on the grounds that after openly speaking against
153
him in the past, I later mentioned him respectfully in my correspondence.

One thing at least is certain here: I have never spoken with Hutten about

Aleander; besides, he was still in Rome when we talked in Brabant last, and

at that time no one suspected he was about to come out against Luther. There-

fore, whatever Hutten relates here, he relates from rumors, and anyone with
154
any sense at all knows how much they can be relied on.

129. Nevertheless I would like to clarify the matter. While with Aleander

in Venice, I was not only on friendly but even on intimate terms with him.

I admired his erudition and loved his temperament, the more so as he had

zealously promoted Greek letters among the French. And then, when he had

already been chosen to attack Luther in our parts, he conceived against me -

while he was still in Rome - I know not what sort of anger, about which I
was informed by a letter of his to the Bishop of Liège. ¹⁵⁵ The cause of
his anger was the first letter I had ever written to Luther, and this at
¹⁵⁶
his own request.

130. Upon his arrival, indeed before he had even entered Brabant, someone
with the most pernicious of tongues got hold of him and completely poisoned
his mind - a thing I had never supposed would happen. Thus at first Aleander
seemed to avoid any contact with me, suspecting God knows what about me.
Finally, even certain rather unfriendly things he had said about me made
the rounds of Louvain, although as yet they did not contain anything really
harsh.

131. When he returned again to that city where he had sucked in the poison -
the Emperor had in the meantime left there for Cologne - the same viper in-
jected more venom into his mind, already ill disposed toward me. In Cologne,
therefore, I heard from many different sources that he was talking most
¹⁵⁷
hostilely about me to those in high places and also at well-attended banquets.
At first I was not able to find out where he was staying, but finally, having
tracked down his lodgings, I sent a servant to tell him that I wanted to
speak with him. In a pleasant and cheerful mood, he invited me to lunch, an
invitation I declined, but right after lunch I arrived for the interview.

132. He received me with extreme politeness and we conversed for several
hours, mutually expostulating with one another, for he had also been informed
that I had said many rather unfriendly things about him. This charge was
not wholly groundless since I had complained to several people that, although
he had been sent to oppose Luther, he was raving against me as if the Luther
affair really pertained to me. After our mutual expostulations, we parted
with a kiss, a sign of our former friendship.

133. When once again certain courtiers wrote me that at the Diet of Worms

he had undertaken some dire things against me, I sent my secretary to him
with a letter in which I quite frankly expostulated with him, and I also
wrote to his patron, the Bishop of Liège, about the same matter. Aleander
158
wrote back justifying himself.

134. After the adjournment of the Diet he returned to Brussels and I went
to see him. We conversed for nearly five hours, during which time - as is
the habit of his open mind and candid speech - he poured out against me
nearly the same accusations Hutten now throws in my face: I had told every-
159
body he was a Jew by birth, I was concocting his ruin, and similar nonsense.
Thus those honest and brave German friends eventually brought down all his
ill-will against me.

135. First and foremost let me say, however, that neither my friendship
with nor my enmity against Aleander had anything whatsoever to do with the
Luther business; he was my friend before Luther's name was ever heard of.
Nor did I become hostile toward him because of Luther, but because he had
reproached me without cause, so my friends said, and involved me in the
hateful affair.

136. And if those poisonous tongues had permitted my friendship with Aleander
to remain unimpaired, the Luther affair would possibly have taken a less
hateful turn, and smoke and fire, which only irritate the minds of men, would
not have broken out anew in so many cities. After being angered with him
for trying to ruin me, why would I not have again become his friend once he
had redirected his efforts toward removing the danger? He himself swore to
me in Brussels that he was doing just that, and afterwards, when I had returned
to Germany, I found out from those who were our go-betweens in this matter
that his words were not untrue.

137. What disgrace is it, however, if in my books I did commend Aleander
as a master of erudition in three languages? This praise I conceded to him

179

openly, even when our enmity was at its worst. And although certain people

conceded to me pre-eminence in the Latin language, even this praise I yielded

to him, adversaries though we were. 160

138. Hutten praised him even more profusely in the very letter in which he

strangles him, saying it grieved him that Aleander possessed qualities he

could envy. 161 Is there anything more splendid for Aleander than to have

his enemy extol his knowledge as worthy of envy? I at least praised him

more moderately. And later Aleander boasted to me about this hommage Hutten

had paid him.

139. I shall frankly state what I think: just as that wretch who incited

Aleander against me deserves the worst possible treatment at my hands, in

like measure I would willingly regain the friendship of such a man, given

the opportunity, without seeking from him the slightest advantage for myself.

Moreover, since this does not pertain in any way to the Luther affair, just

what is Hutten complaining about? As far as I am concerned, he can hate

Aleander as much as he wants to.

140. And further, when Hutten says, "He loved you in an unparalled manner

and you hold him dear; you live with him on most agreeable terms and at

times prolong your conversations until well into the night; and you have

even mutually agreed to travel to Rome together", 162 these are his inventions,

not my statements! For indeed what I related in my letter to Laurinus about

my intimacy with Aleander was written not to prove how great my friendship

with him was, but was directed rather against those who were spreading the

rumor that my departure was really a flight, and I wanted to make it clear

that I had left openly, as everyone was well aware.

141. Although it is not true, let us just assume I did wish Aleander ill,

since he wished me the same, and my friendship with him was feigned, so that

he might harm me less and in this manner I might also hold in check certain

180

theologians bent on undermining everything I was doing - now then, will

Hutten be so indignant with me if, to protect my welfare, I employ a certain

cunningness injurious to no one?

142. There was in Louvain a certain raving Dominican who had promised in

a morning sermon to reveal some strange things about me immediately after

lunch. I secretly advised Aleander about this and he sent a messenger to

the friar, a most perverse brawler at that, to silence him. Now who would

not call it prudence to utilize even one's enemies in defense of one's own

cause? 163   Indeed, because of our recently restored intimacy, certain

theologians lost much of their boldness.

143. And what is more, not only was nothing said against Hutten in all our

conversations, but I greatly praised his disposition and genius, to the

indignation of both Caracciolo and Aleander - and this after the Diet of

Worms, when Hutten's situation had worsened considerably.

144. Finally, what is more appropriate for humanity, to honor one's enemies

in one's writings and thus possibly appease their ill-will, or to write

such violent and more than hostile pamphlets as Hutten has written against

a friend who not only was well-disposed toward him but deserved to be well

treated and still wishes to deserve such treatment? 164

145. Still another charge: in my letter to Laurinus I relate that a rumor

has been circulated here that the Roman Pontiff had written some sort of

pamphlet or other against me. 165   Hutten does not hesitate to swear that I

only invented this in order to cast further odium on the Lutherans. Is

there indeed any form of perverse wantonness he would not immediately impute

to his friend?

146. But what if there are many honest men here who know that this rumor

had actually been spread around? And what if I have letters from learned

friends in Augsburg and Constance in which they report that it is quite well-known that the Pope publicly condemned my books in Rome? And what if they possess letters from me asserting that I did not believe this at all - what, I repeat, is the only conclusion possible if not that everyone will have to recognize how shameless Hutten really is?

147. But did I not have the audacity to praise the Pope who formerly wished me ill and who thus far has done nothing to merit any praise? Now, what Hutten writes might be true - I do not know; I only know that no such report was ever brought to me, nor did I ever expect such a thing from him. While we were both staying at Louvain we were the best of friends and, as he himself writes, our fellowship was one of studies. Furthermore, I was never aware of any unfriendly feeling on his part toward me.

148. What, however, do I praise in him other than the good hope which his age, his constant integrity and his erudition offer us? This is encouragement, not praise. I do praise his past accomplishments, concerning which I can be refuted if I am wrong; concerning his future deeds I prophesy only
166
good.

149. Consequently, who cannot see how inappropriately Hutten applied his
167
insipid jest, "But this you will do, O Timon". Nonetheless, I do not doubt in the least that Hutten fancied himself wonderfully amusing. But in the past, Hutten asks, did I not state that not much good was to be expected of him? Since I never spoke to Hutten about the Pope, how shameful of him to accuse me before the tribunal of the world of something he had only heard from some drinking buddy! I did say that I feared he would not be very favorable toward Luther, but about the rest I never said a word, although he did indicate his desire to cause even the Roman Curia to bear better fruit.

150. He says, further, that plans were being made to arrest me as a heretic. That this was being discussed and desired by certain raving monks, I do not doubt. Among the princes, however, this was never considered. Even in Spain

I had friends who were very close to the present Pontiff, and in Rome too, while Leo was still alive, but ones very different from Hutten. At the Emperor's court I had some very important men as friends, whom I did not even suspect were friends at all and from whose letters I was better informed about what was going on than was Hutten who, being in hiding, knew only

168

what some scandalmongers reported to him on the sly.

151. I have in my possession articles submitted to the Emperor after being annotated by Glapion in his own hand. There is absolutely no mention of heresy there, nor anything that even borders on heresy. I have a letter of Chancellor Gattinara which does state there was a suspicion about certain books which, because of their charming style, seemed to be mine, but there was nothing heretical or of the nature of Luther's writings in them.

152. But in that same letter to Laurinus I do mention Joannes Glapion

169

without deserving any insult, for I do not bestow any praise on him.
Here Hutten reveals his gift for exaggeration when he says: "What, Glapion? Oh, so you are trumpeting even his praises?" In point of fact, however, my very words were: "Concerning the Reverend Father Joannes Glapion, who was the Emperor's court preacher, etc.". This is the fanfare with which I sing the man's praises.

153. But what he adds is even more shameless: "You who execrate the man's wickedness...". Since I never spoke nor wrote a single word to Hutten about Glapion, some drinking buddy must have supplied him with this lie too. And yet from gossip of this kind he fabricated such a false accusation against a friend. But here again he has me speak about Glapion in words which would never occur to me even in my dreams. Once - this was in Brussels after the Diet of Worms - when I happened to meet Glapion, I did greet him, but with just a couple of words; for the rest, any business between us had been con-ducted by letter. What he contrived or carried out against Luther, I do not

know; I know for certain, however, that whatever he did was not done at my instigation.

154. I must frankly admit that although I could never bring myself whole-heartedly to trust the man, neither did I ever bear him any hostile feelings. However, I know that more than once he showed himself an active friend on my behalf at the Emperor's court.

155. But is it not strange that after only one conversation our sharp-sighted friend, a veritable Lynceus, 170 can depict Glapion for us as though they had eaten together every day for years and years? 171 From what prudent men have told me about Glapion, as well as from his letters to me, I too was able to form a judgment about his character, and I dare say that even if Hutten had lived with Glapion for ten years, he still would not have really known him. And I could not help laughing when I read in Hutten's pamphlet that I was the very image of Glapion, and this right after he attributed to him an extraordinary cunningness; and yet, if Glapion were as Hutten depicts him, then a camel is no more unlike a fox than is Erasmus unlike Glapion. But about my own character I will speak elsewhere.

156. Hutten is also offended because in a letter of mine I remarked in passing that Silvester Mazolini had written civilly and lovingly to me. 172 I did not judge him worthy of any special mark of respect, however, for all I say is: "the well-known Silvester Mazolini," to which I add that his letter to me was written most civilly. Oh, what extraordinary flattery! "But," Hutten will say, "you write this because of your ill-will toward Luther." On the contrary, I wrote this to show that there was a reason for me to consider going to Rome. If I did so greatly desire to stir up ill-will toward Luther, there are other ways of doing so. Luther always despised Mazolini - this at least is certain.

157. Furthermore, in my Catalogue I call Marino Caracciolo "Reverend Father

Papal Nuncio to the Emperor," without saying anything else about him except
that he had urged me above all to write against Luther.[173]   Hutten, however,
calls him an evil man. Even if he is evil, how does this concern me? I
never said he was a good man, although he was a good and obliging friend to
me until this tragedy destroyed all friendships. Hutten is likewise offended
because somewhere or other I mentioned Eck, without insulting him, I believe,
and so he invents a former judgment suitable for his purposes, but one I
never advanced.[174]

158. Still more intolerable to Hutten is the fact that in a letter I praised
the Dominican Jacques Lefèvre.[175]   What kind of person he is now, I do not know,
but while at Louvain he assured me that he was about to found a college at
Augsburg for the teaching of languages and good letters; and he showed me
his authorization from Emperor Maximilian. He also spoke more than hostilely
about some of Luther's foremost enemies, as well as about the Roman Curia
itself. His gentle manners were pleasing, and in his theology he seemed
remarkably erudite. That was why I could not refuse him some letters of
recommendation. At Cologne, too, while the Emperor was staying there, he
paid his respects to us and left behind - with both the Cardinal of Mainz
and with me - a very fair judgment about Luther, written in his own hand.[176]

159. In all this, with what else can Hutten reproach me except perhaps
simplicity and candor of spirit? If Lefèvre is now the kind of person Hutten
claims he is, I would never have suspected such cunningness in a German.
Nor indeed could I have guaranteed what kind of person he would later become,
any more than I could have prevented Hutten, whom I praised so highly before
and praised with all my heart, from turning out to be the kind of person he
reveals himself to be in this pamphlet, of which no gentleman approves.[177]

160. Moreover, the friendship between Johann Heigerlin, a Canon of Constance,
and myself existed long before the world ever heard of Luther.[178]   If I were

185

to renounce the friendship of everyone who opposes Luther, scarcely one would remain of those to whom I owe everything. Heigerlin did write a book against Luther, but he did not write it at my instigation. I am supposed ¹⁷⁹ to have said on occasion that his book deserved to be thoroughly smeared with excrement; whoever reported that to Hutten certainly deserves the same treatment, for neither did I ever hear anyone say such a thing nor did such a thought ever enter my mind, not even in my dreams!

161. In Constance I read no more than the preface and I praised the author's restraint. The only passage I read - although I did not peruse it - refuted what Luther had written to the effect that now at long last Rome has decided in favor of the immortality of the soul. I am not so bold as to pronounce on a book I have not perused. ¹⁸⁰ Besides, not to like a book written against Luther, does not mean to approve of him.

162. Ludwig Baer was both a sincere friend and a faithful patron of mine long before Luther was known to the world and I consider his favor one of my good fortunes, since by virtue of his many exceptional qualities he is the foremost ornament of this city. ¹⁸¹ He defends his theological position in such a manner that he is yet favorable to good letters and to promoting peace; and although he by no means approves of everything Luther is doing, he is still not at all hostile to the cause of reinforcing the Gospel.

163. But if Hutten has decided to take offense at everyone who is not well disposed toward Luther, why has he attacked only this one man, when in this matter such people are innumerable? And yet, Baer is not a man to distort any position Luther has rightly taken, as many others do, nor has he stupidly vociferated against anyone. One thing he certainly is not: a curialist. Still, Hutten attacks this man's name in such filthy language and with so much harshness, as if he had killed his own father, whereas Baer has never said a word against Hutten's affairs, his name or his friends.

164. With him Hutten associates Johann Gebwiler, who, whatever he is, is

182

anything but a curialist.   I have never been on intimate terms with him,

so much so that he has never even visited at my home, nor do I know where

his is located; nor has either of us ever greeted the other on the street.

And yet, so badly informed by his scandalmongering friend, Hutten writes:

"Moreover, such men you allow in your house and consider them worthy of

183

daily conversations - but me you exclude!"

165. I have already mentioned on what intimate terms I was with Gebwiler;

and Baer, both my friend and neighbor, at times scarcely visited me once

in a space of two months. Daily conversations indeed! But why impute this

nonesense to Hutten? Such was the report from the producer of this melodrama.

But those who read these things and know what the truth is - what are they

going to think?

166. In this same letter I am also supposed to have treated Latomus,

Baechem and John Briard in part ambiguously, in part hypocritically, whereas

184

formerly I used to censure them.   When we were in league together against

the enemies of languages and good letters, I admit that in my letters I

sometimes complained to friends about the obstinate conspiracy of certain

individuals against better studies. Nevertheless, I waged war against them

in such a way that I was always prepared to make peace when the opportunity

presented itself.

167. Therefore, I always spared Latomus, hoping that he would desist;

Baechem I never flattered; Briard was neither uncultured nor adverse to

good letters, but irascible by nature, and thus he was goaded by certain

monks and theologians into staging this hateful tragedy. But by prodding

him on so far, they urged him to his death, for he was weak of health, unable

to endure anger and unaccustomed to injury.

168. After his death the present tragedy became all the more violent - a

clear proof that some moderation was largely due to him. Furthermore,

what I had written about him was that, although universally praised, he was
185
never sufficiently praised.   Even this the theologians at Louvain could

not read without laughing, because he, as Vice-chancellor of the university,

was praised there daily in festive eulogies. In keeping with his nature, he

was not hostile toward me, for of all of them he alone counselled reconcilia-

tion with the theologians. In doctrine and discernment he far surpassed

everyone, and shortly before he died, he even assured me of his peace and

friendship, again an act quite like him.

169. And finally, Hutten fears that I might also become reconciled with
186
Edward Lee.   I admit frankly that I would not mind doing this if he would

only evince an attitude worthy of friendship. In Calais, having met him by

chance, I greeted him and we shook hands - why not, since the quarrel between
187
us had been settled?

170. In any event, the assistance received from Germany contributed nothing

of moment against Lee. When some German friends wrote me that, even against

my will, the Germans were about to tear Lee to pieces, I at first advised

against such action; if I could not prevent them from doing this, I admonished

them to proceed with arguments rather than abuse and especially to refrain

from affronting the whole English nation. This was done, nevertheless, and

I vehemently disapproved of it.

171. I have resolutely and constantly condemned this dialogue directed against
188
Lee   and later I suppressed an enormous bundle of rather hostile letters

from various scholars; copies were made for the perusal of only two of my

friends, Dorp and More, while to certain individuals, who kept exhorting me

to publish them, I responded that I had decided to remain silent in the future,

if only Lee would do likewise. Here, dear reader, you have all that was

enough to embitter Hutten's heart; from this you can see there is nothing which ought to have sundered even an ordinary friendship.

172. I now will broach what he claims to be the chief source of the whole quarrel. However, I must be careful not to please Hutten too much, lest in fleeing Scylla I am swept into Charybdis. [189] He presents the case by joining two most obvious untruths: formerly I had been a member of Luther's party, but now I am combating the cause of the Gospel with all the powers at my command. [190] The truth is I have always abhorred that party and I have never ceased promoting the cause of the Gospel as loyally as I can.

173. This is what he claims, however, in indeed high-sounding but rather shameful words: "Was it not only a short time ago that you aided us in putting the Roman Pontiff in his place, with a vengeful pen castigating Rome itself as a cesspool of depravity and crime? Did you not curse papal bulls and indulgences and damn ecclesiastical ceremonies? Was it not you who scourged the curial system and execrated canon law and pontifical pronouncements? In short, did you not mercilessly flay the entire hypo-critical structure of that estate? And now this same Erasmus has entered into common alliance with the enemy?" [191]

[192]

174. And in another place he says: "But yesterday you exhumed piety, you brought the Gospels back from their dungeons into the light of day and [193] restored faith and religion; now all of a sudden you openly avow the desire to trample this selfsame work underfoot, to expel, overthrow and utterly annihilate it!" Well now, let anyone who can, say that his accusa-tions are not shameless! It is in such a manner that Hutten sums up his case and he repeatedly hammers home his assumptions and exaggerates them with ever varying words, as if what is groundless of itself can become true by constant and bold repetition. [194] To accomplish this he marshals all the batteries of his eloquence, all its force and all its violence. But where the very basis of an argument is inane and worthless, the more time and labor

are lost, the noisier the speech is.   For here, in such a serious

matter, one cannot allow what Quintilian censured even in feigned contro-

veries (although it was customary), namely that one arbitrarily accuse an

196

opponent of something to which he is supposed to respond.

175. Oh, how he torments himself in his efforts to discover what reasons

could have caused me to forsake a cause so holy for one so impious! And

then it was his difficult task to prove that what he assumed to be true

really was. To aid him in this, our violent orator had nothing to say

except: "Certain people informed me." Vigorously and harshly he denounces

me for having abandoned and betrayed the cause of the Gospel and for having

deserted to its enemies; having been corrupted by money, I then began with

all the powers at my command to attack good men, evangelical truth and

197

public liberty.   However, what he thus assumed, should either have been

agreed upon between ourselves or demonstrated with appropriate arguments

before he unleashed these terrible passions of his.

176. In so many letters and writings and attestations I have constantly

198

declared that I do not want to be involved with any party whatsoever.

I gave many reasons why I had decided on this position, but I did not state

them all. In this matter my conscience in no way accuses me before Christ,

my judge. In the midst of such great upheavals in human affairs and even

such great dangers to both reputation and life, I was moderate in my counsel

so as to be neither the cause of any disturbance, nor support any cause of

which I did not approve, nor anywhere betray evangelical truth.

177. How is it that Hutten is offended because I do not declare myself in

favor of Luther as he has done? Three years ago, while in Louvain, I made

it quite clear in an appendix to my _Colloquies_ that I was and would always

199

remain adverse to that party.   And not only did I personally oppose it,

but to the utmost of my ability I have exhorted as many friends as possible to do likewise; and I will not desist in doing so.

178. I call partisan that zeal which swears, as it were, by everything Luther has written, is writing now or will write in the future, a stance which often impresses even good men. I have even openly declared to all my friends that if they cannot love me unless I am a "Lutheran," then they may adopt any attitude they wish toward me. I love my freedom and I neither desire nor am able to serve any party.

179. Luther's party, Hutten says, ought not to have been deserted, if only for the sake of my friends, of whom he claims that several deserve my gratitude and who could not be separated from Luther any more than from truth itself.   ^200   What friends he is talking about, I do not know. I do see, however, that there are many who were formerly most devoted to Luther, but now some of them remain silent, while others cannot bear the name Lutheran to be mentioned, and yet others now condemn what at first they approved of.

180. If any friend of mine ever meant so much to me that, just to please him, I surrendered myself body and soul to Luther's party, then I grant him, I have not deserted the party; but in like measure, if anyone ever saw me so drunk that I wholly approved of Luther, then without protest I will allow him to call me a miserable coward instead of Erasmus.

181. Little wonder if I refuse the name of Lutheran, since I cannot see anyone else who can endure being called one. That Hutten only reluctantly calls himself a Lutheran should not seem strange, since Luther himself does not recognize him as a disciple and even shuns his services; and, unless my guess is wholly amiss, Luther prefers me as an adversary to Hutten as a defender.   ^201   But perhaps Hutten's affairs are in such a state that the name Lutheran would be to his advantage, since it is the only thing that protects and nourishes him at the moment.

182. Hatred for Luther never prompted me to condemn anything that he spoke rightly, nor will love for him ever make me approve of anything he says that seems wrong to me. [202] Even if I had formerly sworn allegiance to him or to his associates, I should be congratulated for having recovered from that folly. [203] Now, this whole affair was begun against my advice, as is well known to some who used to be fervent Lutherans, although what they are now, I do not know.

183. The very first letter I wrote to Luther made clear what I feared in him: his writings lacked moderation and evangelical gentleness and I criticized the obstinacy of his assertions. And now I find these qualities all the more lacking in him, since the books he writes appear more violent with each passing day, directed as they are against even the most powerful [204] princes, whom it is not advantageous to anger, no matter who they are.

184. I sometimes said to friends that, to my regret, I had doubts about Luther's disposition, although I never made any definite pronouncement. Until now my judgment of Luther has gone only thus far, but in this my statements have been most consistent, in what I have written or said, in private or in public. Where then is this extraordinary inconsistency of [205] mine? I fear rather that my consistency displeases them more.

185. "But neglecting everything else, I am now wholly carried away against Luther." Hutten must have heard this fable from some drinking buddy or [206] other; on the other hand, he could have learned from that Achates of his, Eppendorf, that at the time nothing was further from my mind than what he now accuses me of, for by then I had already begun my <u>Paraphrase of the</u> [207] <u>Gospel according to Luke</u> and was wholly engaged in the work when Hutten, [208] our defender of the cause of the Gospel, began this tragedy.

[209]
186. "But in my <u>Catalogue</u> I promise three dialogues against Luther"! Let him quote to me from my own writings this phrase "against Luther"! I

do speak of the "Lutheran affair," but I call my work more correctly a comparison rather than a disputation. And what I say is that they are conceived rather than composed, and I have not yet decided to complete them. Should I complete them, I would submit them only to those who urged me to write them. In the meantime, I warn the reader not to form any premature judgment from this promise.

187. So, first of all, I did not promise these dialogues; but, if I did promise them, it was not to the masses but to the Pope and the Emperor, who would decide whether they ought to be suppressed or published. I also promise they will evince the utmost impartiality toward Luther. How can Hutten then possibly know if these dialogues will extol Luther or abuse him? Either one is possible since in them someone will take Luther's part.

188. Already I can hear certain people saying: "In the meantime you keep us in suspense because you will not openly say what you think about Luther." In the first place, I do not have enough time to peruse the vast amounts Luther has written, and had I enough time, deciding about the whole affair is far beyond my ability. How should I decide? If I wholly condemned Luther, I can see very well what party I would be encouraging and how many good men I might destroy; on the other hand, total approval of him would first of all be presumptuous, since I should not sanction what I do not understand, and then it would mean rushing into a party to which so many belong with whom I 210 want to have nothing to do.

189. Those who hate Luther will hate him even if I remain silent; and those who support him are not demanding my opinion so as to hear an impartial verdict, but only to count on one more partisan. If I were to divide my opinion, conceding certain points to each side, I would only be torn apart by both sides and accomplish nothing but stirring up further discord. Thus it seemed more advisable to me to say nothing until, without partiality,

princes and scholars sought such counsel that would promote the truth of the Gospel and the glory of Christ without tumult.

190.   While trying to appear humorous, Hutten most graciously says that a word of truth had escaped my lips, as happened to Caiaphas, [211]   when I stated that no one could suppress the whole of Luther's teaching without simultaneously bringing about the utter collapse of a good part of evangelical purity and public liberty - just as if I had not always borne witness to this with resolute consistency in what I said and what I wrote! And it is indeed a source of torment for me to see his followers defend his cause as if they themselves do not wish to preserve this purity and this liberty, although what is true in Luther's teaching stems not from him but from Christ.

191.   Let us just assume that I am writing against Luther: am I not free to do so, since I never had any agreement with him and, against my advice, he began the whole affair and is still carrying it on? And let us also assume that in the beginning I did favor Luther: does this mean then that I have to approve of everything he writes, just because his first works pleased me? What if Luther were later to write against articles of the faith: would Hutten still forbid me to write against him?

192.   Now, why does Hutten rage so violently against those who write against Luther - after all, what is the difference between "arguing with" or "writing against" him? Luther himself challenges people to argue with him! If his doctrine is true, it will shine even more brilliantly by being contradicted, just as gold is purified by fire; but if it is false, it deserves to be attacked by everyone; and if it contains a mixture of false and true, then [212] it should be purified.

193.   Will I then immediately overthrow the entire Gospel if I argue with Luther about every Christian being a priest or all the works of the saints being sins? Luther himself does not dread my assault, nor that of anyone

else; on the contrary, courageously he waits for Erasmus to come forth.
Why then does Hutten start such an uproar? By doing so, does he not render
Luther's doctrine suspect, just as though he believed that it could stand
only if no one shook it?

194. I say these things not because I have any desire to dispute with
Luther - even if I had time to do so - but in order to answer Hutten's charges.
I have played the role of a Vertumnus, a Proteus and a Polypus;[213] I have
turned like a weathercock and have done and suffered everything so as not
to be dragged into this gladiatorial arena.[214] To those who dragged me to
court I have made my excuses with clasped hands and bent knees;[215] dangers
which threatened me from the other side I have in part avoided, in part
warded off, in part ignored; I have shunned the Emperor; money and honors
offered me I have consistently refused; and to so many monarchs, princes
and friends who summoned me into the fray I have excused myself.

195. "Now those who incite you against Luther," Hutten says, "are either
very powerful or very evil, or both."[216] All the more reason for Hutten to
admire my consistency, since those who are very powerful can easily destroy
one as well as protect him; those who are very evil willingly injure others;
and those who are both are even more formidable.[217] None of this has so
far constrained that weak and feeble Erasmus, who is easily swayed by any
breeze whatsoever!

196. Hutten further ridicules me because I wrote that the whole world was
sharpening its pen against Luther,[218] and he threatens that soon some
Lutherans will be sharpening their pens against me; he also demands to be
shown this "other, anti-Lutheran world," just as if this present world were
all on his side. Should I perhaps just enumerate here the many who have
already written against Luther? Among the Italians there is Silvester
Mazolini, Thomas Todiscus, Jacob de Vio and Catarinus; among the Germans Eck

and a certain Minorite of Leipzig whose name I have forgotten, Goclenius,
Jacques Lefèvre and Hoogstraten; among the French the whole Sorbonne and the
Augustinian Giustiniani; at Louvain Latomus, Johannes Turenhout and the
Dominicans Eustathius and Vincentius; at the imperial court there is
Marlianus, Bishop of Tudela, and Remacle d'Ardenne, the Emperor's con-
fidential secretary; among the English the King himself, John, Bishop of
Rochester, and a certain third person who is so antagonistic that he could
point a threatening finger even at Luther; among the Spaniards Stunica and
Caranza; then add to these Leo's bull of excommunication and the Emperor's
declaration of outlawry. Furthermore, there are many who have not yet
published their disputations against Luther, many who haven't finished them
yet and many who are unknown to me.

219

197. Now I recount these things only to show that Hutten ridiculed my
hyperbole without cause. Moreover, books by Lutherans written against me
frighten me so little that I am only sorry one has not appeared every three

220

years. Indeed, at times I even thought of suborning someone to provoke
some eminent Lutheran into doing just that, for nothing else could so easily
have freed me from ill-will. Hutten is nothing if not a Lutheran, but the

221

woeful dribble he writes is anything but a diatribe against me. Furthermore, I never had such a poor opinion of the Lutherans that I would have
suspected any one of them would decide to write such vile accusations against
someone else, nor do I believe Luther himself hates me so much that he would
approve of such a book directed against me; and yet, even if he had approved
of it, it would hardly upset me.

222

198. But, in the meantime, like another Metius, I shall remain silent,
awaiting the outcome of the war; for which perfidy I am worthy of being torn
limb from limb. If he deserves such evil who, by his labors and at his own

223

expense, zealously strives to be of benefit to both parties, what will he deserve who, through his fulminations and his stupidity, injures both parties - stirring up the one which he cannot control and aggravating the other by crushing ill-will; indeed, most grievously injuring the one which he boasts to support, while promoting the one whose enemy he claims himself to be?

199. And yet, unlike Metius, I have not remained idle; on the contrary, with continued zeal I advance the cause of the Gospel wherever I can. [224] Let the young fight; as for me, I am already preparing myself for that day which will summon me before the tribunal of Christ, a day which, although no one will escape it, cannot now truly be far off for me. [225]   I see the whole affair full of such hatred and such reviling that it is very difficult to maintain the tranquility of a Christian spirit in the midst of it. While meditating upon my Paraphrases I feel the agitation of my mind subside and myself become better than I was. There are some in both parties who are thankful to me and openly acknowledge that they have benefited from these vigils of mine.

200. Hutten also admits there are things of greater benefit I can do than write against Luther, and he exhorts me to do them. Why then disturb me with such letters while I am attending to these matters? He accuses me of elusiveness because I express myself variously in my correspondence; [226]   does he really want me to fit the same shoe on every foot, to say the same thing to everyone, ignoring as it were the variety of my correspondents as well as the diversity of the subjects and the times? [227]

201. Confronted with such differences of opinion and such divergent efforts, how can one possibly avoid expressing certain things only indirectly? Hutten will say: "Then silence would have been better." Oh, had I only been allowed to remain silent! But I was so pressed upon, beset and overwhelmed that I was finally forced to dispel the ill-will against me. How often does St. Paul not alter his style - now flattering, now reproving, now imploring,

now threatening, ignoring many things? Inconsistency does not lie in this, but in changing one's goals, which for St. Paul were always one and the same, whatever his tone or his countenance.

202. If anyone can show that I have altered my initial purpose, then let him accuse me of inconsistency! The matter itself, however, proves that I always realize my plans, promoting good letters and endeavoring to restore a purer and simpler theology 228 - and this I shall continue to do as long as I live, whether Luther is my friend or my enemy, for I consider him to be but a man who can err as well as induce into error. Luther will pass away like all the rest of us; Christ, however, remains for all eternity.

203. If Luther is truly led by the Spirit of Christ, I pray that Christ may abundantly bless what he is doing; if this is not the case, however, I can only lament this public misfortune. In a haughty manner Hutten passes judgment on our mutual attitudes; according to him, Luther loves me with all his heart, while I am most unfairly disposed toward him. 229 Oh, 230 the ungrateful man who refuses to return the love of one who loves him! I will not comment here at all on Luther's attitude toward me, nor will I discuss the very unfriendly letters he has written about me to his friends. In a matter of this nature one should not take personal feelings into consideration, and what is of moment is not how much Erasmus agrees with Luther, but how much Christendom agrees with the teachings of the Gospel.

204. Were I to take personal inconveniences into account, there is no one deserving my hostility more than Luther: he has heaped so much abuse on me and my books; he has either completely destroyed nearly all my friendships or infected them with bitterness; and he has seriously harmed good letters, which I have always defended, as well as the ancient authors whose authority I am endeavoring to restore. But all human considerations are to be discarded when the glory of Christ and the purity of the Catholic faith are at stake.

198

If Luther, or anyone else, were only to promote these things, I would gladly sacrifice my books, all my possessions and even my life.

205. And just where did Hutten discover Luther's attitude toward me? It was undoubtedly reported to him by some drinking buddy or other, who had heard it from someone else, who in turn had heard it from someone else; having changed hands some twenty times, the rumor finally reached him, and on such sources as these he based his pamphlet.
231

206. And he knows hardly more about my attitude toward Luther. "But at times you speak out against Luther," Hutten will claim. For me this is nothing new. Like another Carneades, I will occasionally argue both for and against Luther during the same banquet - sometimes just for the fun
232
of it, thus fishing for what this person or that one thinks, and at other times also learning something. On my part, however, such argument never degenerates into bitterness, for I am able to listen to all sides with impartiality.

207. I enjoy this lack of restraint at banquets or in conversations with friends and often make use of it immoderately, judging the temperaments of others by my own. However, so as not to acquit myself of all shortcomings, I admit this is my principal one, so implanted in me by nature that I can
233
scarcely overcome it,   although more than once I have learned by experience that some people forget the many things they themselves have said very freely, but remember what I might have said; this they repeat to others and on occasion they even use it against me, not without, so to speak, exaggerating and distorting it. Now really, whatever is said over one's cups should be
234
written in the wine!

208. While at the table, how often have we not bestowed the imperial authority on Pope Julius and the pontificate on Emperor Maximilian, or united in marriage the orders of monks and nuns? Then again, we made of

them an army to oppose the Turks or settled them as colonies on newly dis-

covered islands. In short, we altered the whole order of the universe.

Our decrees, however, were inscribed not on tablets of iron, but in wine,

235

so that, the revelry over, no one could remember who had said what.

209. It is an even greater boorishness to contrive an accusation from those

things which friends, who rely on our fidelity, say to us freely and jokingly

in their letters. I used to have some intimate friends who later became

mortal enemies of mine and have stopped at nothing to bring about my

destruction; they, however, have never suffered from what they told me in

private while our intimacy lasted, nor have I ever used any part of their

letters to attack them. Were I to do so, I would consider myself worthy to

be expelled from the society of men and thrust into the company of wild

236

beasts.

237

210. Nevertheless, he calls that letter to Laurinus a hateful attack.

Let him cite just one hateful word directed against Luther! There is no

mention made of heresy, nor of a heretic. I call the whole matter a tragedy,

I call it a disagreement and an uproar, words I could likewise have used in

speaking of any cause involving the Gospel. I was only trying to placate

certain Lutherans who, lacking judgment, are being carried away by an un-

restrained passion and at the slightest unfounded rumor stir up such tragedies.

211. Let us note here what reason Hutten invents for his shameless charge:

I am so ill-disposed toward Luther because I began to envy him his renown

238

after his books were in the hands of almost more people than mine were!

I do not envy Luther his reputation; indeed, I would prefer to be more

239

obscure than the humblest inhabitant of Caria than to have his reputation.

If he suffers it for the love of Christ, he suffers more than death, and it

would be unreasonable for any good man to envy him. But if this is not the

case, then one would have to be mad to envy anyone such a reputation.

212. If I had my way, I would prefer to have my works read forever and in every country rather than just snatched up as in a passing craze; but if they do not merit the reader's approval because of their inner worth, I will not lift a finger in their defense, even if no one reads them. "But," as they say, "even children in the cradle are learning to invoke Luther's name."[240] It would be far better for them to learn to invoke the name of Jesus! And yet, where these children are supposed to be, I do not know - perhaps Hutten saw them in the fortress of his friend Franz von Sickingen? For my part, I experience daily how many powerful, learned, serious and good men execrate the name of Luther, men whose erudition and purity of life are such that I could hardly suspect them to err from passion or lack of judgment.

213. Nor about the Holy See have I ever spoken inconsistently.[241] I have never approved of its tyranny and rapacity or its other vices, about which good men have universally complained for a long time now. Indulgences, however, I have never wholly condemned, although I have always detested the shameless trafficking connected with them.[242] And my books bear witness in many places to what I think about ceremonies.

214. Where indeed have I ever condemned Canon Law or the decrees of the Popes? Now, what "putting the Pope in his place" means I do not quite understand.[243] I assume Hutten will admit at the outset that there is a Church in Rome, for the multitude of bad Christians there cannot render it any less a Church - were this so, no Church would exist anywhere. I also believe this community is orthodox, for in spite of some impious individuals, the Church resides at least in its good members. I assume, further, that he will grant this Church a bishop and allow him metropolitan status, since there are so many archbishops in those areas where no apostle ever visited, while Rome after all did have both Peter and Paul, indisputably the two

greatest apostles. Now what is so unreasonable about granting the Roman

Pontiff the primacy among metropolitans? But no one has ever heard me

defend the enormous power which they have usurped over the centuries.

215. Hutten, however, cannot endure a corrupt Pope; do we not all desire

that the Pope be worthy of his Apostolic See? But if he is not, should

he be deposed? According to this line of reasoning, all bishops who do

not worthily perform their duty, would then have to be deposed. "For

many years now the world's greatest evils have flowed out of Rome." Were

it only possible to deny this charge! But now we have a Pope who, I believe,

endeavors with all the power at his command to restore to us a purified

Holy See and Curia. Hutten doubts this, although there are many indications
244
which offer some hope; and, as St. Paul says, charity hopes all things.

216. Now, if Hutten has declared war on vices and not men, let him hasten

to Rome and assist the Pontiff, who is endeavoring to do just what he him-

self is striving after. But Hutten has declared war on the Roman Pontiff

and all who support him. Could he actually have declared war on this good

Pope? If so, what will he do to those who support him, even if against

their will? What will he do to the Emperor, who has wholly allied himself

with him? Now, if Hutten considers war to consist in laying fields to

waste, razing cities to the ground, pillaging wealth and dispossessing

rightful owners of their property, he has thus far accomplished nothing but

to curse the Pope. Why, he has not injured even one Roman fly; unless of

course he consideres those to be butchered on the spot against whom he

hurls his insults!

217. He ought to consider, however, whether it is advantageous to incite
245
those one cannot quell. The Roman Curialists have always desired such

enemies as Hutten. Now, if the Curia cannot be cured except by the tumults

of war and by undermining and throwing everything into confusion - things which Hutten cannot possibly do - then it would be far better to leave

"the slumbering evil" undisturbed rather than to stir up the fetid bog to
246
the detriment of the whole world.

218. I would like to find out from Hutten, however, whom he has in mind

when he says "we" and "us," for he frequently uses these pronouns. Perhaps

he means everyone who supports Luther in any way whatsoever and wishes evil

to the Roman Pontiff? Now, as I see it, this class of men is quite varied:

there are indeed certain learned men who, in my opinion, are not in the

least evil, but who both approve of the greater part of what Luther says

and would wish to see the power of the Roman Pontiff curtailed; instead of

a worldly prince they would wish to have a teacher of the Gospel, a father

instead of a tyrant;

219. they would also desire to have the tables of the buyers and sellers
247
in the temple of the Lord overturned   and see restrained the intolerable

shamelessness of the indulgence hawkers, the horde of petty ecclesiastical
248
bureaucrats,   and the fabricators of dispensations and papal bulls; they

would desire ceremonies to be greatly reduced and the striving after true
249
piety greatly increased;   they would wish the power of the Gospel, which

is now almost out of style, to be restored and the dogmas and opinions of

men to yield to the authority of Holy Scripture; they would wish that human

ordinances be not preferred to the precepts of God nor that scholastic
250
decrees of whatever nature have the strength of a divine fiat;

220. they grieve that Christians are burdened with certain human ordinances,
251
as for instance those concerning the choice of food,   the great number of
252
holy days,   the reservation of certain cases, the degrees of consanguinity

or spiritual relationship; they would further like certain human fancies to

yield to the public good, for example mutual agreement should be enough for
253
two people to be joined in matrimony;   they would desire that our consciences

be rid of the too many nets in which they are now entangled   and that

sermons be free and holy; they would desire that bishops, now in great

measure little more than worldly princlings, be true bishops and that monks -
a class more worldly than any other - be true monks.

221.   These men support Luther because he seems to have energetically

attacked on all these points.   Although no pact binds me to these men, our

old friendship based on a mutual love of good letters does remain, even if

we do not agree in all things.   There is not one of them, however, who
approves of what Hutten is doing, not even Luther himself.

222.   On the other hand, there are certain ignorant individuals of no dis-

cernment and of impure life, detractors, obstinate and unmanageable people

who are wholly dedicated to Luther, although they neither know nor observe

what he teaches.   They constantly quote the Gospel, but at the same time

they neglect prayers and ceremonies; they eat whatever they please and curse

the Roman Pontiff.   That's the type of Lutherans they are!

223.   In the end the princes and magistrates will be compelled to suppress

their disorderly tumults and ill-advised suggestions.   And thus it will be

their fault if even those things about which everyone rightly complains are

not corrected.   Their commitment to the Gospel is also generally made over

their cups.   They are as a rule so absolutely stupid they do not even realize

that they themselves are the greatest hindrance to that cause which they

support, and whoever wishes to aid them will have to deceive them, just as
a doctor must deceive a mad man when giving him some medicine.

224.   I personally want nothing to do with this type of individual.   Even
Hutten does not seem to approve of them, since he calls them clowns.

There are others whom I suspect of not really supporting the Gospel - all

they yearn for is pillaging - but under the pretext of doing so they are
mere brigands.   Luther himself does not approve of these people.

225. They operate on quite different principles, namely whoever can put
forward some claim or other to noble rank [260] is allowed to attack travellers
on public highways and rob them or lead them into captivity and, when he
has exhausted his money on drink, prostitutes and gambling, [261] he is
allowed to declare war on anyone who suits his fancy. These are definitely
not Luther's principles.

226. There may be some people who, having squandered and lost everything,
style themselves Lutherans so as to find patrons by using this name. [262]
Now, would Hutten be prepared to defend all of these individuals? It would
seem so, for as soon as I mention certain Lutherans, he becomes violent. [263]
If I complain that some Lutheran stole my purse while I was travelling, [264]
can Hutten possibly assume responsibility for the theft?

227. He charges further that I once viciously attacked him personally;
this puzzles me since he neither cites the passage nor mentions the nature
of the attack. I can only say that whatever I wrote, I certainly did not
intend to hurt Hutten, whom I favored as a friend of good letters. And
even if things were as he alleges - which is not the case - would this
justify such slanderous abuse on his part? Had he covertly attacked me ten
times, I would have ignored it. [265]

228. But when he summons me back to his party, what does he want me to
join? Is it good men living according to the Gospel? I would willingly
hasten to such if they were pointed out to me. If he knows men who, in
place of drink and prostitutes and gambling, derive pleasure from reading
the spiritual authors or from holy discussions; who swindle no one out of
money owed to him, but generously give to the needy that which is not owed
to them; those, moreover, who do not speak ill of the innocent, but rather
with a gentle response mollify abuse heaped upon themselves; those who
neither bring force to bear on anyone nor threaten any with violence, but,

on the contrary, repay injury with kindness; those, further, who stir up

no discord but, mindful of the words of Christ "Blessed are the peace-

makers," [266] bring peace and harmony wherever they can; men who do not

boast of their own good deeds nor seek praise for their misdeeds or those

committed by others, but attribute to Christ rather all the glory of deeds

well done; [267] I repeat, if he knows such men, endowed with truly evangelical

virtues, let him point them out and he will see me join them.

229. As it is, I indeed see Lutherans, but of those who live the Gospel,

I see none or very few. Therefore, just as I do not withhold my friendship

from those learned men who with moderation and discernment support Luther,

in like measure I do not cease to consider as friends those in the other

camp who with a pious heart take Luther to task, but with moderation and

discernment. For indeed, even though their judgment may be in error, their

pious disposition has nonetheless persuaded them that because of Luther's

teachings innumerable souls will perish.

[268]

230. And yet on occasion I admonish both sides if I think they are fanatic.

It is not my purpose here, however, to pass judgment on Luther, but only to

respond to Hutten's calumnies. How can my courteous friendship with others

harm Luther? At times it may even benefit him.

231. The Reverend Father John, Bishop of Rochester, has written an enormous

volume against Luther. [269] For a long time now I have known this true man -

a singular friend and a most constant patron indeed. Will Hutten now perhaps

demand that I renounce this friendship because he has written against Luther?

232. Almost all learned men were my friends before anyone ever heard of

Luther. [270] Later on some began to support Luther - nevertheless, I did not

renounce my friendship with them on that account. Some of them, however,

changed their minds again, and now they do not think well of Luther at all -

neither on this account have I stopped considering them my friends. Nor do hang in the balance, waiting to fly into the arms of the victorious party.

233. What can I hope to obtain from Luther's party? I have constantly refused whatever the other party offered - and of the two, it is the more powerful. I must preserve some tranquility of mind and, as far as possible, try to remain impartial, thus to be of service to many when the occasion arises. 271 In the meantime I have sincerely and ardently desired to see the strength of the Gospel and the glory of Christ flourish throughout the whole world. 272 The Lord Himself will look after me. 273 I expect no happiness in this life; nevertheless, I would die with a more contented soul if I could only see the cause of Christ victorious.

234. But to return to the Roman Pontiff, about whom Hutten accuses me of thinking differently now than I used to think. "You praise this Pope," he says, "and in turn you are praised by him." 274 I do praise him, but many indications have led me to hope that he will in all sincerity promote the glory of Christ. Even so, my praises are very moderate. Could Hutten be so indignant because in my writings I praise with a few words such a good Pope - a former friend of mine who even now wishes me well - while in these same writings I praise him so often, in so many words and so magnifi- cently - even in such a serious work as my <u>Annotations to the New Testament</u>? 275 Why does he not call me a flatterer for doing that?

235. Moreover, the Pope sent me two briefs, the second written more lovingly than the first. 276 I welcomed them all the more gratefully because several of my old friends had prophesied my certain downfall once the present Pope had been elected. In this they were mightily deceived. And although no further advantage is likely to accrue to me from these apostolic letters, should I despise them? Hutten of course considers this mere cunningness.

236. With defenses such as these Erasmus must protect himself. To protect himself, Hutten has fortresses and fortifications, troops and guns, smoke

and fire and swords, proclamations and wars. My defense, however, rests wholly upon the favor of good men and certain influential people. Yes, I make use of this favor, but only on behalf of the commonweal, for were I to consider only myself, I would pursue other paths.

237. Perhaps Hutten is so brave because he no longer has anything for the safety of which he must fear. As for myself I cannot deny that I fear for my writings, [277] from which even Hutten admits a great many people have derived extraordinary profit. [278] I do not wish to jeopardize this profit through some rashness on my part, and if I guard myself it is only to remain of service to others.

238. He also reproaches me because the Pope and Cardinal Schiner praise me when addressing me - as he says, "He praises you to your face"! [279] - as if I should consider it a fault to be praised by such men, even though I personally interpret their praise as an admonition. Perhaps I should have endeavored rather to be praised by Hutten?

239. Now is it really so odd to praise one to whom we write? Does St. Paul not praise the Romans when he writes to them? "Erasmus," he says, "has surrendered himself to the Roman Pontiff." [280] What does he mean? Was I ever at war with him and thus in need of surrendering? Was I not equally devoted to Leo, hardly a lauded Pope?

240. Hutten also claims that I have promised never to desert the honor of the Roman See. [281] I did write this, but to those to whom I had been accused of conspiring with Luther against the Roman See. Does this mean, however, that I have promised to defend the tyranny and greediness and the other evils which Hutten hurls in the face of the Papal court? On the contrary, more than once I have stated that the dignity of the Pope and his See is rooted in apostolic virtue; it is this dignity which I promise not to desert. [282]

241. As for overthrowing the Gospel, as Hutten says, [283] I do not believe

that any Pope, least of all the present one, would beg my assistance, and

if one demanded this of me, I would not comply.

242. Neither fear nor favor of any prince will ever have such power over

me that I would knowingly oppose the truth of the Gospel or the glory of
                   284
Christ.   Nonetheless, I think it a matter of some prudence to maintain

the favor of princes so as not to desert evangelical truth. The result of

the current issues will establish which one of us has more rightly promoted
                              285
the cause of the Gospel.

243. At times, however, by speaking ambiguously I deliberately deceive, so

that many believe I am arrogating to the Roman Curia the right to tyrannize

and plunder and traffic in matters sacred and profane alike. In times of

danger it is permitted to deceive by ambiguity - even King David once feigned
          286
madness   - but, lest anyone be further deceived, let me state directly

that I shall not desert the Roman See unless it deserts the glory of Christ,

and I shall support it to the utmost of my ability if it endeavors by honest
                              287
means to promote the Gospel.

244. Although I have expressed myself in this manner in many places, Hutten

ignores them. He has selected only those passages he can distort, or rather,

I suspect, informers have pointed them out to him, for I cannot believe he

has sufficient leisure to read my works, engaged as he is in so many domestic

and military enterprises.

245. Even more intolerable for Hutten is what I wrote somewhere to the
                                                  288
effect that every honest man supports the Roman Pontiff.   He fails to see

that this statement followed logically from my argument: I at once won the

Pope's favor and transferred the odium of any misdeeds to certain others who

conducted the Pope's affairs rather poorly. Nor is what I wrote false, for

he truly supports the Pope who desires to see him overflow with apostolic

gifts. Thus one might possibly hate Leo and still support the Pope, for to

support the Popes' wrongdoing is not to wish them well!

246. Hutten also reproaches me because I state that all of Christendom has
for so many centuries rendered obedience to Rome. 289 This is true and may
God grant that it continue forever, provided Rome itself promotes the cause
of Christ! Hutten will shriek that it will never happen; 290 we, however,
still hope for the best, especially from the present Pope.

247. What, I ask you, is more holy, to obey the authority of the Roman
Pontiff or to follow that of Hutten? This is precisely the parallel toward
which my remarks were directed, including the statement about the Pope's
authority being acknowledged by the whole world for many centuries - a statement for which Hutten rebukes me. 291 In my own defense, I beg forgiveness
if, being a man unlearned in controversial matters, I follow the authority
of the Roman Pontiff rather than the authority of this person or that one.
For some a pronouncement by Luther is sufficient grounds for faith: I have
spoken! If Luther claims this, he is mad; if he does not, it is they who
are mad.

248. It is certainly well-known that in later years even the Greek Church
conceded authority to the Roman Pontiff. 292 By the term "world," however,
I understand the majority of Christians, although Hutten, in the manner of
a sophist, objects that the antipodes have not yet used the phrase: the
Roman Pontiff. But even granted that the primacy of the Pope does not stem
directly from Christ, it would nonetheless be expedient for one to have
precedence in authority over the others - an authority, however, far removed
from any sort of tyranny.

249. I wrote somewhere that the authority of the Roman Pontiff must be considered sacred. 293 I would not hesitate to say the same about each and every
bishop, provided they command nothing impious, for then they would cease to
be bishops. It can hardly be emphasized enough how dangerous it is for the
laity to become accustomed to mocking the commands of their bishops under

the pretext that they are evil men, for soon nobody would listen to the good bishops either.

250. He also reproaches me because I somewhere stated that not even death could separate me from the Roman See,[294] a statement I had to make, for at the time I was accused of having conspired against it. So what? Is this to condone the tyranny or the vices of the Roman Court?

251. Hutten then adds that it was shameless of me to write this, since I had so often deviated from the Roman See.[295] On the contrary, it is he who shamelessly invents this accusation, for my writings proclaim the very opposite. Just because I have criticized the Roman See, does not mean that I have deviated from it. For that matter, there are those among Luther's opponents who condemn the fact that up to now the Popes have been so venal, but this does not mean they have abandoned the Roman See. If criticism entails separation, then both the Emperor and the present Pope must have withdrawn from the Roman See, since both are considering means for eliminating its vices.

252. He likewise rebukes me for having written somewhere, "Who would not support the man who by his evangelical virtues represents Christ for us?"[296] Why does Hutten so misrepresent what I said?[297] I merely stated what the qualities of the Pope ought to be and the extent to which we should support him.[298] I am then accused of using a figure of speech. And what does it really matter, if the subject and the times demand such a figure?

253. Where indeed have I ever said that I could heal these dissensions?[299] If I only could, they would not last till tomorrow! But "Cry out!" Hutten urges me, "Do not cease to do so! Declare to the people their transgressions!"[300] I have cried out more boldly than I should have, for only he who is himself free from sin should decry the sins of others.[301] If I chastise the sins of others with moderation, it is because I am only too well aware of my own many weaknesses.[302]

254. Let Hutten cry out, a man of purity, in whom no stain of sin can be censured! I am not Isaiah. Besides, the latter was commissioned to cry out against the people, [303] whereas Hutten commands me to cry out against the princes. Now it is written, "Thou shalt not speak ill of the prince of thy people." [304] There is a great difference between God commanding Isaiah to cry out and Hutten commanding Erasmus to do so. A cry is useless, however, if it provokes nothing but upheavals and incites tyranny.

255. Moreover, till now I have not ceased to cry out in my writings, wherver there was some hope of betterment. Even my _Paraphrases_ are a form of crying out, for what is the light of the Gospel if not a refutation of our darkness? Let the impartial man judge which is more beneficial, Hutten's ranting or my silence. Besides, when have I ever deserted Christendom, if I was able to be of service?

256. Furthermore, princes will not allow themselves to be censured by just anyone, since this is the duty of bishops. [305] And it is also proper that it be done in secret rather than publicly. And too, for whom do I assume such labors, which are beyond my age and health?

257. "If you are so eager to restore harmony between the parties," Hutten asks, "why do you so viciously attack one of them?" [306] In one place he calls me another Metius, and now he claims that I am exerting all my powers against one of the parties. [307] Now just where am I supposed to have started all this? Only in my letter to Laurinus, directed against certain over-particular individuals, did I claim the right of disputing with Luther - first, should it prove necessary, and then without vindictive abuse, armed only with evidence from Holy Scripture and substantial arguments.

258. Hutten also complains that Luther's lot is only reviling abuse and shouts of disapproval. Why then does he rave so against one who promises that, should he dispute with Luther, he will refrain from reviling and shouts

of disapproval and, in the spirit of a peaceful conversation, will proceed solely with evidence from Holy Scripture and sound logical arguments? For this is all I have promised, and I have done so in such a way as to make it sufficiently evident that I will not act unless there is some evident hope of betterment.

259. Now, the same things that offend me in Luther's writings, namely his unrestrained abusive language and his arrogance, also offend those who are most devoted to him. I did not conceal this displeasure even from Duke Frederick of Saxony when I met him in Cologne, stating so in the presence of Georg Spalatin - and this even before the <u>Babylonian Captivity</u> had appeared.[308] They replied that in his sermons and lectures he was the most gentle of men; I rejoiced and approved, adding, however, that it would be preferable to instill such gentleness in those writings which fly to the ends of the earth, since his voice reached only a few. They promised they would try their best to get him to do so.

260. Hutten himself does not deny that Luther lacks modesty and gentleness. "But," he says, "what does that have to do with his cause?" Hutten is the last one who should ask such a question. Does he not everywhere maintain that Luther's cause is just and holy and pious? Then he ought to be terribly angered by a fault that alienates the hearts of so many.

261. If from the very beginning Luther had explained his position simply and gently, abstaining from that which at first sight cannot be tolerated, then no tumult would have arisen.[309] If he were my brother, three or four times over, and if I approved of his whole teaching, I still could not but strongly disapprove of so much fierceness in asserting his opinions and the harsh abuse he is always prepared to use.

262. I simply cannot convince myself that the spirit of Christ - than which nothing is more gentle - dwells within that heart from which so much bitterness gushes forth. And would to God my feelings were wrong! "But even the

213

spirit of the Gospel admits of some irritation," some will say. Agreed, but it is a different kind of irritation; and, besides, it never lacks the honey of charity to temper the gall of reproach.

263. I hear Peter angrily reproaching Simon, "May your money be damned to perdition along with you! Do you believe that God's gift can be bought with money?" ^{310} The vileness of the deed forced this reproof from the most gentle of all the apostles. But this is now the seasoning of comfort: "Do penance for your sin and beg God that He might perhaps forgive you this ^{311} thought of your heart."

264. Luther, on the other hand, whose arguments are so sparing and so close, knows neither moderation nor limitation in his insults, and he repeatedly amuses himself with mockery and biting remarks where there is no occasion to do so. For instance in his treatise directed against the King of England; whom did he think he was addressing when he said, "Come forward, Lord Henry, ^{312} and I shall teach you"?   The King's book was at least written in Latin, and not unlearnedly either; and yet there are those who strangely enough consider such silly jokes humorous.

265. Hutten complains that by having held out some hope of an imminent dispute with Luther, I inspired the princes as it were to unite in a re- ^{313} newed attack against him.   But it is he himself with his pointed pen who provokes everyone against him, and imitates the Scyrian she-goat, mentioned in the proverbs of the Greeks, who wildly overturned the pail of good milk ^{314} she had given.

266. Hutten also gnaws away at a statement I made somewhere to the effect that "It is not in the spirit of the Gospel to drag anyone into one's camp by cunning and force, for in the past Christians used to hide those who were exposed to danger, but they admitted no one into their fellowship except of his own accord and if he begged for admittance. Now, however,

certain Lutherans have tried to ensnare me by many tricks so as to prevent
315
any escape."

267. He maintains that this is pure fabrication unless I can name those
316
who tried to do such a thing.   Well then, let Hutten himself explain
317
just what they were doing who published that first letter I wrote to Luther,

or those who had printed and spread around certain hateful passages they

extracted from my books and then translated into German, publishing in an

even more unfriendly manner certain other things as well? And what were

they doing who made public a letter I secretly wrote to the Cardinal of
318
Mainz - a letter they never delivered to him?   What else, if not trying

to procure some pledges from me with no possible escape? I only mention

those things that are rather well-known, but if I wanted to I could also

relate many other facts.

268. I have noticed that almost everyone who supports Luther's faction,

acts just like those who fall into the water - he grabs hold of anyone he

can and tries to drag him into his danger, even a would-be rescuer. Similarly,

at every opportunity the Lutherans endeavor to involve everyone they can in

the common danger, even those who could free them from it.

269. Let Hutten explain to us what he was thinking when he wrote, "You
319
will write no better books, if indeed you write any more,"   and then let

him deny that there are those who tried to drag me into their camp by force!

No matter what I do, he says, my feet are firmly planted in the Lutheran

faction, for my books will fight for them even if I should happen to desert
320
the party.   I beg you, dear reader, how can anyone who writes such things

and threatens with I know not what secret letters, have the effrontery to

demand that I reveal the names of those who tried to drag me into the Lutheran

faction by tricks and by force? Now, the man who constantly, indeed per-

petually opposed all factions and was the first to warn against this dangerous

business, is this the same man who has his "feet firmly planted in the

Lutheran faction"?

270. What is in my books I cannot deny and till now I have been able to
defend it without Hutten's support. Although I now have so many distinguished
enemies, should my books not enjoy the same honor accorded to Luther's
writings if they teach the same things Luther teaches? "They will fight for
us," Hutten says; [321] but for whom, might I ask? This pronoun "us" occurs
so frequently in Hutten's mouth, and yet he is acknowledged neither by
Luther nor by any Lutheran who is the least bit prudent.

271. Of similar nature is Hutten's threat that if any misfortune should
befall the Lutheran party, then the victorious party will in no way treat
me more gently than "the rest of us." [322] But in point of fact I did not
declare war on the Roman Pontiff, nor did I write annotations against the
Papal bull, [323] nor declare myself protector of the Lutheran faction, nor
oppose the Emperor's edict.

272. Now just what does he mean by "if some misfortune should befall the
Lutheran party"? Is the party opposed to Luther not already wholly
victorious and dominant? And have I not thus far exposed myself unarmed
to everyone? What has happened to Erasmus? The Emperor and Ferdinand
have honored him and the Pope offers him both friendship and fortune. Only
certain madmen roar against him, arch-enemies of good letters whom Hutten
wanted to please with this little work of his - and he did.

273. And yet, those who pursue Hutten do not so much throw all this in
his face as certain other things, in view of which Hutten himself admits
that we were never brothers-in-arms. But from those who are his friends
in these matters he has far more to fear than from the Pope, against whom
he has long since declared war. [324]

274. How violently he harasses me, however, because somewhere I wrote
that the truth does not always have to be stated and that it makes a great

difference how it is stated. To quote him: "...this sacrilegious utterance of yours ought to be shoved down your throat again (indeed, the matter at hand compels me to express this with some animus) if those who now force heretics to recant or send them to the stake, properly did their job." [325]

275. When Christ first sent forth the apostles to preach the Gospel, He forbade them to announce that He was the Christ. [326] Now if the Truth It- self ordered that a certain truth be left unspoken for the time being - a truth which it is necessary to know and profess as a condition for salvation - is it then so unheard of if I stated that on occasion the truth is to be held back?

276. And did not Christ also remain silent before that wicked council which had assembled in the house of Annas and Caiaphas? "If I tell you," He said, "you will not believe Me." [327] It was the truth He was to tell. Why, therefore, did He remain silent? Because He knew that His words would be to no avail. And did He not likewise remain silent before Herod?

277. It was not enough that He did this; He taught that others should do so as well. "Do not give that which is sacred to dogs," He said, "nor cast pearls before swine." [328]

278. When Christ commanded the apostles to leave a city which showed it- self unworthy of the preaching of the Gospel, did He not in effect command them to remain silent about what is true? In his first sermon Peter referred to Christ as a man, about His divinity he said nothing. [329] Paul did the same thing in Athens, where he preached the true wisdom to the saints; among the weak, however, he remained silent about the truth. [330]

279. Paul refers to the apostles as the stewards of the mysteries of God. [331] Now, he who dispenses something, does he not offer certain things while retaining certain others, the better to ensure the progress of his listeners?

Why were not all the mysteries of the philosophy of Christ immediately revealed to the catechumens? Precisely because they were not yet able to comprehend them.

280. Nonetheless, in that particular passage I was not speaking about the articles of faith, but about Luther's paradoxes and about his insults of the Pope. Suppose I am firmly convinced that the feast of Easter is not being celebrated on the proper day; now what would be preferable, to defend this truth at the cost of great tumult throughout the world or to remain silent?
332

281. If I were to defend the cause of some innocent man before an all-powerful tyrant, would I disclose the whole truth, thereby betraying the cause of the innocent party, or would I not conceal many things? Hutten, a courageous man wholly committed to the truth, would, I imagine, plead in this way: "O you most infamous tyrant, you have already slain so many subjects far better than you; is your cruelty still not sated? Must you also snatch this innocent man from our midst?" Those who rage against the Roman Pontiff in their seditious books do not defend Luther's cause any more skillfully.
333

282. Or again, if Hutten were trying to obtain from an impious Pope the priesthood for one worthy of it, he would probably write something like this: "Oh impious Antichrist, you annihilator of the Gospel and oppressor of public liberty, you flatterer of princes, you so often shamefully bestow the priesthood on shameful individuals, and more shamefully sell it, give the priesthood to this worthy man; at least this time it will not be wrongly bestowed!" You laugh, dear reader, but yet these people promote the cause of the Gospel no less unwisely.

283. I did not say, however, that all truth was to be left unsaid, nor forever, but only at times. Now, is nothing ever to be said if the Roman

Pontiff is the Antichrist? Suppose he were! Did Hilary not remain

silent for a long time before he wrote against the Arians? He admits this

and justifies himself.

335

284. When Cyprian was about to be beheaded for Christ, and the Prefect

accused him of having conspired against the majesty of the Emperor, did he

answer: "We rightly conspire against him, for he is a worshipper of demons,

an enemy of God and an heir of eternal fire"? Not at all; he denied rather

that he was an enemy of the Emperor, and asserted that on the contrary, for

the sake of public tranquility, he daily prayed for his well-being. To

speak the truth in such a manner was only proper for a Christian bishop.

336

285. Moreover, when defending his cause, how did Hilary write to Constantius?

Did he not remain silent about many things, conceal many things, phrase

many things more flatteringly than the Emperor deserved? And again, how

337

did Paul defend his cause before Felix, Festus and Agrippa? Did he not

conceal some of the truth on these occasions? And did he not speak the

truth with the greatest courtesy?

286. What then is so sacrilegious in this statement of mine that it should

be shoved down my throat or worthy of the stake? Is Hutten not ashamed to

338

incite such tragedies over such trifles?

287. Furthermore, I have no doubt whatever that everyone will view as

ridiculous those things he has dreamed up about my departure for Rome, my

reception by Cardinals, the festive triumphs in my honor and the pious

339

gifts. He would have invented these things less foolishly, had I only

completed my preparations for this trip to Rome.

288. And then all of a sudden my accuser turns into an advisor, urging

340

me not to trust simulated friends. Oh, what a friendly heart, so

solicitous for my welfare! But there is no call for such counselors. I

know far better than Hutten what is happening in Rome.

289. It is also humorous that in the end, after having proven not a single thing he alleged, his affection for me moves him to call me back again and to lament my fate. [341] Immediately afterwards he pities me, doubting all the same that I am worth his pity. [342] And all the while, in his naiveté, he believes he is deceiving everyone.

290. What, however, is more foolish than to call me back from where I have never been and to summon me to where I am already? He calls me back from the party of those most evil men who support the tyranny of the Curialists, overthrow the truth of the Gospel and obscure the glory of Christ; and yet it is against those very men that I have always waged war. He invites me, on the other hand, to join his party, although I am still not certain where he stands.

291. In this I am indeed compelled to find Hutten lacking in judgment, since throughout his diatribe he portrays me as a man most vain, fickle and inconsistent, one who can be tempted back into the opposite party with nothing more than a morsel of bread - so feeble, timid and bloodless is Erasmus! What need is there then to invite such a one to join the party of strong men, this "friend for a day," whose assistance, should he persevere, would be worth no more, as the Greeks say, than that of a fig-tree? [343]

292. Enough has already been said, I believe, about Luther and the Pope. This might be the proper place, however, to answer a few things about my character, which Hutten promised to lay bare completely. [344] I fear though that in his little treatise he has disclosed more about his character than mine; he might perhaps have acted more advisedly, had he endeavored to conceal his own character rather than reveal that of others. [345]

293. Now what is more impudent than that Hutten should set himself up as the censor of my character, a man who never enjoyed any intimacy with me since he met me only a couple of times and was a guest of mine only once or at most twice? Let those who have lived with me on intimate terms and for

220

a long time pass judgment on my character!

294. He approves of my instruction but disapproves of my character and he warns the Germans against imitating it. All right then, let the usefulness of our lives be divided between us; let German youth derive its instruction from me but take Hutten as its ideal of character! ³⁴⁶ But let this also be a unique example of German integrity: since you are unable to harm any enemy, you suddenly cut the throat of a friend with such writings and, what surpasses all barbarity, from this very same friendship you fashion the dart with which to pierce your friend, or as the saying goes "cut out a whip from the ox's own hide." ³⁴⁷

295. For had I not embraced Hutten with sincere benevolence, he would not have had the means to hurt me. Nonetheless, I am more indignant at the one who goaded Hutten into this, for he too would not have had the opportunity to hurt me had he not been one of my intimate friends. ³⁴⁸ But he will receive his due when he betrays himself. ³⁴⁹ Till then, however, in the spirit of Terence's maxim "What I know, I ignore." ³⁵⁰

296. Afterwards, Hutten banishes me to my French Germany, ³⁵¹ although he himself has no truly secure place in Germany and prefers to be a clandestine guest of the Swiss rather than a German among Germans. I will make no further comment on the fact that he refers to the citizens of Brussels as German-French, for they are indisputably French, or that he exiles me from Germany, as if by living in Basle I were actually in Germany.

297. If Hutten obtains supreme sovereignty all over Germany, so that he has the power to banish whomever he desires, he still ought to be more partial to me since I was born between the estuaries of the Rhine, albeit closer to France than to Germany.

298. I entered Germany only once or twice in my life and then, in passing through, I visited a couple of cities situated not far from the Rhine,

namely Frankfurt some time ago and more recently Freiburg; nor do I have
352
any desire whatsoever to travel further into the country.

nor have I ever
299. I was never a burden to Germany / requested anything from her,
353
unless he is a burden who through his labors promotes public education;

nor am I presently living here so as to plunder anyone, but rather to
354
favor good letters and the cause of the Gospel at my own expense.   I did

welcome the friendship of the Germans, but now, thank God, I need the

generosity of none of them.

300. I have personally never boasted of my character, and even now as an

old man I must daily contend with it; nevertheless, I rejoice that I am
355
free of those vices which Hutten so liberally attributes to me   - and

this I can prove by the testimony of all those with whom I have lived on

an intimate basis.

301. Hutten at first describes me as timid - so weak-minded, in fact,

that I am almost afraid of my own shadow. He ought to remember, however,

that bravery is a far cry from foolhardiness: to attempt what one cannot
356
accomplish, to provoke when unable to coerce is madness, not bravery.

302. There is a certain type of gladiatorial bravery that bursts forth in

mere physical energy. Our lyrical Horace wisely wrote:

> Strength wanting in prudence collapses under its own weight.
> 357
> Strength moderated, even the gods raise in higher degree.

And yet, if one carefully considers the outspokenness found in my writings,

he will censure me in places for my temerity rather than my timidity.

303. Now note how zealously unfair he is toward me: Hutten, who is no

different now than he ever was, wants to be considered a formidable man,

but me he calls timid because, without betraying the truth of the Gospel,

I fear the Emperor and the Pope. He himself, however, when he was in Brussels,

did not dare to stay because, as he said at the time, Hoogstraten might just

222

happen to run into him; but at that time Hoogstraten was neither a Prior nor an Inquisitor nor was he supplied with any Papal bulls or warrants!

304. He was so afraid of this unarmed lion that he stealthily stole away; and yet it is I who am the timid one because I do not everywhere provoke so many enemies with foolish insults? - men who wished me ill even before Luther appeared on the scene and who are now armed with so many edicts and Papal bulls and even troops? It is sometimes wise to fear so as not to have to be afraid. If Hutten had done so before, he would not now have to fear everything,[358] but would be loved by most and feared by many. Moreover, contempt for one's enemy has never worked to anyone's advantage.[359]

305. What was more outspoken than my treatise on the duties of a Christian prince?[360] And I personally delivered it into the hands of Emperor Charles! Hutten considers himself brave if, from behind a secluded corner, he hurls a few words at this one or that and then, as they say, having thrown his dart, he flees.[361]

306. I do not see why I should greatly regret having had this type of courage since thus far it has proven adequate in so many sicknesses and labors, in so many misfortunes and tragedies; it has given me the strength to despise both the insults and injuries of my enemies and to refuse the wealth and honors offered me by kings; and despite so many turmoils and dangers it has never failed me in my zeal to be well-deserving in the cause of public education. Hutten boasts, however, that he strove to inspire me with courage - he would do far better to curtail his own courage and add to his judgment.

307. Hutten claims that one should even be willing to die for the truth of the Gospel. I too would not refuse to do this if the occasion demanded it.[362] But for Luther or Luther's paradoxes, I am not yet ready to die.

308. The dispute is not about articles of faith but whether the primacy

of the Roman Pontiff stems from Christ; whether the College of Cardinals is an essential part of the Church; whether confession was instituted by Christ; whether the regulations of bishops can bind under pain of mortal sin; whether free will contributes anything to man's salvation; whether faith alone is enough for salvation; whether any works of man can be called good; whether the mass can in any way be called a sacrifice. 363 364

309. For such as these, which are after all only topics of scholastic debate, neither would I dare to condemn someone to death, nor would I wish to risk my own life. I might choose to become a martyr for Christ, if He gave me the strength to do so, but a martyr for Luther I do not wish to be.

310. That I left Brabant and refrain from going to Rome is just prudence, not fear. I knew that if I stayed there, I would have to enter the arena against Luther. "But," Hutten will say, "had you not already decided what would have to be done if the Emperor ordered you to write against Luther?" 365 All right, then let Hutten tell me!

311. Suppose the Emperor had spoken to me as follows, which without a doubt he would have done: "Erasmus, we are convinced that, because of your erudition and your literary skill, you are the man who can accomplish the most; and, further, you are held in high esteem by the scholars of Germany. Aid our efforts, therefore, in suppressing this pestilential Lutheran heresy and your services will be most amply rewarded by us." What answer could I have given to that? That I did not have the time? Or that my strength was not sufficient to perform what his Majesty demanded?

312. He might have insisted: "We have been fully informed by learned men of your abilities; we request and demand that you comply with our pleasure in this matter. You will not only find favor in our eyes but at the same time you will free yourself from the false suspicion, leveled against you more than once, of being a supporter of Luther's impiety." Now, let Hutten

224

tell me how I should have answered!

313. If I had promised to do this, I would have had to forsake everything else and become involved in this tragedy. I would have been compelled to serve as a mere clerk for certain monks and theologians, whom I know only too well, and I could not have written my _Paraphrases_ and some other things the reward for which, I hope, will not be confined to this world alone.

314. But had I flatly refused, I would have rushed headlong into a hornet's nest and obvious destruction. To where could I have fled? To Hutten's stronghold? to Wittenberg? And would I not then have lost my few possess-
366
ions? My age and health do not permit me to wander about or live in poverty nor to hide somewhere or flee from place to place. Therefore, if I have kept quiet it was to avoid becoming enmeshed in this inextricable
367
labyrinth and yet not forsake the cause of the Gospel.

315. I am not yet fully convinced that evangelical truth is on Luther's side. If Hutten is such a staunch supporter of the truth and ready to die for it, then why does he flee and hide? Let him go to Rome or the Netherlands - there he will obtain the longed-for martyr's crown!

316. So much for the feebleness of my courage which I still would not exchange for ten times Hutten's courage, greater though it may be than that of Achilles. Enough has already been said, I believe, about my constancy, a quality which does not consist in always saying the same thing, but in always pursuing the same end.

317. Now, since a German should not speak evasively, let Hutten answer these questions: When he left here, did he travel on the direct, public road to Mühlhausen? And when he left Mühlhausen, did he do so in broad
368
daylight?

318. Everywhere he describes me as a most vain person and a shameless liar;
369
for himself he claims an adamantine devotion to truth. With respect to

225

this quality, however, I yield to but few. Even as a little boy - almost

instinctively, as it were - I hated liars, and this before I ever knew what

a lie was. And even now I am so repelled by this type of person that the
370
very sight of them makes me start.   Those intimates who know my character
my home
well from sharing my life or frequenting/   will testify to this.

319. Those who know me more intimately, even attribute to me as a singular

failing my all too free tongue incapable of concelaing the truth. This

is also the principal reason for my having retired from life at court,

where, willingly or not, one has to keep quiet about much that is shameful
371
and unfair.

320. He further accuses me of impoliteness and even infidelity toward my

friends. What he terms impoliteness, I do not know. To accompany visitors

about or escort them home; to invite them to dinner or accept invitations;

to observe similar customary courtesies with everyone - this is beyond my

health and is something the many labors I am engaged in will not allow.

Nevertheless, as impolite as I am supposed to be, I still spend more than
372
half my time writing letters to answer, greet or recommend friends.

321. Perhaps on occasion I have refused a dinner invitation from someone on

account of my health. Often, however, and to my great detriment, I have

accepted. To please affectionate friends, I have frequently acted foolishly,

a compliance I have often regretted.

322. Let any friend come forward, however, to whom I have ever refused

faithful counsel, to whom I have refused aid when it was seriously needed!

"But some, with an oath, have complained of my infidelity." Not even an

enemy has ever accused me of infidelity, nor would I now hesitate to call

upon all my friends to reveal when I have not kept my promises, or whom by
373
lies and fraud I have deceived, or whose secret I have ever betrayed.

323. I can indeed assert, and justifiably so, that very few are more stead-

fast in their friendship than I. Had I only been as fortunate or as cautious in forming my friendships as I am faithful in maintining them!

324. I have never harbored resentment against anyone whom I once truly loved with all my heart; I just terminate our intimacy. Only some terrible crime would cause me to break off a friendship. By way of example let me cite one or two such cases.

325. A few years ago I wrote a letter to the Cardinal of Mainz condemning certain theologians of Louvain. I sent the letter in a sealed envelope, addressed to a man known by no one better than by Hutten, and I charged him to deliver it if he thought it fit, or otherwise to burn it or throw it into the river. Since he was a member of the Cardinal's household and, as I thought, one of his privy councillors, I believed he would better know the Prince's mind. But what happened? The letter was printed and publicized
without ever being delivered to the one to whom it had been written.

326. This enkindled a grievous ill-will against both the Cardinal and me in that country. Besides, the papists were already preparing a triumph, boasting I could no longer escape them. So, greatly angered, the Cardinal demanded the letter I had written to him, which by then had already made the rounds for fully three months. In response to his sharp demand, he finally received it, half-mangled and smudged with printers' ink.

327. As was bound to happen, the Prince was very annoyed by the matter and very indignant with me, suspecting that the guilt was mine. I am inventing nothing here. Afterwards in his letters the Cardinal complained to me about the whole affair.

328. What an uproar Hutten would have made if I had done something like that to him! First of all, fidelity to a commission placed in the hands of a friend was betrayed; then, the publication of the letter harmed a cause which could have been fostered had the letter been read in secret; both a
were
friend and a well-deserving patron/burdened with ill-will; and finally, such

a great prince, who was my friend, became my enemy.

329. Although I openly reproached that man with the matter in only a couple of words, he, admitting the whole thing with a modest smile, said that it was due to the carelessness of the Bishop's secretaries. Afterwards, as impolite as I am, I did not say another word about it, and I even refused to admit what I suspected about him.

330. But later that same person undertook something far more impolite and dangerous to me; still, I never complained about it nor did I begin to be any less a friend - I only decided to be more cautious in the future.

331. Was it also not extremely unfriendly of him to excerpt certain carping passages from my books, translate them into German and have them published? I had not written these things for the masses and they were not intended to be read out of context. Here, too, I briefly expostulated with him by a letter in which I said: "I have heard that it was you who did this. Perhaps such a disservice was inspired by friendship, but I rejoice nonetheless that my enemies do not have as much talent for hurting me." [376] Content with this rebuke, I allowed our former friendship to remain undisturbed.

232. How many similar stories could I not cite?! Nonetheless, no matter how impolite and discourteous I am supposed to be, I still have not withdrawn my friendship from anyone. If any man can truly lay to my charge just one such action, then I will admit as true everything of which Hutten now falsely accuses me.

333. Let him then bring forward those friends who on their word of honor accuse me of infidelity [377] and I will easily reduce them to silence. If I allowed myself to suspect Hutten of things to the same degree that he allows himself to accept as fact all these "crimes" of mine, I would suspect as pure fiction his repeated assertions "Some say ...," or "I heard in France..."; [378] why does he not also add "recently I dreamed that ..."?

334. He attributes to me an insatiable thirst for glory and fame.   If

this were so, I would long ago have entered the service of the Roman Curia,

where an enormous harvest of glory was offered to me; or I would have

frequented the Imperial Court, to which I have been invited more than once,

and accepted the riches and honors held out to me. I would have chosen

glorious themes bound to win me applause. As it is, I have obstinately

refused those subjects which promise glory and hold fast to my inglorious

leisure, tackling rather those themes which shine before the world least of

380

all.

335. Hutten, I imagine, judging my attitude by his, is unable to believe

me when I swear that, if I could, I would most willingly give up whatever

fame I may have, or that if I had known what a burden fame can be, I would

381

have followed Epicurus' injunction: "Live your life in seclusion!"

336. I am also accused of bragging about the letters written to me by

princes and the praises of others bestowed on my lucubrations. And from

this Hutten concludes I am a most vain, that is a most hollow person - for,

I suspect, that is what he means. But in fact I have revealed barely a

tenth of the letters which princes and scholars write to me, and these I

have mentioned now and then only to protect myself against the shamelessness

of detractors; for I am able to fight against them with no other weapons and

I can make a stand against their depravity with no other defense, except,

as I have said, with my own innocence and the good-will of princes and learned

382

men.

337. I have never boasted that the most illustrious Prince Ferdinand has

repeatedly honored me with the most courteous letters or that he sent me a

very generous gift which I neither sought nor expected. I have not boasted

that the King of France has often invited me to his court under the most

honorable conditions, writing to me in his own hand, although I am told, he has not written three autograph letters in all since his coronation; or that

the King of England did the same thing only a short time ago. Thus within a

few months I have received letters from four monarchs of the earth - the

Emperor, the Kings of France and England, and Prince Ferdinand. Had Hutten

received these letters, oh, what boasting and bragging he would have trumpeted
383
before us!

338. To be sure, he himself writes to the Emperor, to Cardinals and Apostolic

Nuncios; but who of them has ever answered him? He may just as well write

to the inhabitants of heaven or hell. To praise the benevolence and generosity

of princes toward me is not, however, a matter of boasting, but of gratitude.

339. Furthermore, regarding the praises of scholars, I have boxes full of

their laudatory epistles and more are sent daily from every side. Sometimes

I do not even read them, for there is no type of letter which pleases me less.

Where indeed do I acknowledge or swallow the praises rendered to me? Have I

not rather always disclaimed these pompous praises which certain people

lavish on me, rejecting them with my head and hands and feet and my entire
384
body?

340. According to Hutten I am also so envious that I can bear neither the

flourishing fame of those who lived before me nor the budding fame of men

younger than I. From the testimony of all who, through an intimacy of long

standing, have become acquainted with my character and carefully observed it -

this same character which Hutten has criticized after only a few conversations

with me - I shall prove that I am as far from envy as I am from lying.

341. I ask you now, who in his books has praised more men (whether older or

younger) than I, and praised them more fully and sincerely? Concerning a great

many of them, the world would never have known their names, had they not

appeared in my writings. But Hutten objects that in doing this I praise many

who are unworthy. Is "envious" really the word for the man who sins in this regard? And, too, who has worked as much as I have to restore the ancient authors? Is this then envy of one's elders?

342. Who has paid greater tribute to Lorenzo Valla, Ermolao Barbaro and Angelo Poliziano, whom the preceding generation considered as masters in the world of letters?³⁸⁵ To Rudolf Agricola and Alexander Hegius I owe practically nothing, but do I not fully praise them in a work everyone believes will long endure?³⁸⁶ Have I not everywhere praised Reuchlin beyond measure?³⁸⁷

343. And have I not always revered Ulrich Zasius, not to mention Thomas Linacre and William Grocyn?³⁸⁸ Whom among my contemporaries have I not highly esteemed of my own free will? Do I grudgingly praise the merits of Guillaume Budé?³⁸⁹ And even though he violently attacked me, who has ever praised Jacques Lefèvre more sincerely than I?³⁹⁰ In short, the list of the names of friends mentioned in my works is all but endless!

344. As for Hutten, have I envied his rising star? My countless praises of him belie this accusation, praises which he himself has forced me to retract because of that pamphlet.³⁹¹ Who has commended him more often, more sincerely or more lovingly? And what sort of reward did I ever expect in return? But of course, the envious always treat others this way!

345. Many I praise because of their promising talents, many just to encourage them. To whom have I ever preferred myself or with whom have I had even a couple of words about pre-eminence in knowledge? To whom have I not willingly conceded the praise which Hutten bestowed upon me more than anyone else? Whom have I ever attacked before first being violently attacked by him? And these I have thus far treated in such a manner that through me they have become more famous.

346. My works have contributed something important to the promotion of Greek letters among our contemporaries, and yet do I not publicly admit and rejoice at the fact that countless young scholars are coming to the fore who surpass me by far? Oh, unheard-of envy indeed!

347. Even though someone else might have wanted to accuse me of envy, it certainly was not proper for Hutten to do so, since I am almost alone in having commended him wholly without envy. I alone have conferred more praise on Hutten than all of his friends ever did, but he, my friend, in turn has heaped more accusations on a friend than all my enemies have done till now or than he has ever hurled against any enemy of his. In his letter to me he nonetheless called his expostulation extremely gentle, considering the abomination of my crimes. Ah, what a sweet man!

348. To whom have I not extended a helping hand if he were striving for some honorable goal? That I could not assist many was the fault of my circumstances, not my good-will. Whomever I could promote, I have done so by praising or commending them, or such similar courtesies. I have even supported some who were rather ill~disposed toward me, solely because they served learning.

349. Were I to cite here the letters of those who thank me for my sincerity, Hutten would scream that I am the most vain man on earth. But they in turn would shout back that of all false accusers Hutten is the most shameless.

350. When I was in Brabant, from my meager income I gave more generously to students in one year than many who boast of their wealth received from their family estates. That is how much I envy younger scholars! I will not betray nor reproach anyone for the little service I rendered, for I consider that in giving I received benefit, if I gave to a deserving man; 392 and these will testify on my behalf how shameless Hutten's accusations are.

351. "You believe that no one can compare with you in eloquence," Hutten 393 says. But actually I will bear it with great equanimity if countless numbers are ranked above me, and there are indeed many who rightly can be.

352. With similar shamelessness he depicts me as some sort of chameleon, 394 an extraordinary master of every form of pretence and dissembling. How

232

little does Hutten know the real Erasmus in such matters, since nothing is more difficult for him than to pretend or dissemble; he is rather simple and straightforward by nature, to the point of being foolish; his tongue is dangerously free; in short, he is so unaccustomed to deceiving anyone with feigned flattery that it is a fault of his to be more severe in his words
395
than in his heart.
396
353. "You will never again deceive me with your airs," Hutten says. Pray, on what occasion was he ever deceived by my airs? It was he rather who deluded me by his countenance, for around me he showed an astonishing
397
modesty and restrained the impudence of his tongue. Therefore, either he has undergone a certain strange metamorphosis or his former behavior was
398
admirably feigned.

354. May I perish utterly if I had believed that so much vanity, shame-lessness, rudeness and malice were to be found in all of Germany as are
399
contained in that one pamphlet. Because of this, however, I am not about to be adverse toward any German, nor on account of one hostile friend will
400
1 appreciate my honest friends any the less.
401
355. He is also not ashamed to call me repeatedly another Gnatho, although my writings are so plain-spoken. There is consequently the danger that any-one who reads these many praises bestowed on Hutten in my books will indeed ridicule me as a mere Gnatho flattering a Thraso.

356. Here, too, I am forced to find Hutten lacking in good judgment. He wants to be considered the defender of Germany's reputation, but if my books are filled with praises of the Germans, does he not then detract from the weight of all these praises by passing me off as a vain, crafty and frivolous flatterer?

357. Nevertheless, in this not one word of flattery was said; far from it. Even all the homage I paid to Hutten came from the bottom of my heart. I

liked his talents and his flowing style, and, with more study, experience

and age, I expected something exceptional from him.   Am I, therefore, a

flatterer because he deceived not only me but everyone to whom I praised him?

358. But I am too flattering when I write to princes! At times, to be sure,

I speak very freely to them, when the subject demands it. However, it is no

doubt advisable to treat lions gently, and Holy Scripture teaches that we

owe reverence to princes.   But where do I so flatter them as to betray

truth?

359. Who has been of greater service to truth, I who express myself too

flatteringly, or certain others whose abuse borders on frenzy? Kings and

queens, who in the past read nothing but fabled romances, now have the

Gospels in their hands, they consult sacred writings and rejoice to learn

something about the mysteries of the philosophy of Christ.

360. Let Hutten tell us to what extent his abuse has been useful! He

flatters blamelessly who flatters not to help himself, but another. If I

sought to gain something from princes, then my flatteries would be suspect.

As it is, I seek nothing, or if I do, it is not for me but for the advance-

ment of public education.

361. And yet, it is not always flattery if one praises princes; for to

the good praise is due, and to praise the mediocre or those who show some

promise is but to encourage the progress of virtue, and to praise the bad

is to admonish them about their duties, but without offending them. All of

this I explained at length some time ago in a letter to Jean Desmarais.

Erasmus has always been this kind of Gnatho.

362. I, too, could call the Popes Antichrists, the bishops idols and the

princes tyrants, as others do; but I do not consider it worthy of a good

man to assail good men with insults, instead of rendering them their due

respect; and it is sheer madness to provoke evil men with abuse, since one

cannot curb them once they are angered.

363. Following the example set by the ancient Doctors, I have dedicated my works in part to personal friends, in part to princes. I have never allowed my friends even to thank me for the dedication, let alone tried to extort something from them; and from princes I have never begged anything, 405 so much so that nobody would believe how few have ever given me anything on that account. I could go into detail here, were it not that I fear I might offend someone; at another time, perhaps, I might do so anyway.

364. And yet, since one needs many things in the course of life, he who by honest study seeks to share in the liberality of princes acts more excusably than one who borrows money from friends and never repays it, or buys 406 merchandise for which he never pays, or who blackmails innocent people.

365. What gall on his part to accuse me of incivility and discourtesy, since he makes it quite evident in his pamphlet that he himself does not possess a bit of courtesy! Even the Scythians treat old age with deference, and wild beasts, too, know their obligations; why, even bandits and pirates value friendship! Hutten acknowledges the exceptional friendship binding us. He also acknowledges as eminently profitable my efforts on behalf of the public welfare and as not insignificant those on his own behalf. Nevertheless, provoked by no injury to himself, he has torn asunder all the bonds of gratitude, and he, a young man, has spewed upon one advanced in age so many insults and contentions and quarrels; he has struck my ears, my face and my mouth; he has dragged me around and spun me like a top; in short, he has 407 treated me as if I were a slave purchased at auction, and not Erasmus.

366. Hutten has also convinced himself that somewhere on the face of the inhabited earth, there lives someone so savage and ferocious that he would not execrate such great savageness on his part. And, I imagine, he considers his character to be that of the Spartans and the Massilians, a character 408 which German youth should learn to imitate from him.

367. At one time such was my disposition toward Hutten that I believed were anyone to come forward to attack me, he would risk his own life to avert the blow. [409] I spoke about him to my friends with tenderness, I offered him my services, deplored his adverse fate and was even solicitous about his future well-being.

368. Now this priest of humanity has with such a pamphlet ambushed, as it were, a friend whom he had always honored most reverently, whose grey hair he ought to have respected and whose services on behalf of public education, not to mention those rendered him, he acknowledges.

369. He has declared war on the papists, but in truth he wages war against the Muses and the Graces. The sword he directed at his enemies remains bloodless, the pen directed at his friends drips with blood. I do not know on what account I ought to forgive him for accusing me of being the instigator of all the present tumults and then, with the conflagration raging, of denying my deed and trying to curry favor with the enemy. [410]

370. I imagine that Hutten will even go so far as to make me the instigator of all the crimes he is committing on land and sea under the auspices of Mars. Now, in a letter he wrote to me recently he said that no one goaded him into action, nor would he allow himself to be goaded by anyone. [411] If this is so, how can he have the effrontery to accuse me of being the manipulator of everyone, since I have no influence with him at least and his vigorous spirit will not allow itself to be goaded by any man?

371. Aside from dinner conversations, written in wine, and my <u>Colloquies</u>, [412] in which friends are jesting among themselves, I have always - as I have said before - advocated moderation whenever a matter demanded serious consideration. I warned Reuchlin against offending the Religious Orders and I deplored the passionate violence of his <u>Apologia</u>. I imagine my letters to him can still be found among his papers and they will show that I am telling the truth. [413]

372. I felt the same way about Luther and I have already mentioned the advice I gave to the Count of Neuenahr.[414] Concerning Hutten I will reveal none of the secrets of our friendship; I will repeat only what he himself wanted the whole world to know through his published books.

373. While we were both at Louvain, he requested a private interview with me - this was the only one I ever had with him. He immediately began to discuss his intention to declare war on the papists. At first I thought he was joking and so I asked him what assurance of victory he had, since the Pontiff was so powerful in his own right, besides having the support of so many princes.[415]

374. After he had answered my question, I replied that the matter was both violent and dangerous and, although it might be honest, it was nonetheless foolish to attempt something when there was no hope of success.[416] Then I added that, however it might be, I did not want to hear any more about the matter, for my primary concern was to benefit public education with my labors;[417] and I advised him not to become involved in whatever others might dare to do. That is the way I goaded Hutten!

375. Long before this, when he had published some immoderately unrestrained books, I admonished him in a letter to restrain the freedom of his pen, that[418] he might continue to enjoy the favor of his prince. In his reply to me he said that he would follow my advice. Had he only done this, he would not now have to hide and flee from place to place, but could live as an influential man among the most influential and would be a person whom one could love without suffering the ill-will of others.

376. Even before this, when we met and conversed for the first time in Mainz, he showed me his Reuchlin's Triumph, a truly beautiful poem.[419] I recommended that he not publish it, and this for two reasons: first, so that no one could scornfully - and deservedly - accuse him of celebrating a victory before the battle was won, as the Greeks say;[420] and secondly, so that he

would not embitter Reuchlin's enemies any more than they already were,
since his cause was still fraught with the greatest danger. However, if he
would not comply with my request, he should at least delete my name from the
poem.

421

377. Several months later he visited me again, this time in Frankfurt.
As soon as we were together, I asked him if he had remembered my advice.
He answered that he had remembered it well and had firmly resolved to follow
my counsel in all things.

378. Not long afterwards the poem appeared anyway, along with a truly
magnificent wood-cut depicting Reuchlin's triumph, both of which accomplished
nothing but to make Reuchlin more hated than he was and further provoke his
enemies, who were raving quite enough on their own. I do not doubt that
Reuchlin himself disapproved of the whole affair. I am not discussing here
what his enemies deserved, but what would have been advantageous for Reuchlin's
cause.

379. My counsel was always of this sort, as soon as the matter demanded serious
advice. No agreement ever bound me to Hutten, except one - our mutual compact
under the laws of the Muses to combat the enemies of the classical languages
and good letters.

380. I admit that I did not wholly support Luther's opponents, for I saw
that, were they to prevail, they would become insufferable; and even now I
would not want to see them gain total victory. In the beginning I did not
disapprove of the Lutheran drama, but I have always disapproved of its performance.

381. Although it is not true, let Hutten just pretend that in the beginning,
when everyone was applauding Luther, especially the scholars of Germany, I
too supported him and that I confided to Hutten, as an honest friend, the
secret thoughts of my heart. What then could be more discourteous, once he

for no reason became my enemy, than for him to broadcast my confidences far and wide and reproach me with them before the whole world?

382. So as to please the Muses, Hutten calls his vicious accusations an "Expostulation." However, to expostulate with someone is to remonstrate as a friend in private, hoping thereby to be given satisfaction.[422] But without warning me first, Hutten accuses me before the whole world, and he is so impudent that he believes he can write such things without injuring our former friendship.

383. He may have whatever friends or enemies he likes, but I personally want nothing more to do with the type of person his letter reveals him to be. I had already responded to the chief points about which he claimed to be so angered, for he had discussed them at length in his letter to me.[423] In the meantime, however, this "Expostulation" reached Zurich, after passing through the hands of many here in Basle.

384. I explained to him that the reason why I had refused to see him privately was other than he suspected; I vindicated my letter to Hoogstraten; I explained that I had never even dreamed of accusing Reuchlin of anything; I made it clear that I had changed my mind in no way about Luther's case, nor had I ever been one of his partisans, and yet I was wholly committed to promoting the cause of the Gospel; I stated further that I had thus far written nothing against Luther, but were I to write against him in the future, I would use no insults, but only sound arguments and evidence from Holy Scripture.

385. My modesty and fairness would be such that not even Luther could be offended. I pointed out that his resolution would be disadvantageous not only to the cause of the Gospel, but also to the pursuit of the liberal arts and even to his own affairs, as they currently stood.

386. I wrote to him at that time about these things and many others. His learned friends also advised him against publishing such a book, among them

239

even Eppendorf, as Hutten himself admits.

387. Making light of all this advice, however, he published his book, which brought greater joy to no one more than to those who are the most hostile toward Luther, the classical languages and good letters, men whom Hutten thoroughly detests, if what he says is true. Oh, how insolently these people will exult! And what will they not say among themselves! "Ah, there is Erasmus' much vaunted Hutten: may he enjoy him! There is
425
that gift of genius with whom he fell in love: may he enjoy it! Yes, let him kiss the gracious charms of that diction he has extolled so often!"

388. There are even those who claim that Hutten was hired to write against Erasmus by Hoogstraten, Baechem or some of their associates. This seems more than probable to me, since somewhere or other he jests appropriately
426
enough that he had scented the bait the Pontiff had tossed out. In my opinion, however, the bait he smelled was tossed out rather by monks and theologians, for the whole affair is not of recent origin - it is an old boil that only now has had the chance to drain its pus.

389. Several months ago friends wrote me that some sort of a book was being prepared against me. I expected some minor dispute concerning Luther's teachings; now I see that this work was spawned elsewhere and enlarged as it were with the tagged-on rags of denunciations supplied by others. This must be so since on the whole the style is so uneven, whereas that part he wrote
427
in leisure is far more carefully worked out.

390. Which is more honorable, however, to accept a reward from the Emperor and the Pope for disputing with Luther, or to accept payment from monks for attacking a friend with such insults? Therefore, let Hutten honestly tell us what little morsel the monks and theologians tossed out to make him bark at me and I will then confess what I received from the Emperor and the Pope for writing against Luther.

391. He will perhaps deny it, but it is highly probable, indeed certain, that no one has ever done the enemies of Luther and good letters a greater favor than Hutten has done with his diatribe. I am supposed to have burdened Luther with ill-will because I addressed the theologians at Louvain as Reverend Fathers; but it is he himself, Luther's champion, who has afforded his enemies the greatest pleasure with this spectacle of his. Nothing has ever given them a better opportunity to swagger and sneer or done more to bolster their courage than this book of Hutten's.

392. It seems to me I already see the sworn enemies of good letters and a more sound theology everywhere exulting, leaping madly about and congratulating one another - Baechem and Vincentius at Louvain; in Paris two theologians
428
in particular, the one Guillaume Duchesne, the other Natalis Beda; Theodorich of Nijmwegen with his shabby crew in Cologne; and perhaps also Edward Lee along with Henry Standish in England.

393. All of them are preparing a triumph for Hutten and for themselves, applauding and acclaiming him: "Bravo, courageous Knight, strike again! For our sake, slay that Erasmus who has shaken the foundations of our supremacy by introducing new languages and letters. Onward! With more books like this render these letters (which some falsely call "good") hateful in the eyes of princes and youth by letting them see what virulence is concealed within them and that they are good only for calumniating honest men or in-
429
citing insurrections!   Betray the mysteries of the bacchanalian poets; spit, blow snot, piss and shit in this spring of the Muses, so that afterwards no one will want to drink from it. And if you want to defile it in all these ways at the same time, just immerse your whole body in it! Whatever you have done to offend us in the past we forgive, if you but continue what you have begun."

394. Oh, fortunate Hutten! Now he will receive congratulatory letters from these new friends, countless gifts will be sent to him, magnificent

rewards will be offered.   Whether all of this has already happened, I

am not yet certain; but these assumptions are closer by far to the truth

than what he fabricated about my going to Rome and the Cardinals welcoming
me with open arms.

395. For, although provoked in so many ways, I have thus far written

nothing against Luther; whereas Hutten, without any provocation, has written

such a malicious book against a friend through whose praise many who have

never met him have yet come to know and love him.
396. What else could have compelled him to write such a malicious diatribe?

I have shown that the reasons he alleges are of no account, something that

of itself was evident to prudent and unbiased men, even to those who support

Hutten. What did he hope to gain by this book? Did he write it just for

fun? It would have been better had he chosen some other theme if he only

wanted to be humorous. Maybe he just wanted to perfect his style? This he

could have done without drawing his sword against a friend who had been and

was still ready to be of service to him.

397. Or, as someone said, maybe he wanted to bequeath to posterity a perfect
example of his eloquence, a swan song as it were,   just as Cicero did with

his _Phillipics_. If this is what he wanted, he ought to have chosen a subject

important in its own right, one which by its usefulness would commend itself

to posterity. As it is, by his choice of subject he has done the greatest

harm to his reputation, assuming of course that he takes it into consideration
at all.

398. Maybe he was trying to deter me from writing against Luther? Nothing

in fact could have provoked me more quickly to do so. But far be it from me

either to undertake or discontinue anything in such a weighty matter, merely

for Hutten's sake. Things must really be going badly for Luther if after

being forced back to the triarian line of defense and reduced to such a
miserable anchor,   he has to be defended by such books.

399. Maybe he wanted utterly to destroy me? What, however, could be more barbaric than to feel that way about someone who neither suspected anything nor deserved such hatred? Among other Scythian expressions, all of them testifying to his extraordinary brutality, he is said to have cried out exultantly: "Erasmus will really be layed low by this book."[436] And now, since I did accidentally fall victim to a sunstroke, Hutten is undoubtedly rejoicing and congratulating himself.

400. I trust he does not believe, however, that I am so cowardly that I would become sick, even if fifteen such books were written against me. This diatribe of Hutten's will in fact regain for me many friends whom he is alienating from himself; what friends he will attract to his side, he will shortly discover. How great indeed to please a few dull-witted Lutherans ever ready to applaud! Yet he has but few friends of this kind and, if some of them are a little wiser, he will soon have even fewer.

401. He boasts that he was surrounded here by hosts of Lutherans,[437] and for the hospitable reception accorded him he profusely thanks this city in which I have now been living for almost two years and have yet to meet any-one who wants to be called a Lutheran; a city furthermore in which by official decree it has been forbidden for anyone to teach in public anything contrary to the Gospel, even with the support of Luther's authority.

402. Moreover, I am not so sure there is not something to the suspicion of those who repeatedly tell me that Hutten gave up being a Knight to become a sedentary and write such books for profit, in fact a two-fold profit, since he is paid by those who commission his work and then is paid off by those against whom he writes to keep him from publishing his books.

403. Even though he is an enemy, I feel sorry for Hutten if his fortune has sunk so low.[438] I hear that even the printer paid him something for his work! But enough about Hutten, lest I produce something harsher than a sponge. I

just wanted him to realize that I too could wield a sharp pen, had I not

chosen to maintain my customary restraint rather than imitate his example.

404. Thus far I have never quarreled with anyone whom I once loved with all

my heart, nor have I ever given vent to the fury of my pen even against

those who attacked me most hatefully. Were I prone to such petulance, I

would prefer an opponent who had never been my friend or one in more fortunate

circumstances. It is unworthy to quarrel with a friend and cruel to ridicule

someone in misery.

405. Since Hutten's example is obviously so detestable, it remains only for

me to exhort all those devoted to good letters to refrain from a similar

intemperance, lest good letters be reduced to something hateful. They are

called the humane studies - let us then see to it that they are not dis-

possessed of this honorable name through any fault of ours. Similarly, they

will be what they are styled - good letters - only if they make us better and

if they serve the glory of Christ.

406. They were not reintroduced into the schools in order to drive out the

older disciplines, but rather to help them be taught more purely, more

pleasantly. But now there are almost as many dissensions in the schools as

there are in the churches, for most of those who eagerly promote classical

languages and good letters want to see them alone advanced, to the exclusion

of all other studies. On the other hand, those who steadfastly fight to

maintain the older studies, strive with all their might to destroy and annihilate

more refined letters.

407. Should we not, therefore, merge our individual gifts so as to help

each other, rather than hinder one another by foolish contentions? Let

those accomplished in good letters seek earnestly to recommend them through

their own virtuous, chaste and agreeable conduct and ennoble them by the

acquisition of more weighty disciplines! And those yet unaffected by good letters, let them add this beauty to their studies!

408. Were mutual concord to prevail, no one would lack anything; through
443
dissension, however, we cannot enjoy even that good which is ours already.

Let each of us, therefore, from the greatest to the least, endeavor to bring
444
about peace and concord among Christians.   As things stand now, we possess

neither the peace that this world can give, since everything is seething

with passion because of the wars raging everywhere, nor do we possess the

peace of God, on account of the violent disagreement of our opinions, nor

is there anywhere to be found honest friendship or fraternal charity. On

the contrary, because of this most vile fermentation all things have been

corrupted.
445
409. Whoever likes this age, may he enjoy it; to me it seems most miserable.

Let those who support the cause of the Gospel do so simply and prudently,

without recourse to clandestine conspiracies or abusive books directed against

the Pope or the Emperor - such things only foster more good-will toward them

and incite ill-will against the Gospel. Discarding all obstinacy and human

ambitions, let those who are learned confer among themselves about what can
446
be done to heal the universal dissensions;   and those things that would

seem to promote the welfare of the Christian people and the glory of Christ,

let them indicate these to the Pope and the Emperor in private correspondence;
447
and let them honestly engage in this work, as if before the face of God.

410. The truth of the Gospel is more readily fostered in this way than it

is with never-ending quarrels. For while we endlessly dispute about whether

man can perform good works, we have absolutely no good works at all; as long

as we bitterly fight about whether faith alone, without works, saves man, it

will happen that we obtain neither the fruit of faith nor the reward for
448
good works.

411. Moreover, certain things are of such a nature that, no matter how true

they might be, it is not convenient to preach them openly to the people. For example, "free will" is nothing but an empty word; every Christian is a priest and can thus forgive sins and consecrate the body of Our Lord; righteousness is imputed to faith alone, our works contribute nothing. To cast these paradoxes among the laity, what does it accomplish other than to create dissension and strife? 449

412. Once again I would implore the spiritual and the secular princes to esteem their own feelings and private interests less than the common good and the glory of Christ. This is the will of Jesus Christ, and if we do this He will protect and bless all that we do. 450

413. Let him to whom the spirit of Jesus imparted the gift of deeper insight, share it honestly and with all gentleness, bearing and tolerating those who cannot immediately grasp what is taught, just as our Lord Jesus tolerated for so long the weakness of His own disciples until they better understood Him.

414. Princes and bishops are men who can make mistakes and be deceived. Is it not far more profitable to lead them gently to the knowledge of truth rather than embitter them with reproaches? Let those who claim to have found spiritual knowledge in Luther's camp consider well that they too are men, subject to the same evils as Popes and princes. Of themselves, neither crown nor miter produces evangelical wisdom, I admit, but then neither does an ordinary cap or belt.

415. Those who believe they possess the gifts of the spirit must not despise civil authority. Princes, on the other hand, no matter how powerful or important they are, should not disregard the truth of Christ, however lowly the person is who preaches it - the apostles themselves were of humble origin. We tend to accept a remedy for the body offered by the most insignificant, uneducated man or even by any woman; should we then reject a cure for the soul just because it is prescribed by those of lowly birth? 451

416. Let everyone in both parties put aside personal desires and, with shared hopes, implore the Spirit of Peace, lest Christianity, reduced already to such critical circumstances, be wholly destroyed through our mutual dissensions!
452
Let us not continue to flay and mangle one another like wild beasts and deadly fish, thus providing a joyous spectacle for both Satan and the enemies of the name Christian!

417. There is agreement among us concerning all the basic articles of faith transmitted from the early Church; why, therefore, should the world be torn asunder because of such strange paradoxes, some of which by their very nature cannot be fully understood, others that can be argued either for or against, and still others that, considering their importance, contribute little to
453
the improvement of morals?

418. Our Christian life is overwhelmed on every side by most inane wars, by tumults, highway robberies, quarrels, hatreds, disparagements, deceptions, guile, excesses, violent desires; nothing anywhere is sound, and yet, disregarding all this, we fight among ourselves as to whether the primacy of the Roman Pontiff was ordained by Christ.

419. Let each side attempt to bear with the other, for affability will result in friendship, whereas obstinacy only provokes strife. What will the end of all this be if one side has nothing but tumults, quarrels and invectives, the other nothing but condemnations, papal bulls, pronouncements and autos-da-fé?

420. What is so great about burning to death some poor wretch who has to die anyway? To teach him and convince him of his error - that is something great. Not even retractions affect anyone all that much, for is it not evident that a man would prefer to be shamed rather than burned alive?

421. And how unpraiseworthy that a bishop, who is supposed to teach the philosophy of the Gospel, should have more power than a satrap as regards

the things of this world, while as regards the things of the faith he has
nothing but pronouncements, imprisonments, executions and autos-da-fé?[454]

422. No bishop should ever be ashamed of serving Christian charity, just as no apostle was ashamed of doing so, nor should any scholar be annoyed at rendering the bishops their due respect. I offer this advice to both parties as one who has pledged his loyalty to neither but wishes well to both.[455]

423. I, for my part, am preparing myself for that day which will summon me before the judgment seat of Christ,[456] and for that reason I choose to retire from those contentions in which one can hardly be engaged without striking or being struck and thus lose some part of the tranquility of the Christian spirit.[457] I turn instead to those things which will calm my emotions and soothe my conscience.

424. In this respect I feel that working on my _Paraphrases_ will be of great benefit to me. Thus it grieves me all the more that because of this quarrel I have lost six whole days in reading Hutten's false accusations and then wiping off the muck he threw on me. Farewell, honest reader, whoever you are. The End.

Notes: *Sponge*

1. Allen, Ep. 1378 (Bö, II, 262-263).

2. "Turpe silere" (Ad, 613F-614B: it is disgraceful for one to remain silent when advice is needed and can be given); on the <u>Adagia</u> cf. Allen, XII, pp. 16-17; on Hutten, Allen, II, p. 155 and XII, pp. 113-114; on Zwingli, Allen, XII, p. 189.

3. "Corrumpunt mores bonos colloquia parva" (Ad, 388D-389D: evil morals are easily imbibed and thus one must beware of the company one keeps); cf. Allen, Ep. 1379, ll. 6-7: "... dem ich ... weder mit worten noch wercken verletzt hab ..."

4. "Altera manu fert aquam" (Ad, 1041E-F: a person may seem to be a friend but in secret he is planning to harm you).

5. In this instance Erasmus should perhaps have remembered some of his own adages concerning rash judgments: "Ex uno omnia specta" (Ad, 100D-E); "Ollae amicitia" (Ad, 190C-D); "Una hirundo non efficit ver" (Ad, 299C-F); "Pannus lacer" (Ad, 515C-E).

6. "Sapiens sua bona secum fert" (Ad, 1055D-E; Phillips, p. 134: since our true riches and security reside within our souls, we cannot escape from the evils in our lives by merely changing our abodes).

7. "Salem et mensam ne praetereas" (Ad, 225B-E: hospitality is a sign of friendship, and neither should be violated).

8. "In Care periculum" (Ad, 226D-227C; Phillips, p. 123: the Swiss are indeed an honorable people); Allen, Ep. 401, p. 225, Ep. 404, p. 234 and Ep. 1378, p. 310.

9. "Difficila quae pulchra" (Ad, 410C-411C: it is easy to sow discord but almost impossible to bring about peace and harmony).

10. Allen, Ep. 1389 (Bö, II, 263-265).

11. "Minutula pluvia imbrem parit" (Ad, 112A: if we disregard slight evils they

will grow into large ones); "Omnes sibi melius esse malunt quam alteri" (Ad, 147A-C: charity begins at home).

12. "Extra lutum pedes habes" (101A-B: one is indeed lucky if he can extricate himself from some enterprise that at first seemed advantageous but in the end would cause great harm).

13. "Ut sementem feceris, ita et metis" (Ad, 325F-326C: what you sow, that you will reap).

14. "Virum improbum vel mus mordeat" (Ad, 332B-F: one cannot be unjust toward a whole nation because of the evil actions of just one rogue); cf. par. 354 below. Anacharsis was a Scythian prince who went to Athens about 594BC to study. He was a friend of Solon and a man of great ability. A number of aphorisms were ascribed to him and he is credited with having invented the bellows, the anchor and the potters' wheel (cf. Harper's, p. 76; Seneca, Epistolae, XC).

15. "Ne bos quidem pereat" (Ad, 1049A-1054B; Phillips, pp. 368-380: bad neighbors can ruin our lives; friends should be chosen with care and judgment but friendships, once established, should not be broken off lightly; praise of Archbishop Warham as a friend and benefactor; a bad life can bring odium on good letters - a defense of Greek studies as a method of perfecting all branches of knowledge); cf. pars. 58, 393 below.

16. "Bene plaustrum perculit" (Ad, 226C-D); Plautus, Epidicus, IV, ii, 22.

17. "Ut lupus ovem amat" (Ad, 1120E-1121A: said of one who pretends regard for someone he is about to destroy).

18. "Sustine et abstine" (Ad, 617A-B: bear and forebear - it is best for all concerned if one suffers and yet remains silent).

19. "Piscator ictus sapiet" (Ad, 38B-C: a sad experience can be a very good teacher); "Exiguum malum, ingens bonum" (Ad, 571A-B: a wise man will learn from his misfortunes).

20. "Ne quid nimis" (Ad, 259E-260E: be moderate in your praise and censure of others).

21. Plutarch, Solon, XXXI, 3; Cicero, De senectute, VIII, 26; on Solon (c. 638-c. 559BC), the famous Athenian lawgiver, cf. Harper's pp. 1476-1477.

22. "Non bene imperat, nisi qui paruerit imperio" (Ad, 25E-26C: one must learn to have command over his passions); "Taurum tollet qui vitulum sustulerit" (Ad, 90D-E: since the force of habit is so strong, one must learn to check his vices in his youth); "Naturam expellas furca, tamen usque recurret" (Ad, 617B-E: habits become second nature); "Nucem frangit qui e nuce nucleum esse vult" (Ad, 671B-C: nature demands that we must labor for what we desire).

23. "Felix qui nihil debet" (Ad, 637D-F: debts are the cause of many evils in our lives; because of them we must blush for shame, hide from our friends, flee our homes, cheat others and eventually beg).

24. On the idea that unjustly procured riches are generally squandered on vices cf. "Male parta, male dilabuntur" (Ad, 294F) and "Qui multa rapuerit, pauca suffragatoribus dederit, salvus erit" (Ad, 472D-E; Phillips, p. 108). In Greek legend the Danaides were the 50 daughters of Danaus (grandson of Poseidon and founder of Argos; he was the ancestor of the Danai or Argives, a term used by Homer to denote the Greeks in general) on whose command 49 of them slew their husbands and, according to later versions, as a punishment for their crime they were condemned in Hades to pour water into sieves (cf. Harper's, p. 468).

25. "Festina lente" (Ad, 397B-407D; Phillips, pp. 171-190: among other things Erasmus discusses the need for self-discipline, the avoidance of over-indulgence and flatters, the need for all to promote the common good, etc.; to act upon impulse is to rush into heedless action).

26. "Mandrabuli more res succedit" (Ad, 92F-93B: an ill-conceived project cannot possibly succeed); "Mustelam habes" (Ad, 99E-F: said of persons for whom

251

everything seems to turn out wrong); "Mali corvi malum ovum" (Ad, 343E-344E: a bad egg is bound to produce a bad bird); "Similes habent labra lactucas" (Ad, 386D-387C: a sordid man is bound to commit sordid actions).

27. For "birds-of-a-feather" references cf. "Aequalis aequalem delectat" (Ad, 78D-79D; Phillips, pp. 83, 122); "Caput sine lingua" (Ad, 390E-F; Phillips, p. 131); "Furemque fur cognoscit et lupus lupum" (Ad, 510A-B).

28. "Cum larvis luctari" (Ad, 91B-C: it is disgraceful to contend with the dead).

29. Undoubtedly a reference to Eppendorf; on Eppendorf cf. Allen, XII, p. 88.

30. Since the Sponge is almost twice the length of the Exp. one is tempted to wish that Erasmus had called to mind the following adages: "E multis paleis, paulum fructus collegi" (Ad, 100A: much labor but little profit); "Non est ejusdem, et multa et opportuna dicere" (Ad, 106A-C; Phillips, p. 384; cf. Proverbs, X, 19: "In multitude of words there wanteth not sin"); "Manum de tabula" (Ad, 120B-D: too much explaining obscures the issue).

31. "Veritatis simplex oratio" (Ad, 145F-146C: truth does not need the ornament of many words); "Flamma fumo est proxima" (Ad, 189A-B: where there is smoke, there is fire); "Mendacem memorem esse oportet" (Ad, 514A-B: a liar needs a good memory but one who tells the truth never needs to fear being discovered); "Vino vendibili suspensa hedera nihil opus" (Ad, 589C-D: good actions are their own interpreters, they need no rhetoric to adorn them).

32. The sarcasm of this remark becomes more than evident when compared with the many references to Eppendorf in Erasmus' correspondence, colloquies and adages (cf. Allen, XII, p. 88). Among others cf. "The Cheating Horse-Dealer" (Col., pp. 245-249; LB, I, 756A-757D: the Latin title "Hippoplanus" is a pun on Eppendorf's name); "The Ignoble Knight or Faked Nobility" (Col., pp. 424-432; LB, I, 834D-837F: a caricature of Eppendorf and a satire on the greedy German nobility in general); "Terrae filius" (Ad, 328E-329C: on persons of obscure descent and the new self-made man); "Proterviam fecit" (Ad, 349E-350E; Phillips,

p. 130: a ludicrous picture of the young German nobility; the name "Ornithooplutus Isocomus" is an approximate Greek rendering of Eppendorf's name); "Argivos vides" (Ad, 970E-F: ridicule of a small town boy who adds the name of a larger city to his name so as to impress others); Allen, Ep. 1122, p. 303, Ep. 616, Ep. 1371, pp. 299-300; Smith, pp. 383-386. Thompson points out that Erasmus also wrote a counter-part to "The Ignoble Knight" in his colloquy "The Lover of Glory" (Col., 478-488; LB, I, 857E-862D) and that echoes of Erasmus' sentiments are to be found in Xenophon, Cyropaedia, I, vi, 22, and Memorabilia, II, vi, 39; Cicero, De officiis, II, xii, 43; Montaigne, De gloire (cf. Col., p. 478); cf. also pars. 6 and 25 below.

33. "Ad felicem inflectere parietem" (Ad, 118D-119E: we should assist our friends who are in need or danger, but this does not mean that we must hazard our own destruction).

34. "Altera manu fert lapidem, altera panem ostentat" (Ad, 309C-E: of one who gains our confidence only to destroy us in the end).

35. "Frons occipitio prior" (Ad, 77E-78D: those who are to benefit most from any undertaking are the ones who will manage it best).

36. "Herculana balnea" (Ad, 510E-511B: Germans seem to spend all their time in over-heated rooms ("hypocaustis")). "Inns" (Col., pp. 147-152; LB, I, 715F-718D: on the perils of travel in Germany, the perpetual drunken state of the Germans, and their filthy, over-heated rooms).

37. Böcking suggests that the doctor in question was a certain Osvaldus Berus (cf. Bö, II, p. 267, n. 8) and refers the reader to Bö, II, p. 213 for possible corroboration of this assumption. Bö, II, p. 213 does discuss Ludovicus Berus (Ludwig Baer) and in note 8.9 gives a reference to a book I was unable to locate, i.e. Athenae Rauricae (Catalog. professor. acad. Basil. ab 1460 ad 1778). Basle: Serini, 1778. It is possible that an Osvaldus Berus is discussed in this volume but if he is, one can but wonder why Böcking

did not cite the exact pagination. In any event, the work Hutten is
supposed to have written against this doctor does not seem to be extant.

38. "Nuces relinquere" (Ad, 194E-195B: a man must give up childish amusements
and employ himself in more manly pursuits); "Honos alit artes" (Ad, 330F-
331B; Phillips, p. 387: one should not hide one's light under a bushel;
cf. also Matthew, V, 15 and Luke, XI, 33).

39. "Things and Names" (Col., pp. 382-388; LB, I, 820C-822C: the discussion between the speakers, Beatus Rhenanus and Boniface Amerbach, centers around the
contrast between appearances and reality); "Vita mortalium brevis" (Ad, 943B:
since our lives are so short we should use our time so that in the end there
with
is nothing/which we can reproach ourselves); on Beatus Rhenanus cf. Allen,
XII, pp. 49-50; on Amerbach, Allen, XII, pp. 40-41.

40. "Ignem ne gladio fodito" (Ad, 17C-E: do not further irritate an angry person
with words of reproof - try rather to appease him; when his passion subsides
he might listen to your remonstrance).

41. "Lucrum malum, aequale dispendio" (Ad, 793C-E: that which is useful is also
honest).

42. On Capito cf. Exp. pars. 85, 93; on Reuchlin, Exp., pars. 96-97; on the
theologians of Louvain, Exp., pars. 113-114.

43. "Lupi illum priores viderunt" (Ad, 296C-E: said of the bold of tongue who
suddenly become less talkative and intrusive); on Sickingen cf. Allen, XII,
p. 168.

44. "Argentanginam patitur" (Ad, 269B-D: about the power of money to bribe even
a good man).

45. "Matura satio saepe decipit, sera semper mala est" (Ad, 358B-C: do things
at the right time, not too early, not too late).

46. "Ira omnium tardissime" (Ad, 265D-266C; Phillips, pp. 51, 386: anger is the
last emotion to grow old, although benefactions are forgotten immediately; a

comparison between Ate and Lucifer: Ate was expelled from Heaven by an angry Jove as Lucifer was by an angry Jehovah).

47. "In caducum parietem inclinare" (Ad, 605C-D: concerning trust in a false friend who in the end betrays that trust); "Amicitias immortales esse oportet" (Ad, 1060A-B; Phillips, p. 127: friendship is something that was meant to last forever; one "Ate" does more harm than 100 "Litae" (prayers personified as a goddess); anger is the last passion to cool down).

48. "Leonem larva terres" (Ad, 239E-F: concerning those who try to frighten someone of superior intellect by merely making a lot of noise).

49. "Mature fias senex" (Ad, 93B-C: one should give up the irregularities of his youth in time to enjoy a pleasant old age; the pleasures of the senses are the causes of all disease); "Aranearum telas texere" (Ad, 169C-D: we only waste our time and money in the pursuit of frivolous objects).

50. Exp., pars. 17, 66.

51. Concerning something that is not to the purpose cf. "Nihil ad versum" (Ad, 199B-F); "Nihil ad Bacchum" (Ad, 541D-542D); "Non-sequiturs" (Col., pp. 422-424; LB, I, 834A-D), cf. also par. 91 below.

52. Exp., par. 18.

53. "Inter malleum et incudem" (Ad, 33B-C: concerning one who is so surrounded by evils that he cannot win no matter what he does).

54. Exp., pars. 20-21.

55. Concerning the necessity of deliberation before action cf. "Sub omni lapide scorpius dormit" (Ad, 163E-164B); "Festina lente" (Ad, 397C-407D; Phillips, pp. 171-190; cf. n. 25 above); "In nocte consilium" (Ad, 462B-C); "Antequam incipias, consulto" (Ad, 512F-513A).

56. "Ut sementem feceris, ita et metes" (Ad, 325F-326C; Phillips, p. 387; cf. also Psalm CXXVI, 5, Galatians, VI, 8 and 1 Corinthians, IX, 11: what you sow, that shall you reap).

57. Exp., par. 22.

58. Cf. n. 8 above; "Artem quaevis alit terra" (Ad, 275B-E: an educated man is at home anywhere); on the universal recognition of Erasmus cf. below pars. 37, 38, 55, 129, 147, 150, 153, 158, 161; on Erasmus and Basle cf. Allen, XII, pp. 48-49.

59. "Cor ne edito" (Ad, 17E-18E: do not let cares gnaw at your heart; the greatest misfortune is not to be able to bear misfortune).

60. "Foenum habet in cornu, longe fuge" (Ad, 59A-C: flee from those who are of a quarrelsome, malevolent disposition); "Similes habent labra lactucas" (Ad, 386D-387C; Phillips, p. 50: a hard pupil needs a hard master). This claim by Erasmus would seem to be rather exaggerated!

61. Exp., pars. 13, 22, 45, 62.

62. Cf. Bö, II, 168-169.

63. Christiern II, King of Denmark, cf. Allen, IV, p. 568, n. 30; on Christiern cf. Allen, XII, p. 70.

64. "Hic bonorum virorum est morbus" (Ad, 902A-C; Phillips, p. 265: envy, greed, ambition - these are the downfall of even good men).

65. Cf. Bö, I, 162, v. 11 and p. 171, par. 2.

66. "Conscientia mille testes" (Ad, 394D-E: an evil conscience needs no accuser); "Quod quis culpa sua contraxit majus malum" (Ad, 990E-991A: the evil caused by your own deeds presses most heavily on your mind); cf. also par. 51 below.

67. Concerning the idea of the young trying to teach their elders cf. "Sus Minervam" (Ad, 43A-F); "Caecus caeco dux" (Ad, 312E-313A); "Plaustrum bovem trahit" (Ad, 273A-B); "Ante barbam doces senes" (Ad, 784D-785B); cf. also pars. 59 and 365 below.

68. "Tertius Cato" (Ad, 330A-B: concerning the man who affects more gravity and scantity than he has); "Sapientum octavus" (Ad, 330B-C: concerning the man who claims to be a censor of the morals of others though he himself is immoral).

In 1514 Erasmus edited the <u>Disticha Catonis</u>, a collection of moral precepts erroneously attributed to Cato the Censor (cf. Allen, II, Ep. 298). Marcus Porcius Cato the Elder or the Censor, 234-149BC, was a Roman statesman, general and writer. He sought to restore the integrity of morals and simplicity of manners of the early days of the Roman Republic. As public censor in 184BC he was very severe. He advocated the Third Punic War and in every speech before the Senate his concluding words were the now famous statement "Ceterum censeo Carthaginem esse delendam" (cf. Harper's, pp. 298-300; Plutarch, <u>Cato</u>).

69. "Lingua, quo vadis?" (Ad, 460C-D: a turbulent tongue can cause confusion and distress); "Lingua bellare" (Ad, 694B-F: to rage and threaten with a violent tongue is the only recourse a coward has).

70. "Quid de quoque viro, et cui dicas, saepe caveto" (what is said in mixed company usually finds its way back to the one talked about, cf. Horace, <u>Epistolae</u>, I, 18, 68); cf. also pars. 130-132 below.

71. Cf. Allen, Ep. 2918 (Erasmus states that he never had had any intention of coming to grips with Luther since it would have served no good purpose to provoke him with books attacking him personally or his views; he further states that he had always clearly expressed his love for the Church and that he prided himself on never having joined any sect or party); cf. also par. 176 below.

72. "Fucum facere" (Ad, 201D-202B and n. 66 above: concerning those who deceive others with false pretense); Exp., pars. 1-4; on Laurinus cf. Allen, XII, pp. 122-123.

73. Cf. Introduction, n. 27.

74. I was unable to locate the letter in which Hutten is supposed to have stated this; cf., however, Introduction, n. 30.

75. "Verecundia inutilis viro egrenti" (Ad, 613B-E: bashfulness is of no use to a man in need).

76. "Hostis non hostis" (Ad, 817F: concerning those who prefer hostile acts to expostulation).

77. Cf. n. 74 above.

78. The letter referred to was either never written by Eppendorf or has been lost - in any event, I was unable to find any trace of it.

79. "Refutantis laudem immodicam" (Ad, 909B: said by one who finds himself treated with too much adulation - a check on immoderate commendation); cf. also par. 137 below; on Erasmus and classical studies, languages and literature cf. Allen, XII, pp. 104-105, 113, 121, 126.

80. Cf. n. 15 above ("Ne bos quidem") and par. 393 below.

81. "Caput artis decere quod facias" (Ad, 1054B-D; Phillips, p. 125: there are some things that not everyone can do, e.g. a young man reprove an older one); cf. also par. 40 above and par. 365 below.

82. "Corrumpunt mores bonos colloquia parva" (Ad, 388D-389D; Phillips, p. 388: even good men can be corrupted by evil speech; cf. I Corinthians, XV, 33).

83. Concerning the idea of retracting one's former opinion and praising that which was previously condemned cf. "Ex eodem ore calidum et frigidum efflare" (Ad, 309E-310D; Phillips, p. 386); "Palinodiam canere" (Ad, 356A-D); cf. also pars. 73, 92, 117, 121, 127, 128 below.

84. Exp., par. 58; Allen, Ep. 1006; Allen, XII, p. 111.

85. Destructio Cabale seu Cabalistice perfidie ab Ioanne Reuchlin Capnione iampridem in lucem editae. Cologne: Quentel, 1519 (cf. Allen, Ep. 1006, pp. 44-45).

86. Cf. par. 119 below.

87. Exp., par. 58.

88. Exp., par. 165.

89. Concerning opposing an adversary with his own weapons cf. "Malo nodo malus quaerendus cuneus" (Ad, 70F-71A) and "Baeta tum hyeme, tum aestate bona"

(Ad, 887E-F); cf. also par. 142 below.

90. Concerning Erasmus' ideas on learning and eloquence cf. among others "A Short Rule for Copiousness" (Col., pp. 614-620; LB, I, 670A-672B: this treatise was written first in 1499 and then expanded in 1512 as De duplici copia verborum ac rerum (LB, I, 3A-110D; Donald B. King and H. David Rix, trls. and eds., Desiderius Erasmus of Rotterdam: On Copia of Words and Ideas. Milwaukee, Wis.: Marquette University Press, 1963; the later version was written as a textbook to be used by John Colet in his newly founded school for boys; on Colet cf. Allen, XII, pp. 73-74). A complete program for education was written in 1511 in his treatise De ratione studii (LB, I, 521A-530B), complemented in 1529 by De pueris instituendi (LB, I, 489A-516A); cf. further "The Art of Learning" (Col, pp. 458-459; LB, I, 849C-850D: and Erasmus' edition of Lorenzo Valla's Elegantiae (LB, I, 1069A-1126C; Allen, Ep. 23, p. 108); Woodward, Desiderius Erasmus Concerning the Aims and Method of Education; Hanna H. Gray "Renaissance Humanism: The Pursuit of Eloquence," Journal of the History of Ideas (New York), XXIV (1963), 497-514; cf. also n. 353 below.

91. Exp., par. 58.

92. "Animus habitat in auribus" (Ad, 1066B-C; Phillips, p. 127: a word of accusation can kill as readily as a sword or poison); cf. par. 119 below.

93. "Lydius lapis sive Heraclius lapis" (Ad, 215B-E: on people with an acute judgment who can easily solve difficult problems); on Hermann Busch cf. Allen, XII, p. 61, on Neuenahr, Allen, XII, pp. 144-145.

94. "Vel caeco appareat" (Ad, 331B-E: even a blind man can see something so obvious).

95. "Facile, cum valemus, recta consilia aegrotis damus" (Ad, 249D-250A: how easy it is for us to see the faults of others but not our own).

96. Triumphus Capnionis (pub. 1518; cf. Bö, III, 413-448). "Capnion" is a Greek rendering of the German word "rauchig" from which "Reuchlin" is probably

derived: that Reuchlin himself used the name Capnion, cf. Allen, Ep. 290, p. 556, 1. 30.

97. "Mortuum flagellas" (Ad, 172D: on reproving a man who is innocent of the crimes with which he is charged).

98. Cf. n. 83 above.

99. Concerning those who detract from the character of another in order to enhance their own reputation cf. "Nosce teipsum" (Ad, 258D-259E; Phillips, pp. 10-12); "Te ipsum laudas" (Ad, 627D-628A); "Athos celat latera Lemniae bovis" (Ad, 768A-D); on Erasmus and Reuchlin cf. Allen, XII, pp. 160-161.

100. Exp., par. 68.

101. I wish to thank my friend Keith Palka of the University of Michigan for drawing my attention to the following reference: Dante, Purgatorio, XVII, 115-117; cf. also the Dante reference, n. 450 below.

101a. On those who incautiously give information which can be harmful to themselves and those who relate what they have heard at banquets cf. "Hirundinem sub eodem tecto ne habeas" (Ad, 22A-23A); "Turdus ipse sibi malum cacat" (Ad, 49C-F); "Fenestram aperire" (Ad, 152B-C); "Ovem lupo commisisti" (Ad, 155C-F); "Odi memorem compotorem" (Ad, 262A-F); "Aut bibat, aut abeat" (Ad, 862B); "Fores aperire" (Ad, 862B).

102. "Tuum tibi narro somnium" (Ad, 677F-678A: said of one who pretends to have an intimate acquaintance with the personal affairs of another); cf. also Exp., par. 105.

103. Allen, Ep. 1078, p. 205, n. 38; "Eadem mensura" (Ad, 41E-42A; Phillips, p. 384: with what measure you mete, it shall be measured to you; cf. Matthew, VII, 2).

104. Allen, Ep. 1082 (Introduction); cf. par. 372 below.

105. Hermann Busch, Vallum humanitatis. Cologne: Nic. Caesar, 1518; cf. Allen, Ep. 830, p. 296.

106. Terence, Hecyra, I, ii, 37: on Terence (c. 185-159BC), a Roman comic poet, cf. Harper's, pp. 1538-1542.

107. "Ama tanquam osurus, oderis tanquam amaturus" (Ad, 434A-F: never reveal your vices to others for they could use this information against you; in like measure, never reveal what others say to you in their correspondence); cf. par. 209 below.

108. Exp., par. 70.

109. Matthew, V, 23-24.

110. Herodotus, III, 153-160; M. Justinus, *Epitoma historiarm Philippicarum Pompei Trogi*, I, 10. Zopyrus was a famous Persian subject of Darius who mutilated himself and then fled to the Babylonians and told them that he was a victim of the cruelty of the Persian king. The Babylonians placed him in charge of their troops and he immediately delivered Babylon to Darius' vengeance. As a reward for his self-sacrifice - and the betrayal of the Babylonians - Darius made him satrap of Babylon for life (cf. Harper's, p. 1685).

111. Exp., pars. 76-78; on Erasmus and Brabant cf. Allen, XII, p. 57.

112. Exp., par. 77.

113. Cf. n. 51 above; "Quid ad Mercurium" (Ad, 768E: what has this to do with the matter before us?).

114. Cf. Introduction, n. 5; Allen, XII, p. 88; *Declarationes ad censuras* (LB, IX, 936E-937C); on changing his views cf. n. 83 above; Exp., pars. 81-83; on Erasmus and Cologne cf. Allen, XII, p. 74.

115. "Convivio magistrorum" (Bö, VI, 3-5); cf. Stokes, pp. 291-294.

116. Although Erasmus did as a rule attack only abuses and not individuals (cf. "Ollas ostentare" (Ad, 460D-461D; Phillips, pp. 355-357: a defense of his *Praise of Folly*, stating that he had attacked only vices and not people since he wished only to admonish against wickedness)), he did at least twice attack a person by name, cf. "Esernius cum Pacidiano" (Ad, 580F-583C; Phillips, pp. 361-368: a satirization of Henry Standish (d. 1535), a Franciscan preacher at the court of Henry VIII; cf. also "Auriculam moricus" (Ad, 1191D:

Standish is referred to as an old Scotist and a member of the "triarii," the Old Guard)) and the more famous *Julius Exclusus a Coelis*. Concerning this satire cf. Paul Pascal, trl. and ed., *The Julius Exclusus of Erasmus*. Bloomington, Ind.; Indiana University Press, 1968; J.K. Sowards, "The Two Last Years of Erasmus: Summary, "Review and Speculation," *Studies in the Renaissance* (New York), IX (1962), 161-186; Roland H. Bainton, "Erasmus and Luther and the Dialog Julius Exclusus," *Vierhundertfünfzig Jahre lutherische Reformation. 1517-1967*. (Festschrift für Franz Lau zum 60. Geburtstag). Göttingen: Vandenhoeck und Ruprecht, 1967, pp. 17-26); on Froben cf. Allen, XII, pp. 96-97.

117. Allen,   Ep. 622; on Caesarius cf. Allen, XII, p. 62.

118. *Dialogus novus et mire festivus* (Bö, VI, 301-316).

119. It is impossible to know exactly which dialogues Erasmus had in mind, although Böcking assumes that they were included in the later editions of the EOV (cf. Bö, II, p. 278, n. 18).

120. "Oleum camino addere" (Ad, 71E: to irritate those one cannot appease is but to add fuel to the fire).

121. *Hochstratus ovans dialogus festivissimus* (Bö, VI, 461-488).

122. Allen, Ep. 1165, p. 395, n. 22, Ep. 1195, p. 459, n. 4 and Ep. 1083, p. 211, n. 23.

123. Exp., pars. 85-94; Erasmus on Hebrew cf. Allen, XII, p. 108; on Capito cf. Allen, XII, p. 64.

124. "Ne bos quidem pereat" (Ad, 1049A-1054B: a more or less frank discussion of himself by Erasmus - his goals, methods of procedure, ideals, etc.); cf. n. 15 above.

125. Cf. Introduction, ns. 4-5.

126. On bringing together arguments that have no relevence cf. "Ex harena funiculum nectis" (Ad, 175C-E and 601A-B); "In eburna vagina, plumbeus gladius" (Ad,

272C); "Arena sine calca" (Ad, 508A); cf. par. 172 below.

127. Erasmus' annotated translation of the New Testament is to be found in LB, VI, the Paraphrases in LB, VII. One version of the Paraclesis is in LB, VI, 5-8, an enlarged version in LB, V, 137D-144D; the Apologia is in LB, VI, 17-19; the Ratio verae theologiae in LB, V, 75A-138C. The various Prefaces and the Ratio have appeared in a critical, bi-lingual edition, cf. Gerhard B. Winkler, trl. and ed., Erasmus von Rotterdam: Vorreden zum Neuen Testament/Theologische Methodenlehre, Aus. Schr., Vol. III, 1967. An English version can be found in Olin (TB), pp. 92-106; for a French translation with Introduction cf. Pierre Mesnard, "Le Paraclesis d'Erasme," Bibliothèque d'Humanisme et Renaissance (Paris), XIII:1 (April, 1957), 26-42. For a discussion of the Ratio cf. Bouyer, Erasmus and his Times, pp. 157-175. Concerning the publication of the Novum Instrumentum and the Annotations, as well as the attacks Erasmus suffered because of his labors cf., among many others, the following: August Bludau, Die beiden ersten Erasmus-Ausgaben des Neuen Testaments und ihre Gegner (Part I - on the publication, Part II - on the attacks); Marvin Anderson, "Erasmus the Exegete," Concordia Theological Monthly (St. Louis, Mo.), XL:11 (Dec., 1969), 722-733; Rabil, Erasmus and the New Testament, esp. pp. 115-155; C.A.L. Jarrott, "Erasmus' Biblical Humanism," Studies in the Renaissance (New York), XVII (1970), 119-152; C.A.L. Jarrott, "Erasmus' 'In principio erat sermo': A Controversial Translation," Studies in Philology (Chapel Hill, Uni. of North Carolina)LXI:1 (Jan., 1964), 35-40; Pierre Mesnard, "Humanisme et Théologie dans la controverse entre Erasme et Dorpius," Filosofia (Torino), XIV:4 (Nov., 1963), 885-900 (for an English translation of Erasmus' letter to Dorp in defense of his biblical studies cf. Olin (TB), pp. 55-91; the original version is in Allen, Ep. 337; cf. also Allen, Ep. 304 (from Dorp) to which Ep. 337 is a response and Ep. 347 (again from Dorp) replying to Ep. 337); Béné, Erasme et Saint Augustin, pp. 289-333

(on the attacks by Jacob Latomus); Etienne, _Spiritualisme érasmien et les théologiens louvanistes_, pp. 163-186; Mann, _Erasme et les débuts de la réforme française_, Chs. 2-3; Renaudet, _Etudes érasmienes_, Ch. 6 (on the attacks by the Sorbonne); Allen, Ep. 1037, pp. 108-111 (on the attacks by Edward Lee in 1520); Bataillon, _Erasme et l'Espagne_, pp. 98-105 (on the attacks by Spanish critics); Renaudet, _Erasme et l'Italie_, pp. 225-237 (on the attacks by Italian critics); on the New Testament cf. Allen, XII, pp. 26-27, 33-34, 54-55, 145; on theologians, Allen, XII, p. 175.

128. Exp., pars. 96-110; the letter to Fisher, Allen, Ep. 1129, 11. 6-14; on Duke Ulrich I of Württemberg cf. Allen, XII, p. 187.

129. On being adaptable like a polypus cf. "Polypi mentem obtine" (Ad, 62E-64C; Phillips, p. 384); "Omnium horarum homo" (Ad, 144A-D); "Polypi caput" (Ad, 396E-397B); "Polypi" (Ad, 519A-D).

130. "Aquilae senecta" (Ad, 355C-F: about old men in vigorous health).

131. "The Apotheosis of that Incomparable Worthy, John Reuchlin" (Col., pp. 79-86; LB, I, 689E-692E: celebrates the Christian scholar as a hero in the campaign against obscurantism).

132. On the other hand, however, cf. Erasmus' comments in "Suam quisque homo rem meminit" (Ad, 979F-980A: never allow others to perform any business that concerns you directly); on Salius cf. Allen, IV, p. 299, n. 10.

133. "Quicquid in buccam venerit vel in linguam venerit offundere" (Ad, 209F-210A: on those who display bravery merely by offending someone).

134. Exp., par. 112.

135. "Orci galea" (Ad, 700C-701D: said of those who incite others to villainy but do not want themselves implicated in it); cf. par. 369 below; on Louvain cf. Allen, XII, pp. 128-129.

136. Exp., par. 113 and n. 83 above. Theophrastus (c. 372-c. 287BC) was a Greek philosopher and disciple of Aristotle whom he succeeded as head of the Peripatetic School. He is best remembered for his 30 short _Characters_ - vivid

vignettes on human types and personalities (cf. Harper's, p. 1567).

137. "Camelus saltat" (Ad, 630A-B: the "camel" is a play on the word Carmelite; Baechem was a Carmelite prior who had denounced the Colloquies for containing heretical ideas - cf. Allen, Ep. 878, p. 416, n. 13. Erasmus defended himself before the Theological Faculty of Louvain - cf. Allen, I, I, pp. 24, 1. 36-25, 1. 31 and Ep. 1301 pp. 90-94); Exp., par. 114.

138. "Non est beatus, esse qui se nesciat" (Ad, 1054D-F; Phillips, p. 126: lack of self-knowledge is an all but incurable disease).

139. Cf. par. 68 above.

140. Cf. n. 92 above.

141. Cf. par. 126 below.

142. On the idea of not interfering in the disputes of others cf. "Extra telorum jactum" (Ad, 147E-148B) and "Oderint, dum metuant" (Ad, 676D-F).

143. Cf. n. 83 above.

144. The Opinion was entitled Sententiae condemnatoriae magistrale nomen. Cologne, 1513 - cf. Josephus Hartzheim, Prodromus Historiae Universitatis Coloniensis (quo exhibetur synopsis actorum et scriptorum a Facultate Theologica pro Ecclesia Catholica et Republica). Coloniae Augustae Agrippiensium (Cologne), 1759, p. 15.

145. Exp., par. 116.

146. "Ansam quaerere" (Ad, 152C-F: about looking for a handle or club with which to beat an adversary).

147. Allen, Ep. 1033, p. 103, 11. 148-150; for an English translation of this letter cf. Olin (TB), pp. 134-145; on Albrecht of Mainz cf. Allen, XII, p. 37.

148. Concerning those people who speak confidently about that which they do not know cf. the following adages: "Invita Minerva" (Ad, 44A-B); "Barbae tenus sapientes" (Ad, 104D-E); "Ne sutor ultra crepidam" (Ad, 228A-C); "Velocem tardus assequitur" (Ad, 287E-288C); "Illotis pedibus ingredi" (Ad, 354A-C);

"Illotis manibus" (Ad, 354C-355C); "Inter pueros senex" (Ad, 1002E); cf.
par. 188 below.

149. Exp., par. 117; concerning Erasmus' comments on the Dominicans cf. Allen,
Ep. 1006, p. 43, n. 4 and Ep. 1875, p. 167, 11. 138-154: Erasmus blames
the Dominicans for goading Luther into a position he would not otherwise
have taken; on the Dominicans cf. also Allen, XII, p. 83, on the Franciscans,
Allen, XII, p. 95.

150. Erasmus' writings are filled with rather negative comments about the religious
and monasticism - among many others cf. the following: "The Soldier and the
Carthusian" (Col., pp. 127-133; LB, I, 708A-710D: the military is evil, the
monk here is good and intelligent, although more learned than spiritual (cf.
Surtz, The Praise of Wisdom, pp. 112-114, 294-299); Ecclesiastes (1535) (LB,
V, 1068E: one should not condemn an entire class or profession); "The
Seraphic Funeral" (Col., pp. 500-516; LB, I, 866E-873B: Erasmus here calls
into question some of the basic tenets of the monastic life, especially the
idea that the celibate life is holier than the lay estate; cf. also "The
Sermon" (Col., pp. 462-478; LB, I, 850D-857E) and "The Girl with no Interest
in Marriage" (Col., pp. 99-111; LB, I, 697C-701B)); Erasmus condemned as
superstitious the idea that a monk's habit could ward off the devil (cf.
Ratio (LB, V, 136C-D), De praeparatione ad mortem (LB, V, 1305E) and Allen,
Ep. 447, p. 305, 11. 508-509); since he admired the Franciscans, he said that
the references to them in the Colloquies were there not to censure them but
to correct their weaknesses (cf. Allen, Ep. 2700, pp. 79, 1. 19-82, 1. 150 and
the praise accorded them in the Apotheosis of Reuchlin (Col., pp. 79-86; LB,
I, 689E-692E)); there are more bad monks than good ones (cf. Suppulatio
errorum Beddae (1526) (LB, IX, 647D-E) and Declarationes ad censuras (1532)
(LB, IX, 894D)); Erasmus was tricked into becoming a monk (cf. Allen, Ep.
296, pp. 564-573 and Ep. 309, pp. 29-32 - a jaundiced view of what monastic

266

life was really like); De contemptu mundi (LB, V, 1239A-1262F: Chs. 1 through 11 are written in praise of the monastic life and describe the perils of the secular life; Ch. 12, however, is almost a complete reversal of what was said in the preceeding 11 chapters and it is generally believed that this last chapter was written much later (1521?); "The Well-to-do-Beggars" (Col., pp. 203-217; LB, I, 738A-744E: clothes do not make the monk; also further comments on the supposed distinction between the religious and the secular states); Ecclesiastes (LB, V, 823F-824A: a devout village priest is more estimable than many monks whose lives have made them lazy and dissolute); Olin (TB), pp. 164-191; on the Declarationes, cf. Allen, XII, p. 19, on monks in general, Allen, XII, p. 140.

151. Cf. n. 83 above.

152. Exp., par. 118.

153. Concerning Aleander cf. Exp., pars. 119-122; n. 83 above; Allen, XII, pp. 38-39.

154. "Pluris est oculatus testis unus quam auriti decem" (Ad, 602A-D: the testimony of one eyewitness is better than that of ten who know from hearsay only); cf. par. 205 below.

155. This was in 1507; concerning the unsettled course of the friendship between the two cf. Allen, Ep. 1195, p. 460, n. 47 and Ep. 256, pp. 502-503; the Bishop of Liège was Erard de la Marck (cf. Allen, Ep. 738 (Introduction), pp. 167-168 and Allen, XII, p. 81).

156. Allen, Ep. 980.

157. Cf. n. 20 above.

158. This letter does not seem to be extant.

159. The reference to Aleander as a Jew can be found in Erasmus' colloquy "Penny-Pinching" (Col., pp. 488-499; LB, I, 862D-866E) in which Aleander is portrayed as Verpius, i.e. the circumsized one. This colloquy is in reality a defense of Erasmus' Ciceronianus (1528; LB, 973A-1026C; cf. Allen, XII, pp. 18-19;

for an English version cf. Izora Scott, trl. - ed., _Ciceronianus or a Dialogue on the Best Style of Speaking_. New York: Columbia University Press, 1908; reprinted in _Controversies over the Imitation of Cicero as a Model for Style_. New York: Columbia University Press, 1910, pp. 19-130.) in which Erasmus ridiculed the pedantic imitation of Cicero by many Humanists - especially those in Italy - and denounced the blatant paganism of these modern "Ciceronians" (cf. Allen, XII, p. 71). The French and Italian Humanists were outraged and Erasmus was attacked in turn in the treatise _Oratio pro M. Tullio Cicerone contra Erasmum Roterodamum_ (written 1529, published 1531) in which, among other things, Erasmus was charged with being a drunkard while living in Venice. At first Erasmus thought that Aleander had written the _Oration_ (cf. Allen, Ep. 2736, p. 125, 1. 12; Ep. 2565, p. 370, 11. 25-26; Ep. 2575, p. 391, 11. 5-6, Ep. 2587, p. 407. 1. 11; cf. also Theodor Brieger, _Aleander und Luther (1521)_ (Die vervollständigten Aleander-Depeschen, nebst Untersuchungen über den Wormser Reichstag). Gotha: A. Perthes, 1884, pp. 51-54). In reality the _Oration_ was written by the Italian Humanist Julius Caesar Scaliger (cf. Vernon Hall, "Life of Julius Caesar Scaliger," _Transactions of the American Philosophical Society_ (Philadelphia), New Series, XL:2 (1950), 85-170, esp. 96-114). In the colloquy Erasmus excoriates _en passant_ the niggardliness of the Aldine household (Antronius in the dialogue is Andreas Asulanus, Aldus' father-in-law; cf. also "Acolo non ficu" (Ad, 1093D-E; Phillips, p. 133: on the odd diet of the Italians)), a family he had formerly eulogized in the 1508 edition of the _Adagia_ (cf. "Haud equidem sine mente reor sine numine" (Ad, 402C-406C - the part 403B-406C was added in 1526: a eulogy of Aldus as a great printer and fosterer of learned studies and a praise of Froben as his "Northern successor")). On Italy and the Italians cf. Allen, XII, p. 115, on Scaliger, Allen, XII, p. 165.

160. Cf. n. 79 above.

161. <u>Invectiva in Hieronymum Aleandrum</u> (Mar. 1521; Bö, II, 12.16, esp. p. 16, par. 32).

162. Exp., par. 121; on Erasmus and Rome cf. Allen, XII, p. 162.

163. Cf. n. 89 above.

164. On the idea that kind words are the best medicine for an afflicted spirit and that they can turn away wrath cf. "Aegroto dum anima est, spes est" (Ad, 526D-527A), and "Animo aegrotanti medicus est oratio" (Ad, 744D-745C).

165. Exp., pars. 125-127; on Adrian VI cf. Allen, XII, p. 35.

166. "Dies adimit aegritudinem" (Ad, 556B-D: time not only cures all afflictions but it also brings all things to perfection).

167. Exp., par. 127; concerning deception through flattery cf. "Demulcere caput" (Ad, 725D-E); "Obtrudere palpum" (Ad, 855C-D). Timon, called the Misanthrope, lived during the Peloponnesian Wars (second half of the 5th century BC). As a result of disappointments and the ingratitude of his fellow men, he withdrew completely from the world except for his association with Alcibiades. He is said to have died because he refused to allow a doctor to attend to his broken leg (cf. Harper's, p. 1585; Lucian, <u>Timon</u> and Shakespeare's drama <u>Timon of Athens</u>).

168. "Coenare me doce" (Ad, 840E: do not try to teach others that which you do not know yourself); cf. n. 148 above.

169. Exp., pars. 128-133; on Glapion cf. Allen, XII, p. 102.

170. In Greek mythology Lynceus was the husband of Hypermnestra, the only one of the 50 daughters of Danaus to spare her husband after Danaus had ordered them all to be killed. Lynceus was among the heroes of the Argonaut expedition. He had such keen eyesight that he could look into the earth and espy buried treasure (cf. Harper's, p. 985).

171. The original Latin says: "had eaten bushels of salt together"; on salt and eating together as signs of intimacy and hospitality cf. "Panem ne frangito"

(Ad, 23D; Phillips, p. 383); "Salem et mensam ne praetereas" (Ad, 225B-E; Phillips, p. 385); "Ne a chytropode cibum nondum sacrificatum rapies" (Ad, 231F; Phillips, p. 386); "Nemini fidas nisi cum quo prius modicum salis absumpsens" (Ad, 411D-412D); "Salem et fabam" (Ad, 832E; Phillips, p. 383); "Velut in cratere" (Ad, 1023F-1024A; Phillips, p. 390); "Sal et mensa" (Ad, 1160E-F; Phillips, p. 150).

172. Exp., par. 134.

173. Exp., par. 135; on Caracciolo cf. Allen, XII, p. 64.

174. Exp., par. 136; on Eck cf. Allen, XII, p. 85.

175. Exp., par. 137.

176. I can find no reference to this treatise anywhere else; for some reason it was probably never printed.

177. "Cura esse quod audis" (Ad, 990A: endeavor to be what you desire to be esteemed).

178. Exp., par. 138; on Heigerlin cf. Allen, XII, p. 90.

179. Exp., n. 82.

180. On not censuring a book one has not read, or passing a hasty judgment about something cf. "Aethiopem ex vultu judicio" (Ad, 348C); "Summis naribus olfacere" (Ad, 385A); "Non statim decernendum" (Ad, 914D-E); "Prius antidotum quam venenum" (Ad, 1024B-C); "Non statim finis appareat" (Ad, 1066E-1067A).

181. Exp., par. 139; on Ludwig Baer cf. Allen, XII, p. 52.

182. Exp., par. 139; on Gebwiler cf. Allen, VI, p. 218, n. 129.

183. Exp., par. 140.

184. Exp., Pars. 141-142; on Latomus cf. Allen, XII, p. 122, on Baechem (Egmondanus), Allen, XII, pp. 85-86, on Briard (Atensis), Allen, XII, p. 58.

185. Exp., n. 87.

186. Exp., par. 143; on Lee cf. Allen, Ep. 765 (Introduction), XII, p. 123.

187. Allen, Ep. 1037 (Introduction, pp. 108-111).

188. Conradus Nastadiensis (pseudonym for Wilhelm Nesen), _Eruditi adulescentis_
Chonradi Nastadiensis Germani Dialogus saneque festiuus bilinguium ac
trilinguium, siue de funere Calliopes, etc. Paris: Resch, 1519 (?) (cf.
Allen, Ep. 1061, n. 505 for a discussion of the authorship of the book and
why Wilhelm Nesen published it under his brother's name; the book was
immediately reprinted in Schlettstadt: Schurer, 1520); cf. also Justus
Jonas, _In Eduardum Leum quorundam e sodalitate literaria Erphurdien._
Erasmici nominis studiosorum Epigrammata. Moguntiae (Mainz), 1520. Cf.,
however, Allen, Ep. 998, 11. 61-71 (to Edward Lee, 15 July 1519: Erasmus
threatens him with the proposed attacks by German scholars unless he (Lee)
desists from his attacks on Erasmus).

189. "Evitata Charybdi in Scyllam incidi" (Ad, 183A-184C: on escaping one evil
only to fall into another). Charybdis is a whirlpool on the coast of
Sicily opposite Scylla, a huge rock on the Italian coast. In legend the two
were believed to be the abodes of two monsters who seized vessels traversing
the narrow Straits of Messina (cf. Harper's, pp. 1431-1432; Homer, _Odyssey,_
XII, 73-110, 235-259, 430-444).

190. Exp., pars. 144-147; Allen, Ep. 1228, pp. 568, 1. 46-569, 1. 51: Erasmus
promises Archbishop Warham that he will read Luther's works and see what he
can do for the dignity of the Roman Pontiff and the tranquility of the
Christian religion); on Luther and/or Lutherans cf. Allen, XII, pp. 130-133.

191. Exp., par. 33.

192. Exp., par. 150.

193. On the Gospels as the basis of the religious life and true piety cf., among
others, _Enchiridion militis christiani_ (LB, V, 1A-66C; Hajo Holborn, ed.,
Desiderius Erasmus - Ausgewählte Werke. München: C.H. Beck, 1933, pp. 1-136;
Aus. Schr., Vol. I, pp. 56-375; for an English translation cf. John P.
Dolan, trl. and ed., _The Essential Erasmus_. New York: Mentor-Omega Books,
1964, pp. 24-93; Allen, XII, p. 21). For a discussion of the treatise cf.

Rabil, pp. 52-58; Bainton, pp. 65-71; Phillips (2), Ch. 2; Auer; Kohls (1), Vol. I, Ch. 3; Béné, pp. 127-186. On true piety as opposed to superstition cf. "The Shipwreck" (Col., pp. 138-146; LB, I, 712B-715F; cf. also LB, IX, 942C-E, 1086C-F); "Exorcism or the Specter" (Col., pp. 231-237; LB, I, 749A-752E); "Alchemy" (Col., pp. 238-245; LB, I, 752E-756A); "Beggar Talk" (Col., pp. 248-254; LB, I, 757D-759D); from Folly (LB, IV, 441C-441D); on images and indulgences cf. Allen, XII, p. 114.

194. "Laterem lavas" (Ad, 169D-E: on those who use rhetoric or verbiage only to make that which is false appear to be true).

195. "Thesaurus carbones erant" (Ad, 346E-347A: on those who exert great labor only to realize something of little worth).

196. Quintillian, Institutio oratoria, XII, i, 35; Marcus Fabilus Quintilianus (c. 35-95AD) was a Roman rhetorician and teacher. His most famous work, Institutio oratoria, is an elaborate treatise on the goals and methods of education and literary criticism (cf. Harper's, pp. 1356-1357).

197. On the power of bribes and flattery cf. "Fumos vendere" (Ad, 128D-130A; Phillips, p. 51) and "Auro loquente nihil pollet quaevis oratio" (Ad, 786D-F).

198. Cf. n. 71 above; Allen, Ep. 1041, p. 121, l. 13: "Ego nec Reuchlinista sum nec ullius humanae factionis".

199. Allen, Ep. 1041 (a letter appended to Marten's enlarged edition of the Colloquiorum formulae (c. Nov. 1519) (cf. Ep. 909, Introduction) and described on the title-page as "Contestatio adversus seditiosas calumnias"); on the Colloquies cf. Allen, XII, pp. 18-19.

200. Exp., par. 144.

201. "Praestat habere acerbos" (Ad, 1020B-C: it is better to have an open enemy than a false friend).

202. Allen, Ep. 872, pp. 409, l. 12-410, l. 19: on Erasmus' initial favorable impression of Luther and his theses (Oct. 1518).

203. "Satius est recurrere quam currere male" (Ad, 347B-C: it is better to desist and reverse one's position than to remain in error).

204. "Contra stimulum calces" (Ad, 131A-C: it is foolish to contend with persons capable of inflicting greater injury on you than you can on them).

205. "In quadrum redigere" (Ad, 368E-F; 1210B-C: to "act upon the square" is to act consistently).

206. Achates was a companion and friend of Aeneas in his wanderings and was styled by Vergil as the "fidus Achates"; his fidelity has now become proverbial (cf. Aeneid, I, 188).

207. Paraphrase of the Gospel According to Saint Luke (LB, VII, 279A-488F); cf. also "The Sermon or Merdardus" (Col., pp. 462-478; LB, I, 850D-857E) in which Erasmus rebukes the Imperial Court preacher Medardus for attacking his (Erasmus') interpretation of a passage in the "Magnificat" (Luke, I, 46-49; cf. LB, VII, 292D and LB, VI, 225F-227C). Medardus preached at the Diet of Augsburg (1530) before King Ferdinand of Hungary and Erasmus was soon informed of the attack (cf. Allen, Ep. 2408, pp. 86, 1.7-87, 1. 18) as well as the rebuke Medardus received from the Bishop of Vienna (cf. Allen, Ep. 2503, pp. 278, 1. 1 - 279. 1. 5). In the colloquy the man's name is changed from Medardus (mustard) to Merdardus (excrement).

208. In a letter to Gerard Geldenhauer (9 Sept. 1520, Allen, Ep. 340, 11. 25-26) Erasmus stated that the whole "tragedy" was begun by the stupidity of certain monks and their hatred of good letters. Later he blamed the Dominicans for goading Luther into his heretical positions (Allen, Ep. 1875, p. 167, 11. 138-154). In a letter to Jodocus Jonas (13 June 1521, Allen, Ep. 1211, pp. 508, 1. 13 - 514, 1. 243; Olin (TB), pp. 164-191), on the other hand, he eulogizes the Franciscan Vitrier. Erasmus was always willing, however, to throw little digs at monks in general - witness his statement (attributed to the Franciscans of Cologne, but found only in Erasmus' letter)

273

that it was he "who laid the egg that Luther hatched" (Allen, Ep. 1528, p. 609, 1. 11).

209. Exp., par. 204 and n. 125; on the "Catalogue" cf. Allen, XII, p. 18.

210. Cf. par. 123 above.

211. Exp., par. 222.

212. "Aurum igni probatum" (Ad, 982E-983B; Phillips, p. 390; I Peter, I, 7: on gold that is tried in fire).

213. On Vertumnus cf. Exp., n. 76; in classical mythology Proteus was a sea god who had the power to assume many different shapes. If he was caught and held fast through his many changes, he would be compelled to answer questions truthfully. In one legend, Menelaus, on his return voyage from Troy, caught Proteus and held him until he told Menelaus how to return home (cf. Harper's, pp. 1323-1324); on Polypus cf. n. 129 above; cf. also "Proteo mutabilior" (Ad, 473B-474A; Phillips, p. 388; Psalm XCI, 6: on protean changes).

214. "Prudens in flammam mitto manum" (Ad, 852B: do not put your hand into the fire, i.e. do not become embroiled in contentions).

215. "Compressis manibus" (Ad, 415C; Phillips, p. 388; Proverbs, XXIV, 33: with folded hands, i.e. in a manner of supplication).

216. Exp., par. 205.

217. "Inimicus et invidus vicinorum oculus" (Ad, 722D-723A; 1127B: an enemy is really like an extra eye since his enmity puts one on his guard - a man does not act incautiously if he knows that he is being watched).

218. Exp., par. 162.

219. Undoubtedly a reference to Thomas More's anti-Luther treatise Eruditissimi viri Guilelmi Rossei (pseudonym of Thomas More) opus elegans ... quo pulcherrime retegit ac refellit insanas Lutheri calumnias: quibus inuictissimum ... regem Henricum euis nominis octauum ... insectatur.

<u>excusum denuo diligentissime</u> ... <u>adiunctis indicibus opera</u> ... Ioannis

Carcellij (Richard Pynson): Londini, 1523; on Mazolini (Prieras) cf.

Allen, XII, p. 137; on Todiscus (Radinus), Allen, IV, p. 409; on de Vio,

Allen, XII, p. 183; on Catarinus, Allen, XII, p. 66; on Eck, Allen, XII,

p. 85; on Goclenus, Allen, XII, p. 103; on Lefèvre (Faber Stapulensis),

Allen, XII, pp. 90-91; on Hoogstraten (Hochstrat), Allen, XII, p. 111;

on the Sorbonne, Allen, XII, p. 150; on Guistiniani, Allen, III, p. 278,

n. 356; on Louvain, Allen, XII, pp. 128-129; on Latomus, Allen, XII, p. 122;

on Vincent Theodorici, Allen, XII, p. 175 and Allen, IV, Ep. 1196, p. 463;

on Marlianus, Allen, XII, p. 135; on Remacle (Rimaclus), Allen, II, p. 241;

on Henry VIII, Allen, XII, p. 109; on Fisher, Allen, XII, p. 93; on Thomas

More, Allen, XII, pp. 141-142; on Stunica, Allen, XII, p. 172.

220. "Manum non verterim, digitum non porrexerim" (Ad, 120F-121B: I do not give

a straw what they say about me).

221. "Elephantus non capit murem, nec aquila muscas" (Ad, 359B-C: a brave man

does not fight with cowards nor does an intelligent mind concern itself

about the censures of insignificant scribblers); cf. par. 404 below.

222. Exp., par. 210.

223. "Herculi labores" (Ad, 707C-717B; Phillips, pp. 190-209: concerning works

which are useful to others but bring only envy to the doer - this is the

attitude Erasmus seems to have assumed toward his own labors; envy can be

compared with the Lernean Hydra).

224. On the idea that perseverance will eventually win out cf. "Fortes fortuna

adjuvat" (Ad, 88B-D); "Multis ictibus dejicitur quercus" (Ad, 331E-F);

"Non statim finis apparet" (Ad, 1066E-1067A; Phillips, p. 127).

225. "Mors omnibus communis" (Ad, 923B: we should frequently meditate on the

fact that eventually we must all die).

226. Exp., par. 123.

227. "Eodem collyrio mederi omnibus" (Ad, 1127B-C; Phillips, p. 390: to lack the power to be all things to all men is the same as using the same medicine for all diseases).

228. On the defense of good letters cf. the new critical edition of the Antibarbari (LB, X, 1691C-1744E; Allen, XII, p. 17) in J.H. Waszink, et al., eds., Opera omnia (recognita et adnotatione critica instructa notisgue illustrata). Amsterdam: North-Holland Publishing Co., 1969, Vol. I, pp. 1-138; Rabil, pp. 20-25. Erasmus' thoughts on a pure and simple theology are stated best in his Enchiridion and Ratio verae theologiae, cf. ns. 127 and 193 above.

229. Exp., 202.

230. "Asinum sub froeno currere doces" (Ad, 167D-E: on doing the impossible, among other things obtaining affection without returning it).

231. Cf. par. 128 and n. 154 above.

232. Carneades of Cyrene (c. 214/212 - 129/128BC) was the founder of the Third New Academy and, following the scepticism of Arcesilaus, taught that knowledge is impossible and thus there is no criterion for truth (cf. Frederick Copelston, A History of Philosophy. Westminster, Md.: The Newman Press, 1950, Vol. I, pp. 414-417; Cicero, De finibus, V, vi, 16-17, De natura deorum, I, ii, 4-5, v., 11, II, lxv, 162, III, xii, 29, xvii, 44; Lactantius, Divinae institutiones, V, 14).

233. "A teneris unguiculis" (Ad, 283A-B: we are born with certain character traits and often there is nothing we can do to alter them).

234. Cf., however, Erasmus' discussion of the adage "In vino veritas" (Ad, 267B-268C: wine opens the heart and we speak what we think).

235. Cf. "The Poetic Feast" (Col., pp. 158-176; LB, I, 720D-727F: a portrayal of a scholars' feast in which learned stories are narrated and biblical exegesis and textual criticism are discussed without rancor or personal abuse).

276

236. Cf. par. 84 and n. 107 above.

237. Exp., par. 32.

238. Exp., par. 35; "Cognatio movet invidiam" (Ad, 1136D: familiarity breeds contempt or we envy only those who have better success than we do, never those who are our inferiors).

239. On Caria (a later province on the eastern border of the Roman Empire) as a symbol of something completely useless cf. Homer, Illiad, IX, 378; as a symbol of bellicosity, Allen, XI, p. 174.

240. Exp., par. 200.

241. Exp., pars. 33, 118, 168-169; Allen, XII, pp. 70, 149, 156.

242. Concerning Erasmus' negative views on indulgences, relics, pilgrimages, etc. cf. "Artem quaevis alit terra" (Ad, 275B-E; Phillips, pp. 37, 125); "Mithragyrtes non daduchus" (Ad, 1135B); "Rash Vows" (Col., pp. 4-7; LB, I, 639A-640C); "A Pilgrimage for Religion's Sake" (Col., pp. 285-312; LB, I, 774C-787D); "On the Utility of the Colloquies" (Col., pp. 625-627; 902D-903A).

243. Exp., par. 93.

244. I Corinthians, XIII, 7.

245. On the idea of not interfering with those in high places or fighting against those with superior strength cf. "A fabis abstineto" (Ad, 18B-19D); "Irritare crabones" (Ad, 50D-51B); "Malum bene conditium ne moveris" (Ad, 51C-D); "In caelum jacularis" (Ad, 179D-E); "Ne gladium tollas mulier" (Ad, 568A-B); "Dentem dente rodere" (Ad, 593A); "Clavam extorquere Herculi" (Ad, 990C-E); cf. par. 301 below.

246. Erasmus' hatred of war and the ravages which follow in its wake is expressed again and again in his writings - among many others cf. "Sero sapiunt Phryges" (Ad, 37F-38B; Phillips, p. 124); "In seditione vel Androclides belli ducem agit" (Ad, 480C-E); "Spartam nactus es, hanc orna" (Ad, 551D-55D; Phillips,

pp. 300-308); "Bellum haudquaquam lachrymosum" (Ad, 590F-591C; Phillips, p. 113); "Ut fici oculis incumbunt" (Ad, 653E-655C; Phillips, pp. 358-361); "Dulce bellum inexpertis" (Ad, 951B-970E; Phillips, pp. 308-353); Querela pacis (LB, IV, 625-642; for a critical edition cf. Aus. Schr., Vol., V, pp. 359-451; an English version in Dolan, Essential Erasmus, pp. 174-204; a French translation and analysis by Elise Bagdat, La 'Querela Pacis' d'Erasme. Paris: Presses Universitaires de France, 1924; José Chapiro, Erasmus and Our Struggle for Peace. Boston: Beacon Press, 1950 (Introduction, translation of the text and notes by Chapiro)); "The Soldier and the Carthusian" (Col., pp. 127-133; LB, I, 708A-710D); "The Funeral" (Col., pp. 357-373; LB, I, 810A-817C); "Charon" (Col., pp. 388-394; LB, I, 822C-824D); "Cyclops" (Col., pp. 415-422; LB, I, 831C-833F). Erasmus also attacked war and military matters in his Julius Exclusus, Praise of Folly and the Institutio principis Christiani; cf. also Allen, Ep. 288, pp. 551-554, Ep. 858, pp. 365 and 371, Ep. 1756, p. 420, XII, p. 28.

247. "Fabarum arrosor" (Ad, 1085B-D: on the sale of public offices, with reference also to the bribes openly offered to those who elect the Popes and Emperors).

248. The original speaks of the shamelessness of the "indulgentiariorum, compositionariorium, dispensationariorum, bullariorum", i.e. those functionaries in charge of papal indulgences, decrees, dispensations and bulls.

249. "Culicem colant" (Ad, 948A-C; Phillips, p. 27: to stress trifles and ceremonies is to forget the nature of true piety); Allen, Ep. 858, p. 364, 1. 97 (Christ requires of us nothing but a pure and sincere life); Isaiah, I, 10-17 (God desires only a pure heart, not sacrifices; cf. also Psalm, L).

250. "Ventres" (Ad, 657C-658C; Phillips, pp. 80, 151: an outburst against medieval glosses); Allen, Ep. 858, p. 365, 1. 144 (matters of faith should be expressed as concisely and simply as possible).

251. "A Fish Diet" (Col., pp. 312-157; 787D-810A: on Christian liberty versus

"Judaic legalism", i.e. the contrast between the Law and the Gospel or the "letter" and the "spirit"; in this regard cf. also Allen, Ep. 1887, pp. 199,1.9 - 200, 1. 21.); De interdictio esu carnium (LB, IX, 1197A-1214E: on fasting and Erasmus' hatred of fish; cf. also Allen, Ep. 1353, pp. 262-270 and Declarationes ad censuras (LB, IX, 949E-953A)); "The Profane Feast" (Col., pp. 591-614; LB, I, 660A-670A: on fasting cf. pp. 599-607); "On the Usefulness of the Colloquies" (Col., pp. 634-635); Allen, Ep. 1300, p. 88, 11. 29-37 (the fasting urged by Christ must be distinguished from the dietary regulations under the Mosaic Law); Allen, Ep. 1301, p. 93, 11. 60-67 (Erasmus questions whether prelates can obligate Christians on such matters under pain of sin; cf. Declarationes ad censuras (LB, IX, 933B-934B); Allen, XII, p. 91.

252. "Ignavis semper feriae sunt" (Ad, 586E-587C; Phillips, pp. 267-269: for the lazy it is always a holiday; on the evils which follow upon too many feast days - they lead men to evil pastimes and are a plague on the Church); cf. also Erasmus' exegesis of Romans, XIX, 1-6 (LB, VI, 639E-640E); similar sentiments are expressed by Martin Luther in his An Open Letter to the German Nobility, cf. Three Treatises. Philadelphia: Fortress Press, 1960, pp. 73-74.

253. Erasmus' writings are replete with discussions about the various aspects of married life, virginity and the religious life; among others cf. Institutio christiani matrimonii (1526; LB, V, 615A-724B; in the defense of same cf. LB, IX, 937C-938A); Vidua christiana (1526; LB, V, 724B-766E); "Mulierum exitia" (Ad, 689D-F; Phillips, p. 119: upholds the personal rights of women, their intellectual interests, etc.); "Courtship" (Col., pp. 86-98; LB, I, 629E-697C); "The Girl with no Interest in Marriage" (Col., pp. 99-111; LB, I, 697C-701B: Erasmus denies that celibacy is superior to the married state; cf. also his statement "Angelica res est virginitas, at humana quaedam res est

coniugium" (LB, I, 419F) and Allen, Ep. 604, p. 17, n. 10); "The Repentant Girl" (Col., pp. 111-114; LB, I, 701B-702B: a girl becomes a nun against the advice of others but quickly repents her decision and leaves the convent since she realizes that she was not called to that state in life; cf. also LB, IX, 941E-F); "Marriage" (Col., pp. 114-127; LB, I, 702B-708A: sound advice on the essential ingredients of a happy marriage; the girl involved is Jane Colt, the husband is Thomas More; cf. Allen, Ep. 999, p. 18, 11. 168-171; cf. Telle, Erasme et le septieme sacrement, pp. 153-184, 329-340 and Surtz, The Priase of Wisdom, pp. 228-257); marriage is spiritually beneficial (LB, V, 692E), Christ did not enjoin celibacy (LB, IX, 1201C), why pretend that concubinage is better than marriage? (LB, IX, 1201A-1202A); "The Young Man and the Harlot" (Col., pp. 153-158; LB, I, 718D-720D; for a defense of his treatment of the penitent harlot cf. Allen, Ep. 2037, p. 460, 11. 22-25 and Allen, Ep. 2300, pp. 408,1.109 - 409, 1. 114); "The Abbot and the Learned Lady" (Col., pp. 217-223; LB, I, 744E-746D: Erasmus praises learned women and urges that all girls be educated; cf. his praises of Thomas More's educational methods - Allen, Ep. 1233, pp. 578,1.103 - 579, 1. 149; cf. also Institutio christiani matrimonii (LB, V, 716C-717B)); "The New Mother" (Col., pp. 267-285; LB, I, 766A-774C: advice on the care of babies and the education of children); "A Marriage in Name Only" (Col., pp. 401-412; LB, I, 826E-830E: a tirade against parents who force their children to marry for wealth or position even though the partner is diseased, here with syphilis; cf. also Allen, Ep. 1593, p. 137, 11. 85-90 and "Inns" (Col., p. 150), Institutio christiani matrimonii (LB, V, 667A-668D)); cf. also Hutten's treatise on syphilis, written from first-hand experience, De morbo Gallico (1519; Bö, V, 399-497).

254. "Summum jus summa injuria" (Ad, 374D-375A: to adhere unwaveringly to the letter of the law can quickly kill its spirit); that Erasmus considered the

cult of saints and relics to be such a danger cf. "The Shipwreck" (Col., pp. 138-146; LB, I, 712B-715F), but more especially "A Pilgrimage for Religion's Sake" (Col., pp. 285-312; LB, I, 774C-787D); cf. further Allen, Ep. 2037, pp. 460,1.26 - 461, 1. 29 and Allen, Ep. 2443, p. 163, 11. 220-221.

255. On false piety, ignorance of the clergy, more attention to ecclesiastical garb than true piety, money-grubbing in the Church, etc. cf. "Barbae tenus sapientes" (Ad, 104D-E); "In diem vivere" (Ad, 322D-F); "Illotis manibus" (Ad, 354C-355C; Phillips, pp. 265-267); "A mortuo tributum auferre" (Ad, 432D-433A; Phillips, pp. 37, 96, 225); "Ut fici oculis incumbunt" (Ad, 653E-655C; Phillips, pp. 358-361); "Leonis exuvium super Crocoton" (Ad, 849E-850A; Phillips, p. 265); "Quod volumus sanctum est" (Ad, 1101F-1102A; Phillips, p. 132).

256. Cf. Introduction, n. 44.

257. On the idea that it is a waste of time to admonish the illiterate or the immoral person and that one is wholly lost when by his efforts he causes that which he wanted to prevent cf. "Cyclops, or the Gospel Bearer" (Col., pp. 415-422; LB, I, 831C-833F: a thrust at Oecolampadius (p. 417) and the Anabaptists; cf. also Allen, Ep. 2149, pp. 137,1.4 - 138, 1. 50); "Cibum in matellam ne inmittas" (Ad, 19E); "Nullus sum" (Ad, 130D-E and 1199A); "Surdo oppedere" (Ad, 169C); "Surdo canis; surdo fabulam narras" (Ad, 178C-E); "Anulus aureus in naribus suis" (Ad, 271F-272C).

258. Exp., par. 194.

259. "Malum vas non frangitur" (Ad, 1007D: an evil man who is watchful can often seize many of the world's goods which a good man deserves but does not have).

260. On the idea that we should all conform to the station of life into which we were born and a satire on the poor/try to emulate the rich cf. "Tecum habita" (Ad, 255D-E); "Intra tuam pelliculam te contine" (Ad, 256F-257D); "Simia simia est, etiamsi aurea gestet insignia" (Ad, 265A-C); "Fluvius cum mari

certas" (Ad, 360C-D); "Caput artis decere quod facias" (Ad, 1054B-C).

261. On Erasmus' negative views on gambling cf. "Knucklebones, or the Game of Tali" (Col., pp. 432-441; LB, I, 838A-841F); "Si crebro jacias, aliud alias jeceris" (Ad, 72F-73C); "Nec uno dignus" (Ad, 305F-306B); "Non Chius, sed Cius" (Ad, 451C-F); "Aut ter sex, aut tres tesserae" (Ad, 511B-D); "Chius ad Coum" (Ad, 630B-D); "Midas in tesseris consultor optimus" (Ad, 682F-683A).

262. "Nec obolum habet, unde restim emat" (Ad, 131E: on those who have completely dissipated their wealth or patrimony).

263. "Odit cane pejus et angue" (Ad, 676F-677A: like a mad dog who passionately hangs on to an object, this type of man will allow no single word to be said against the object of his passionate love).

264. "Sponde, noxa praesto est" (Ad, 260E-261A: one cannot be responsible for the actions of everyone else).

265. "Non inest remedium adversus sycophantae morsum" (Ad, 592C-D: since there is no remedy against slander, one ought to treat it with contempt - innocence will vindicate itself in the end).

266. Matthew, V, 9.

267. LB, VII, 808D-E, 816F-817A (we are all guilty of sin and evil, any good that we do should be acknowledged as of Christ).

268. Erasmus should perhaps have recalled the adages "Duabus sedere sellis" (Ad, 262F-263A: by trying to please both parties, one ends up despised by both) and "Ne Jupiter quidem omnibus placet" (Ad, 626E-627A: no matter what you do, like Jupiter you cannot please everyone); cf. also par. 416 below.

269. Assertionis Lutheranae confutatio per ... Ioannem (Fisher) Roffensem Episcopum, etc. In aedibus... Michaelis Hillerii: Apud inclytam Antwerpiam, 1523; on Fisher cf. Allen, XII, p. 93.

270. "Ubi amici ibi opes" (Ad, 121E-122A: it is better to have friends than wealth for true friends constitute riches).

271. On our duty to aid those in need cf. "Tollenti onus auxiliare, deponenti

282

nequaquam" (Ad, 20D-21A) and "Par pari referre" (Ad, 41A-E).

272. For a concise expression of Erasmus' view of Christian Humanism as the "cause of Christ" cf. "The Godly Feast" (Col., pp. 46-78; LB, I, 672B-689E).

273. That we should live from day to day and not worry about tomorrow, since Christ will look after us cf. "In diem vivere" (Ad, 322D-F; Phillips, p. 387) and "Ultra peram sapere" (Ad, 842F-843A; Phillips, p. 389).

274. Exp., pars. 39, 127, 156, 188.

275. Cf. Introduction, n. 10; on the <u>Paraphrases</u> cf. Roland H. Bainton, "The Paraphrases of Erasmus," <u>Archiv für Reformationsgeschichte</u> (Gütersloh), LVII:1-11 (1966) 67-76; Joseph Coppens, "Les idées reformistes d'Erasme dans les Préfaces aux Paraphrases du Nouveau Teastament" in <u>Scrinium Lovaniense</u>. Ed. by Etienne van Cauwenbergh. Gembloux: Duculot (Series: Louvain. Université catholique), 1961, pp. 344-371; E.J. Devereux, "The Publication of the English 'Paraphrases' of Erasmus," <u>Bulletin of the John Rylands Library</u> (Manchester), LI (1969), 348-367; Rudolf Padberg, "Glaubenstheologie und Glaubensverkündigung bei Erasmus von Rotterdam, dargestellt auf der Grundlage der Paraphrase zum Römerbrief" in <u>Verkündigung und Glaube</u>. <u>Festgabe für Franz X. Arnold</u>. Ed. by T. Filthaut and J.A. Jungmann. Freiburg: Herder, 1958, pp. 58-75; Rabil, pp. 128-180; Margaret Roper's translation of Erasmus' exegesis of the Lord's Prayer is reprinted in <u>Moreana</u> (Angers), VII (1965), 9-63; Hermann Schlingensiepen, "Erasmus als Exeget auf Grund seiner Schriften zu Matthäus," <u>Zeitschrift für Kirchengeschichte</u> (Stuttgart), XLVIII (1929), 16-57; Winkler, <u>Erasmus von Rotterdam und die Einleitungsschriften zum Neuen Testament</u>; Allen, XII, pp. 26-27.

276. Allen, Ep. 1324 (1 Dec. 1522) and Ep. 1138 (23 Jan. 1523); cf. Exp., par. 39.

277. "Spontanea molestia" (Ad, 1055C-D; Phillips, p. 126: like children, books are one's own responsibility and must be defended and improved).

278. Exp., pars. 71, 219-220.

279. Exp., pars. 39-40; on Schiner cf. Allen, XII, p. 166.

280. Exp., par. 146.

281. Exp., par. 158.

282. "Sileni Alcibiadis" (Ad, 770C-782C; Phillips, pp. 269-296: Christ is like a Silenus - poor on the outside but rich in spirit; the apostles followed their Master in this, so should all bishops and popes; there is more wisdom in a simple soul taught by the Holy Spirit than in all the great Doctors of the Church; scripture and the sacraments also resemble a Silenus - simple and plain and yet spirit-filled; popes rich in the world's goods are in no way like Christ for they tend to oppress the Church for the sake of wealth - the same is true of all bishops; warring princes are a plague on Christendom; let bishops be like Christ and not robber barons; popes are soldiers but their fight is against pride, lust, simony, anger, irreligion, etc.; there follows then a discussion of the true virtues of popes and bishops); cf. par. 252 below.

283. Exp., par. 148.

284. Exp., pars. 45, 206-207.

285. "Tempus omnia revelat" (Ad, 527F-528E: time will tell the truth); "Res indicabit" (Ad, 815C-F: the event will show where the truth lay).

286. I Book of Kings, XXI, 13-15.

287. "Bonus dux bonum reddit comitem" (Ad, 333C-F: where there is a good master, there are also good servants).

288. Exp., par. 160.

289. Exp., pars. 161-162.

290. Exp., par. 160.

291. Exp., par. 161.

292. Exp., par. 162.

293. Exp., pars. 118, 158, 177.

294. Exp., par. 169.

295. Exp., par. 169.

296. Exp., par. 188.

297. "Toto coelo errare" (Ad, 48B-C: one can be wrong in his opinion and mistake the meaning of a passage).

298. Cf. n. 282 above; on the Paraclesis cf. n. 127 above.

299. Exp., par. 183.

300. Exp., par. 184.

301. "Nosce teipsum" (Ad, 258D-259E: if one truly knows himself he will be slow in censuring others).

302. "Quo transgressus" (Ad, 935A-F: on the necessity of self-examination).

303. Isaiah, XL, 6.

304. Exodus, XXII, 28.

305. "Salem lingere" (Ad, 891D-E: on reproving the vices of the great; not only teach but also witness to the truth!).

306. Exp., par. 232.

307. Exp., par. 210.

308. "Babylonian Captivity of the Church", trl, by A.T.W. Steinhäuser, in Martin Luther: Three Treatises. Philadelphia: Fortress Press, 1960, pp. 115-260; on Duke Frederick cf. Allen, XII, pp. 95-96, on Spalatin, Allen, XII, p. 170.

309. "Caudae pilos equinae paulatim evellere" (Ad, 331F-332B: deliberation is more effective than violence).

310. Acts of the Apostles, VIII, 20.

311. Acts of the Apostles, VIII, 22.

312. Erasmus' quotation "Veniatis, domine Henrice, ego docebo vos" is not a direct quotation of Luther's original statement, cf. "Accede, gloriose Thomista, ad ferulam, docebo te, quid sit pugnare dogmata" in Contra Henricum Regem Angliae (1522: D. Martin Luthers Werke. Kritische Gesamtausgabe (Weimarer

Ausgabe). Weimar: Hermann Böhlaus Nachfolger, 1907, Vol. X, 2. Abt., p. 189, 11. 19-20.

313. Exp., pars. 153, 206-208.

314. "Capra Scyria" (Ad, 373A-C; Zenobius, II, 18 (Leutsch, Vol. I, p. 36)).

315. Exp., par. 191.

316. Exp., par. 193.

317. Cf. n. 156 above.

318. Cf. Introduction, n. 37.

319. Exp., par. 220.

320. Exp., par. 222.

321. Exp., pars. 218, 229-230, 269.

322. Exp., pars. 210-215.

323. Bulla decimi Leonis contra errores Martini Lutheri et sequacium (Bö, V, 301.334; on the various editions cf. Bö, I, 61-62).

324. "Quae uncis sunt unguibus, ne nutrias" (Ad, 21C-D: do not cherish a deceitful person as a friend for eventually he will also turn on you); cf. par. 288 below.

325. Exp., par. 180; this remark was made in a letter to Spalatin, cf. Allen, Ep. 1119, 11. 40-41 ("Not always is the truth to be put forth. And it makes a difference in what manner it is put forth").

326. Matthew, XVI, 20.

327. Luke, XXII, 67; Annas was appointed High Priest by Quirinus, Proconsul of Syria, in c. 7AD and was deposed by Valerius Gratus, Procurator of Judea, in 14 AD. His son-in-law Caiaphas became High Priest in c. 27 AD. The first hearing of Jesus was held before Annas who then sent Him bound to Caiaphas (cf. Luke, III, 2, John, XVIII, 13, Acts, IV 6). Caiaphas presided at the council which condemned Jesus to death and took part in the trial of Peter and John (cf. Matthew, XXVI, 57-68, Acts, IV, 6).

328. Matthew, VII, 6.

329. Acts, II, 14-40.

330. Acts, XVII, 17-31.

331. I Corinthians, IV, 1.

332. "Bos in lingua" (Ad, 268C-269B: on those who, either through fear or prudence, do not make their opinions known; also on those who are bribed into silence).

333. "Inscita confidentiam parit" (Ad, 1066C-E: Phillips, p. 127: those who are the most violent are the least artful and those who know the least have no modesty in stating their ideas because they believe they know everything).

334. St. Hilary (c. 283/285-13 Jan. 368) was a Gaulish prelate and theologian, noted primarily for his writings against the Arian heresy. He was elevated to the bishopric of Poitiers in 353. His chief writings are the treatises De Trinitate and De Synodis. He was declared a Doctor of the Church in 1852 (cf. Catholic Encyclopedia (1910 ed.), VII, 349-350). The Arians were the followers of Arius, a deacon of Alexandria, who in the 4th century maintained that the Son is of a nature similar to but not the same as that of the Father, thus denying the divinity of Christ. This teaching was condemned in 325 by the Council of Nicaea.

335. St. Cyprian (c. 200-14 Sept. 258) was a Church Father, bishop and martyr. As bishop of Carthage (from 248 to his death) he urged compassion for the Christian apostates who fell away from the Church during the persecutions under Decius in 250. He distributed all his wealth to the poor and worked unceasingly for Church unity. His manifold theological writings are said to have later exercised a great influence on St. Augustine. He was beheaded under Valerian (cf. Catholic Encyclopedia (1910 edition), IV, 583-589).

336. Flavius Julius Constantius (6 Aug. 317-3 Nov. 361) was the third son of Constantine I (the Great) and Roman Emperor from 353 to 361. He personally

favored the Arian sect and consequently banished all orthodox bishops. He died while marching to attack his cousin Julian (later called the Apostate) who, as Caesar in Gaul (from 355 to 361), had been proclaimed Emperor by his soldiers (cf. <u>Oxford Classical Dictionary</u> (2nd edition), p. 282).

337. Felix, Roman governor, resident in Caesarea (cf. Acts, XXIII, 122-135, XXIV, 1-27); Festus, governor after Felix (cf. Acts, XXV, 1-12, XXVI, 24-32); Agrippa, i.e. Herod Agrippa II, son of King Herod mentioned in Acts, XII, 1-25 (cf. Acts, XXV, 13-27, XXVI, 1-32).

338. Concerning slight offenses treated as serious crimes cf. "Litem parit lis, noxa item noxam parit" (Ad, 333C) and "Elephantem ex musca facis" (Ad, 359A-B).

339. Exp., par. 155.

340. Exp., par. 157; cf. also par. 273 and n. 324 above.

341. Exp., pars. 226-228.

342. "Quid nisi victis dolor" (Ad, 583F-584C: pity and friendship are emotions incompatible with one another); cf. par. 403 below.

343. Macarius Aesopus, VII, 83 (Leutsch, Vol. II, p. 210); "Ficulnus" (Ad, 295F-296C, esp. 296B).

344. Exp., pars. 237-238.

345. On those who readily criticize others but do not recognize their own short-comings cf. "Tuis te pingam coloribus" (Ad, 153C-D); "Aedibus in nostris quae prava, aut recta gerantur" (Ad, 254E-255C); "In se descendere" (Ad, 255C-D); "Festucam ex alterius oculo ejiare" (Ad, 256D-F; Matthew, VII, 1-5).

346. "The Old Men's Chat, or the Carriage" (Col., pp. 189-203; LB, I, 732E-738F: good examples are to be followed, bad ones shunned; basically the Erasmian program for leading a good life).

347. Plutarch, <u>Moralia</u>, 1090F ("Disputatio qua docetur ne suaviter quidem viri posse secundum Epicuri decreta", VI, 4); Macarius Aesopus, III, 69 (Leutsch, Vol. II, p. 162).

348. "Malo accepto stultus sapit" (Ad, 38E-39E: some men must suffer before
they learn).

349. "Cornix scorpium" (Ad, 50B-C: those who plot evil for others will find
that it often recoils on themselves); "Malum consilium consultori pessimum"
(Ad, 73C-74E: evil counsel is most pernicious to those who give it);
"Captantes capti sumus" (Ad, 372B-C: if one ridicules another he will himself soon become the object of ridicule); "In lagueos lupus" (Ad, 372D-E:
a crafty man ploting against someone else will in the end fall victim to
his own mischief).

350. Terence, The Eunuch, IV, iv, 54-55 ("Si sapis, quod scis, nescis").

351. Exp., par. 236; on Erasmus and Holland cf. Allen, XII, p. 112.

352. Cf. the colloquy "Inns", n. 36 above; Allen, XII, pp. 100-101.

353. Concerning Erasmus' views on education cf. n. 90 above; cf. further "Off
to School" (Col., pp. 43-45; LB, I, 654A-F: on the pedagogical methods of
the 16th century); "The Whole Duty of Youth" (Col., pp. 30-41; LB, I, 648E-
653D: a eulogy of St. Paul's school for boys founded by John Colet (on
Colet cf. Allen, Ep. 1211, pp. 514, 1. 244-527, 1. 633; for an English version
cf. Olin (TB), pp. 175-191; on Colet's works cf. Harbison, pp. 55-90) and
Erasmus' concept of the life and training of the ideal student: love God
as father, injure no one, practice charity, be long-suffering, start each
day with prayer, study good letters, eat properly, relax sufficiently, sleep
enough but never too much, pray with the mind (meditate on Scripture), avoid
bad company, believe in Scripture and the Creed and let the theologians argue
about non-essentials). Erasmus wrote the following works specifically for
Colet's school: De copia (LB, I, 3A-110D); Concio de puero Jesu (LB, V,
599B-610A); Institutum hominis christiani (LB, V, 1357D-1359F: a revision
in Latin verse of a small catechism written originally by Colet); two prayers,
cf. Precationes (LB, V, 1209C-D). Concerning the basis of a humanistic
education and methods for learning cf. also "The Art of Learning" (Col.,

pp. 458-461; 849C-850D) and <u>De recta latini graecique sermonis pronuntiatione</u>
(LB, I, 922E-923C).

354. "Quarta luna nati" (Ad, 58A-B: on those whose labors benefit the world but are of no advantage to the individual himself).

355. "Ne gustaris quibus nigra est cauda" (Ad, 15D-E: avoid a bad reputation by never doing that which you must later repent).

356. Cf. par. 217 above; "Non est cujuslibet Corinthum appellere" (Ad, 150D-151E: deter those who are trying to do something beyond their power); "In saxis seminas" (Ad, 170D-E) and "Oleum et operam perdiri" (Ad, 171E-172C: it is a waste of time and energy to try to obtain the impossible); "Ne Hercules quidem adversus duos" (Ad, 197C-198C: an answer given by one censured for not doing the impossible; where much is well done, small errors should be overlooked); "Ultra vires nihil aggrediendum" (Ad, 919F-920A: be cautious in attempting to do what you cannot possibly accomplish).

357. Horace, <u>Odes</u>, III, iv, 65-67; on Horace (65BC-8BC) cf. Harper's, pp. 843-846.

358. "Virum improbum vel mus mordeat" (Ad, 332B-F: a guilty conscience fears everything and everyone).

359. "Inest et formicae et serpho" (Ad, 562F-563A) and "Habet et musca splenam" (Ad, 829F: even a weak enemy is not to be despised and, therefore, he is a wise man who offends the least).

360. <u>Institutio principis christiani</u> (LB, IV, 561A-612A; Allen, XII, p. 25; a critical edition appeared in Aus. Schr., Vol., V, pp. 111-357; for an English version cf. Lester K. Born, trl. and ed. <u>The Education of a Christian Prince</u>); on princes cf. Allen, XII, p. 157.

361. Horace, <u>Odes</u>, II, xiii, 17.

362. "Ad finem ubi perveneris, ne velis reverti" (Ad, 19E-F: if one gives up toward the end of a struggle, all his efforts are lost; nevertheless, be willing to die when the time comes); on martyrdom cf. Allen, XII, p. 136.

363. "Principium dimidium totius" (Ad, 85C-F) and "Dimidium plus toto" (Ad, 364C-366C: well begun is half done; in moral matters, the desire to be good is in great measure the means of becoming good).

364. Cf. par. 280 above and par. 417 below.

365. Exp., pars. 164, 228.

366. "Optimum obsonium labor senectuti" (Ad, 797B-C: it is disgraceful for the aged to be too solicitous about their worldly possessions).

367. "Suo jumento sibi malum accersere" (Ad, 48C-D) and "Auribus lupum teneo" (Ad, 190F-191C: do not entangle yourself in affairs with which you cannot cope nor meddle in a strife which is not your concern).

368. Cf. Introduction, n. 26.

369. Exp., pars. 6, 61.

370. On Erasmus' hatred of liars cf. "Pseudocheus and Philetymus, or the Dedicated Liar and the Man of Honor" (Col., pp. 133-137; LB, I, 710D-712B); "Things and Names" (Col., p. 386; LB, I, 821E); "Sympathy" (Col., p. 527; LB, I, 878E-F); LB, IV, 442D-443A (from Praise of Folly).

371. On Erasmus' views concerning court life cf. "Fumos vendere" (Ad, 128E-130A) and "Thus aulicum" (Ad, 130A: the promised rewards of a court life are titillating but volatile); "Mono satisfacere" (Ad, 210B-211C; Phillips, p. 34: those in power want pleasant praise, not useful criticism); "Simia in purpura" (Ad, 264E-265A: courtiers are nothing more than decorated monkeys on parade); "Periculosum est canis intestina gustasse" (Ad, 530F; Phillips, p. 110: it is dangerous to expose one's moral character to the licentious atmosphere of a court life); "In ostio formosus" (Ad, 867C-868A; Phillips, 110: for their own gain courtiers flatter their kings who themselves are nothing but robbers); "Quibus nec ara nec fides" (Ad, 890E-891A; Phillips, p. 110: courtiers keep faith with neither God nor man); "Expedit habere plura cognomina" (Ad, 894D-F: courtiers will do anything for personal gain).

372. "Amicorum communa omnia" (Ad, 13F-14F: on the qualities of true and lasting friendship).

373. "In utramvis dormire aurem" (Ad, 307B: a clear conscience can rest in peace for it has nothing to fear); cf. n. 358 above.

374. "Ne cuivis dextram injeceris" (Ad, 17B: since true friendship demands an object worthy of love, i.e. a person of good moral character, true friendship is rare; therefore, do not give your hand in friendship to just anyone).

375. Concerning this letter to Albert cf. Introduction, ns. 17 and 37; the letter was often printed together with Erasmus' first letter to Luther (Allen, Ep. 980). In this instance one cannot help but wish that Erasmus had called to mind the following adages: "Refricare cicatricem" (Ad, 253A-B: it is ill-natured of one to revive the memory of a past injury); "Ne malorum menineris" (Ad, 445A-F: do not revive the memory of troubles that are past); "Quae dolent ea molestum est contingere" (Ad, 982D-E: it is a breach of good manners to remind someone of a fault or folly he wants to forget).

376. The letter to which Erasmus refers here does not seem to be extant.

377. Exp., pars. 111-112, 120.

378. Exp., par. 89.

379. Exp., par. 34.

380. "Ut possumus, quando ut volumus non licet" (Ad, 313E-314B: happiness lies in moderating our desires and being satisfied with what we have).

381. Epicurus, V (Fragments), D (from uncertain sources), 86; cf. also Epicurus, Fragments, No. 201 (Seneca, Epistulae ad Lucilium, Ep. XVI, 7: "Si ad naturam vives, numquam eris pauper; si ad opiniones, numquam dives); Fragments, No. 209 (the time when, most of all, you should withdraw into yourself is when you are forced to be in a crowd). On retirement from the world cf. De contemptu mundi (written c. 1489, published 1521; LB, V, 1239 - 1262 (cf. also LB, V, 1257A-1259A: a development of the idea of Christian

Epicureanism wherein pleasure is in the soul, not in the body): Chs. 1-11
treat of the miseries of the world and the flesh and the happiness to be
derived from the solitary life; Ch. 12, added later, contradicts everything
said in the first eleven chapters; cf. "Introduction" to the English version
of the De contemptu mundi, trl. by Thomas Paynell. A facsimile reproduction
of the Berthelet edition of 1533, with an Introduction by William James
Hirten. Gainesville, Fla.: Scholars' Facsimiles and Reprints, 1967, pp.
v-xliv); "The Epicurean" (Col., pp. 535-551; LB, I, 882B-890B: on the
teachings of ancient philosophy enriched by Christian insights; pleasure is
the end of life, but intellectual pleasure is the most desirable; this can
best be cultivated in simplicity of life and retirement from the active
world; those who live most simply, live most righteously and thus are most
happy; a true Christian is therefore a true Epicurean; cf. D.C. Allen, "The
Rehabilitation of Epicurus and His Theory of Pleasure in the Early Renaissance,"
Studies in Philology (Chapel Hill, N.C.), XLI (1944), 1-15; Surtz, The Praise
of Pleasure, esp. pp. 9-42: a discussion of the Epicurean principles in St.
Thomas More's Utopia (II, 6ff.), wherein it is stated that the highest earthly
happiness is the practice of virtue, i.e. living in accordance with right
reason which leads to eternal bliss, the ultimate end of all virtue; Marie
Delcort and Marcelle Derwa, "Trois aspects humanistes de l'épicurisme
chrétien," in Colloquium Erasmianum (Actes du Colloque international réuni
à Mons du 26 au 29 octobre 1967 à l'occasion du cinquième centenaire de la
naissance d'Erasme). Mons: Centre Universitaire de l'Etat, 1968, pp. 119-
133). For similar ideas cf. "The Godly Feast" (Col., pp. 46-78; LB, I,
672B-689E: a Christian appreciation of what is good in pagan ethics) and
"In aere piscari, in mare venari" (Ad, 174D-E: it is useless to attempt to
combine the incompatible - business and the quiet life, sensual pleasure and
happiness, etc.). The idea that the monastic life is the most truly Christian

Epicurean form of life (cf. LB, V, 1257C) was drastically revised in "The Girl with no Interest in Marriage" (Col., pp. 99-103; LB, I, 697C-701B).

382. "Frustra Herculi" (Ad, 594C-E: no one will listen to ill spoken of a man whose integrity and moral character are generally known and revered).

383. "Ipse semet canit" (Ad, 576D-E: a caution against vain boasting; although a man is not praised by others, his own conscience will know what he deserves); "Tanquam Argivam clypeum abstulerit ita gloriatur" (Ad, 648E-F: said of one who boasts about and magnifies insignificant exploits); on Charles V, cf. Allen, XII, pp. 67-69, on Henry VIII, Allen, XII, p. 109, on Francis I, Allen, XII, pp. 94-95, on Ferdinand of Austria, Allen, XII, pp. 91-92.

384. "Oculis ac manibus" (Ad, 1163D-E; Phillips, p. 390: to grasp (or reject) something in all possible ways); cf. John, XV, 25.

385. On Valla cf. Allen, Ep. 26, pp. 113-115, Ep. 29, pp. 119-120, Ep. 182, pp. 407-412 (Erasmus defends Valla's views); Ep. 304, pp. 14, 15, Ep. 337, p. 112 (Valla's influence on Erasmus' New Testament work (LB, X, Index Generalis - Valla is quoted some 22 times in Erasmus' Annotations to the New Testament); Ep. 2172, p. 185 (Erasmus' debt to Valla); Epitome Desiderii Erasmi Roterodami in Elegantiarum Libros Laurentii Vallae (LB, I, 1069A-1126C); In Latinam Novi Testamenti Interpretationem ... Adnotationes. Ed. by Erasmus. Paris: Badius, 1505 (cf. Allen, I, I, p. 14 and I, IV, p. 64 and Ep. 2172, p. 185). On Barbaro cf. Allen, II, p. 532, VIII, p. 186, X, p. 94, XI, p. 177, XII, p. 47; on Poliziano, Allen, II, pp. 376, 532.

386. On Agricola cf. Allen, I, I, p. 2, Ep. 480, p. 365, Ep. 2073, p. 533, XII, p. 36; LB, I, 1014A and V, 920F-921A (praise of Agricola), LB, IV, 78B (on his industry), LB, V, 497F (on his piety); "Canis in balneo" (Ad, 166C-167D; Phillips, p. 50: a tribute to Agricola); cf. Spitz, pp. 20-40; on Hegius cf. Allen, I, pp. 48, 55, 57, 106, 384-388, XII, p. 108.

387. Cf. Introduction, ns. 4 and 5; Allen, XII, pp. 160-161.

388. On Zasius cf. Allen, Ep. 862, p. 384 (Erasmus praises his Latin style),
Ep. 1352, p. 261 (Erasmus' dedication to Zasius); on Linacre, Allen, I, IV,
pp. 59, 62, Ep. 232, p. 472 (among Erasmus' English circle of friends),
Ep. 118, p. 274 (praised by Erasmus), Ep. 350, p. 139, Ep. 388, p. 198,
Ep. 502, p. 420 (Erasmus doubts his friendship), Ep. 541, p. 489 (he is
praised as the most eloquent medical writer in England), XII, p. 125; on
Grocyn, Allen, I, I, pp. 5, I, III, p. 55 (concerning his relations with
Erasmus), Ep. 118, p. 273 (praised by Erasmus), I, IV, pp. 59, 67 (listed
among Erasmus' English friends), Ep. 520, p. 441, Ep. 540, p. 486 (Erasmus
praises his Greek scholarship), XII, p. 106.

389. On Budé cf. Allen, I, IV, p. 67 (concerning his services in the cause of
learning), Ep. 480, p. 365 (compared to Agricola), Ep. 531, p. 460 and Ep.
1479, p. 515 (praised as a Greek scholar), Ep. 529, p. 455, Ep. 531, p. 460
(surpassed the Italian humanists), Ep. 1111, p. 283, Ep. 2468, p. 235, Ep.
3048, p. 215 (again praised by Erasmus), XII, pp. 59-60.

390. On Lefèvre cf. LB, VI, 244D, 282C, 722C, 739E, 777F, 783D, 853D, 884C;
Allen, XII, pp. 90-91.

391. Cf. Introduction, n. 35; Allen, XII, pp. 113-114.

392. "Bis dat qui cito dat" (Ad, 330C-F: benefits are esteemed not as much for
their intrinsic value as for the readiness with which they are bestowed).

393. Exp., par. 95.

394. Exp., pars. 229-230; cf. also "Chamaeleonte mutabilior" (Ad, 805E-806B) and
"Trochi in morem" (Ad, 1128E-1129B: censure of the cameleon-like mutability
of disposition).

395. "Lingua quo vadis" (Ad, 460C-D; Phillips, p. 388: concerning the power of
the tongue to soothe or to injure; cf. also Epistle of James, III, 4 and
Proverbs, XVIII, 21).

396. Exp., par. 231; "Tecum habita" (Ad, 255D-E) and "Intra tuam pelliculam te

contine" (Ad, 256F-257D: be what you are and do not put on airs or pretend
to be more than you are).

397. "Aliorum medicus, ipse ulceribus scates" (Ad, 564D-E and 1032A-B: concerning
those who rail against vices in others to which they themselves are subject).

398. Exp., par. 38.

399. Cf. Allen, Ep. 1376 (to Pirckheimer, 19 July 1523).

400. Cf. n. 14 above.

401. Exp., pars. 170, 229; Gnatho is a character in Terence's play The Eunuch -
a boastful, insolent miles gloriosus.

402. "Sine cortice natis" (Ad, 313C-F: with age and experience you no longer
need a master for you can perform great deeds on your own).

403. Cf. n. 304 above.

404. Allen, Ep. 180 (to Jean Desmarais, i.e. Joannes Paludanus, (Feb. 1504);
often printed with the Desiderii Erasmi Roterodami ad Philippum Panegyricus
(cf. LB, IV, 507A-554F and Allen, XII, pp. 26, 153); cf. also Allen, Ep.
179 (to Nicholas Ruistre, (Feb. 1504) - the Preface to the Panegyric); on
Desmarais/Paludanus cf. Allen, XII, p. 149.

405. Even a cursory reading of Erasmus' correspondence to friends and patrons
will suffice to demonstrate that he frequently did speak of and complain
about his poverty, especially between 1498 and 1515; among many others cf.
Allen, Eps. 80, 95, 115, 128, 139, 145, 146, 153, 154, 227, 237, 240, 242,
250, 266, 281, 295, 350; both Colet (Allen, Ep. 230, p. 471, 11. 32-46) and
Linacre (Allen, Ep. 237, pp. 478,1.54 - 479, 1. 59) reproached Erasmus for
his begging habit). On the other hand cf. the adage "Emere malo, quam rogare"
(Ad, 120D-E: it is better to work for and purchase something than to beg
for it).

406. "Pecuniae obediunt omnia" (Ad, 144D-145F; Phillips, p. 129: what is more
hateful than lying or perjury? - yet many do so; vows are frequently taken

and just as frequently broken; money borrowed and never returned is little more than thievery).

407. Cf. n. 67 and par. 59 above.

408. "In sola Sparta expedit senescere" (Ad, 1002E-1003B: even the warlike Spartans respected the aged).

409. Cf. Introduction, n. 8.

410. "Orci galea" (Ad, 700C-701D: said of those who incite others to acts of villainy but do not want themselves to be seen as involved in them); cf. par. 115 above.

411. Cf. Introduction, n. 30.

412. In 1522 Nicolaus Baechem attacked the Colloquies for containing heretical ideas (cf. Allen, Ep. 1299, pp. 86,1.54 - 87, 1. 71, Ep. 1300, pp. 88, 1.14 - 89, 1, 42) and in May 1526 the Sorbonne officially censured the work (the censure was not published until 1531), citing 69 passages as either erroneous or contributing to the corruption of youth. In 1532 Erasmus wrote a rebuttal to the Sorbonne's censure, his Declarationes ad censuras (LB, IX, 928D-954E) in which the individual charges are stated and his reply to each. After the 1526 censure Erasmus wrote his De utilitate colloquiorum (Col., pp. 623-637; LB, I, 901D-908F) and appended it to each successive edition of the work. For a succinct digest of the De utilitate cf. Allen, Ep. 1704, p. 333, 11. 23-38.

413. Cf. Introduction, n. 5.

414. Cf. par. 82 and n. 103 above.

415. Cf. Introduction, ns. 20 and 21.

416. "Nosce tempus" (Ad, 289A-290D: although of itself an action might be good, if done at the wrong time it could be the cause of great harm).

417. "Mala ultro adsunt" (Ad, 1002A: misfortunes come fast enough of themselves - do not go in search of them; this is exactly what one does if he meddles in

quarrels which do not concern him).

418. Allen, IV, Ep. 1119 (to George Spalatin, 6 Jul. 1520).

419. Cf. Introduction, n. 5.

420. Plato, _Lysis_, 205, d; Diogenianus, III, 62 (Leutsch, Vol. II, p. 47).

421. Bö, I, p. 44, par. 38 (Hutten to J. Fuchs, 13 Jun. 1515); cf. Introduction, n. 6.

422. Matthew, XVIII, 15.

423. Cf. Introduction, n. 29.

424. I was unable to discover any document in which Hutten admitted this or was said to have done so.

425. "Habet" (Ad, 977B: he has what he wanted, may he enjoy it; also, he has received his just deserts).

426. Exp., pars. 41-42, 145, 153, 156, 263-264.

427. "Canis festinans caecos parit catulos" (Ad, 459B-E: that which is done hastily is done imperfectly).

428. For an attack on his enemies at the Sorbonne, especially Natalis Beda (Bédier) cf. "A Meeting of the Philological Society" (Col., pp. 394-400; LB, I, 824D-826E); cf. also "The Sermon" (Col., pp. 462-478; LB, I, 850D-857E: an attack leveled especially against Peter Sutor who is caricatured as an ignorant obscurantist); "A Fish Diet" (Col., pp. 351-353; LB, I, 808A-810A: a slap at Beda's predecessor at College Montaigu in Paris (on his predecessor, Standonck, cf. Renaudet, _Préréforme_, pp. 114-161); on Erasmus' scorn of the medieval method of philosophy and glosses cf. Allen, _The Age of Erasmus_, pp. 33-65.

429. Erasmus' writings are literally saturated with his arguments in defense of classical studies and a true theology as opposed to the hair-splitting inquiries of the later scholastics. From the Adages cf. the following: "Rudius ac planius" (Ad, 42E-43A; Phillips, p. 124: some theologians discuss

the most common subjects but introduce logical subtleties merely to appear learned); "Quot homines tot sententiae" (Ad, 114A-D; Phillips, pp. 117, 125: true piety can indeed flourish without the hair-splitting subtleties of merely so-called theologians); "Multi thyrsigeri, pauci Bacchi" (Ad, 263E-264B; Phillips, p. 53: it is not the gown that makes the theologian nor the cowl that makes the monk); "Unico digitulo scalpit caput" (Ad, 311B-C: too many monks and theologians pay more attention to their dress than their character endowments); "Illotis pedibus" (Ad, 354A-C; Phillips, pp. 37, 51, 265: a mastery of the classical languages is a prime requisite for a study of theology; mere dabblers in the field have no authority to speak about the mysteries of our faith); "Illotis manibus" (Ad, 354C-355C; Phillips, pp. 265-267: to attempt to interpret the Divine Scriptures without a knowledge of Hebrew, Greek and Latin is to touch the subject with dirty hands and thus to pollute it; trivial syllogisms are no substitute for a thorough classical education); "Elephantus non captat murem" (Ad, 359B-C; Phillips, p. 263: would-be theologians who are ignorant of the classical languages lack the greater part of the means for learning); "Impossibilia captas" (Ad, 370A-C; Phillips, pp. 82, 263: there is no true learning without a foundation in classical languages); "Summum cape et medium habebis" (Ad, 491F-492B; Phillips, pp. 111, 264: although Aristotelean philosophy can be used to justify anything, it should be obvious that those who are satisfied with something mediocre quickly fall below the level of mediocrity); "Prius duo Echini amicitiam ineant" (Ad, 547F-548A; Phillips, p. 264: there is little agreement between the prickles of so-called theologians and good letters); "Turpe silere" (Ad, 613F-614B; Phillips, p. 125: because of their ignorance there are many who should remain silent (in theological matters), but in order to appear eloquent and learned they nonetheless insist on making a lot of noise); "Qui nimium properat, serius absolvit" (Ad,

299

842A-E; Phillips, p. 82: without a knowledge of Greek, philosophy is impossible); "Tam perit quam extrema faba" (Ad, 1041C-D; Phillips, p. 264: true theology is perishing because it is being handled by the most ignorant of people); "Equi dentes inspicere donati" (Ad, 1059C-F; Phillips, pp. 7, 126: never look a gift horse in the mouth - here a thrust at the ingratitude of the theologians for his efforts to supply them with an emended version of the Greek New Testament); "Ver ex anno tollere" (Ad, 1067E-1068A; Phillips, p. 128: to deprive the year of spring is analogous to the endeavors of some to suppress the study of languages and good letters); cf. also n. 15 and par. 58 above.

430. "Noctua volat" (Ad, 57E-58A: concerning those who obtain their own advantage by means of bribery).

431. Exp., pars. 155-156.

432. "Hinc illae lachrymae" (Ad, 138F-139A: on discovering the true causes of an action which one has tried to conceal).

433. Martial(is), Epigrams, XIII, 77.

434. "Spem pretio emere" (Ad, 524D-F: on paying a very high price for a supposed future benefit).

435. Gregorius Cyprius, III, 77 (Leutsch, Vol. II, p. 118).

436. The source of this remark has completely eluded me!

437. Exp., pars. 22, 195.

438. Exp., par. 254 and n. 342 above.

439. "Et meum telum cuspidem habet acuminatum" (Ad, 102E-F: although I do not want to fight, I can and will give back to you what you give to me).

440. Cf. par. 197 above.

441. "Aequalis aequalem delectat" and "Simile gaudet simili" (Ad, 78D-79E: like interests are drawn together for their mutual benefit).

442. "De fructu arborem cognosces" (Ad, 348C-D; Phillips, pp. 387-388: the real value of a man is proven by his actions); cf. Matthew, VII, 15-20.

443. Allen, Ep. 1352, pp. 260,1.147 - 261, 1. 169 (to Pope Adrian VI, Mar. 1523: force will not stop the Lutherans any more than it did the Wycliffites).

444. Allen, Ep. 1334, p. 177, 1. 217: "Summa nostrae religionis pax est et unanimitas"; "Multa novit vulpes, verum echinus unum magnum" (Ad, 187E-188F: the advice of one sensible man is worth far more than many discordant opinions).

445. Contrast with this Hutten's joyous exclamation: "Oh century! oh scholarship! It is a joy to be alive, etc." - cf. Introduction, n. 76.

446. "Senis mutare linguam" (Ad, 93F-94D: although you cannot teach an old dog new tricks, each one should do what he is qualified to do).

447. "Occultae musices nullus respectus" (Ad, 295B-E: concealed talents are of use to no one - they must be shared for the benefit of all).

448. "Sero sapiunt Phryges" (Ad, 37F-38B: too frequently many people fail to see in time the advantage of some specific measure of action or precaution, and then it is too late to adopt it).

449. "In seditione vel Androclides belli ducem agit" (Ad, 480C-F: a warning against those theologians who do nothing but stir up strife among the laity).

450. Dante, Paradiso, III, 85: "En la sua voluntade è nostra pace"; Erasmus' hatred of war has already been mentioned (cf. Institutio principis christiani, Querela pacis, Sileni Alcibiadis, Dulce bellum inexpertis, etc.); cf. further "Charon" (Col., pp. 388-394; LB, I, 822C-824D: on contemporary politics, his hatred of war and a further "complaint of peace"); Erasmus dedicated his Paraphrases of the Gospels to four monarchs: Emperor Charles V, Francis I, Henry VIII and Prince Ferdinand of Austria, calling on each to seek for peace (cf. Allen, Ep. 1255, pp. 5-7, Ep. 1333, pp. 164-172, Ep. 1381, pp. 313-322, Ep. 1400, pp. 352-361); he also stated that a Christian teacher could never approve of war (LB, II, 964B) and that the most unjust peace is preferable to the most just war (Allen, Ep. 1156, pp. 373, 11. 13-15, Ep. 1211, pp. 524, 1.557 - 526, 1. 614); on Erasmus and peace cf. Rudolf Liechtenhan, "Die

politische Hoffnung des Erasmus und ihr Zusammenbruch," in <u>Gedenkschrift</u>

<u>zum 400sten Todestag des Erasmus von Rotterdam</u>. Hrsg. von der Historischen -und

Antiquarischen Gesellschaft zu Basel. Basel: Braus-Riggenbach, 1936, pp.

144-165 and Adams, passim.

451. "Saepe etiam est olitor valde opportuna locuutus" (Ad, 220E-221E) and "Viam

qui nescit ad mare ... eum oportet amnem quaerere" (Ad, 633A-C: even a fool

or a humble person can sometimes give good advice about that which they are

informed - do not despise such advice).

452. "Dimidium plus toto" (Ad, 364C-366C: the half you have is better than the

whole you do not possess; therefore, it is better for the Roman Church to

concede some points to the reformers than to lose the whole of Christian

unity and thus diminish its authority); cf. par. 230 above.

453. Concerning Erasmus' belief that only non-essentials were the source of the

evils that were sundering Christendom, cf. "An Examination Concerning Faith"

(Col., pp. 177-189; LB, I, 727F-732E; Thompson published a critical edition

of this short work, cf. <u>Inquisitio de fide</u>. New Haven: Yale University

Press, 1950: since both Catholics (Aulus in the dialogue is Erasmus) and

Luther/Lutherans (Barbatius in the dialogue) agree on the basic creed (cf.

Erasmus' <u>Symbolum</u> (LB, V, 1133A-1196E) - an exegesis of the Creed), why

should they flay one another because of matters not essential to salvation?).

For a discussion of Erasmus' views of Luther prior to writing his <u>De libero</u>

<u>arbitrio</u> (1524; Allen, XII, p. 96) cf. Thompson, <u>Inquisitio de fide</u>, pp. 1-49

and Gottfried G. Krodel, "Luther, Erasmus and Henry VIII," <u>Archiv für</u>

<u>Reformationsgeschichte</u> (Gütersloh), LIII (1962), 60-78; cf. esp. n. 96); cf.

also Erasmus' <u>De sarcienda ecclesiae concordia</u> (LB, V, 469A-506D; translated

into English with Introduction and notes by Raymond Himelick, <u>Erasmus and</u>

<u>the Seamless Coat of Jesus</u>. Lafayette, Ind.: Purdue University Press, 1971);

"De lana caprina" (Ad, 133D-E: why dispute about non-essentials?); "Latum

302

unguem" (Ad, 184E-185B: about those who agree on basics but fight acrimoniously about slight differences); Allen, XII, pp. 20-21.

454. "In Pursuit of Benefices" (Col., pp. 7-11; LB, I, 640C-641E: Erasmus scourges the buying and selling of Church offices and the wealth of the Church, especially in Rome where, it is said, not one good man can be found); "Suum cuique pulchrum" (Ad, 74E-76C; Phillips, pp. 125, 264: some people claim that they are pious although in reality they are steeped in vices; these same individuals, however, rage against such vices in others); "Bonus dux bonum reddit comitem" (Ad, 333C-F: some bishops who demand sincere religion and piety from their flocks are themselves far from these goals); "Spartam nactus es, hanc orna" (Ad, 551E-555D; Phillips, pp. 300-308: if you are a bishop, act like a bishop instead of a satrap; fulfil your station in life and, being content with your lot, use your talents and means to promote goodness in others; let your inner greatness arouse your neighbor's wonder, your goodness their love).

455. "Ad consilium ne accesseris, antequam voceris" (Ad, 103C: do not offer advice until it is required, but when danger threatens we must warn our friends whether they want our advice or not).

456. On the art of dying cf. Erasmus' Declamatio de morte (LB, IV, 617A-624A) and his De praeparatione ad mortem (LB, V, 1293D-1318D; Allen, XII, p. 20); for a contrast between hypocritical ostentation at the time of death and a simple, deeply Christian piety cf. "The Funeral" (Col., pp. 357-373; LB, I, 810A-817C).

457. "Scarabeus aquilam quaerit" (Ad, 869A-883F; Phillips, pp. 229-263: although this essay is primarily a violently anti-monarchical treatise which excoriates the despotism of princes, the unscrupulousness of courtiers and the devastations of war, Erasmus makes the statement that it is better not to fight against the contentious (i.e. beetles) lest in the struggle one becomes as defiled as they are (Phillips, p. 263)).

INDEX I: SECONDARY LITERATURE

Eckert, Willehad Paul: Int., ns. 10, 57, 59, 61, 62, 68, 73, 79
Eckert/Imhoff: Int., ns. 5, 76
Eggers, Kurt: Int., n. 80
Ergang, Robert: Int., n. 70
Etienne, Jacques: Sp., n. 127

Fechter, Heinrich: Int., n. 80
Ferguson, Wallace K.: Int., n. 72
Förster, Richard: Int., n. 70
Francke, Kuno: Int., n. 81
Friedenthal, Richard: Int., n. 80, Exp., n. 75
Fritsche, Franz: Int., n. 57
Froude, James A.: Int., n. 55

Galley, A.: Int., n. 57
Gay, Peter: Int., n. 70
Gebhardt, Georg: Int., ns. 63, 67
Geiger, Ludwig: Int., ns. 3, 4, 5, 40
Gerrish, Brian A.: Int.,n. 57
Gewerstock, Olga: Int., n. 70
Gilmore, Myron: Int., n. 61
Glöckner, Gottfried: Int., n. 61
Goedeke, Karl: Int., n. 40
Gray, Hanna H.: Sp., n. 90

Hagen, Karl: Int., n. 77
Halkin, Leon E.: Int., n. 60
Hall, B.: Int., n. 27
Hall, Vernon: Int., n. 159
Harbison, E. Harris: Int., n. 61, Sp., n. 353
Hardison, O.B.: Int., n. 61
Heep, Martha: Int., n. 70
Heer, Friedrich: Int., ns. 21, 58
Himelick, Raymond: Sp., n. 453
Hoffmann, Manfred: Int., ns. 66, 67
Holborn, Hajo: Int., ns.1,3, 8, 9, 20, 21, 55, 56, 57, 83, Sp., n. 193
Hottinger, Johann Jacob: Int., ns. 26, 46, 52
Huizinga, Johan: Int., ns. 55, 57, 59
Hutton, W.H.: Int., n. 57
Hyma, Albert: Int., n. 72

Imhoff, Christoph von: Int., ns. 5, 76

Jacob, E.F.: Int., n. 61
Jarrott, C.A.L.: Sp., n. 127
Jensen, De Lamar: Exp., n. 75
Joachimsen, Paul: Int., ns. 77, 78
Jones, Rosemary: Int., n. 21

Kaegi, Werner: Int., ns. 1, 11, 83
Kaiser, Walter: Int., n. 59
Kalkoff, Paul: Int., ns. 11, 20, 21, 56, 57, 77, 80, 82, 83
Keim, C. Th.: Int., n. 5

Kieser, Carl: Int., ns. 27, 36
Köhler, Walter: Int., n. 62
Könneker, Barbara: Int., n. 59
Koerber, Eberhard von: Int., n. 80
Kohls, Ernst Wilhelm: Int., ns. 27, 58, 61, 62, 68, Sp., n. 193
Kolde, Th.: Exp., n. 8
Krebs, Manfred: Int., n. 6
Krodel, Gottfried: Int., n. 44, Sp., n. 453

Laible, Wilhelm: Int., n. 58
Lesowsky, Winfried: Exp., n. 31   *343,*
Leutsch, Ernst Ludwig von: Exp., n. 140, Sp., ns. 314, 347, 420, 435
Liechtenhan, Rudolf: Sp., n. 450   ∧
Locher, Gottfried W.: Int., n. 43
Lortz, Joseph: Int., n. 21

Marc'hadour, Germain: Int., n. 15
Mee, Charles L.: Int., n. 42
Mesnard, Pierre: Exp., n. 31, Sp., n. 127
Mestwerdt, Paul: Int., ns. 58, 61
Murray, Robert: Int., n. 72

Nauwelaerts, M.A.: Int., n. 24
Newald, Richard: Int., ns. 55, 59, 74 (cf. Drewinc), 75

Olin, John C.: Int., ns. 42, 63, Sp., ns. 127, 147, 150, 208, 353

Packer, J.I.: Exp., n. 31
Padberg, Rudolf: Int., n. 61, Sp., n. 275
Pascal, Paul: Sp., n. 116
Paulus, N.: Int., n. 40
Payne, John B.: Int., ns. 63, 66
Paynell, Thomas: Sp., n. 381
Petry, Ray C.: Int., n. 61
Pfeiffer, Rudolf: Int., n. 61
Pflugk-Harttung, Julius von: Int., n. 34
Phillips, Margaret Mann: Int., n. 65, Sp. n. 193 (and *passim*, i.e. Adages)
Planck, Gottlieb J.: Int., n. 29
Popkin, Richard H.: Int., n. 58

Rabil, Albert: Sp., ns. 127, 193, 228, 275
Rand, Edward Kennard: Int., p. 1
Renaudet, Augustin: Int., n. 63, Sp., ns. 127, 428
Reynolds, Ernest E.: Int., n. 15
Ritter, Gerhard: Int., n.57
Rouschausse, Jean: Int., n. 41
Rüdiger, Horst: Int., n. 56
Rupp, E. Gordon: Exp., ns. 31, 75
Russell, Juga: Int., n. 56

Schlingensiepen, Hermann: Sp., n. 275
Schnürer, Gustav: Int., n. 83
Schottenloher, Otto: Int., n. 65
Schwiebert, Ernest George: Exp., n. 75
Scott, Izora: Sp., n. 159

Achates: Sp., n. 206
Achilles: Sp., par. 316
Aeneas: Sp., n. 206
Alcibiades: Int., pp. 3, 14, 24, Exp., n. 72, Sp., n. 167
Alcmene: Exp., n. 37
Alexander the Great: Sp., par. 75
Amphitryon: Exp., n. 37
Anabaptists: Sp., n. 257
Anacharsis: Sp., Pref. II, par. 65, n. 14
Annas: Exp. n. 131, Sp., par. 276, Sp., n. 327
Arcesilaus: Sp., n. 232
Arians: Sp., par. 283, Sp., ns. 334, 336
Aristotle: Exp., n. 62, Sp., n. 136
Aphrodite, Hera and Athena: Exp., n. 124
Apostolus: Exp., n. 140
Arminius: Int., pp. 30, 31, Exp., n. 79
Asia: Exp., par. 162
Ate: Int., p. 13, Exp., par. 235, n. 141, Sp., n. 46
Athens: Exp., par. 114, n. 72, Sp., Pref. II, par. 278, n. 14
Augsburg: Sp., pars. 146, 158

Babylonians: Sp., par. 88
Basle: Int., pp. 7, 8, 9, 11, 12, 13, 33, ns. 5, 21, 24, 25, 26, 38, 55,
          Exp., pars. 1, 4, 22, 26, 30, 93, 139, 195, 198, Sp., Pref. II,
          pars. 3, 14, 34, 46, 47, 92, 112, 162, 296, 383, n. 58
Bible, Books of the:
          Exodus: Sp., n. 304
          Book of Kings, First: Sp., n. 286
          Isaiah: Exp., n. 113, Sp. par. 254, ns. 249, 303
          Psalms: Sp., ns. 56, 213, 249
          Proverbs: Sp., ns. 30, 215, 395
          Gospel of St. Matthew: Exp., ns. 110, 13, 134, Sp., ns. 38, 103,
              109, 266, 326, 328, 345, 442
          Gospel of St. Luke: Exp., n. 110, Sp., ns. 38, 327
          Gospel of St. John: Exp., n. 131, Sp., ns. 327, 384
          Acts of the Apostles: Exp., n. 131, Sp., ns. 310, 311, 327, 329,
              330, 337
          St. Paul, I Corinthians: Sp., ns. 56, 82, 244, 331
          St. Paul, Galatians: Sp., n. 56
          St. Paul, II Timothy: Exp., n. 115
          St. Peter, I: Sp., n. 212
          St. James: Sp., n. 395
Brabant: Exp., par. 79, Sp., pars. 31, 70, 89, 90, 94, 112, 128, 130, 310,
          350, n.110
Bruges: Int., p. 9, Sp., par. 38
Brussels: Int., p. 6, Sp., pars. 134, 153, 296, 303

Cacus: Exp., par. 69, n. 39
Caiaphas: Exp., par. 222, n. 131, Sp., pars. 190, 276, n. 377
Calais: Sp., par. 169
Camillus, Marcus Furius: Exp., n. 96
Caria: Sp., par. 211, n. 239

Carneades: Sp., par. 206, n. 232
Cato the Censor: Sp., par. 41, n. 68
Cicero: Exp., ns. 42, 136, Sp., par. 397, ns. 21, 32, 159, 232
Claudianus: Exp., n. 65
Cologne (Köln): Int., pp. 2, 7, 9, n. 3, Exp., pars. 82, 113, 116, Sp.,
            pars. 92, 94, 95, 115, 116, 121, 131, 158, 259, ns. 110, 208, 392
Constance: Exp., par. 138, Sp., pars. 25, 146, 160, 161
Constantine the Great: Sp., n. 336
Constantius: Sp., par. 285, n. 336
Curia: Int., p. 7, Exp., pars. 12, 14, 33, 118, 124, 125, 154, 179, 224,
            258, n. 6, Sp., pars. 127, 149, 158, 173, 215, 217, 243, 290,
            ns. 308, 334
Cyprian, St.: Sp., par. 284

Danaides: Sp., Pref. II, n. 24
Danaus: Sp., ns. 24, 170
Dante: Sp., ns. 101, 450
Darius: Sp., n. 110
David, the King: Sp., par. 243
Decius: Sp., n. 335
Democritus: Exp., par. 162, n. 101
Diet of Augsburg: Int., p. 28, Int., n. 79, Sp., n. 207
Diet of Worms: Int., p. 6, Exp., par. 120, Exp., ns. 8, 74, Sp., pars.
            133, 134, 143, 153
Diogenianus: Sp., n. 420
Dominicans (cf. BdG, IV, 177-178): Int., p. 2, Int., n. 5, Exp., pars.
            108, 117, 137, Sp., pars. 84, 120, 125, 126, 142, 196, Sp., ns.
            149, 208

Ebernburg: Exp., par. 131
England: Exp., par. 81, Sp., pars. 103, 104
Epicurus: Sp., par. 335, Sp., n. 381
Erfurt: Int., p. 19
Eris: Exp., par. 202, Exp., n. 124

Felix, Festus, Agrippa: Sp., par. 285, Sp., n. 337
France: Exp., pars. 81, 89, Sp., pars. 37, 129, 297
Franciscans (cf. BdG, IV, 215-217): Sp., ns. 149, 150, 208
Frankfurt am Main: Int., p. 2, Sp., pars. 298, 377
Freiburg: Int., n. 24, Sp., par. 278

Germany: Exp., pars. 13, 45, 60, 63, 69, 71, 80, 113, 120, 124, 125, 129,
            141, 168, 195, 206, 236, Sp., Pref. II, Sp., pars. 55, 58, 74,
            99, 100, 108, 112, 136, 170, 284, 297, 298, 299, 311
Gnatho: Exp., par. 229, Exp., n. 106, Sp., pars. 355, 361, Sp., n. 401
Good letters (classical studies, languages, etc.): Int., p. 7, Int., n. 14,
            Exp., pars. 88, 113, 137, 139, 152, Sp., Pref. II, Sp., pars. 57,
            60, 103, 126, 128, 158, 166, 346, 348, 379, 387, 391, 393, 405, 406,
            407, Sp., ns. 79, 228
Gospel Scripture, evangelical piety, etc.): Int., pp. 7, 16, 19, Exp., pars.
            25, 131, 144, 148, 150, 159, 167, 168, 173, 182, 185, 188, 191,
            192, 196, 201, 223, 245, 251, 252, Sp., Pref. I, II, Sp., pars.
            17, 18, 59, 60, 126, 162, 172, 174, 175, 185, 189, 193, 199, 203,
            210, 219, 222, 223, 224, 228, 229, 233, 241, 242, 243, 257, 262,
            275, 278, 282, 290, 299, 303, 307, 314, 358, 359, 384, 385, 409,
            410, 421, Sp., ns. 193, 251

Greece: Exp., par. 162
Gregorius Cyprius: Sp., n. 435

Harpies: Exp., par. 113, Exp., n. 61
Hebrew: Exp., pars. 85, 86, 92, 93, 95, Sp., pars. 18, 97
Helen of Troy: Exp., n. 124
Hercules (Heracles): Exp., pars. 69, 146, Exp., ns. 37, 38, 39, 91, Sp., ns. 93, 223, 245, 356
Herodotus: Sp., n. 110
Holland: Exp., pars. 76, 236, Exp., ns. 44, 142, Sp., pars. 296, 315, Sp., n. 351
Homer: Exp., ns. 61, 141, Sp., ns. 189, 239
Horace: Exp., par. 137, Sp., par. 302, Sp., ns. 70, 357, 361
Hydra: Exp., pars. 69, 113, Sp., n. 223
Hypermnestra: Sp., n. 170

Ingolstadt: Exp., par. 97, Sp., par. 102
Italy: Exp., par. 236

Jesus Christ: Int., pp. 15, 24, Exp., pars. 160, 181, 182, 184, 186, 188, 196, 209, 218, 245, 248, 256, Sp., pars. 60, 127, 175, 189, 190, 202, 203, 204, 211, 212, 228, 233, 234, 242, 243, 246, 248, 252, 275, 276, 278, 279, 284, 290, 308, 309, 359, 405, 412, 413, 415, 418, 423, Sp., ns. 249, 253, 267, 272, 273, 282, 327, 334
Jews: Exp., pars. 92, 120
John the Baptist: Int., p. 10
Julian the Apostate: Sp., n. 336
Julius Caesar: Exp., n. 29
Justinus, Marcus: Sp., n. 110

Lactantius: Sp., n. 232
Landstuhl: Int., pp. 8, 18
Leipzig Disputation: Int., p. 5
Livy: Int., n. 11, Exp., ns. 39, 96, 128
Louvain (Louvain theologians): Int., pp. 2, 4, 6, 7, 9, Int., ns. 5 (Ep. 1217), 19 (Ep. 1217), 21 (Ep. 1217), 24, Exp., pars. 113, 116, Exp., n. 63 (Eps. 1217, 1301), 108 (Ep. 1217), 111 (Ep. 1217), Sp., pars. 18, 95, 101, 111, 115, 116, 118, 120, 121, 130, 142, 147, 158, 168, 177, 196, 325, 373, 391, 392, Sp., ns. 42, 135, 137 (Ep. 1301), 144, 219, 251 (Ep. 1301)
Lucian: Int., p. 26, Int., n. 70, Exp., ns. 72, 146, Sp., n. 167
Lucifer: Sp., n. 46
Lynceus: Sp., par. 155, Sp., n. 170

Macarius Aesopus: Sp., ns. 343, 347
Mainz: Int., pp. 2, 3, 27, Int., ns. 11, 16, Exp., par. 137
Mars: Int., p. 4, Exp., n. 124, Sp., par. 370
Martial: Sp., n. 433
Massilia: Sp., par. 366
Menelaus: Sp., n. 213
Metius: Exp., par. 210, Exp., n. 128, Sp., pars. 198, 257
Montaigne: Sp., n. 32
Mühlhausen: Int., pp. 8, 11, 13, Exp., par. 30, Exp., n. 19, Sp., pars. 11, 42, 317
Muses and Graces: Sp., par. 369

Nyx: Exp., n. 124

Omphale: Exp., par. 146, Exp. n. 91
Ovid: Exp., n. 39

Parmeno: Sp., par. 83
Peleus and Thetis: Exp., n. 124
Persius: Exp., n. 65
Pfaffenkrieg: Int., pp. 8, 16, 30, Int., n. 79, Exp., n. 8
Plato: Exp., par. 114, Exp., n. 62, Sp., par. 117, Sp., n. 420
Plautus: Sp., n. 16
Plutarch: Exp., n. 96, Sp., ns. 21, 68, 347
Polypus: Sp., par. 194, Sp., ns. 129, 213
Pontius Pilate: Exp., n. 134
Pope (Papacy, Roman Pontiff, Apostolic See, cf. BdG, IV, 476-480): Int.,
        pp. 15, 30, 31, Exp., pars. 146, 158, 160, 169, 232, Sp., Pref. 1,
        Sp., pars. 22, 31, 33, 39, 89, 125, 127, 128, 135, 145, 146, 147,
        149, 150, 159, 160, 168, 169, 171, 173, 177, 187, 188, 189, 192,
        214, 215, 216, 218, 222, 224, 234, 235, 238, 239, 240, 241, 245,
        246, 247, 248, 249, 251, 252, 258, 265, 271, 272, 273, 280, 282,
        283, 292, 303, 308, 362, 372, 388, 390, 409, 414, 418, Sp., ns.
        190, 247
Poseidon: Sp., n. 24
Priam, King of Troy: Exp., n. 68
Proteus: Exp., par. 230, Sp., par 194, Sp., n. 213
Pythagoras: Int., n. 3

Quintilian: Sp., par. 174, Sp., n. 196
Quirinus: Sp., n. 327

Rhine River: Sp., pars. 297, 298
Rienzi, Cola di: Int., p. 29
Rome: Exp., pars. 33, 121, 125, 126, 138, 139, 145, 149, 155, 157, 159, 171,
        192, 202, 203, 205, 206, 262, 263, Sp., pars. 104, 128, 129, 140,
        146, 147, 150, 156, 161, 173, 215, 216, 246, 287, 288, 310, 315,
        Sp., n. 162

St. Augustine: Sp., ns. 27, 335
St. Cyprian: Sp., n. 335
St. Hilary: Sp., pars. 283, 285, Sp., n. 334
St. Jerome: Int., pp. 1, 2, Int., n. 5
St. John: Exp., n. 131, Sp., n. 327
St. Paul: Exp., par. 186, Sp., pars. 201, 214, 215, 239, 278, 285
St. Peter: Int., p. 24, Exp., n. 131, Sp., pars. 214, 263, 278, Sp., n. 327
Saul: Int., p. 10
Schlettstadt: Int., pp. 8, 12, Sp., par. 42
Scylla and Charybdis: Sp., par. 172, Sp., n. 189
Scyria: Sp., par. 314
Scythia: Sp., Pref. II, Sp., pars. 365, 399, Sp., n. 14
Seneca: Sp., n. 14
Shakespeare: Exp., n. 72, Sp., n. 167
Sinon: Exp., n. 68
Socrates: Int., pp. 3, 14, 24
Solon: Sp., Pref. II, Sp., ns. 14, 21
Sorbonne: Int., p. 9, Exp., par. 93, Sp., par. 196, Sp., ns. 127, 219, 428

INDEX III: CORRESPONDENTS AND/OR CONTEMPORARIES OF ERASMUS

Adrian VI, Pope (i.e., Adriaan Florisze, of Utrecht, 1459-1523; Professor of theology and Vice-Chancellor of Louvain, tutor to young Charles V, Bp. of Tortosa, Cardinal, Viceroy of Spain, elected Pope in 1522: cf. Allen, I, 380, ADB, X, 302-308, BNB, II, 596-605 (v. Boeyens), EB, I, 216, NNBW, I, 25-29, Pastor, IX / passim in Bataillon, MHL, X-XIII, UTM / BdG, IV, 477-478, V, 260-261), Int., n. 21 (Ep. 1352), Exp., pars. 125-127, 138, Exp., n. 26 (Ep. 1338), Sp., pars. 145-150, Sp., ns. 165, 276 (Ep. 1324), 388 (Ep. 1352), 443 (Ep. 1352)

Agricola, Georgius (i.e., Georg Bauer of Glauchau, Saxony, 1494-1555; Teacher and principal in Zwickau, writer on mining and Galen, correspondent with Erasmus after 1531: cf. Allen, VI, 142, ADB, I, 143-145, MHL, XI, 576, EB, I, 386, NDB, I, 98 / BdG, I, 4-5, III, 3-6, V, 4, VII, 499), Sp., n. 71 (Ep. 2918)

Agricola, Rodolphus (i.e., Rudolf or Roelof Huusman or Huisman, of Baflo, Friesland, c. 1442-1485; Dutch Humanist, called the "father of German Humanism", master of Latin and Greek, musician, draughtsman, translator of the Classics, urged Hebrew studies, set the style for the "universal man and the Italianate German"; cf. ADB, XLV, 709-710, EB, I, 387, MHL, X, 148-158, NDB, I, 103, NNBW, IX, 12-16, Spitz, 20-40 / passim in MHL, X-XIII), Sp., par. 342, Sp., ns. 386 (Eps. 480, 2073), 389

Albert, Margrave of Brandenburg, Archbp. of Magdeburg, Cardinal Archbp. of Mainz (Albertus, Marchio Brandenburgensis, 1490-1545; Patron of art and letters, friend of Erasmus and center of the eye of the Reformation through his relationship with Tetzel, the indulgence hawker: cf. Allen, III, 84, ADB, I, 268-271, EB, I, 496-497, NDB, I, 166-167 / passim in MHL, X, XI, UTM/BdG, III, 275, 278, VII, 348), Int., pp. 3, 4, 5, 6, 13, 14, 27, 28, Int., ns. 5 (Ep. 1033), 11 (Eps. 661, 745), 17 (Ep. 1033), 19 (Ep. 1152), 20, 21 (Ep. 1152), 35 (Ep. 745), 37 (Ep. 1033), 40 (Ep. 1033), 54 (Eps. 745, 968, 1009), Exp., par. 137, Exp., ns. 79 (Ep. 1152), 80 (Ep. 1152), Sp., pars. 36, 122, 158, 267, 325-327, 329, 375, Sp., ns. 147 (Ep. 1033), 375

Alciato (Alciati), Andrea (of Milan, 1492-1550; Lawyer and professor of law, writer of legal treatises and commentaries on the Classics (esp. Tacitus), teacher of Greek, said to have been the greatest legal mind in Italy of the times: cf. Allen, IV, 611, DBI, II, 69-77, EB, I, 522, MHL, XI, 442-443 / passim in MHL, XI, UTM/BdG, I, 11, VII, 499, Ono, 16), Sp., n. 389

Aleander, Girolamo (Girolamo Aleandro, of Motta in Friuli by Venice, 1480-1542; Learned scholar in the classical languages, teacher in Paris, Papal Librarian and Papal Legate to Germany in 1520 and 1538, Archbp. of Brindisi, Cardinal, aided Erasmus in Venice with the publication of his Adages: cf. Allen, I, 502, ADB, I, 329-332, DBI, II, 128-135, EB, I, 538 / passim in Bataillon, MHL, X-XIII, Renaudet (2) and (4), UTM / BdG, I, 11-13, V, 7, Ono, 17), Exp., pars. 119-122, 135, 152, Sp., pars. 128-143, Sp., ns. 153, 155 (Eps. 256, 738, 1195), 159 (Eps. 2565, 2575, 2587, 2736)

Amerbach, Basilius (of Basle, c. 1488-1535; Studied law under Zasius, took some part in his father's printing house, not too distinguished a career: cf. Allen, II, 66, ADB, I, 397, NDB, I, 246 / passim in MHL, X, Renaudet (2) / BdG, I, 17, VII, 9-10), Int., p. 8

Amerbach, Bonifacius (of Basle, 1495-1562; Studied law under Zasius, taught at Basle, also active as a lawyer there, intimate friend of Erasmus, executor of Erasmus' will: cf. Allen, II, 237, ADB, I, 397-398, NDB, I, 247 / passim in MHL, X-XIII, Renaudet (2), UTM / BdG, I, 17, VII, 9-10), Sp., ns. 159 (Ep. 2575), 388 (Ep. 862)

Ammonius, Andreas (Andrea Ammonio/Andreas de Harena, of Lucca, c. 1478-1517; Friend of Erasmus, secretary to Lord Mountjoy and Latin secretary to Henry VIII: cf. Allen, I, 455, DNB, I, 363, Emden (0,2), 8 / passim in Renaudet (4), UTM / BdG, VII, 70, Ono, 28), Sp., ns. 388 (Ep. 232), 405 (Eps. 240, 250, 281, 295)

Anthonisz, Jacob (Jacobus Antonii Middelburgensis, of Middelburg, fl. c. 1502; Doctor of Canon Law and Vicar-General to Henry of Bergen, Bp. of Cambrai: cf. Allen, I, 358, BWN, I, 327, NNBW, III, 37-38), Sp., n. 405 (Ep. 153)

Ardenne, Remacle d' (Remaclus or Rimaclus, of Florennes, 1480-1524; Teacher and writer, collaborator with Aleander at the Diet of Worms: cf. Allen, II, 241, BNB, I, 365-366, XIX, 8-11 / passim in MHL, X), Sp., par. 196, Sp., n. 219

Atensis, cf. Briard, Jan

Aytta van Zwichem, Wigle van (Viglius Zwuichemus Phrysius, of Zwichem, 1507-1577; Statesman of the Netherlands, Councillor to Margaret of Austria, Charles V and Philip II, entered the priesthood in 1562, founded a college at Louvain in 1567: cf. Allen, VIII, 56, ADB, XXXIX, 699-703, BNB, I, 590-594, BWN, I, 464-471, MHL, XI, 145-150, NNBW, II, 46-52 / passim in MHL, X-XII / BdG, II, 412-413, V, 288), Sp., n. 159 (Ep. 2736)

Baechem (Bachem), Nicolaas (Carmelita Egmondanus or Edmondanus, of Egmond near Alkmaar, c. 1462-1526; Prior of the Carmelite House in Louvain, obstinate opponent of Erasmus, attacked his N.T. translation for containing heresy: cf. Allen, III, 416, BNB, I, 616-618, MHL, X, 460-461, NNBW, I, 206 (v. Bachem) / passim in Bataillon, MHL, X-XIII, Renaudet (4), UTM), Int., n. 40, Exp., pars. 141-142, Sp., pars. 118, 122-123, 166-167, Sp., ns. 137 (Ep. 878), 184, 388, 392, 412 (Ep. 1299)

Baer (Ber), Ludwig (of Basle, 1479-1554; Professor of theology at Basle, twice Rector of the University, anti-Reformation friend of Erasmus: cf. Allen, II, 381, ADB, II, 45-46, DS, I, 508-509, NDB, I, 525), Exp., pars. 93, 139, Sp., Pref. I, Sp., pars. 38, 47, 101, 162-163, 165, Sp., ns. 37, 181, 257 (Ep. 2149) .

Barbaro, Ermolao (of Venice, 1454-1493/94; Professor of philosophy in Venice, diplomat, Patriarch of Aquileia: cf. Allen, I, 293, DBI, VI, 96-99, EB, III, 382 / passim in MHL, X, Renaudet (2) and (4)), Sp., par. 342, Sp., n. 385

Barland, Hubert (of Baarland, Zeeland, d. after 1544; Student of Vives in Louvain, with Erasmus in Basle in 1528, wrote on medicine, translated Galen: cf. Allen, VII, 545, BNB, I, 722-723 (fl. 1528-1544), BWN, II:1, 27-28, MHL, XI, 518-523, NNBW, I, 220-221 (v. Baerland) / passim in MHL, X-XIII), Sp., n. 385 (Ep. 2172)

Batt, Jacob (of Bergen, c. 1464-1502; Teacher in Bergen and secretary to the Town Council, early friend and patron of Erasmus: cf. Allen, I, 131, BWN, II:1,

175, NNBW, VIII, 57 (v. Battus) / passim in MHL, X, XI, Renaudet (2) and (4)), Sp., n. 405 (Eps. 80, 95, 128, 139, 146)

Beatus Rhenanus (i.e., Beat Bild, of Schlettstadt, 1485-1547; Worked for Amerbach and Froben for 15 years, supervised Erasmus' publications: cf. Allen, II, 60, ADB, XXVII, 383-386 (v. Rhenanus), EB, XXIII, 233 (v. Rhenanus), MHL, X, 391-392, NDB, I, 682 / passim in MHL, X, XI, Renaudet (2) and (4), UTM / BdG, II, 175-176, V, 83, 230), Int., ns. 6 (Ep. 327), 14, Sp., pars. 15, 42-50, 54, Sp., ns. 39, 388, 389

Beda, Natalis (i.e., Noël Bédier, of the diocese of Avranches in Picardy, d. 1536/37; Supporter of Standonck (q.v.) at Montaigu, Syndic of the Faculty of Theology in Paris, attacked Lefèvre and Erasmus, retired to Mont-S.-Michel after an attack on Marguerite of Navarre, sister of Francis I: cf. Allen, VI, 65, BU, III, 478-479, MHL, I, 533-534, NBG, V, 118 / passim in Bataillon, MHL, I, X, XI, XII, Renaudet (2) and (4), UTM), Sp., n. 428

Bergen, Antonius van (of Bergen, 1455-1531/32; Abbot of St. Bertin at Saint-Omer; cf. Allen, I, 334, NNBW, IX, 50-51 / passim in MHL, X (v. Berghes), Renaudet (2) and (4), UTM), Sp., n. 246 (Ep. 288)

Bergen, Hendrik van (of Bergen, d. 1502; 1480 Bp. of Cambrai, patron of Erasmus: cf. Allen, I, 160 / passim in MHL, X, Renaudet (2), UTM), Sp., n. 405 (Ep. 154)

Blount, William, cf. Mountjoy

Bombasius, Paulus (i.e., Paolo Bombace, of Bologna, 1476-1527; Teacher of Greek and secretary to Cardinal Pucci and Clement VII: cf. Allen, I, 443, DBI, XI, 373-376 / passim in Renaudet (4), UTM / Ono, 122), Int., n. 54 (Ep. 1411)

Botzheim, Johann von (of Sasbach/Alsace, c. 1480-1535; Doctor of Canon Law, Humanist writer, Canon of Constance, intimate friend of Erasmus: cf. Allen, I, 1, ADB, III, 208-209, NDB, II, 490 / passim in MHL, XII, UTM / BdG, I, 62, VII, 21), Int., p. 12, Int., ns. 26 (Ep. 1934), 27 (Ep. 1331), 29 (Ep. 1934), 30 (Ep. 1934), 33 (Ep. 1934), 54 (Ep. 1335), Exp., ns. 73, 81 (Ep. 1335), 94, 125 (Allen, I, 1), Sp., par. 54, Sp., ns. 76a, 137 (Allen, I, 24-25), 386 (Allen, I, 2), 388 (Allen, I, 5, 55, 59, 67)

Briard, Jan (Jan Briaert/Joannes Briardus Atensis, of Beloeil/Hainault, d. 1520; Professor of theology and Vice-Chancellor of Louvain, moderate conservative, friendly with Erasmus although he feared his views: cf. Allen, III, 93, ADB, III, 327, BNB, III, 47-50, BU, V, 510, MHL, X, 301-303, NBG, VII, 371-372 / passim in MHL, X-XII), Exp., pars. 141-142, Sp., pars. 166-168, Sp., n. 184

Brunfels, Otto (of Mainz, c. 1488-1534; Writer of educational treatises, at first attacked Dorp and Luther but then joined Zwingli in Zurich, friend of both Erasmus and the Reformation, died as a medical doctor in Basle: cf. Allen, V, 367, ADB, III, 441, NDB, II, 677 / BdG, I, 74, V, 31), Int., p. 18, Int., ns. 28 (Responsio ad spongiam Erasmi), 45 (Eps. 1405, 1406, 1614), 54

Budé, Guillaume (of Paris, 1467/68-1540; Translator of Greek texts, secretary to Francis I, persuaded the King to found the Collège de France trilingue, defended the study of Greek against charges of heresy: cf. Allen, II, 227, BU, VI, 109-112, EB, IV, 749-750, MHL, I, 456-458, NBG, V, 718-725 / passim in Bataillon, MHL, I, X, XI, Renaudet (2) and (4), UTM), Int., ns. 21 (Ep. 1184), 76, Exp., n. 48 (Ep. 778), Sp., ns. 253 (Ep. 1233), 343, 365 (Ep. 480), 389 (Eps. 480, 529, 531, 1111, 1479, 2468, 3048, Allen, I, 67)

Burbank, William (d. 1531; Student at Cambridge, secretary and chaplain of Wolsey, aided in converting the monastic property into the foundation of Wolsey's Cardinal College at Oxford: cf. Allen, IV, 333, Emden (C), 106-107 (Gulielmus Burbancus)), Sp., n. 276 (Ep. 1138)

Busch (or van dem Busche), Hermann (of the Castle of Sassenberg near Münster, 1468-1534; Teacher and wandering Humanist, 1522 turned to theology, 1526-1533 taught at the new Reformed university of Marburg, wrote his famous treatise Vallum humanitatis in defense of the humanities as an aid to the study of theology: cf. Allen, III, 296, ADB, III, 637-640, MHL, X, 478-484, NDB, III, 61 / passim in MHL, X-XI / BdG, I, 89-90, V, 36), Int., pp. 2, 18, Exp., par. 58, Sp., pars. 63, 69, 83 (Vallum), Sp., ns. 93, 105 (Ep. 830, Vallum)

Caesarius, Jan (of Jülich, c. 1468-1550; Teacher of Greek in many centers of Germany, friendly with many Reformers but stayed within the Church: cf. Allen, II, 172, ADB, III, 689-691, MHL, X, 281, NDB, III, 90 / passim in MHL, X-XI), Exp., ns. 36 (Ep. 808), 46 (Ep. 622), Sp., par. 94, Sp., ns. 117, 208 (Ep. 1528)

Cajetan, cf. De Vio, Tommaso

Camerarius, Joachim (i.e., Joachim Kammermeister, of Bamberg, 1500-1574; Friend of Erasmus then follower of Luther, taught the Classics 1526 to 1574, writer of commentaries on the Classics, comedies, histories, biographies, etc.: cf. Allen, V, 555, ADB, III, 720-724, MHL, X, 274, NDB, III, 104 / passim in MHL, X-XIII / BdG, I, 104, V, 44, VII, 41, 502), Int., n. 44

Camillo, Giulio (of Forlì, 1480-1544; Teacher of Greek and student of Oriental languages, invented a mysterious "cabinet of knowledge", patronized by Francis I: cf. Allen, IX, 479, BU, VI, 480, NBG, VIII, 336-337), Exp., par. 154

Cammyngha, Haio (Haye van Cammingha/Haio Caminga Phrysius, of Friesland, c. 1503-1558; 1529-1530 member of Erasmus' household in Basle: cf. Allen, VII, 532, BWN, III, 45, MHL, XI, 455-460 / passim in MHL, XI-XIII), Sp., n. 386

Campegio (Campeggio), Lorenzo (of Bologna, 1472-1539; Bp. of Feltre and then Bologna, canonist and twice Papal Legate to England, sent to England in 1528/29 in the matter of the King's divorce: cf. Allen, III, 573, DNB, III, 850, EB, V, 134, EI, VIII, 598, Lauchert, 614-619 / passim in Bataillon, MHL, X-XIII, Renaudet (4), UTM / BdG, I, 105, V, 44, VII, 41, Ono, 169), Int., ns. 19 (Ep. 1167), 21 (Ep. 1167), 38 (Ep. 1167), Exp., ns. 94 (Ep. 1167), 98 (Ep. 1167), 105 (Ep. 1167), 114 (Ep. 1167), 120 (Ep. 1167)

Capito, Wolfgang (i.e., Wolfgang Faber or Fabricius Köpfel, of Hagenau, c. 1478-1541; Cathedral preacher in Basle, Dean of the Faculty of Theology there, Hebrew scholar, aided Erasmus with his N.T. translation, went over to the Reformation and withdrew to Strasburg: cf. Allen, II, 333, ADB, III, 772-775, EB, V, 282, NDB, III, 132 / passim in MHL, X, UTM / BdG, I, 111-112, V, 45-46, VII, 42), Int., n. 5, Exp., pars. 85-93, Sp., pars. 18, 97-101, Sp., ns. 42, 122 (Eps. 1083, 1165), 123, 388 (Ep. 541)

Capnio, cf. Reuchlin

Caracciolo, Marino (of Naples, c. 1469-1538; Bp. of Catania, Cardinal, Papal Nuncio
    to Emperor Maximilian, governor of Milan, urged Erasmus to write against
    Luther: cf. Allen, III, 390, NBG, VIII, 651 / passim in Renaudet (4) /
    Ono, 178), Exp., pars. 135, 152, Sp., pars. 143, 157, Sp., n. 173

Carondelet, Jean de (of Dôle, 1469-1544; Councillor of Margaret of Austria and
    Charles V, Archbp. of Palermo, President of the Privy Council of the
    Netherlands, patron of Erasmus: cf. Allen, III, 257, BNB, III, 348-350,
    BU, VIII, 31, MHL, I, 139, NBG, VIII, 819 / passim in Bataillon, MHL, I,
    XI-XIII), Sp., n. 444 (Ep. 1334)

Carranza, Sancho (Sanctius) (of Miranda in Navarre, fl. 1496-1523; Teacher at Alcalá,
    major-domo of Alexander VI, critic of Erasmus: cf. Allen, V, 53, HHE, II,
    54-57 / passim in Bataillon), Sp., par. 196

Cat(h)arinus, Ambrosius (i.e., Lancellotto de' Politi, of Siena, c. 1484-1553;
    Lawyer and Bp. of Minori, influenced by Savonarola, attacked Luther, Erasmus
    and Cajetan: cf. Allen, V, 50, Lauchert, 30-133 / BdG, I, 115-116, VII,
    43, Ono, 195), Sp., par. 196, Sp., n. 219

Celtis, Conradus Protucus (i.e., Konrad Pickel (Bickel), of Wipfeld near Schweinfurt,
    1459-1508; German Humanist, neo-Latin poet and playwright, professor at
    Ingolstadt and Vienna, encouraged the study of the Classics by founding
    sodalities in Cracow, Budapest and Heidelberg, wrote historical works and
    on versification: cf. ADB, IV, 82-88, EB, V, 653, NDB, III, 181-183, Spitz,
    81-109 / passim in UTM), Int., p. 30, Int., n. 2

Charles V, Emperor (Caesar Carolus quintus, 1500-1558, Emperor, 1519-1556; cf. EB,
    V, 899-905 / passim in Bataillon, MHL, X-XIII, Renaudet (2) and (4), UTM /
    BdG, III, 38-66, V, 405-408, VII, 321-327, 521), Int., p. 31, Int., ns. 20,
    21, 79, Exp., pars. 128, 131, 152, Exp., n. 8, Sp., Pref. I, Sp., pars.
    31, 37, 111, 150-154, 157, 187, 194, 196, 216, 251, 272, 303, 305, 310,
    311, 312, 334, 390, 409, Sp., ns. 383, 388 (Allen, I, IV), 389 (Allen, I,
    IV), 450 (Ep. 1255)

Choler (Koler), Johannes (of the Canton Grisons, fl. 1508-1541; Provost of Passau,
    intimate friend of the Fuggers, Provost of Chur, follower of the Reformers:
    cf. Allen, VIII, 228, AK, V, 96, DS, IV, 386, MHL, XI, 149, 496), Int.,
    n. 24 (Ep. 2470), Sp., n. 159 (Ep. 2565)

Christiern (Christian) II, King of Denmark (1481-1559, King between 1513-1523,
    expelled by his subjects in 1523 and then imprisoned for life in 1532 when
    he tried to regain his throne by force: cf. Allen, IV, 333, 568, EB, VI,
    274-276 / passim in MHL, X-XII, UTM), Sp., n. 63

Cles, Bernard (Bernhard/Bernhardus von Cles, 1485-1539; Great statesman and prelate,
    advisor to Maximilian and Ferdinand, governor of Verona, Cardinal, Bp. of
    Trent, patron of Erasmus: cf. Allen, V, 275, ADB, IV, 324-325, MHL, XI,
    392 / BdG, III, 521-522, VII, 44), Exp., n. 81 (Ep. 1357)

Colet, John (of London, c. 1466-1519; Leader of the Humanist movement in England,
    teacher at Oxford, Dean of St. Paul's, founder of St. Paul's School, close
    friend of Erasmus: cf. Allen, I, 242, DNB, IV, 777-784, EB, VI, 681-682,
    Emden (O,1), I, 462-464 / passim in Olin (TB), Renaudet (2) and (4), UTM /

BdG, I, 228 (No. 5655), Sp., ns. 90, 208 (Ep. 1211), 353, 405 (Eps. 227, 230, 237)

Croke, Richard (of London, c. 1489-1558; Pupil of Erasmus in Paris, taught Greek in England and on the Continent, Canon of Henry VIII's College, Oxford (Christ Church): cf. Allen, I, 467, DNB, V, 119-121, Emden (0,1), I, 515-517, MHL, X, 274-277 / passim in MHL, X-XII, UTM), Exp., n. 45

Crotus Rubianus (Rubeanus) (i.e., Johannes Jäger, of Dornheim/Thuringia, c. 1480-1545; Humanist and theologian, mentor of Hutten in Erfurt, contributed to the EOV (some 38 letters), friend of Luther, advisor to Albert of Mainz: cf. ADB, IV, 612-614, NDB, III, 424 / passim in MHL, X, UTM / BdG, I, 144, V, 57, VII, 52), Int., p. 2, Int., n. 7

Desmarais (Desmarez), Jean (Joannes Paludanus, of Cassel near Saint-Omer, d. 1525; Public rhetor in Louvain, Scribe of Louvain, friend of Erasmus: cf. Allen, I, 398, BNB, XVI, 517-518 (v. Paludanus), MHL, X, 184-186 / passim in MHL, X-XI, Renaudet (2, esp. pp. 428-429), UTM), Sp., par. 361, Sp., n. 404 (Ep. 180)

De Vio, Tommaso OP (of Gaeta, Naples, c. 1470-1534; General of the Dominican Order, Cardinal, Bp. of Gaeta, Papal Legate in Germany, bulwark of the papacy: cf. Allen, III, 429, EB, IV, 961, EI, XII, 703 (v. Caietano), Lauchert, 133-177 / passim in Bataillon, MHL, X, XIII, Renaudet (2) and (4), UTM / BdG, I, 94, V, 38, VII, 32, 501), Int., p. 4, Int., n. 79, Sp., par. 196, Sp., n. 219

Dierckx, Vincent Theodoricus (Vincentius Theodorici OP, of Beverwijk near Haarlem, c. 1481-1526; Dominican at Paris, edited part of Aquinas' Summa, taught at Louvain, Inquisitor of the Utrecht diocese, with Baechem bitterly opposed to Erasmus: cf. Allen, IV, 463, MHL, X, 464-465 / passim in Bataillon, MHL, X-XI, Renaudet (4)), Sp., pars. 118, 196, 392, Sp., n. 219

Dorp, Martin (Maarten Bartholomeuszoon, of Naaldwijk, c. 1480-1525; Professor of philosophy and theology at Louvain, anti-Erasmian writer: cf. Allen, II, 11, BNB, VI, 138-141, BWN, IV, 290-291, MHL, IV, 61-408, X, 187-188, 215-222, 502-505, NNBW, IV, 519 / passim in Bataillon, MHL, X-XIII, Renaudet (2) and (4), UTM), Int., n. 60 (Ep. 337), Sp., par. 171, Sp., ns. 127 (Eps. 304, 337, 347), 385 (Eps. 304, 337)

Duchesne, Guillaume (Quercus/Quernus/Querquo Normannus, d. 1535; Doctor at the Sorbonne, leader of the Faculty of Theology, with Beda responsible for the Determinatio against Luther, Inquisitor and heresy-hunter: cf. Allen, IV, 447, Féret, II, 62 / passim in Renaudet (2)), Sp., par. 392

Eck, Johann (i.e., Johannes Maier, of Egg or Eck, 1486-1543; Doctor of theology, professor in Ingolstadt, anti-scholastic, published the papal bull against Luther in 1520: cf. Allen, III, 208, ADB, V, 596-602, EB, VIII, 884-885, NDB, IV, 273 / passim in MHL, X-XII, UTM / BdG, I, 207-210, V, 73-74, VII, 65), Exp., par. 136, Sp., pars. 157, 196, Sp., n. 219

Egmondanus, cf. Baechem

Egnatius, Baptista (i.e., Giambattista Egnazio (orig. Cipelli), of Venice, 1473-1553; Edited many of the Classics for Aldus, taught at Venice: cf. Allen, I, 523, BU, XII, 311-312, EI, X, 386 (v. Cipelli), MHL, XIII, 494, NBG, XV, 735-736 / passim in MHL, XII, Renaudet (2) and (4) / Ono, 285), Int., n. 9 (Ep. 588)

Eleutherius (prob. Sebastian Franck, of Donauwörth, q.v.), Int., n. 54 (Ep. 2441)

Eobanus Hessus, Helius (i.e., Helius Eobanus Koch or Coci, of Halgehausen in Hesse, 1488-1540; Lecturer on the Classics in Erfurt, professor of history at Marburg: Allen, III, 411, ADB, XII, 316-318, MHL, XI, 32-37, NDB, IV, 543 / passim in MHL, XI, XII, UTM / BdG, I, 219, V, 77, VII, 68), Int., pp. 17, 19, Int., n. 14

Eppendorf, Heinrich von (of Eppendorff near Freiburg/Meissen, 1496-1551; Follower and friend of Hutten, antagonistic to Erasmus for many years, patron of good letters and translator from the Greek: cf. Allen, IV, 303, ADB, VI, 158, MHL, X, 492, NDB, IV, 548 / passim in MHL, X-XII), Int., ns. 29, 33, 54, Exp., par. 26, Sp., pars. 4-23, 43, 48, 50, 54, 56, 185, Sp., ns. 29, 32 (Eps. 1122, 1371, Allen, IV, 616), 78, 386

Erasmus of Rotterdam (c. 1466-1536; cf. ADB, VI, 160-180, EB, IX, 727-732 (v. also Index, p. 289), NDB, IV, 554-560, Spitz, 197-236 / passim in MHL, X-XIII, UTM / BdG, I, 221-235, V, 77-84, VII, 68-75, 504-506):
Erasmus on:
buying of Church offices, Sp., n. 454
celibacy, Sp., n. 253
Christian Humanism, Sp., n. 272 (cf. BdG, IV, 283-292, V, 81, VII, 72)
court life, Sp., n. 371 (cf. BdG, IV, 278-279)
cult of saints, Sp., n. 254 (Eps. 2037, 2443) (cf. BdG, IV, 269)
dying, Sp., n. 456
education, Sp., ns. 90 (Ep. 23), 353 (Ep. 1211) (cf. BdG, I, 230, 233, IV, 193-194, V, 79)
fasting, Sp., n. 251 (Ep. 1353)
gambling, Sp., n. 261
good letters, Sp., n. 429 (cf. BdG, I, 230, 231, VII, 72)
goals of his life, Int., p. 10, Sp., n. 124
holy days, Sp., n. 252
law vs. spirit, Sp., ns. 251 (Ep. 1887), 254 (cf. BdG, VII, 74)
marriage vs. celibacy, Sp., n. 253 (Eps. 999, 1233, 1593, 2037, 2300) (cf. BdG, VII, 72)
martyrdom, Sp., n. 362
monasticism, Sp., n. 150 (Eps. 296, 309, 447, 2700) (cf. BdG, IV, 91-92, 374-375)
non-essentials, Sp., n. 453
peace, Sp., n. 444 (Ep. 1334) (cf. BdG, I, 235, IV, 651-652, V, 80)
piety, Sp., ns. 249 (Ep. 858), 193, 255 (cf. BdG, I, 230, IV, 219)
princes, Sp., n. 360
retirement from the world, Sp., n. 381
virginity, Sp., n. 253
war, Sp., ns. 246 (Eps. 288, 858, 1756), 450 (Eps. 1156, 1211, 1255, 1333, 1381, 400) (cf. BdG, IV, 389-390, VII, 74)

Erasmus, works of:
Adagia, Int., ns. 61, 65, Sp., n. 2 et passim (cf. BdG, I, 224, VII, 69, MHL, XI)
Antibarbari, Int., ns. 58, 62, Sp., n. 228 (cf. BdG, IV, 78)
Apotheosis of Reuchlin, Sp., par. 109, Sp., ns. 131, 150 (cf. BdG, VII, 70)
Catalogus omnium Erasmi lucubrationum, Exp., ns. 73, 94, 125, Sp., pars. 157, 186, Sp., ns. 137, 209, 386, 388 (cf. BdG, I, 227)
Ciceronianus, Sp., n. 159 (Eps. 2565, 2587, 2736) (cf. BdG, I, 227, 229, VII, 71)

Colloquia (cf. Thompson (1)), Int., ns. 4, 56, 62, Sp., pars. 17, 371,
   Sp., ns. 32, 36, 39, 51, 90, 131, 137, 150, 159, 193, 199
   (Ep. 909), 207, 235, 242, 246, 251, 253, 254, 257, 346, 352,
   353, 381, 412 (Eps. 1299, 1300, 1704), 428, 450, 453, 454, 456
   (cf. BdG, I, 228, V, 80, VII, 71, MHL, XI)
Compendium vitae Erasmi (cf. Allen, I, 46-52, BdG, V, 80, VII, 71)
Concio de puero Jesu, Sp., n. 353
Coniugii matrimonii, Sp., n. 253 (Ep. 604, p. 17, n. 10) (cf. BdG, IV,
   182-184, VII, 74)
Declamatio de morte, Sp., n. 456
Declarationes ad censuras Lutetiae vulgatas, Sp., ns. 114, 150, 251, 412
De contemptu mundi epistola, Int., n. 62, Sp., ns. 150, 381
De duplici copia verborum ac rerum commentarii duo, Sp., n. 353 (cf. BdG,
   VII, 1, 71)
De formando studio (De ratione studii), Int., n. 61, Sp., n. 90
De interdictu esu carnium, Sp., n. 251
De libero arbitrio, Exp., n. 31, Sp., n. 453 (cf. BdG, I, 225, IV, 752,
   VII, 70)
De praeparatione ad mortem, Sp., ns. 150, 456
De pueris statim ac liberaliter instituendis, Sp., n. 90 (cf. BdG, I,
   228, VII, 72)
De recta latini graecique sermonis pronuntiatione dialogus, Sp., n. 353
De sarcienda (amabili) ecclesiae concordia, Sp., n. 453 (cf. BdG, I, 228)
De utilitate colloquiorum, Sp., n. 412
Dulce bellum inexpertis, Sp., n. 450 (cf. BdG, VII, 70)
Ecclesiastes, Sp., n. 150
Enchiridion militis christiani, Int., p. 23, Int., n. 62, Sp., ns. 193,
   228 (cf. BdG, I, 229, V, 79, VII, 71)
Hyperaspistes diatribae adversus servum arbitrium Lutheri, Exp., n. 31
   (cf. BdG, VII, 73)
Inquisitio de fide, Sp., n. 453 (cf. BdG, VII, 72)
Institutio principis christiani, Int., p. 23, Sp., par. 253, Sp., ns. 246,
   360, 450 (cf. BdG, I, 231, 235, IV, 221, V, 81)
Institutum hominis christiani, Sp., n. 353
Julius exclusus, Int., n. 5, Sp., ns. 116, 246 (cf. BdG, I, 229, V, 80,
   VII, 73)
Moriae encomium, Int., pp. 21, 24, 25, Int., ns. 59, 60, Sp., ns. 116,
   193, 246, 370 (cf. BdG, I, 229, V, 80; VII, 71)
Novum Instrumentum (New Testament; cf. BdG, I, 232-233, IV, 92-96, 463,
   VII, 73, MHL, X-XI): Annotations, Int., n. 10, Sp., par. 234,
   Sp., n. 252 (BdG, I, 230, V, 80); Paraphrases, Sp., pars. 185,
   199, 255, 313, 424, Sp., ns. 127 (Eps. 304, 337, 347, 1031),
   207, 275, 450; Translation, Int., ns. 16, 60, 76, Exp., pars.
   88, 93, Sp., par. 101, Sp., ns. 127, 385
Opera omnia (new edition), Sp., n. 228
Paraclesis ad christianae philosophiae studium, Sp., ns. 127, 298 (cf.
   BdG, I, 233, VII, 73)
Precationes (prayers), Sp., n. 353
Querela pacis, Int., n. 62, Sp., ns. 246, 450 (cf. BdG, I, 233, V, 83,
   VII, 74)
Ratio verae theologiae methodus, Int., pp. 3, 24, Sp., ns. 127, 150, 228
   (cf. MHL, X, 303-304 et passim)
Sileni Alcibiadis, Int., n. 65, Sp., ns. 282, 450
Supputationes errorum in censuris Natalis Bedae, Sp., n. 150
Symboli explanatio, Sp., n. 453
Vidua christiana, Sp., n. 253

Faber Stapulensis, cf. Lefèvre d'Etaples

Fabri (or Faber), Joannes, cf. Heigerlin

Ferdinand of Austria (Ferdinandus, Caroli Caesar germanus, 1503-1564, Emperor,
1558-1564: cf. ADB, VI, 632-644, EB, X, 261-262, NDB, V, 81-83 / passim
in UTM / BdG, I, 222, III, 66-75, V, 408, VII, 327), Int., ns. 21, 79,
Exp., n. 8, Sp., pars. 272, 337, Sp., ns. 207, 383, 450 (Ep. 1333)

Fisher, Christopher (d. 1511; Notary for Archbp. Warham, Bp. of Elphin 1506: cf.
Allen, I, 406, Emden (0,1), II, 686-687 / passim in Bataillon, Renaudet (2),
esp. p. 478 and (4), p. 39, MHL, XI, esp. p. 41), Sp., n. 385 (Ep. 182)

Fisher, John (of Beverly, c. 1459-1535; Confessor to Lady Margaret, the mother of
Henry VIII, Chancellor of Oxford, Bp. of Rochester, martyrer: cf. Allen,
I, 469, DNB, VII, 58-63, EB, X, 427-428, Emden (C), 229-230 / passim in
Bataillon, MHL, X-XI, Renaudet (2) and (4), UTM), Int., ns. 5 (Ep. 413),
40 (Ep. 889), 41 (Ep. 1129), Exp., par. 97, Exp., ns. 47 (Ep. 413), 49
(Ep. 413), 52 (Ep. 1129), 54 (Ep. 1129), Sp. pars. 102, 104-106, 111, 196,
231, Sp., ns. 128 (Ep. 1129), 219, 269, 405 (Ep. 242)

Fisher, Robert (d. by 1511; Lawyer, churchman, Canon of Windsor: cf. Allen, I, 188,
MHL, XI, 365 / passim in Renaudet (2) and (4)), Sp., n. 388 (Ep. 118)

Francis I, King of France (1515-1547: cf. Allen, VII, 234, EB, X, 934-935 / passim
in UTM), Int., n. 11, Sp., par. 337, Sp., ns. 383, 450 (Ep. 1400)

Franck, Sebastian (of Donauwörth, 1499-1542; Prodigious writer on history and religious
topics, joined the Nürnberg Reformers, translated Erasmus' _Encomium Moriae_
into German: cf. Allen, IX, 153, ADB, VII, 214-219, EB, XI, 4, NDB, V, 320-
321 / passim in UTM / BdG, I, 263-266, V, 92, VII, 79-80), Int., n. 65

Frederick III, the Wise (Federicus sacri imperii elector, Kurfürst von Sachsen, 1463-
1525; Electoral Prince of Saxony, champion of Luther and the Reformation:
cf. Allen, II, 579, ADB, VII, 779-781, EB, XI, 60, NDB, V, 528-530 / passim
in MHL, X, esp. p. 534, XI, UTM / BdG, III, 448-452), Int., p. 31, Int.,
ns. 21, 79, 80, Sp., par. 259, Sp., n. 308

Froben, Johannes (of Hammelburg/Franconia, c. 1460-1527; Took over Amerbach's printing
house, Erasmus' publisher in Basle: cf. Allen, II, 250, ADB, VIII, 127-128,
EB, XI, 237, NDB, V, 638-640 / passim in MHL, X-XIII, Renaudet (2) and (4),
UTM / BdG, I, 272, V, 94, VII, 81), Exp., n. 89, Sp., Pref. II, Sp., pars.
52, 93, 119, 125, Sp., ns. 116, 159

Gattinara, Mercurino Arborio (of Gattinara/Piedmont, 1465-1530; Minister of Margaret
of Austria, President of the Council of Burgundy, Chancellor of Castile for
Charles V, Cardinal, friend of Erasmus: cf. Allen, IV, 359, ADB, VIII,
418-419, EI, XVI, 450, MHL, XI, 287 / passim in Bataillon, MHL, XI-XII,
Renaudet (4), UTM / BdG, I, 283, V, 98, VII, 84, Ono, 43-44), Int., n. 54
(Ep. 1700), Exp., n. 79 (Ep. 1150)

Gebwiler, Johannes (of Kolmar, fl. 1469-1523; Professor at Basle 1504-1523, three
times Rector of the University there: cf. Allen, VI, 218, AK, II, 266, DS,
III, 339), Exp., par. 139, Sp., pars. 164-165, Sp., n. 182

Geldenhauer, Gerard (Gerardus Noviomagnus, of Nijmegen, c. 1482-1542; Secretary to
the Bp. of Utrecht, professor of history at Marburg, Humanist writer,
promoted the Reformation: cf. Allen, II, 379, ADB, VIII, 530-531, BWN,
VII, 77-79, NNBW, VI, 550 / passim in MHL, X-XI, UTM / BdG, I, 285), Int.,
ns. 5 (Ep. 1141), 40 (Ep. 1141), Sp., n. 208

George, Duke of Saxony (1471-1539; Opponent of Luther and the Reformation in his
territory: cf. ADB, VIII, 684-687, NDB, VI, 224-227 / passim in MHL, X-XI,
UTM / BdG, III, 453-456, VII, 72, 367-368), Int., n. 21 (Eps. 1313, 1526)

Gerard, Cornelis OSA (Aurelius/Aurotinus, of Gouda, fl. 1489-1524; Humanist writer:
cf. Allen, I, 92, BNB, VII, 780 / passim in MHL, X-XI, Renaudet (2) and (4)),
Sp., ns. 90 (Ep. 23), 385 (Eps. 26, 29)

Gillis (Gilles), Peter (Petrus Aegidius Gillis, of Antwerp, 1486/87-1533; Corrector
for Marten's press, chief secretary to Antwerp, edited many Classics, works
by Erasmus and More's Utopia: cf. Allen, I, 413, ADB, I, 125 (v. Aegidius),
BNB, VII, 780-783, BWN, I, 99, MHL, XI, 66-67, NNBW, VII, 5-6 (v. Aegidius) /
passim in MHL, X-XIII, UTM), Int., n. 1 (Ep. 332)

Giustiniani (Giustiniano), Agostino (of Genoa, 1470-1536; Scholar of Oriental languages,
Almoner of Francis I, translator from the Greek, Bp. of Nebbio/Corsica: cf.
Allen, III, 278, EB, XII, 55, EI, XVII, 384), Sp., par. 196, Sp., n. 219

Glapion, Jean OFM (of Normandy or Maine, d. 1522; Provincial of the Franciscans of
Burgundy, confessor of Charles V, aided Aleander at the Diet of Worms: cf.
Allen, V, 47, BNB, VII, 805 / passim in Bataillon, MHL, XI-XII), Exp.,
pars. 128-133, 152, Exp., ns. 73, 74, Sp., pars. 151-154, Sp., n. 169

Glareanus, Henricus (i.e., Heinrich Loriti, of Mollis, Canton Glarus, 1488-1536;
Supporter of Reuchlin, teacher in Basle and Paris, edited Roman histories:
cf. Allen, II, 279, ADB, IX, 210-211, MHL, XI, 499, NDB, VI, 425-426 / passim
in MHL, X-XIII, Renaudet (2) and (4) / BdG, I, 292-293, V, 102, VII, 86),
Int., n. 25, Sp., par. 54, Sp., ns. 76a, 253 (Ep. 604)

Goclenius, Conradus (i.e., Konrad Gockelen, of Mengeringhausen/Waldeck, c. 1489-1539;
1519-1539 taught Latin at Louvain, devoted to Erasmus: cf. Allen, IV, 504,
ADB, IX, 308-312, MHL, X, 484-487, XII, 94-104, NDB, IX, 308 / passim in
MHL, X-XIII, Renaudet (4), UTM / BdG, II, No. 26264), Int., ns. 26 (Ep.
1437), 29 (Ep. 1437), 36 (Ep. 1437), 46 (Ep. 1437), 52 (Ep. 1388), 54 (Ep.
1437), Sp., par. 196, Sp., ns. 159 (Ep. 2587), 219

Grimani, Domenico (of Venice, 1461-1523; Cardinal-Patriarch of Aquileia, Bp. of Porto,
patron of literature and collector of manuscripts: cf. Allen, II, 73, EI,
XVII, 971, Lauchert, 455-458 / passim in Renaudet (2) and (4)), Int., n. 4
(Ep. 334)

Grocyn (Grocin), William (of Colerne/Wiltshire, c. 1446-1519; Teacher of Greek at
Oxford, friend of Colet and Erasmus, fostered the Humanist movement in England:
cf. Allen, I, 273, DNB, VIII, 709-712, EB, XII, 610-611, Emden (0,1), II,
827-830, MHL, X, 171-172 / passim in MHL, X, Renaudet (2) and (4), UTM),
Sp., par. 343, Sp., n. 388 (Allen, I, 5, 55, 59, 67, Eps. 118, 520, 540)

Grunnius, Lambertus (a pseudonym - person unknown), Sp., n. 150 (Ep. 447)

322

Haio, Hermannus (Hermannus Humpius Phrysius, of Hompens or Emden, c. 1500-1540; Peripatetic student and Humanist, translator of the Classics, member of the Council of Utrecht, friend of Erasmus and More: cf. Allen, III, 444, BWN, VIII:1, 88, MHL, X, 393-394, NNBW, X, 320-321), Sp., n. 389 (Ep. 1479)

Hedio, Gaspar (Caspar) (i.e., Kaspar Heyd/Bock or Böckel, of Ettlingen by Karlsruhe, 1494-1552; Preacher in Mainz and Strasburg, moderate Reformer, wrote a history of the Church: cf. Allen, V, 479, ADB, XI, 223-224, NDB, VIII, 188-189 / BdG, I, 330, V, 115, VII, 93), Int., ns. 26, 34 (Ep. 1459)

Hegius, Alexander (of Heek/Westphalia, c. 1433-1498; Pupil of R. Agricola, teacher of Erasmus: cf. Allen, I, 106, ADB, XI, 283-285, EB, XIII, 208, MHL, X, 198, NDB, VIII, 232-233 / passim in MHL, X, Renaudet (2) and (4)), Sp., par. 342, Sp., n. 386

Heigerlin, Johannes (Joannes Fabri of Faber, of Leutkirch/Allgau, 1478-1541; Suffragan-Bp. of Constance, Bp. Vienna, minister of Ferdinand I, promoted Humanism, friend of Erasmus: cf. Allen, II, 189, ADB, XIV, 435-441 (v. Faber, Bp. of Vienna), MHL, XI, 356, NDB, IV, 728 / passim in MHL, XI-XII / BdG, I, 240, V, 85, VII, 77), Exp., par. 138, Sp., par. 160, Sp., ns. 178, 207 (Ep. 2503)

Henry VIII, King of England (1509-1547: cf. DNB, IX, 527-545, EB, XIII, 287-290 / passim in UTM / BdG, IV, 186-188, VII, 418-419), Sp., pars. 196, 264, 337, Sp., ns. 116, 219, 312, 383, 450 (Ep. 1381), 453

Hoogstraten (Hochstrat), Jacob OP (of Hoogstraten, c. 1465-1527; Dominican of Cologne, Inquisitor-General of Cologne, Mainz and Trier, ardent supporter of the anti-Jewish/anti-Reuchlin faction: cf. Allen, I, 556, ADB, XII, 527-529, BNB, X, 77-80, BWN, VIII:2, 1147-1149, NDB, IX, 605-606, NNBW, I, 1152-1155 / passim in Bataillon, MHL, X, Renaudet (2) and (4), UTM / BdG, I, 347, V, 122), Int., pp. 9, 11, 15, Int., ns. 5 (Ep. 1006), 40 (Ep. 1006), Exp., pars. 58-59, 66-78, 108, 112, Exp., n. 32 (Ep. 1006), Sp., pars. 18, 61-71, 76-82, 85-91, 164, 303-304, 384, Sp., ns. 84 (Ep. 1006), 85 (Ep. 1006), 103 (Ep. 1078), 122 (Eps. 1083, 1165, 1195), 219

Hutten, Ulrich von (of Castle Steckelberg near Fulda/Hesse, 1488-1523: cf. Allen, II, 155, ADB, XIII, 464-475, EB, XIV, 14-15, Spitz, 110-129 / passim in MHL, X-XI, UTM / BdG, I, 378-385, V, 131-132, VII, 104, 509), Int., ns. 7 (Ep. 365), 9 (Ep. 611), 12 (Ep. 923), 13 (Ep. 951), 21 (Eps. 1135, 1161), 22 (Ep. 1135), 23 (Ep. 1161), 27 (Ep. 1356), 29 (Ep. 1356), 73 (Ep. 1161), Sp., n. 253 (Ep. 999)

Hutten, works of:
Arminius, Int., n. 79 (cf. BdG, I, Nos. 9215-9215a)
Aula, Int., p. 29, Int., n. 76
Bulla vel bullicida, Int., n. 99 (cf. BdG, IV, 157)
Epistola vitae suae rationem expones, Int., ns. 16, 76 (cf. BdG, I, No. 9236)
EOV, Int., p. 7, Int., ns. 5, 41, Exp., pars. 81-82, Exp., ns. 33, 45, Sp., par. 92, Sp., n. 119 (cf. BdG, I, 382, IV, 190, VII, 419, MHL, X, passim)
Febris prima, Int., p. 4, Int., n. 79
Febris secunda, Int., n. 79
Fortuna, Int., pp. 25, 26, Int., ns. 69, 71, 79
Hochstratus ovans, Int., n. 5, Sp., par. 96, Sp., ns. 121, 122 (Eps. 1083, n. 23, 1165, n. 22, 1195, n. 4)

Inspicientes, Int., n. 79
Invectiva in Hieronymum Aleandrum, Sp., n. 161
Invectiva in Lutheromastigas sacerdotes, Exp., n. 146
Klageschriften (Exhortations), Int., n. 79
Monitor primus, Int., n. 79
Monitor secundus, Int., n. 79
Nemo, Int., pp. 2, 25, 26, Int., ns. 5, 7, 69 (cf. BdG, I, No. 9264)
Phalarismus, Int., p. 4
Praedones, Int., n. 79
Triumphus Capnionis, Int., p. 2, Int., n. 5, Sp., pars. 71, 376, Sp.,
    n. 96 (Ep. 290)
Vadiscus, Int., pp. 30, 31, Int., n. 79 (cf. BdG, I, Nos. 9281-9282)

Jonas, Jodocus (Justus) (i.e., Jodocus/Jost Koch, of Nordhausen/Thuringia, 1493-1555;
    Humanist turned theologian, follower of Luther and Melanchthon, Bp. of the
    Reformed Church of Halle: cf. Allen, III, 413, ADB, XIV, 492-494, EB, XV,
    497, MHL, XI, 34-37 / passim in MHL, X-XII, UTM / BdG, I, 391-392, V, 134,
    VII, 105), Int., ns. 15 (Eps. 999, 1233), 37 (Ep. 1202), Sp., ns. 208
    (Ep. 1211), 353 (Ep. 1211), 450 (Ep. 1211)

Julius II, Pope (i.e., Giuliano della Rovere, of Savona, 1443-1513, Pope 1503-1513;
    cf. EB, XV, 551-552, EI, XVII, 324-325, Pastor, VI-VII/UTM), Sp. par. 208

LaMarck, Erard de (of La Marck/Sedan, 1472-1538; Bp. of Liège, Archbp. of Valencia,
    Cardinal, at first supported Luther but as Cardinal opposed heresy although
    he fought abuses in the Church, patron of Erasmus: cf. Allen, III, 167,
    BNB, XIII, 497-512 (v. Marck) / passim in Bataillon, MHL, X-XIII, Renaudet
    (2) and (4)), Exp., n. 79 (Ep. 1151), Sp., pars. 129, 133, Sp., n. 155
    (Ep. 738)

Lange, Johannes (of Erfurt, d. 1548; Former Austin Friar, follower of Luther, Bp. of
    the Reformed Church in Erfurt: cf. Allen, III, 408, ADB, XVII, 635-637,
    MHL, XI, 135 / passim in MHL, X-XI / BdG, I, 428-429, V, 48, VII, 110), Sp.,
    n. 202 (Ep. 872)

Lasco (Lasky), Jan (of Sieradia, 1499-1560; Polish nobleman, Humanist, Erasmian re-
    former, embraced the Reformation and spent some time in London as the guest
    of Archbp. Cranmer, there he formed a community of Protestant refugees
    before his return to Poland in 1556: cf. ADB, XVII, 736-739, EB, XVI,
    234, MHL, XIII, 145-146 / passim in MHL, X-XII, UTM / BdG, I, 431-432, V,
    149), Int., n. 40 (Ep. 1821)

Latimer, William (birthplace unknown, c. 1460-1545; English scholar, tutor to Reginold
    Pole, active at Oxford, parish priest in Gloucestershire; cf. Allen, I,
    438, DNB, XI, 622-623, Emden (0,1), II, 1106-1107 / passim in UTM), Sp.,
    n. 388 (Eps. 520, 540)

Latomus, Bartholomeus (i.e., Bartholomäus Steinmetz, of Arlon, c. 1498-1570; Teacher
    of Latin and Greek at the Collège de France, annotated Cicero, lectured on
    Horace, etc., strongly orthodox: cf. Allen, V, 1, ADB, XVIII, 14, BNB,
    XI, 425-434, MHL, XI, 591-602 / passim in MHL, XI-XIII / BdG, I, 435, V,
    150, VII, No. 55486), Sp., n. 389 (Dp. 3048)

Latomus, Jacobus (i.e., Jacques Masson, of Cambrai/Hainualt, 1475-1544; Professor of
    theology at Louvain, leader of the orthodox anti-Lutheran faction: cf.
    Allen, III, 519, BNB, XI, 434-438, MHL, X, 324-334 / passim in MHL, X-XIII,

UTM / BdG, I, 435, V, 150, VII, No. 55487), Exp., pars. 141-142, Sp., pars. 166-167, 196, Sp., ns. 127, 184, 219

Laurens, Josse (i.e. Josse Lauwerijns, seigneur of Terdeghem d. 1527; Councillor of Charles V, commissioned to extirpate heresy in Bruges: cf. Allen, V, 84, Bataillon, 240, MHL, I, 184-185 / passim in MHL, I, XI), Int., n. 40 (Ep. 1299), Exp., n. 36 (Ep. 1299), Sp., n. 412 (Ep. 1299)

Laurinus, Marcus (i.e., Marcus Lauwerijns, of Bruges(?), 1488-1546; Dean of St. Donatian's in Bruges, friend of Erasmus and Vives: cf. Allen, I, 432, BNB, XI, 458-459, BWN, XI, 212, MHL, I, 13-14 / passim in Bataillon, MHL, I, X-XII, Renaudet (4), UTM), Int., p. 9, Int., n. 27, (Ep. 1342), Exp., pars. 32, 82, 92, 153, 227, Exp., ns. 2 (Ep. 1342), 3, 24, 26, 28, 43, 69, 71, 73, 81, 94 (Ep. 809), 95, 99, 100, 102, 103, 107, 108, 111, 112, 116, 117, 120, 133, Sp., pars. 51, 89, 140, 145, 210, 257, Sp., n. 72

Lee, Edward (of Lee Magna/Kent, c. 1482-1544; Student of Greek at Louvain, critic of Erasmus' N.T., Royal Almoner, Archbp. of York, sent on embassies for Henry VIII, helped create the Anglican Church free from Rome but hostile to the Continental Reformers: cf. Allen, III, 203, DNB, XI, 788-790, Emden (0,1), II, 1122-1123 / passim in Bataillon, MHL, X, XI, XIII, UTM), Int., p. 5, Int., ns. 16 (Eps. 1037, 1061), 40, Exp., par. 143, Exp., ns. 88 (Eps. 1037, 1061), 89 (Ep. 1037), Sp., pars. 82, 169, 170, 171, 392, Sp., ns. 127 (Ep. 1037), 186, 187 (Ep. 1037), 188 (Ep. 998)

Lefèvre d'Etaples, Jacques (Jacobus Faber Stapulensis, of Etaples, c. 1455-1536; Forerunner of the Reformation in France, translated the Bible into French, attacked by the Sorbonne but protected by Francis I and the Bp. of Meaux: cf. Allen, II, 37, BU, XIII, 475-477 (v. Fabvre), NBG, XXX, 333-339 / passim in Bataillon, MHL, I, X-XIII, Renaudet (2), (4) and (5, pp. 201-216), UTM), Exp., pars. 89, 137, Exp., n. 48, Sp., pars. 158, 159, 164, 343, Sp., ns. 219, 390

Leo X, Pope (i.e., Giovanni de' Medici, 1475-1521, Pope 1513-1521; Second son of Lorenzo de' Medici, the Reformation began during his pontificate, ex-communicated Luther in 1521, honored Henry VIII with the title Fidei Defensor for his book against Luther: cf. EB, XVI, 433-436, EI, XX, 906-908, Pastor, VII-VIII / passim in MHL, X-XIII, UTM / BdG, IV, 478-479), Int., p. 2, Int., ns. 4 (Ep. 335), 5 (Ep. 335), 20, 42, 79, Sp., pars. 196, 239, Sp., n. 323

Linacre, Thomas (of Canterbury, c. 1460-1524; M.D. degree from Padua, physician to Henry VIII, also Humanist scholar: cf. Allen, I, 274, DNB, XI, 1145-1150, EB, XVI, 701-702, Emden (0,1), II, 1147-1149 / passim in MHL, X-XI, Renaudet (2) and (4), UTM), Sp., ns. 388 (Eps. 118, 232, 350, 388, 502, 541), 405

Longland, John (of Henley on Thames, 1473-1547; Dean of Salisbury, confessor to Henry VIII, Bp. of Lincoln, Chancellor of Oxford, maintained the royal supremacy: cf. Allen, VI, 1, DNB, XII, 120-121, Emden (0,1), II, 1160-1162 / passim in UTM), Sp., ns. 253 (Ep. 2037), 254 (Ep. 2037), 412 (Ep. 1704)

López de Zuñiga, Diego (Jacobus Stunica, d. 1530/31; Theologian at the University of Alcalá, Greek and Hebrew scholar, critical of Erasmus' N.T., one of the editors of Cardinal Ximenes' Polyglot: cf. Allen, IV, 621-622, BHN, I, 295-296, Bludau, 125-140, EU, XXI, 161, Paul Kalkoff, in Archiv für Reformationsgeschichte (Leipzig/Gütersloh), III, 70-83 / passim in Bataillon, Renaudet (4) / BdG, V, 266), Sp., par. 196, Sp., n. 219

Luther, Martin (of Eisleben, c. 1483-1546: cf. Allen, III, 517, EB, XVII, 133-140,
        Spitz, 237-266 / passim in MHL, XI-XIII, UTM / BdG, I, 231-232, 458-629,
        IV, 420-422, V, 82, 158-183, VII, 73, 114-161, 510-511), Int., pp. 5, 6, 7,
        9, 10, 14, 15, 16, 17, 18, 21, 31, 32, Int., ns. 5, 14, 19 (Eps. 933, 980),
        20, 21, 34, 37, 38, 40, 42, 44 (Ep. 1443), 54 (Eps. 1443, 1445), 57, 79,
        81, 82, Exp., pars. 31, 35, 47, 57, 74, 75, 116, 120, 125, 126, 131-132,
        134, 137, 138, 152, 162, 165, 167, 168, 169, 170, 172, 173, 174, 175, 178,
        187, 191, 193, 194, 195, 196, 197, 198, 199, 200, 201, 202, 228, 257, 267,
        Exp., ns. 8, 16, 31, 63, 74, Sp., Prefs. I, II, Sp. pars. 31, 48, 78, 89-90,
        121-124, 129, 135-136, 139, 145, 149, 151, 156-163, 172, 177-206, 210, 212,
        218, 221-226, 229-233, 240, 247, 251, 257-272, 280-281, 304, 307-312, 315,
        372, 380-391, 398-401, 414, Sp., ns. 71 (Ep. 2918), 116, 147 (Ep. 1033),
        149, 156 (Ep. 980), 159, 190, 202 (Ep. 872), 208, 219, 252, 308, 312, 323,
        375 (Ep. 980), 443 (Ep. 1352), 453

Lypsius (Lipsius), Martin (of Brussels, c. 1492-1555; Close friend of Erasmus in Basle,
        helped him in editing his works: cf. Allen, III, 185, ADB, XVIII, 839-841,
        BWN, XI, 519 / passim in MHL, X-XIII / BdG, I, 448), Int., ns. 5 (Ep. 2045),
        40 (Ep. 1040)

Manutius, Aldus (i.e., Aldo Manuzio, of Venice, 1449-1515; Head of the famous Aldine
        Press in Venice: cf. Allen, I, 437, EB, XVII, 624-625, EI, XXII, 182-184 /
        passim in Bataillon, MHL, X-XI, Renaudet (2) and (4), UTM), Sp., n. 159

Marlianus, Aloysius (i.e., Alvise Marliano, of Milan, d. 1521; Physician to Archduke
        Philip and Prince Charles, Bp. of Tudela in Galicia, wrote against Erasmus:
        cf. Allen, II, 241, Lauchert, 221-229 / passim in Renaudet (4) / BdG, II,
        10), Exp., ns. 10 (Eps. 114, 1195), 98 (Ep. 1195), 99, 104, 109, 117 (Ep.
        1195), 118, 119, 120, Sp., ns. 122 (Ep. 1195), 155 (Ep. 1195), 219

Maximilian I, Emperor (1459-1519, Emperor 1493-1519: cf. ADB, XX, 725-736, EB, XVII,
        922-923 / passim in MHL, XI-XIII, UTM / BdG, III, 27-38, V, 404-405, VII,
        320-321), Exp., n. 8, Sp., pars. 158, 208

Mazolini (Mazzolini), Silvester (of Priero, referred to as Prieras, c. 1456-1523;
        Vicar-General of the Dominicans in Lombardy, Master of the Papal Palace,
        writer on Aquinas and theology, sought to enlist Erasmus' aid against Luther:
        cf. Allen, III, 409, EI, XXVIII, 238-239 (v. Prierias), Lauchert, 7-30 /
        passim in MHL, X, Renaudet (4) / BdG, II, 153, V, 222), Exp., pars. 41, 134,
        Sp., pars. 156, 196, Sp., n. 219

Medardus (Metardus) (of Kirchen; Court preacher to Ferdinand of Austria (1530),
        attacked Erasmus: cf. Allen, IX, 86, MHL, XI, 250), Sp., n. 207 (Eps. 2408,
        2503)

Melanchthon, Philippus (i.e., Philip Schwarzerd, of Bretten, 1497-1560; Great-nephew
        of Reuchlin, taught Greek in Wittemberg, influenced by Erasmus' N.T.,
        constant aid and champion of Luther: cf. Allen, II, 319, ADB, XXI, 268-279,
        EB, XVIII, 88-89 / passim in Bataillon, MHL, X-XIII, Renaudet (4), UTM /
        BdG, II, 18-48, IV, 487, V, 190-193, VII, 164-170), Int., ns. 17, 20, 21
        (Ep. 1113), 27 (Ep. 1496), 34, 44, 52, 54 (Eps. 1496, 1500, 1523)

Mexia, Peter (i.e., Pero Mejia, of Seville, 1498-1551; Spanish Humanist, wrote
        especially about history and natural history: cf. Allen, VIII, 405, EU,
        XXXIV, 256-257 / passim in Bataillon, MHL, XII), Sp., n. 253 (Ep. 2300)

Meyner, Matthias (of Chemnitz, d.c. 1520; Superintendent of the mines at Schneeberg, friend of Eppendorf: cf. Allen, IV, 302, MHL, X, 494, XI, 39), Sp., n. 32 (Ep. 1122)

More, Thomas (of London, c. 1477-1535; Scholar, lawyer, Chancellor of England, martyr under Henry VIII, intimate friend of Erasmus: cf. Allen, I, 265, DNB, XIII, 876-896, EB, XVIII, 822-826, Emden (0,1), II, 1305-1308 / passim in MHL, X-XIII, Renaudet (2) and (4), UTM / BdG, II, 64-67, IV, 718, V, 82, 199-200, VII, 74, 172-173), Int., ns. 5, 16 (Ep. 1087), 26, 54 (Ep. 1804), Sp., par. 171, Sp., ns. 219, 253, 381, 388 (Eps. 388, 502)

Mountjoy, William Blount, 4th Lord (Baron) of (of Barton/Staffordshire, c. 1479-1534; Friend, pupil and patron of Erasmus, tutor to young Henry VIII, Chamberlain to Queen Catherine, Master of the Mint: cf. Allen, I, 207, DNB, II, 721-722 (v. Blount), / passim in MHL, X-XII, Renaudet (2) and (4), UTM), Exp., par. 152, Sp., n. 405 (Ep. 115)

Mutianus Rufus, Conradus (i.e., Konrad Mut, of Homberg, 1471-1526; Canon at Gotha, led a quiet, studious life, great influence on young Humanists, supported Reuchlin and Erasmus: cf. Allen, II, 416, ADB, XXIII, 108-109, EB, XIX, 99, MHL, XI, 32, Spitz, 130-154 / passim in MHL, X-XI / BdG, II, 82-83, V, 204, VII, 176), Int., n. 60

Nesen, Konrad (of Nastätten near Koblenz, 1495-1560; Studied law at Wittenberg, tutor at the court of Frederick the Wise, Syndic of Zittau, champion of Lutheranism: cf. Allen, VIII, 14, ADB, XXIII, 437-438, MHL, X, 399 / passim in MHL, X / BdG, II, 92), Sp., n. 188

Nesen, Wilhelm (of Nastätten, 1493-1524; Corrector for Froben, head of Latin school in Frankfurt am Main, joined the Reformers: cf. Allen, II, 65, ADB, XXIII, 438-441, MHL, X, 399-401, Dialogus bilinguium, reprinted on pp. 547-574 / passim in MHL, X-XIII / BdG, I, 229, 232, II, 92), Sp., n. 188

Neuenahr (Neuenar), Hermann Count of (1492-1530; Lectured at Cologne on Greek and Hebrew, dedicated himself to the revival of good letters, supporter of Erasmus: cf. Allen, II, 282, ADB, XXIII, 485-486, MHL, X, 436-437 / passim in MHL, X-XIII / BdG, II, 93, V, 206), Int., ns. 5 (Ep. 636), 40 (Eps. 636, 878), Exp., par. 58, Exp., n. 46 (Ep. 636), Sp., pars. 61, 63, 69, 82, Sp., ns. 93, 103 (Ep. 1078), 137 (Ep. 878), 372

Oecolampadius, Joannes (i.e., Johannes Hussgen/Heussgen, of Weinsberg by Würzburg, 1482-1531; Leader of the Reformation in Basle, friend of Capito and Melanchthon, aided Erasmus with the translation of his N.T.: cf. Allen, I, 464, ADB, XXIV, 226-236, EB, XX, 11-12 / passim in MHL, X-XII, Renaudet (4), UTM / BdG, II, 100-102, V, 208, VII, 178-179), Int., p. 19, Int., n. 26, Exp., n. 87 (Ep. 563), Sp., n. 257

Pace, Richard (of Winchester, c. 1482-1536; Dean of St. Paul's, friend and correspondent of Erasmus, wrote an account of a mission to the Swiss on behalf of Henry VIII: cf. Allen, I, 445, DNB, XV, 22-24, EB, XX, 432, Emden (0,1), III, 1417 / passim in MHL, X-XI, UTM), Int., n. 64 (Ep. 1218), Sp., ns. 388 (Ep. 350), 405 (Ep. 350)

Paludanus, cf. Desmarais

Peutinger, Konrad (of Augsburg, 1465-1547; Town Clerk of Augsburg, writer on Roman antiquity, Imperial Councillor to Emperor Maximilian: cf. Allen, II, 41, ADB, XXV, 561-568, EB, XXI, 338, MHL, XIII, 432-433 / passim MHL, X, XIII / BdG, II, 133-135, V, 217, VII, 189), Exp., n. 79 (Ep. 1156), Sp., n. 450 (Ep. 1156)

Pfefferkorn, Johannes (of Cologne, 1469-1524; A converted Jew who with the aid of the Dominicans in Cologne sought to convert all Jews, opposed by Reuchlin in a long and bitter legal process (1507-1521), attacked unmercifully in the EOV: cf. Allen, II, 381, ADB, XXV, 621-624 / passim in MHL, X, Renaudet (2), UTM / BdG, II, 136, V, 217, VII, 104), Int., n. 5

Philip, Landgrave of Hesse (1504-1567; Champion of the Reformation, founded the University of Marburg: cf. Allen, VIII, 126, ADB, XXV, 765-783, EB, XXI, 388-389, NDB, II, 499-500 / passim in MHL, XII / BdG, III, 188-198, V, 421, VII, 340-341), Exp., n. 8

Pirckheimer, Willibald (of Eichstadt, then Nürnberg, 1470-1530; Public official of Nürnberg and great Humanist scholar and educator: cf. Allen, II, 40, ADB, XXVI, 810-817, Spitz, 155-196 / passim in MHL, X-XI, Renaudet (4), UTM / BdG, II, 141-144, V, 219, VII, 190-191, 513), Int. pp. 13, 29, Int., ns. 5 (Ep. 694), 16, 24 (Eps. 2158, 2196), 29 (Eps. 1376, 1383), 33 (Ep. 1383), 34 (Ep. 1376), 35 (Ep. 1376), 40 (Eps. 856, 1085), 47 (Eps. 1376, 1383, 54 (Eps. 1376, 1383, 1893, 1991, 1992), 76, 77, Sp., n. 399 (Ep. 1376

Poliziano, Angelo Ambrogini (of Montepulciano/Tuscany, by Florence, 1454-1494; Humanist scholar and poet, considered to be the greatest classical scholar of his age in both Latin and Greek, like Erasmus he too attacked the slavish imitation of Cicero: cf. EB, XXI, 982-983, EI, XXVII, 690-693 / passim in Bataillon, MHL, X-XII, Renaudet (2) and (4)), Sp., par. 342, Sp., n. 385

Poncher, Etienne (of Tours, 1446-1525; Chancellor of the University of Paris, Bp. of Paris, Archbp. of Sens, Aleander was in his service: cf. Allen, II, 454, BU, XXXIV, 51, EB, XXII, 59, NBG, XL, 741-742 / passim in MHL, X-XIII, Renaudet (2) and (4), UTM), Sp., n. 389 (Ep. 529)

Prieras, cf. Mazolini

Radinus Todiscus, Tomaso OP (1488-1527; Dominican, writer on Aquinas, taught philosophy in Rome, opponent of Luther: cf. Allen, IV, 409, Lauchert, 177-199 / BdG, II, 158, Ono, 563 (v. Radini Tedeschi)), Sp., par. 196, Sp., n. 219

Reisch, Gregor (of Balingen/Schwarzwald, d. 1525; Carthusian prior, teacher of Eck, confessor to Emperor Maximilian: cf. Allen, II, 27, ADB, XXVIII, 117 / BdG, II, 167, V, 228, VII, 194), Sp., n. 150 (Ep. 309)

Reuchlin, Johann (Joannes Capnio, of Pfortzheim, 1455-1522; Champion of Hebrew studies, teacher of Greek and Hebrew, Imperial Councillor, cf. Hoogstraten and Pfefferkorn: cf. Allen, I, 555, ADB, XXVIII, 785-799, EB, XXIII, 204-206, MHL, X, 419-424, Spitz, 61-80 / passim in MHL, X-XII, Renaudet (2) and (4), UTM / BdG, II, 169-172, IV, 267-269, V, 228-229, VII, 195), Int., p. 2, Int., ns. 1 (Ep. 300), 3, 4, 5 (Eps. 300,324), 6, 7, 14, 40 (Ep. 300), 41, 76, Exp., pars. 15-17, 24, 58, 77-78, 84-88, 90-110, 137, Exp., n. 49, Sp., pars. 18, 61-63, 69, 73-74, 81, 91, 94-113, 342, 371, 376-378, 384, Sp., ns. 42, 84 (Ep. 1006), 85 (Ep. 1006), 96 (Ep. 290), 99, 128 (Ep. 1129), 198 (Ep. 1041)

Riario, Raffaelle (of Savona, 1461-1521; Cardinal, rival to Leo X in the 1513 conclave, at his request Erasmus wrote his anti-war treatise of 1509: cf. Allen, II, 69 / passim in Renaudet (2) and (4), UTM), Int., n. 4 (Ep. 333)

Rogerus, Servatius (of Rotterdam, d. 1540; Friend of Erasmus at Steyn, later Rector of Marienpoel near Leiden: cf. Allen, I, 77 / passim in MHL, X, XII, Renaudet (2) and (4)), Sp., n. 150 (Ep. 296)

Rosemondt, Godschalk (of Eindhoven, c. 1483-1526; Professor of theology at Louvain, one of the judges who tried and condemned Jan Pistorius, the first Dutch martyr of the Reformation (1525), wrote devotional literature: cf. Allen, IV, 361, BNB, XX, 102-110, NNBW, V, 612-613 / passim in MHL, X-XI), Int., n. 19 (Ep. 1153), Exp., n. 63 (Ep. 1153)

Ruistre, Nicholas (of Le Ruistre/Luxemburg, c. 1442-1509; Secretary at the court of Burgundy, Chancellor of Louvain, Bp. of Arras: cf. Allen, I, 390, BNB, XX, 465-482 (v. Ruter), MHL, X, 8-9 / passim in MHL, X-XII, Renaudet (2)), Sp., n. 404 (Ep. 179)

Russinger, Johann Jacob (d. 1549; Abbot of the monastery of Pfäffer, Switzerland: cf. DS, V, 618 / BdG, II, No. 16908), Int., p. 18

Ruthall, Thomas (of Cirencester, d. 1523; Dean of Salisbury, Bp. of Durham, secretary to Henry VIII: cf. Allen, I, 423, DNB, XVII, 492-493, Emden (0,1), III, 1612-1613 / passim in Renaudet (2) and (4), UTM), Int., n. 6

Sadoleto, Jacopo (of Modena, 1477-1547; Latin scholar, secretary to Leo X, member of the Roman Academy, Bp. of Carpentras, Cardinal, commissioned to aid in the reform of the Church: cf. Allen, V, 572, EB, XXIII, 994, EI, XXX, 425-426, Lauchert, 385-411 / passim in MHL, XI-XIII, Renaudet (4), UTM / BdG, II, 214, VII, 203, Ono, 59), Sp., n. 254 (Ep. 2443)

Salius, Joannes (i.e., Johannes Saltzmann, of Steyer, fl. 1507-1521; Medical doctor, physician to Ferdinand of Austria, professor of medicine in Vienna, wrote treatises on the plague, friend of Reuchlin: cf. Allen, IV, 299), Sp., pars. 111-112, Sp., n. 132

Scaliger, Julius Caesar (b. at the Castle La Rocca on the Lago de Garda, 1484-1558; Physician, Bp. of Agen, soldier, attacked Erasmus' Ciceronianus, writer of Latin verses, a commentary on Aristotle, etc.: cf. Allen, IX, 368, EB, XXIV, 283-284, EI, XXX, 1000, MHL, XII, 29-30 / passim in MHL, XII, Renaudet (4) / BdG, II, 221, V, 239, VII, 204, Ono, 614 v. Scaligero)), Sp., n. 159 (Eps. 2565, 2587, 2736)

Schiner, Matthäus (of Mühlbach, c. 1470-1522; Diplomat, Cardinal-Bp. of Sion (Sitten), aided the Pope in his wars against the French, at his suggestion Erasmus wrote the Paraphrase of Matthew: cf. Allen, II, 307, ADB, XXXIII, 729-737, DS, VI, 20-21, MHL, X, 352 / passim in Bataillon, MHL, X / BdG, II, 232-233, V, 242, VII, 205), Exp., par. 40, Sp., par. 238, Sp., n. 279

Schott, Johannes (of Strasburg, 1477-c. 1550; Strasburg publisher of Humanistic, theological and later Reformation works: cf. Allen, V, 416, ADB, XXXII, 402-404 / passim in UTM / BdG, II, 243), Int., p. 13, Int., n. 34

Schydlowyetz, Christopher (i.e., Krysztof Szydlowiecki, d. 1532; Chancellor of Poland, patron of letters: cf. Allen, VI, 134, MHL, XI, 394 / passim in Bataillon), Sp., n. 253 (Ep. 1593)

Sickingen, Franz von (of Schloss Landstuhl, Ebernburg near Worms, 1481-1523; Defender of Reuchlin, Hutten and Luther, 1519 Imperial Councillor to Charles V, led the dissident knights in the "Pfaffenkrieg": cf. Allen, II, 559, ADB, XXXIV, 151-158, EB, XXV, 36 / passim in MHL, XII, UTM / BdG, I, 384, II, 274-276, V, 254-255, VII, 104, 216), Int., pp. 8, 12, 16, 18, Int., ns. 20, 74, 79, Exp., par. 131, Exp., ns. 8, 74, Sp., pars. 20, 36, 212, Sp., n. 43

Spalatin(us), Georg (i.e., Georg Burkhard, of Spalt by Nürnberg, 1482-1545; Tutor to the son of Duke John of Saxony, chaplain and secretary to Frederick the Wise, translator of the Classics and works of Erasmus into German: cf. Allen, II, 415, ADB, XXXV, 1-29, EB, XXV, 591, MHL, X, 534-536 / passim in MHL, X-XI, UTM / BdG, II, 284-286, V, 258, VII, 217), Int., ns. 21 (Ep. 1119), 44, Exp., n. 10 (Ep. 1119), Sp., par. 259, Sp., ns. 308, 325 (Ep. 1119), 418

Standish, Henry OFM (perhaps from Standish/Lancashire, d. 1535; Court preacher for Henry VIII, Provincial of the Franciscans, Bp. of St. Asaph, renounced papal jurisdiction in England: cf. Allen, III, 21, DNB, XVIII, 880-881, Emden (O,1), III, 1756-1757, MHL, XI, 5), Sp., par. 392, Sp., n. 116

Standonck, Jan (of Mechlin, 1480-1504: Reformer of the College Montaigu, Rector of the University of Paris: cf. Allen, I, 200, BNB, XXIII, 588-599, Renaudet (5), 114-161 / passim in MHL, X, XII, Renaudet (2) and (4)), Sp., n. 428

Stromer, Heinrich (of Auerbach by Chemnitz, 1482-1542; Physician to Albert of Mainz and Duke George of Saxony, Dean of the Faculty of Medicine at Leipzig, attended Erasmus at his death: cf. Allen, II, 554, ADB, I, 638 (v. Auerbach), MHL, XI, 326 et passim / BdG, II, 313), Int., n. 11 (Eps. 614, 631)

Stunica, Jacobus, cf. López de Zuñiga

Sturm, Caspar (dates and place uncertain; Imperial Herald, conducted Luther to the Diet of Worms: cf. ADB, XXXVII, 41-42 / Renaudet (4) / BdG, II, 316-317, IV, 271), Exp., n. 8

Sutor, Petrus (i.e., Pierre Cousturier, of Chemiré-le-Roi/Maine, d. 1537; Carthusian, taught philosophy, strictly orthodox, critical of Erasmus' N.T., Prior of the Sorbonne 1509: cf. Allen, VI, 132, BU, IX, 402-403, NBG, XII, 293 / MHL, XI passim), Sp., n. 428

Theodorich of Nijmegen (in all likelihood Erasmus meant Theodorich of Gouda, fl. 1502-1539; Dutch Carmelite and Prior of his Order, on intimate terms with the Dominicans of Cologne and supported them in their struggle against Reuchlin, he was sent by them and the Theological Faculty of Cologne to gain the support of the Sorbonne - a journey crowned with success when in Dec. 1514 the Sorbonne issued its official condemnation of Reuchlin: cf. NNBW, I, 959, Stokes, p. 5, n. 1. 39 and EOV, letter 1, 11. 35-42), Sp., par. 392

Theodorici, Vincent, cf. Dierckx

Transsylvanus, Maximilianus (of Brussels, d. 1538; A member of the Imperial Chancery of Charles V, traveled with the Emperor and recorded accounts of his travels, supported Erasmus at the Emperor's court: cf. Allen, VI, 33, BNB, XXV, 521-527 / passim in Bataillon, MHLXI / BdG, II, 34, VII, 225), Int., n. 54 (Ep. 1645)

Ulrich I, Duke of Württemberg (1487-1550: cf. ADB, XXXIX, 237-243, EB, XXVII, 567-568 / BdG, III, 543-544, VII, 374), Int., p. 15, Exp., par. 97, Exp., n. 57, Sp., par. 102, Sp., n. 128

Utenhove, Karel (of Ghent(?), d. 1580; A member of Erasmus' household in 1528, 1539 an Alderman of Ghent: cf. Allen, VIII, 42, BWN, XVIII, 33, MHL, XI, 465-473, NNBW, IX, 1148-1149 / passim in MHL, XI-XIII, Renaudet (4) / BdG, VII, 227), Sp., n. 150 (Ep. 2700)

Valla, Lorenzo (of Rome, c. 1407-1457; Italian Humanist scholar, demonstrated the spuriousness of the "Donation of Constantine", wrote Annotations to the N.T., his _Elegantiae_ became a manual of Latin style: cf. EB, XXVII, 861, EI, XXXIX, 923-924 / passim in Bataillon, MHL, X-XIII, Renaudet (2) and (4), UTM), Sp., par. 342, Sp., ns. 90, 385 (Eps. 26, 29, 182, 304, 337, 2172)

Vander Noot, Jérôme (Seigneur de Lutiaux, Risoire et Wuestwezel, c. 1450-1540; Chancellor of Brabant 1515-1531: cf. Allen, V, 88, BNB, XXVI, 374-375), Sp., ns. 251 (Ep. 1300), 412 (Ep. 1300)

Varius, Nicholaus, cf. Wary

Veere, Adolphus of Burgundy, Lord of (c. 1490-1540; Patron of Erasmus: cf. Allen, I, 229, BWN, II:3, 961 / passim in Renaudet (2) and (4)), Sp., n. 405 (Ep. 266)

Veere, Anna van Borssele, Lady of (c. 1469-1518; Patroness of Erasmus: cf. Allen, I, 208, BWN, II:3, 961 / passim in MHL, X-XI, Renaudet (2) and (4)), Sp., 405 (Eps. 80, 145)

Vergara, Juan (of Toledo, 1492-1557; Student of Ximenes, worked on the Complutensian Polyglot, secretary to Ximenes, friend of Erasmus and Vives: cf. Allen, V, 51, BHN, I, 792-794, MHL, XII, 79-80 / passim in Bataillon, MHL, XI-XIII), Sp., ns. 149 (Ep. 1875), 208 (Ep. 1875)

Vincentius, cf. Dierckx

Vitrier, Jean OFM (of Tournai, dates unknown; Warden of a Franciscan monastery near St.-Omer, 1498 some of his writings were condemned by the Theological Faculty of Paris: cf. Allen, I, 372, Olin (TB) / passim in Renaudet (2) and (4)), Sp., n. 208 (Eps. 1211, 1875)

Vives, Juan Luis (of Valencia, 1492-1540; Spanish Humanist and educator, lectured from Alcalá to Oxford, prodigious writer: cf. Allen, III, 508, DNB, XX, 377-379, EB, XXVIII, 152, Emden (0,2), 594-596, EU, LXIX, 713-720, MHL, I, 231-234, XIII, 1-59 / passim in Bataillon, MHL, X-XIII, Renaudet (4), UTM, Woodward / BdG, I, 235, V, 82-83, VII, 75, 230-231), Sp., n. 389 (Ep. 1111)

Volz, Paul OSB (of Offenburg, 1480-1544; Abbot of Hügshofen, followed the Reformers, active Reformer in Strasburg, Erasmus remembered him in his will: cf. Allen, II, 158, ADB, XL, 284-285 / passim in Bataillon, MHL, XII, Renaudet (4), UTM / BdG, II, 363, V, 277, VII, 73), Int., ns. 62 (Ep. 858), 63 (Ep. 858), 67 (Ep. 858), Sp., ns. 246 (Ep. 858), 249 (Ep. 858), 250 (Ep. 858)

Warham, William (of Church Oakley / Malshanger, Hampshire, c. 1450-1532; Bp. of London, Archbp. of Canterbury, Chancellor of England, friend of More, patron of Erasmus: cf. Allen, I, 417, DNB, XX, 835-840, EB, XXVIII, 325, Emden (0,1),

III, 1988-1992 / passim in MHL, XI, Renaudet (2) and (4), UTM), Exp., n. 124 (Ep. 1228), Sp., ns. 15, 190 (Ep. 1228)

Wary, Nicolas (of Marville, D. 1529; 1526 President of the Collegium trilingue, friend of Erasmus: cf. Allen, V, 527, MHL, XI, 298-301, 635-636 / passim in MHL, X-XIII), Sp., n. 246 (Ep. 1756)

Wied, Hermann von (1477-1552; Electoral-Archbp. of Cologne, deposed for active support of Lutheranism: cf. Allen, I, 52, III, 295, ADB, XII, 135-147 / passim in MHL, XI-XIII / BdG, III, 238-241, VII, 345), Sp., n. 388 (Allen, I, 55)

Wiele, Adriaan (of Brussels, fl. 1507-1530; Secretary to Charles V, a member of the Council of Brabant, present at the Diet of Augsburg 1530: cf. Allen, V, 256), Sp., n. 207 (Ep. 2408)

Wimpfeling, Jakob (of Schlettstadt, 1450-1528; Humanist and religious reformer, preacher at Spires and Strasburg: cf. Allen, I, 463, ADB, XLIV, 524-537, MHL, X, 197-198, Spitz, 41-60 / passim in MHL, X, Renaudet (2), UTM / BdG, II, 390-392, V, 283, VII, 235), Int., n. 2 (Ep. 305), Exp., n. 41 (Ep. 1167)

Wolfhart, Bonifatius (Bonifacius Lycosthenes, cf. BdG, 630, No. 14636), Int., n. 33

Wolsey, Thomas (of Ipswich, c. 1475-1530; Dean of Canterbury, Almoner of Henry VIII, Bp. of Lincoln, Archbp. of York, Cardinal, Privy Councillor, Chancellor of England: cf. DNB, XXI, 796-814, EB, XXVIII, 779-780, Emden (0,1), III, 2077-2080 / passim in MHL, X-XI, Renaudet (4), UTM), Int., p. 4, Int., ns. 1 (Ep. 967), 5 (Ep. 967), 14 (Ep. 967), 35 (Ep. 967)

Zasius (Zäsi), Ulrich (of Constance, 1461-1535; Town Clerk in Freiburg, teacher of Latin and professor of law, eminent lawyer, Imperial Councillor, author of numerous legal treatises: cf. Allen, II, 9, ADB, XLIV, 708-715, MHL, XI, 592 / passim in MHL, XI, XIII, UTM / BdG, II, 406, V, 286, VII, 238), Sp., ns. 251 (Ep. 1353), 388 (Eps. 862, 1352)

Ziegler, Jakob (of Landau/on the Isar, c. 1471-1549; Itinerant teacher, joined the moderate Reformers, wrote commentaries on Pliny and Scripture, returned to the Church, Dean of the Faculty of the University of Vienna: cf. Allen, V, 17, ADB, XLV, 175-177 / passim in Bataillon / BdG, II, 409, V, 287), Exp., n. 36 (Ep. 1330)

Zuichemus, cf. Aytta, Wigle van

Zwingli, Ulrich (of the Toggenburg/Switzerland, 1484-1531; Priest, pastor in Glarus, removed to Zurich and became the leader of the Reformation there, died fighting the Catholic cantons in the battle of Kappel: cf. Allen, II, 225, ADB, XLV, 547-575, EB, XXVIII, 1061-1064 / passim in MHL, X-XIII, Renaudet (4), UTM / BdG, II, 414-435, IV, 762, V, 288-291, VII, 239-244, 517), Int., pp. 17-19, Int., ns. 25, 33, 43 (Eps. 1378, 1384), 54 (Eps. 1378, 1384), Sp., Pref. I, Sp., ns. I (Ep. 1378), 2, 8 (Eps. 401, 404, 1378)

The Polemics of Erasmus of Rotterdam and Ulrich von Hutten

ERRATA

Acknowledgement page   Prof. Kaegi's article appeared in 1924 not 1942

p. xii	under Etienne read: de Louvain
p. 10	l. 28, read: St. Donatian
p. 30	l. 4, read: occurred
p. 39	No. 14, l. 28, read: clergy
p. 52	No. 60, l. 7, read: miserrimum
p. 54	No. 76, l. 12, read: exponens
p. 89	No. 124, l. 5, read: attack you...
p. 92	No. 137, l. 22, read: Jacques Lefèvre
p. 127	No. 6, l. 9, read: curtesanus
p. 156	No. 54, l. 26, read: How was...
p. 190	l. 22, read: so as neither to be ..... nor to support
p. 204	l. 3, read: princelings
p. 212	l. 9, read: wherever
p. 226	l. 7, read: concealing
p. 227	l. 1, read: maintaining
p. 249	No. 3, l. 6, read: prava
p. 249	No. 9, l. 24, read: difficilia
p. 251	No. 25, l. 25, read: flatterers
p. 253	No. 32, l. 10, read: De la gloire
p. 257	No. 75, l. 28, read: egenti
p. 258	No. 82, l. 14, read: prava
p. 259	No. 90, l. 11, read: De pueris instituendis
p. 261	No. 110, l. 7, read: Epitoma historiarum...
p. 262	No. 126, l. 28, read: eburnea
p. 266	No. 150, l. 25, read: Supputatio...
p. 267	No. 159, l. 27, read: circumcised
p. 276	No. 228, l. 6, read: notisque
p. 283	No. 276, l. 25, read: Ep. 1338 (23 Jan. 1523)
p. 288	No. 345, l. 22, read: ejicere
p. 289	No. 349, l. 7, read: laqueos
p. 292	No. 372, l. 1, read: communia
p. 293	No. 381, l. 20, read: Delcourt
p. 302	No. 451, l. 5, read: locutus